AF348981

RELIGION AND SECULAR MODERNITY
IN RUSSIAN CHRISTIANITY,
JUDAISM, AND ATHEISM

RELIGION AND SECULAR MODERNITY IN RUSSIAN CHRISTIANITY, JUDAISM, AND ATHEISM

EDITED BY ANA SILJAK

NORTHERN ILLINOIS UNIVERSITY PRESS
AN IMPRINT OF
CORNELL UNIVERSITY PRESS
Ithaca and London

First published 2024 by Cornell University Press

Library of Congress Cataloging-in-Publication Data

Names: Siljak, Ana, 1969– editor.
Title: Religion and secular modernity in Russian Christianity, Judaism, and atheism / edited by Ana Siljak.
Description: Ithaca : Northern Illinois University Press, an imprint of Cornell University Press, 2024. | Series: NIU series in Slavic, East European, and Eurasian studies | Includes bibliographical references and index.
Identifiers: LCCN 2024011166 (print) | LCCN 2024011167 (ebook) | ISBN 9781501778162 (hardcover) | ISBN 9781501778179 (epub) | ISBN 9781501778186 (pdf)
Subjects: LCSH: Secularism—Russia—History. | Christianity—Russia—History. | Judaism—Russia—History. | Atheism—Russia—History. | Russia—Religion—History.
Classification: LCC BL980.R8 R4327 2024 (print) | LCC BL980.R8 (ebook) | DDC 200.947—dc23/eng/20240509
LC record available at https://lccn.loc.gov/2024011166
LC ebook record available at https://lccn.loc.gov/2024011167

Contents

RELIGION AND SECULAR MODERNITY
IN RUSSIAN CHRISTIANITY,
JUDAISM, AND ATHEISM

Introduction
Religion and Secularism in Russia:
A Tradition of Engagement

Ana Siljak

The myth of a unitary "Holy Russia" is powerful both within Russia and without: a foundation of a militant Russian nationalism and a simplistic Western heuristic to explain contemporary Russian politics. Religion in Russia sparked scholarly interest during the post-Soviet revival of religion in the 1990s, and interest intensified in Western public discourse with the start of the war in Ukraine in 2022. The rise in Russian Christian nationalism, the Russian Orthodox patriarch's vocal support of Russian militarism, and official Russia's promotion of a new spiritual "Russian world" have all led to a common perception (shared even by some scholars of Russia) that this current situation is merely the reflection of a thousand-year Russian mythology that has perpetually rested on the firm "belief in Holy Russia" or the "cult of the holy tsar" and has stringently resisted "secularist" ideals such as the separation of church and state.[1]

Contemporary circumstances, however troubling, should not obscure the diversity of voices that are a part of Russian religious and secular experience. Throughout Russian history, in the nineteenth and twentieth centuries in particular, many political figures, writers, theologians, church leaders, and artists debated and discussed the place of religion in the modern world in a manner comparable to the West's. The purpose of this book, then, is to highlight these voices and to reveal the full complexity of the Russian Christian, Jewish, and atheist engagement with secular modernity.

The relationship between religion and secular modernity in the West is a thriving field of study. Over thirty years ago, a perceived global "resurgence of religion" sparked interest in the complicated interaction between the ostensibly secularizing West and the religious cultures that persisted within it. Scholars interrogated long-held assumptions about concepts such as religion and secularization. The binary of secular and religious, once dominant in social-scientific interpretations of modern society, was now challenged from a number of perspectives. Moreover, by recognizing "secularization" theories as predominantly Western, studies of Muslim, Hindu, and other religious communities allowed scholars to compare and contrast the world of Western Christianity with the non-Western, non-Christian world.

Russia has mostly been left out of this scholarly conversation, and few works have compared the Russian and Western approaches to secular modernity. Some of this is a legacy of a twentieth-century bias against Russia's religions as backward, reactionary, and uninterested in engaging with the modern world. But even in the last twenty years, Western scholarship on religion and the secular has mostly overlooked Russia as liminal in the Western/non-Western comparative framework. This is especially true when it comes to Russia's Christian and Jewish traditions: perceived as neither Western nor non-Western, their responses to secularization and secular modernity have been largely ignored by all but specialist historians of Russian religion.

The purpose of this book is to bridge this gap and to use contemporary scholarly insights regarding the complexities of religion and secularism to provide a new, multifaceted perspective on the engagement between religion and the secular in Russia's Christian, Jewish, and atheist traditions. All of these traditions produced theological, philosophical, juridical, and artistic approaches to the challenges of secular modernity, and they were shaped, in turn, by secularizing trends within Russian and Soviet spaces. These traditions have contended with Western ideas imported from abroad, grappled with the religious pluralism of the Russian and Soviet states, and influenced similar debates in the West (especially after Russians found themselves in diaspora after 1917). And the question of the relationship between the religious and the secular has become more evident since the collapse of Communism in 1991.

This book provides a variety of approaches to Christianity, Judaism, and atheism within imperial Russia, the Soviet Union, and the post-Soviet Russian Federation, revealing the intricacies of the "secularization" dynamic throughout the twists and turns of modern Russian history. Now more than ever, as one narrative of Russia's religious history dominates official Russian accounts, alternative perspectives of the relationship between Russian religion and secularism should be highlighted and emphasized.

The "Secularization" Debate in the West: Key Concepts

To understand the relationship between secular and religious in Russia, it is important to delineate the key terms and concepts of the "secularization" debate that originated in and evolved from Western scholarship. The earliest Western uses of the term *secularization* refer to a narrow definition, which describes, in Ian Hunter's words, the "transfer of ecclesiastical property and jurisdiction to civil ownership and authority." By the very early nineteenth century, however, the term had taken on an additional meaning, in part influenced by the French revolutionary project of dechristianization, which went beyond the confiscation of church property and extended to the diminishing of the power and authority of religion in politics and public life.[2] By the mid-nineteenth century, as Phil Zuckerman, John R. Shook, and Joseph Blankholm have convincingly argued, British "secularists" crystallized the modern meaning of the term *secularism*. George Jacob Holyoake and his British Secular Union had a "civic agenda," which was, in Holyoake's words, "a code of duty pertaining to this life, founded on considerations purely human, intended mainly for those who find theology indefinite or inadequate, unreliable or unbelievable." Secularism thus started as an endeavor to find a nonreligious mode of philosophy and action for a modern world. Notably, the term was often used instead of *atheism* in order to incorporate those who did not wish to define themselves as specifically anti-religious, and therefore to invite the inclusion of all people for whom religion was either unimportant or unpalatable.[3] By the end of the nineteenth century, both secularization and secularism referred to a "secular" end: the marginalization of religion in political, social, and cultural life.

By the 1950s and 1960s, the secularization "thesis" emerged to explain what was by then seen as an inevitable process, through which "religion's influence on all aspects of life—from personal habits to social institutions—[was] in dramatic decline." Sociologists, in particular, fell sway to the idea that the marginalization of religion no longer required a comprehensive project, because religion was declining in power so rapidly that, with the increase in knowledge, technology, and mobility in the modern era, it was doomed to disappear.[4]

Secularism and *secularization*, despite their different origins, share a common "myth," as multiple scholars have revealed. For both, the various processes of modernity, including the preeminence of rational calculation and empiricism as forms of knowledge, technological development, social mobility, and political pluralism, were all combining to make the decline of the religious mode of existence inevitable.[5] Charles Taylor has called these types of myths "subtraction stories," in which secularization was no more than the removal of a particular type of thought and practice as human beings "lost, or sloughed off, or liberated themselves from certain earlier, confining horizons, or illusions, or limitations of knowledge." These are the stories sociologists often try to measure by tracking the apparent decline in belief in a deity or a decline in church attendance. Proponents of the secularization thesis often placed societies on a historical continuum, in which those furthest along in the secularization process demonstrated clear markers, such as a separation of church and state, a secular public sphere, religious toleration, and fewer references to religion within the cultural realm, while those that were "behind" in the process found greater degrees of church/state intermingling, fundamentalism, and intolerance.[6]

Since the Enlightenment, *religion* has been defined as an observable anthropological phenomenon with discreet characteristics that apply to all forms of religious faith, one that could be objectively analyzed and measured. Jonathan Z. Smith points out that the Enlightenment was particularly interested in making the adjective *religious* apply to a human "experience or activity" that was but one among many. The Enlightenment challenge was, as Walter Capp argued, to "make religion intelligible by discovering precisely where it is situated within the wide range of interactive human powers and faculties." By the twentieth century, religion was analyzed as a category of "cultural creation," albeit one that referred to "superhuman beings."[7] For William T. Cavanaugh, this category of religion originally assisted in the political project of the separation of church and state, but the contents of this political secular/religious binary expanded, such that religion was associated with the immaterial, supernatural, and irrational and the secular was described as immanent and rational. Moreover, especially in the more triumphalist versions of the secularist project, "religion" became associated with an understanding of the world that was either gradually disappearing or needed to be tightly controlled in order that the secular might flourish.[8]

This tidy understanding of the binary of secular and religious, particularly with its myth of the gradual decline of "religion" and its power, was challenged throughout the second half of the twentieth century, but received its most devastating blow in the late 1990s and the early 2000s, when a "resurgence of religion" was observed throughout the world, which included the rise of various "fundamentalisms" in various countries, the spread of Evangelicalism in the Global South, and the disintegration of avowedly atheist and secular Communist political systems around the world. Peter L. Berger, once himself a proponent of the secularization thesis, wrote his *Desecularization of the World* to precisely document this "resurgent religion" and to explain the "mistakes of secularization theory."[9]

The demise of the unquestioned secularization thesis led to a flourishing of scholarly debate on the possibility of a more complicated understanding of the "secular" and its relationship to religion. Here, Charles Taylor's *Secular Age* became the central text framing the debate. In this book, Taylor attempted to lead his readers away from the simple "subtraction stories" of traditional secularization models and suggested another approach to the contemporary Western secular worldview. In the modern world, according to Taylor, faith "is one human possibility among others." A society or culture is considered secular to the extent that people view the "immanent," or this-worldly, life as the obvious reality and the end of existence and to the extent that references to the "transcendent," or other-worldly, are viewed with skepticism and require justification.[10] For Taylor, the modern secular perspective is not one that is simply emancipated from the shackles of religion, or one that unproblematically rejects a detachable religious worldview. Instead, for Taylor, secularity creates a disquieting modernity, in which humanity is "restless," "fractured," even "schizophrenic," at once happily ignoring the strictures of religious demands and then yearning for higher sacrifices and higher truths.[11] After Taylor, it became impossible for scholars to see the secular as simply what was "left over" after religion diminished. Instead, it needed to be seen as an entire worldview, whose premises and programs needed to be studied and understood as a crucial component of modernity.

Taylor inspired a number of new scholarly works on secularization, including *Rethinking Secularism* (edited by Craig Calhoun, Mark Juergensmeyer, and Jonathan VanAntwerpen) and *Varieties of Secularism in a Secular Age* (edited by Michael Warner, VanAntwerpen, and Calhoun). Authors in these books have questioned the rigid binary of secular/religious and have noted the development of a variety of secularisms and secular modernities.[12]

The interaction between the religious and the secular in the political realms has received the bulk of scholarly attention, and a number of works have challenged the simple subtraction stories implied in the history of concepts such as toleration and the separation of church and state. Talal Asad has influentially traced the genealogy of the concept of "religion" as part of a dominant, rational discourse of political control.[13] Saba Mahmood has pointed out that, in many cases, secularization does not simply expunge religion from politics or society. In her words, "Secularism has sought not so much to banish religion from the public domain but to reshape the form it takes, the subjectivities it endorses, and the epistemological claims it can make."[14] Michael Burleigh has written histories of self-proclaimed secular ideologies such as nationalism and socialism, which became "political religions" that sought to satisfy the human quest for the transcendent and for belonging in an "age without God."[15]

In the case of India, China, Africa, and the Islamic world, the concepts of secularism and secularization have been situated in the complicated narrative of imperialism and colonialism, and the question of native versus imported secularisms has been explored.[16] The question of the secular and secularism in society and culture has received less attention, except when considering educational policies or contentious questions such as the wearing of religious symbols in public.[17] Comparatively little has been done on the interaction between religion and the secular in artistic endeavors, even though this is a field where there are productive conversations about the place of religion in modernity.[18] The history of atheism is a growing field of study, producing a number of works challenging simplistic understandings of unbelief in the modern world.[19]

Given the global nature of the scholarship on secularization and secularism, it is odd that whole geographic regions—Eastern Europe and Eurasia—have been, for the most part, left out of the secularization literature. When speaking of historically Christian contexts for secularization, Western Christianity (Catholic and Protestant) is either implied or explicitly denoted, and Orthodox Christianity is almost entirely excluded. Jewish, Muslim, and Buddhist stories in Eastern Europe and Eurasia are also mostly ignored.[20] This is especially striking, given that these regions underwent some of the most thorough attempted secularization processes in modern times, and post-Communist societies are still struggling with the proper place of religion in newly desecularized contexts.

Sekuliarizatsiia: A Russian History

The history of "secularization" in Russia is, unsurprisingly, tied closely to that of the West. The earliest Russian use of the term *secular* (*svetskii*) has been traced to the narrow description of secular authority (*svetskaia vlast'*) or the white (nonmonastic) clergy.[21] But by the end of the eighteenth century, the terms *secularization* (*sekuliarizatsiia*) and *secularize* (*sekuliarizovat'*) were borrowed directly from Europe to indicate the transfer of ecclesial and monastic property to state control. As such, secularization in Russia, as in Europe, emerged out of an institutional Christian context. During the transformative reigns of Peter I and Catherine II in the eighteenth century, secularization moved beyond the transfer of property and became part of significant reforms borrowed wholescale from Western secular ideas and institutions. Peter's creation of the Holy Synod in 1721 brought the centuries-old relationship between church and state in Russia to an end, replacing the power balance between the tsar and the patriarch with a hierarchical assimilation of the church within the state. Peter's public dismantling and even ridicule of Russian Christian institutions and traditions created a space for a new secular public to develop.[22] The process was continued under Catherine II, who consciously introduced European Enlightenment texts and ideas into the Russian public sphere and added non-Orthodox religions, such as Islam, to the list of religions under the tolerant rule of the secular state.[23] It is during this era of reform that the first uses of the term *religion* (*religiia*) in Russian are found, and the term was used to denote, in Enlightenment fashion, a category that included "one or another faith or confession."[24] Later, in the mid-nineteenth century, the definition of *secularization* was expanded to include a process that was already taking place, namely, the "liberation from spiritual ecclesiastical influence."[25]

In Russia, the idea of a struggle, or binary, between the "secular" and the "religious" worldviews emerged in embryo in the debates between the Slavophiles and the Westernizers in the first half of the nineteenth century, and it was therefore, at the outset, a binary formed in the context of Russian Orthodox culture. Many of the leading Slavophile thinkers defended a "religious" understanding of Russian politics and culture, particularly, as Sergey Horujy has shown, in order to defend their own "theocentric" understanding of the person and his or her relation to politics and society, as opposed to the secular "anthropocentric" view. Strikingly, however, Slavophiles often used derivatives of the generic *religion* (*religiia, religioznoe, religioznost'*) instead of Orthodoxy (*pravoslavie*) and its derivatives.[26] On the other side of the debate, Aleksandr Herzen, a prominent Westernizer, championed the adoption of what he saw as a European-style secularism, believing that progress, especially in Russia, "necessitated the end of religion." Herzen was one of the first in Russia to use the term *secularization* (*sekuliarizatsiia*) positively, to describe a culture and politics freed from religious influence.[27] These debates were not confined to the world of Russian Orthodox Christianity, however, but found parallels in the Russian Jewish world, where the Haskalah movement for Jewish Enlightenment and assimilation similarly affected Jewish intellectuals.[28]

In the second half of the nineteenth century, Russian revolutionaries openly declared themselves against religion and for a society based on a scientific and materialist worldview. Victoria Frede, in her seminal work on atheism and doubt in Russia, has shown that activists in the provinces especially believed that religion bred political passivity and that "self-reliance" could come only with an extirpation of Christian teaching. "The revolution would begin once Russians had dispensed with faith in God." Revolutionaries from Jewish backgrounds similarly revolted against what they perceived to be a retrograde Jewish religious culture. Whether Jewish or Christian, many radicals openly argued for a society free from "superstitions" and "nanny's tales." The postrevolutionary world would be built on the understanding that "there is no hereafter" and that happiness is only in the "here and now."[29]

The most fervent debates regarding religious and secular matters took place at the end of the nineteenth century, in an era of "modernism," when the Russian revolutionaries, the Russian cultural movement of the Silver Age, Russian political figures, and Russian clergy all participated in sometimes bitter struggles over questions of church-state relations, freedom of conscience, toleration, morality, identity, and culture.[30] Many participants openly acknowledged the binary between religious and secular modes of existence. Thus, the revolutionary Piotr Lavrov openly acknowledged that "religious belief" was the obstacle to a proper, scientific, and realistic worldview, and he called for the "establishment of the autonomous secular commune" as the foundation for a future Russian state and society. The only "amulet" against this was "scientific critique."[31] For Vladimir Solov'ev, similarly, there was a marked contrast between the "old, traditional form of religion" and the "modern nonreligious [*vnereligioznaia*] civilization" that was born of the French Revolution and that "believed in man." Solov'ev, however, insisted that the secular or nonreligious phase was a transition between the "religious past" and the "religious future."[32]

By the turn of the century, this binary was codified in the *Brokgauz-Efron Encyclopedia*, published 1890–1907. The term *religion* was given a long entry and preliminarily defined as the "organized worship of higher powers," in which "the undeniable reality of such higher powers" demanded the reverence of the "believing consciousness." To highlight the term's anthropological value, a table and map of the world's religions were appended to the entry. Similarly, the term *secularization* was afforded a detailed history, from its original meaning as the transfer of church property into lay hands to the later, broader inclusion of the transformation of "philosophy and science, literature and art, law and the state, and in general, all of life." Especially in the modern era, the entry stated, the "freedom from the influence of the church" applied to all areas of human life, including a kind of (Charles Taylor–like) immanentist "acceptance of the legitimacy of the joys of earthly existence."[33]

Though the binary between secular and religious became increasingly entrenched in Russian culture, especially at the turn of the century, it was simultaneously being challenged from multiple directions, and sometimes by the same people and institutions that insisted on the divide. Slavophiles, Westernizers, revolutionaries, the Orthodox Church, and Jewish and Christian philosophers endeavored to engage religion with modernity. The Religious-Philosophical Meetings of 1901 were but one example of the attempts to bring together secular intellectuals, artists, revolutionaries, and clerics to discuss the pressing issues in modern Russia, such as religious freedom, toleration, and sexuality. Out of these conversations emerged new ideas about marriage and the family and about human rights, social justice, and the role of art.[34] It was in this era, as Richard Stites and others have pointed out, that the God-seeking and God-building movements explicitly sought a new relationship between religion and the secular in a modern age—the God-seekers wishing to make faith relevant in an age of materialism and empiricism; the God-builders wishing to use religion to further socialist dreams of a brighter future.[35]

The Bolshevik Revolution of 1917 dramatically upended the secular-religious conversation. By 1918, Vladimir Lenin issued a decree formally declaring that "every citizen may confess any religion or profess none at all."[36] A sustained attack on the institutions of the Orthodox Church and other religions, as well as a repression of the clergy, followed. As Catherine Wanner succinctly describes it: "The Soviet Union . . . had policies in place to speed up secularization and the sequestration and renunciation of religion, which included coercion, agitation, and persuasion through propaganda. The rejection of all things religious, in favor of science and progress, became a sustaining national ideal."[37] Because of the continued effort to secularize the Soviet Union, Christianity and Judaism entered into a different kind of engagement with the atheist state. The contributions to *State Secularism and Lived Religion in Soviet Russia and Ukraine*, edited by Wanner, show the variety of Russian responses to the Soviet secularization campaign, including the organization of lay Christians in defense of the Orthodox Church, the retreat of religion into a familial and feminized sphere, and the revival of monasticism after World War II.[38]

Moreover, as scholarship in the last thirty years has pointed out, much of Communist and Soviet ideology and practice was both implicitly and explicitly indebted to a kind of secularization of religious concepts and rituals. Andrzej Walicki and Igal Halfin have both convincingly revealed the eschatology at the heart of both the original Marxist ideology and its Soviet interpretation. Jochen Hellbeck has studied the struggle for self-transformation that was part of the Soviet attempt to create "New Men." Perhaps most importantly, Victoria Smolkin has revealed how the Soviet state, especially under Nikita Khruschev, sought consciously to imitate religious rituals for major life events such as baptisms, weddings, and funerals in order to better proselytize for atheist Communism. Yuri Slezkine is thus following in a long tradition when he speaks of a "Bolshevik millenarianism."[39]

The end of the Soviet Union in 1991 brought with it the resurgence of religion that became a part of a general questioning of the process of secularization. Observers were initially impressed by the dramatic return of religious institutions and ideas into the post-Soviet world. And yet, the story of the return of religion in Russia is now revealed to be more complex than it first seemed. Though the numbers of people who profess to belong to a certain religion (such as Orthodox Christianity) can be quite high, other conventional measures of the strength of religious belief, including regular church attendance, suggest that the level of religious commitment may be much lower. Secular and religious advocates in Russia are still debating the role of the state, public, and culture in determining the direction of modernity.[40]

In short, although the engagement between religion and the secular has undergone various transformations, it persisted throughout the nineteenth and twentieth centuries and has continued through the present day.

The Resurgence of Scholarship on Russia's Religions

For many years, especially during the Soviet era, scholars believed that the secularization thesis had its most convincing proof in Communist states, whose open atheism was often seen as a mere acceleration of the overall secularization process happening elsewhere around the world. Russia's religions in general, and the Orthodox Church in particular, were perceived as especially unable to cope with the secularist assault, given their reactionary nature. The result was, as Valerie A. Kivelson and Robert H. Greene have noted, that prominent history textbooks, for example, "sequestered religion in a decidedly skippable chapter titled 'Religion and Culture' or something similar." Orthodox Christianity, alongside other religions, was viewed "alternatively as a practice of class oppression or of folk custom, devoid of theological, spiritual, or genuine religious content."[41] Similarly, the Jewish question was defined primarily as a question of cultural identity, and the scholarship on secularization and the Jewish question in the Western world has had no robust counterpart in the Russian context.[42] This is not at all to minimize the extraordinary exceptions to this overall trend, including the tireless work of Gregory L. Freeze, Vera Shevzov, Judith Deutsch Kornblatt, and Paul Valliere, which provided extremely important contributions to the history of religion in Russian at a time when few scholars seemed interested.[43]

The "resurgence of religion," combined with the collapse of the Soviet Union, spurred a very welcome increase in scholarship on Russia's religions, especially since 2000. Scholarship on Russian religion moved away from institutional histories to "lived religion," considering narratives of conversion, violence, and confession that intertwined in a multi-faith empire.[44] Vibrant intellectual histories of Orthodox theology, monasticism, and lay practice have revitalized the field of Russian religious thought and culture.[45] Frede, by contrast, has considered the long-neglected story of the development of atheism and nonbelief in Russian history.[46] Since 2018 alone, there has been an incredible growth of new scholarship on Russia's religions, especially Russian religious thought, including contributions by Teresa Obolevitch, Randall A. Poole, and Smolkin, not to mention the indispensable 2020 work *The Oxford Handbook of Russian Religious Thought*.[47]

Although essays and chapters in the literature above have considered the engagement of religion with the secular in Russia, sustained scholarly accounts of the variety of Russian responses to secular modernity are fewer..[48] Wanner's edited book *State Secularism and Lived Religion in Soviet Russia and Ukraine* is one of the few publications that tackles the subject directly, and it is the most thorough work on the Soviet period, especially on the Soviet secularization project.[49] Other works look at separate aspects of the encounter between religion and secular modernity in Russia, including Russian philosophical responses to modernity, religious toleration, freedom of conscience, and human rights; the interrelations between Orthodox, non-Orthodox, and nonbelievers in the context of an increasingly secular state; and the religious elements in the overtly atheist Russian and Soviet revolutionary ideologies.[50] And the scholarship on "lived Orthodoxy" is important for understanding the relationship between religion and the modern.[51] The present book builds on and extends these insights, focusing on the experiences of those living in Christian, Jewish, and atheist cultures in the imperial, Soviet, and post-Soviet Russian spaces.

Secularization and Religion in Russia

Chapters in this collection consider the engagement of Russian Christianity and Judaism with secular modernity from a number of different perspectives. They detail how the state, intellectuals, literary figures, and others placed secular concepts in religious contexts, reevaluated theology and practice to engage with modernity, contested the power of the secular state, and created secular religions. As such, they provide a multifaceted account of faith, nonbelief, and religious practice interacted through two centuries of Russian history. Topics include Christianity, politics, and the state; Christian, Jewish, and atheist intellectuals between the religious and the secular; religion and art; and religion in cross-cultural dialogue. Each chapter will reveal how Russians navigated the complex interactions between the secular and religious—in certain instances, Orthodox thinkers challenged secular modernity by redefining traditionally secular concepts such as "nation." In other circumstances, religious artists appropriated secular ideas and practices (such as those of avant-garde art) for religious purposes, and, finally, in some cases, ostensibly atheist institutions (including the Moscow State Yiddish Theater and the Moscow Methodological Circle) incorporated religious perspectives and frameworks to enrich experience. Taken as a whole, then, the book will show just how complicated the secular-religious interaction has been, and continues to be, within the Russian context.

The first section of the book looks at the relationship between religion and the state in Russian and Soviet history. Challenging the conventional (and often scholarly) assumption of Russian Caesaropapism, this section demonstrates the complicated and changing relationship between religious and state institutions throughout the Russian past. Nadieszda Kizenko looks at the role of confession in Imperial Russia, demonstrating that the use of government power to compel confession was not part of ancient Orthodox custom (it was introduced in the seventeenth century), nor was it particularly "Eastern" (Catholicism used state authorities to compel confession in the sixteenth century). Rather, confession as a tool for making "good citizens" was part of a general project of modernity, one that was not resisted because, according to Kizenko, this hybrid between public good and private devotion fit with the popular understanding of the role of the church in holding the public accountable. Kristina Stoeckl provides a history of the Russian Orthodox Church that considers the historical evolution of two very different understandings of how the institutional church, the Russian public, and the secular political authorities should interact. Both authors complicate prevailing conventional views of the Russian Orthodox Church as a mere appendage of the state, and they challenge the notion of an "Eastern" church untouched by Western modernity.

The book's second section looks at the variety of intellectual responses to religion and the secular that do not fit into easy categories of secular and religious. Kåre Johan Mjør's contribution investigates the Russian religious philosophical struggle with the secular ideology of nationalism. Though scholarly literature suggests that the "nation" became a substitute for belief in God, Mjør shows that religious philosophers in the nineteenth and early twentieth centuries wished to reconsider the nation and nationalism from a Christian perspective, to see whether there was a legitimate, biblical defense of national identity. Peter A. Safronov, by contrast, shows how religious structures and vocabulary developed within ostensibly secular intellectual circles. Operating within a Soviet Communism that demanded the quasi-religious transformation of the individual for the sake of the collective, the dissident Moscow Methodological Circle resisted, but also borrowed from, the state ideology. The circle was held together by the cult of a leader that promised both individual intellectual illumination and collective power—making it into a "secular congregation." Finally, April L. French delves into the very complicated story of Father Aleksandr Men', a Jewish convert to Orthodoxy who stood at the intersection of a variety of identities and ideologies: Jewish, Christian, Communist, nationalist. By appropriating and engaging with Soviet atheist definitions of Jewishness, and by challenging Russian nationalist antisemitism, he sought to promote a genuine Jewish-Christian dialogue in the restricting confines of Soviet secularism.

The third section of the book is devoted to an area often neglected in the debates over the relationship between religion and secularism—literature and the arts. Artistic endeavors provide some of the most fruitful avenues for the exploration of difficult questions relating to the religious and the secular. My chapter begins the discussion with the interrogation of sexuality in the poetry and literature of Zinaida Gippius, whose concept of chaste "infatuation" was developed to challenge the increasingly materialistic and biological emphasis on sexuality prevalent in secular Russian culture at the end of the nineteenth century. Erich Lippman shows how Maxim Gorky's atheist socialism did not exclude, but consciously appropriated, Russian Orthodox Christianity in its "God-building" project. Tatiana Levina counters prevailing notions of Kazimir Malevich as a secular artist, revealing how his experimental, avant-garde art, by promoting "objectlessness," sought a path to the divine. Vassili Schedrin explores how the Moscow State Yiddish Theater, especially in the plays of Solomon Mikhoels, delivered socialist ideas infused with religious messianic beliefs about the Jewish future, rather than with the conventional aspects of socialist propaganda.

The fourth and final section of the book lays out the intersection between the religious and the secular in Russia that had, and continues to have, important effects in cross-cultural dialogue. Alexander Polunov's chapter serves as a cautionary note to all scholars of Russia, by revealing that British observers of Russian religion at the end of the nineteenth century imagined Russian Orthodoxy as an unchanging and anti-modern religion, mostly because they sought refuge from the secularized environment they perceived in their native country. They attempted to fight what they saw as the threat of British secular modernity with visions of "true" Russian religiosity. J. Eugene Clay describes the effect of a small, radically egalitarian, and deeply spiritual Molokan sect on two modernities—Russian and American. In Russia, the Molokans' defiance of the official church of the majority of Russians led them to be labeled as "backward" and unenlightened, while in the United States, their spiritual pacifism caused them to be rejected as racially inferior; in each case, the homogenizing modern state found no room for the committed religious dissenters. Clemena Antonova makes an impassioned plea for a rediscovery in the West of a Russian religious worldview that might provide some new perspectives on the relationship between modernity, religion, and the secular. By using the concept of "fullunity" as a philosophical starting point, scholars can begin to approach a new understanding of religion that is not antithetical to the secular, but which takes it into account. Randall Poole rounds out the volume with his consideration of what he calls a Russian "counter-tradition," one that has encouraged, and should continue to encourage the development of a religious humanism and human rights.

Taken as a whole, this book should be considered a starting point for further scholarship and discussion on religion and secularism in Russia. Each of the book's sections provides promising new directions for research and inquiry, interrogating the complicated relationships between secular and religious that evolved in Russian understandings of politics, ideas, art, and cross-cultural interaction. As such, the book considers Christian, Jewish, and atheist perspectives and provides a framework for further scholarship on the many other religions of the Eurasian space: Islam, Buddhism, Catholicism, and Protestantism. Moreover, the book demonstrates the potential for interesting new scholarship on the influence of Russian discussions of religion and the secular on Western and non-Western cultures.

In looking at the engagement between the secular and the religious, the book will show the multiple ways one could be religious or secular in the Russian and Soviet space. Because the Russian religious world has engaged with secularism for over two hundred years, the literature, ideas, and experiences of this world, documented here, will enrich the Western understanding of Russian religions and also will provide valuable new insights for scholars "rethinking secularism." Moreover, it will give voice to alternative Russian perspectives on Russia's religions and their relationship to secular modernity, to "counter-traditions" even more valuable in a time when one worldview threatens to predominate.

PART ONE

Church and State in Russia and the Soviet Union

CHAPTER 1

Confession and Modernity in Imperial Russia

NADIESZDA KIZENKO

> It was necessary that, in his exile at Romagnano, Fabrizio . . . should hear mass daily without fail, take as his confessor a man of spirit, devoed to the cause of the Monarchy, and should confess to him, at the tribunal of penitence, only the most irreproachable sentiments.
>
> —Stendhal, *The Charterhouse of Parma*

Most of the chapters in this book take as their starting point the middle of the nineteenth century or later. There are good reasons for this approach. The Crimean War, the death of Nicholas I, and Alexander II's Great Reforms changed relations among peoples inside and outside the Russian Empire. I would like to argue, however, that modernity in Russia, in both a secular and a religious sense, goes back rather further. In the Latin West, the requirement of annual sacramental confession, affirmed at the Fourth Lateran Council in 1215 and broadened at the 1563 Council of Trent, has conventionally been taken to signal a new, peculiarly modern, sense of the accountable individual.[1] Similarly, in Russia, the requirement of confession ushered in modernity not in the middle of the nineteenth century, but in the middle of the seventeenth.[2]

With the ascent of the Romanovs to the throne, both Orthodox hierarchs and Orthodox tsars began to express concern that people were not going to confession often enough. They then began a long campaign to get people to do just that. From this point, confession in Russia took on a unique role, different from what it had been in Muscovy and different from what it would become after Soviet rule and beyond. Determining whether one had participated in sacramental confession became a standard element in criminal cases.[3] Mandatory annual confession from the age of seven onward was one of the few experiences that Orthodox Christians of both sexes and all classes in the Russian Empire had in common; it found expression in everything from woodcuts to children's books to Peredvizhniki paintings to the works of Leo Tolstoy, Anton Chekhov, and Fyodor Dostoyevsky. Records and reports of confession persisted through 1917. This interplay formed a distinctive, modern confessional culture that distinguished the experience of Orthodox Christians in the Russian Empire from that of their Orthodox counterparts in the Balkans and in Greece—but *not*, paradoxically, from their Roman Catholic neighbors to the west. This confessional culture is synonymous with modernity.

What made Tsar Aleksei Mikhailovich so intent on having his subjects go to confession at least once a year? Church hierarchs had done so repeatedly; in the fifteenth century, for example, Metropolitan Fotii of Kyiv had urged his clerics to accept their flocks' repentance and confession during all four fasts.[4] Nevertheless, despite centuries of exhortation, many Muscovites did not regularly go to confession and communion. The Jesuit missions and the increasing number of un-Orthodox foreigners in Muscovy started to seem alarming precisely because the Orthodoxy of the Muscovites seemed so shaky.[5] As early as 1627, Patriarch Filaret and Tsar Mikhail Romanov jointly issued a decree forbidding foreigners to have Orthodox slaves and servants. What interests us here is their motivation: "Many [that is, of the Orthodox servants of non-Orthodox foreigners] *die without repentance, without spiritual fathers* [a synonym for *father-confessors*], and during Great Lent and the other church fasts eat meat and all matter of non-Lenten food [*skorom*] against their wills."[6]

This shared concern of both the patriarch and the tsar set the template for the rest of the seventeenth century. From the 1640s onward, Aleksei Mikhailovich and his hierarchs kept appealing to priests and town officials to get laypeople to become more observant. The focus of their concerns was that people were living without spiritual father-confessors, dying without repentance, and not feeling in the least obliged to confess their sins or to receive the body and blood of the Lord. Foreigners were often identified as a particular threat to the piety of the Orthodox. This phrasing appears over and over, whether the writer is a hierarch or the tsar.[7]

This broad trend of an increased emphasis on confession was articulated most forcefully at the Moscow Church Council of 1666–67.[8] Article 11 of that council read: "Instruct your parishioners, men and women and their children, that they should go to their father-confessors for confession often, especially during the four fasts. . . . If someone should go for a whole year without confession, saving for travel or other valid reasons, and the hour of death come upon him, do not bury such a one in church ground nor serve the funeral rites over him; for such a one, while alive, himself separated from the holy Church."[9]

The Old Believer schism played a role as well. Even before the schism, the tsars and patriarchs had already begun attaching greater importance to the sacraments of confession and communion. With the emergence of Old Belief, tsars and hierarchs saw the need to find an effective way of determining whether their subjects were truly Orthodox. What better way of establishing someone's Orthodoxy than knowing whether he or she went to confession and communion to a priest of the official, approved, Orthodox church? After all, dissenters, especially monks and nuns, testified that they refused to go to confession or communion once new liturgical books had been introduced.[10] Laypeople sometimes turned to schismatic priests to hear their confessions.[11] Thus, partly as a result of a perceived threat from foreign representatives of other religious denominations, and partly in response to the Old Believer schism within Russian Orthodoxy, annual confession and communion in an approved Orthodox church became identified as the surest litmus test both of Orthodoxy and of reliability in general.

Confession became even more important under Aleksei's son Peter. Famously, the *Supplement to the Spiritual Regulation* (1722) of Peter I declared that if a priest hearing confessions learned of any treasonous attempts against the emperor or the state and was not able to dissuade the penitent from this nefarious aim, then it was no confession at all; the priest should immediately report the plot to the relevant police authorities. From this point onward, sacramental confession in Russia became the focus around which many modern goals met: on the one hand, education and churching of the ostensibly Orthodox population and, on the other hand, control, that is, increased bureaucratic control over parishes and monasteries and attempted control over what people were thinking and doing. Many historians and theologians have expressed outrage that the seal of the confession was no longer sacrosanct.[12] But this assumes three things: that, if the law were on the books, it would be applied; that Peter's violation of the seal was something new in Russian practice—that, like the rest of Peter's reforms, it characterized the intrusion of the Russian state into what had been the autonomous sphere of the Orthodox Church; and, finally, that this violation of the confessional seal fatally distinguished Russian Orthodox practice from that of the Roman Catholic Church, which had supposedly managed to defend its autonomy and safeguard the confessional seal for over a millennium.

But it is not quite so simple. An intense interest in confession as a way of making good citizens was not new to Peter but was already amply present in Tsar Aleksei Mikhailovich. And the Roman Catholic Church does not provide such a handy or clean comparison. Confession in the Latin West was neither as confidential nor as "silent" as one might think; nor was the element of government compulsion absent. In Passau in 1558, authorities threatened prison for those refusing to confess; in 1612, those residents of Salzburg who refused annual confession and communion had their names sent to the territorial government, not the bishop, for action; in Bavaria, the *Geistliche Rat* (Ecclesiastical Council) continued to seek out and punish the recalcitrant throughout the seventeenth century, keeping lists of the disobedient.[13] What political misbehavior people relayed at confession could lead to arrest; in Speyer, one peasant revolt was foiled because a peasant had mistakenly trusted his confessor.[14] The works of Stendhal, as this chapter's epigraph suggests, provide a vivid illustration of how nineteenth-century Roman Catholics wishing to establish their political bona fides would make a point of mentioning their political convictions in confession.

Thus, rather than focusing on the *Supplement* as an indicator of Russia's "failed" modernity or "otherness," it is more useful to look at how Peter's notorious confessional legislation actually played itself out. Several cases from the decades immediately following the *Supplement* complicate the caricature of Peter as Satan *ex machina*. They also provide valuable insight into how legislation was—or was not—translated into policy.

In 1723, Antipa Evdokimov, a priest from Baku, was accompanying the Moscow and Tobolsk battalions and, like other priests in the empire, received the instruction to report treason heard at confession and swore the loyalty oath. But, unusually, he thought through the implications of the *Supplement* and located several potential traps and loopholes. He decided that no doubt other priests might face the same pitfalls and so sent in his queries to the Holy Synod. He framed his queries as problems.

First, Father Antipa noted, the *Supplement to the Spiritual Regulation* seemed to hinge on the possibility that a potential evildoer would not be dissuaded from his or her aim by the confessor. In that case, as Peter I and Feofan Prokopovich had argued in the *Supplement*, the confession was no confession at all, and there was no confessional seal to break. The father-confessor thus need have no compunction about turning in the intended evildoer immediately. But what, Father Antipa asked, if the penitent did repent? Was he or she simply to be let go without further supplementary interrogation by the police, just in case? Human nature was so changeable.

Second, what if the evildoer repented himself or herself, but had accomplices?

Third, what if the penitent had blasphemed against God, the church, and the sovereign in letters or leaflets he or she had distributed? He or she had repented, well and good—but what about the harm that might come about because of these letters, even though the penitent might not even know about it? What ought the confessor do?

Fourth, what if someone had reproached or criticized the sovereign with inappropriate words or thoughts, but promised not to do so anymore? Should he or she be punished or reported?

Fifth, if someone stole something from the sovereign or the state, great or small, and repented for it—but was not able to compensate for it monetarily, as thieves were meant to do—then what?

These questions are interesting because they show that priests did not simply read government circulars and file them. The Synod's answers show that the priests, too, understood the issues raised. Father Antipa was told that if an initially treasonous penitent at confession wholeheartedly abandoned his or her original evil intent, and no one else was involved, the person should be treated according to the holy canons—that is, absolved—and that no denunciations should be submitted. If the penitent had accomplices at large, he or she should be asked not for their names but for how many there were and where the location of the act harmful to the sovereign or state was meant to occur. In other words, the *Supplement* did not create a "climate of denunciation"; the goal was to prevent assassination attempts and to uncover conspiracies before they can be implemented and thus without breaking the confessional seal.[15]

However, the seal was one thing; absolution was another. The father-confessor was to ask the penitent to personally track down any accomplices and try to dissuade them and to report back the results within a set period of time. Until or unless the penitent succeeded in doing so, there was to be not only no communion of the Holy Mysteries but also no absolution of sins; the penitent was only instructed that, if unable to dissuade his or her comrades, he or she must report them immediately, with the understanding that he or she could then be absolved and not considered an accomplice. But if someone was silent at the prospect of what the Synod called satisfaction (*dovletvorenie*) or if he or she were evasive or promised to quell the evil and did not report back, no matter how sincere the penitence might be, he or she was still to be regarded as a miscreant (*zlodei*).

If the penitent had distributed any seditious or blasphemous letters, he or she was to track them down and destroy them and swear under oath at having done so. If it were not possible to track them down, then he or she must post rebuttals of any previous leaflets (without repeating the original blasphemies or seditions). He or she could then be absolved and the bishop in the area covered by these leaflets informed so that the matter could be dealt with. If anyone *thought*, and only thought, evil against the sovereign and repented of it, he or she could be absolved without further action. Finally, Father Antipa was informed that he was stupid to have raised the issue of not being able to compensate a theft, as canons were clear; such people could be absolved without compensation.[16]

All these details suggest that the instructions regarding the confessional seal in the *Supplement* to the church reform should not be regarded as something self-evident; the details were worked out on an individual basis, and the clerics who were not as cautious as Father Antipa and revealed contents of confessions too hastily could find themselves paying the price. After detailed canonical debates on the penalties for breaking the confessional seal, for example, one priest was executed; another was defrocked, had his nostrils slit, and was sent to Siberia for permanent hard labor.[17] This also shows that the notion of satisfaction introduced by Ukrainian theologians in the seventeenth century lingered well into the eighteenth century.[18] But the confession's social and political use was not limited to treason. Despite confessional manuals' insistence that the seal could be broken only for treason or state security, other eighteenth-century cases illustrate how confession could be used creatively even when treason was *not* involved.

In the reign of Empress Anna Ioannovna, in 1730, Avdotia Ivanova Skvornikova declared her wish to enter a convent, given that she could not have physical relations with her husband because of illness. She was asked whether she had married as a widow or as a maiden, what exactly her ailment was, and how long she ailed thus. More interesting is that she was asked if she was making this request of her own free will or whether she feared being beaten by her husband. Even more interesting for our purposes is that her confessor was also questioned for corroboration. Thus, the assumption here, as in other cases, is that *people will tell the truth at confession* and that what Avdotia had told her confessor could be admitted as evidence if it would mitigate circumstances favorably. In this case, because the confession could have been used to free Avdotia from being pressured to enter a convent by her husband, using it might be argued to be potentially liberating and sympathetic to her freedom rather than an infringement of it.[19]

In a very different kind of case, in 1731, the Synod acted on behalf of an insurance company. It asked a priest who had confessed the merchant Moskvin on his deathbed if Moskvin was guilty of setting fire to a ship containing goods he had insured. The insurance company was reluctant to pay out and wanted every assurance possible that the goods had in fact been on the ship, as Moskvin had not declared them at customs and received the necessary paperwork of inspection. The father-confessor assured them that indeed, Moskvin had regretted the loss of the ship at confession and that it really did contain merchandise and not (as the insurance company suspected) sand; but Moskvin did express regret that he had not filled out the correct customs paperwork. Interestingly, the father-confessor also added that he had asked Moskvin these questions when they were alone, but before he began asking about his sins, so that the discussion was actually just *before* the confession proper and thus not bound by the confessional seal. Although the Synod noted the distinction, they described the discussion as having taken place at confession (*na ispovedi*).[20]

Finally, in 1735, the Synod decided to systematize its confessional practice regarding prisoners held in the Chancellery of Secret Investigations (Kantse-liaria Tainykh Rozysknykh Del). Rather than assigning random priests as confessors on an ad hoc basis, as had been previous practice, the Synod appointed one priest for all the prisoners.[21] Priest Grigorii of the Peter and Paul Fortress Cathedral was now instructed to stop by every day to and from church services to inquire whether there was a prisoner who needed to be confessed or counseled. At each confession, he was instructed to ask whether the prisoner had hatched thievery or treason or other ill intent against Her Imperial Majesty. The *Supplement to the Spiritual Regulation* was mentioned specifically, and the instructions to leave the impenitent without absolution and to report it were transcribed from the *Supplement* nearly verbatim. The innovation was that Priest Grigorii was told to remind the penitent of the Second Coming of Christ and His Dread Judgment and not to subject himself or herself to the torments of Gehenna by making an incomplete confession. Another innovation was elaborating what to do if someone wished to denounce someone else. The penitent was to be told that denouncing someone else out of malice or ill will was a grave sin, especially if the person were innocent. But, if the penitent wished to denounce someone else sincerely and if there was something to denounce him or her for, then this was not and could not be sinful. The other interesting thing is that Priest Grigorii was instructed to keep these last instructions in strict secrecy and not to tell a soul about them, but to act on them "boldly and with common sense." Moreover, if Priest Grigorii did *not* report something he learned at confession, he himself would be executed after "harsh tortures without any mercy." Thus, while the *Supplement to the Spiritual Regulation* had sought to cloak its violation of the confessional seal in the guise of the canons, by 1735 the Synod understood that extorting information about others at confession was not something to publicize.[22] This suggests that, on the one hand, some lingering reservations about using confession as a means of incriminating others remained. On the other hand, as the cases of Skvornikova and Moskvin show, in the decades immediately following the *Supplement* there was little hesitation about using confession as a way of getting to additional information when treason was not involved.

By the nineteenth century, this would change. Any evidence obtained at sacramental confession was deemed inadmissible—because the priest himself might lie, as might the people involved, and because if people thought what they said at confession could be used against them, they might not make a clean breast of it and therefore risk perdition.[23] Thus, the attitude in late imperial Russia was both more cynical and more enlightened. But in the decades after the *Supplement* in the eighteenth century, confession was regarded as a precious and definitive source of information precisely because church and state authorities worked under the assumption that people would *not* lie and that the truths they uttered could and should be used for the benefit of the tsar and the populace.

Why did people not resist this state-sponsored attempt at regulating their religious practices the way they did many of the other reforms Peter sought to introduce? I would frame the argument differently. The most successful part of the Petrine reforms was *precisely* the mandate of annual confession. True, annual confession was not an integral part of popular piety, unlike icons, processions, and the exchange of Easter eggs; these *were*, and because they were, when Peter tried to ban these as being superstitious, people fought him tooth and nail. Annual confession, by contrast, was able to stick precisely because it conformed to what the bishops were trying to do, without interfering with popular piety. From the point of view of the government, in terms of accomplishing basic education, discipline, and surveillance, confession was maximally effective; from the point of view of the populace, it was minimally invasive and corresponded more or less to what they had been told to do all along; from the point of view of the hierarchy, it was essential and desirable.[24] Most importantly, violations of the confessional seal did not affect enough of the population for people to notice. This is the confluence that allowed it to stick.

The structures established by Tsars Aleksei and Peter endured after their creators. Their successors proved just as eager to use confession as a means of creating good imperial citizens. But it would take time to create mechanisms that allowed tracking and investigating everyone. Until the establishment of the consistories in 1801, the authorities focused on groups that both were easiest to notice and seemed to pose the greatest potential risk to good order and setting a good example: the military and the court elite.

Because of the instability created by Peter's legislation on imperial succession, in which the ruler could designate anyone he or she wished as a successor (and given that Tsarevich Aleksei Petrovich had been exposed through confession), rulers most immediately sought to learn whether officers, soldiers, or others were spreading treason. Some anti-imperial plots did emerge as a result of information obtained (or obtained but not reported) at confession. Priest Iakov Savich, for example, was blamed for not reporting the sentiments in favor of Ukrainian independence that the sailor Matviei Nikonov (who later claimed he was drunk) had expressed at confession in 1733; Parfen Frolov repented at confession for his sinful ideas about the empress Anna Ioannovna in 1732 (but was still sentenced to whipping and forced labor); the soldier Ivan

Anikiev was charged with revealing anti–Empress Elizabeth sentiments at his 1752 confession.[25]

After the military, the groups that appear to have been most immediately affected by the larger requirement to confess yearly—and, not coincidentally, easiest to keep track of—were the court, monks, and nuns. The imperial family itself was not only immune from the requirement—it was the most important target. Particularly telling is the role that the confessor played in the relations between the empress Elizabeth and the future Catherine the Great. As Catherine wrote in her memoirs in the beginning of August 1746:

> The Empress had the Grand Duke and me informed that we should make our devotions [that is, go to confession and communion]; we both obeyed her wishes . . . [on] Friday, when it was time to go to confession, the reason for this order [to go to confession] became very clear. Simeon Theodorsky, the Bishop of Pskov, questioned us both a great deal, each one separately, about what had happened between the Chernyshevs and us. But as nothing at all had happened, he was a bit contrite when he saw that with the candor of innocence we told him that there was not even the shadow of what they had dared to suppose. To me he let slip this question: "But then whence is the Empress informed to the contrary?" At this, I told him that I did not know. I suppose that our confessor transmitted our confession to the Empress's confessor, and that he informed Her Imperial Majesty of what had happened, which certainly could not damn us.[26]

Two things are interesting here. First, the decision of when to go to confession was made not by either young spouse, but by the Empress. They accepted her order to do so without question. Second, the purpose of the confession appeared to have been a simple desire for information—and all of this appeared to have been taken for granted by all concerned. Catherine would continue to use this tactic for her own purposes, as when in 1758 she and one of her ladies-in-waiting devised a sure plan to bring her back into Elizabeth's good graces; she pretended to be ill, asked for last rites, and used the confessor (who happened to be the uncle of the lady-in-waiting) to present her side of the story in a conversation that lasted an hour and a half. The tactic worked beautifully, with both the confessor and his niece serving as intermediaries between Catherine and the eventually mollified Elizabeth.[27] Catherine remained conscious of using confession to set a good example; even while traveling one year at the end of Great Lent, she and her court spent Holy Week in prayer and fasting using a "portable" church.[28]

What is surprising is that, while all sides appear to have been aware of what was going on, this does not appear to have undermined the reliability of the confession as a trustworthy source in anyone's eyes. Confession had become a hybrid of private and public, an opportunity both to unburden oneself and sometimes to call attention to something that now had the impress of God's truth.

These elements emerge in the cases of nobility in the diplomatic service. Russian state servitors abroad, as the public face of the empire and on public display, were held to a high standard; any falls from Orthodoxy on their part were castigated with particular severity. In 1744, for example, the Holy Synod noted that, while there were numerous Orthodox Christian diplomats, ministers, and other subjects in Her Imperial Majesty's service residing abroad, the Synod did not know whether they had priests "for confession, both their own and those serving them, and for other Christian duties," and so it asked the College of Foreign Affairs to supply them with a list of all state servitors and their families abroad, as well as of churches and clerics abroad.[29] Noteworthy here is that what alarmed the Synod was that nobles who had spent time abroad, particularly without ready access to the sacraments, might fall away from Orthodoxy and turn to other religions, especially Roman Catholicism.

This was not paranoia. In 1746, for example, Princess Irina Petrovna Dolgorukova and her family came to the attention of the Holy Synod for just this reason. The empress Elizabeth took a lively interest in the case, ordering that the matter be strictly investigated. Showing concern as she did for the "pernicious enticement of their souls," she wanted the Dolgorukovs to be admonished and to affirm them in the faith.[30] Because Dolgorukova initially replied falsely to the empress's questions, she was shown no lenience; she was confined to her house and then assigned public penance.

What had happened was the following. In the 1730s, the confessor of Sergei Dolgorukov, the husband, had already noticed that Dolgorukova consistently shied from going to confession. Year after year, the confessor was unable to include her in the lists he was expected to submit annually about the souls for which he was responsible. She deflected his attempts to exhort her to go to confession, claiming either fulfillment of the obligation elsewhere (though from whom she "could not recall"), or while traveling abroad, or "women's weakness."[31] (This last was a strategically clever loophole; as church custom prohibited women from going to communion while menstruating or otherwise being ritually unclean, as after childbirth, they could and did claim that these happened to coincide with customary times for confession and communion, and thus women had more opportunities than men to beg off.)[32]

After a long and exhaustive investigation, however, it emerged that Dolgorukova was lying and had consistently lied to the men she named as her spiritual fathers. She appeared nowhere in the confessional registers. She had converted to Roman Catholicism and had her children converted as well. Her maid and companion, "Mam'selle Behr," confirmed that her mistress had indeed confessed and communed from a Roman Catholic priest three times in Holland.

This was a scandal on a number of levels. The Dolgorukovs were as prominent as an aristocratic family could be. The "proselytizing" had been prompted by foreign travel, which raised suspicions about the wisdom of such a practice. According to Russian law, anyone born Orthodox had to stay Orthodox; if a child had one Orthodox parent (regardless of sex), that child was to be raised Orthodox.

The relation between husband and wife is striking as well. When Dolgorukov was queried, he claimed complete ignorance. He could not be expected to keep an eye on his wife's every coming and going; they went together to ceremonial religious functions that the court was expected to attend (the birthday and saint's day of the empress, for example); and his wife had never given him cause to question her Orthodoxy. He pleaded ignorance, begged forgiveness, and promised that he would try to "admonish" and "exhort" her.

But these attempts came to naught. The Synod refused to believe that he could have been ignorant of the Roman Catholic priest brought from Holland ostensibly to educate their children; that he could have neglected to notice that she never went to confession or communion in an Orthodox church; and that he was ignorant of the December 16, 1723, legislation forbidding Russians to maintain "foreign religious persons" without express permission of the Synod.

Most interesting here is the decision of the Synod on how to proceed. Dolgorukova and her children were provided with a text disavowing their "Roman delusion" and avowing their adherence to the dogmas and traditions of the Orthodox Eastern Greco-Russian Church. They would then be confessed, but not absolved. Then, on a day specified by Her Imperial Majesty, Dolgorukova and her children, in the court church, would read the text aloud in public before the Gospel and the Cross and before the reading of the liturgy. Once they did that, they would be absolved. They would be communed at the same service. However, given that Dolgorukova had repeatedly shown herself to be shifty, to ensure that both she herself remained Orthodox and others did as a precautionary measure ("so that they who behold this would beware of such evil delusion, and remain firm and steadfast in their native Orthodox Eastern Greco-Russian faith"), she was to be sent to a convent ("to be specified by Her Imperial Majesty") with her daughter for public penance, in hopes that the separation from her luxurious home and the constant company of nuns and Orthodox services would have the desired effect. Dolgorukov and his son were also sentenced to penance in another monastery, on the grounds that he should have kept a better eye on his wife and that he should take some time to reflect on how to bring up his children in an Orthodox way. All were to go to daily morning and evening services and to go to confession and partake of communion ("with suitable Christian preparation") in each of the four church fasts. The priests who had earlier given false information about Dolgorukova's going to confession would be dealt with by the Synod separately and directly.

However, Elizabeth softened the Synod's sentence. While Dolgorukov and his son were indeed sent to the Savva Storozhevskii monastery for a year, Dolgorukova and her daughter, "instead of a penance," were to attend local churches for daily morning and evening services; both parents and children were expected to confess and commune during each of the four fasts. After a year had elapsed, they were all, for all their lives, to maintain their faith unwaveringly—and their confessors and parish priests were to keep a firm eye on them to ensure they did so. Thus, just as not going to confession was a sign that one was dubious, so going to confession both privately and publicly was the surest means of spiritual and social atonement.

By the beginning of the nineteenth century, both the theory and the practice of confession changed relative to that of the eighteenth in one key respect. The establishment of the religious consistories made it possible to track confession far more than before. While priests had been sending in confessional records for decades, the sheer bulk and unwieldiness of those books made them as difficult for Synodal functionaries to sift through as they have for later historians. The consistories became not only screeners of the new reports; they also became the chief forum for parish priests—and their parishioners—to remark on, or denounce, anything that they regarded as troublesome, inappropriate, or disagreeable—and which in their minds required further action from higher powers. Thanks to these records, it became possible to broaden the focus of confession beyond the court and the elites to that of the average parish.

Thus, it may be surprising that the first goal of the consistories regarding confession, as set down by Tsar Aleksei Mikhailovich, was simply to try to get people to go annually. Some of the original problems persisted as well. For all the new information, it was impossible to go after every Orthodox Christian who had missed confession. Overburdened parish priests had only so much time, as did overburdened police. But—and this was the innovation—it was easy to do so once someone was already out of his or her own house and in the hands of the law. *One was far more likely to be assigned a penance for not going to confession, or to be brought up before the consistory for not going to confession, if one had already entered the imperial legal machine for another, secular offense.* That is, if one were already in the hands of the secular legal authorities, then it was much easier to apply the discipline of the religious law as well. If someone was already being questioned for theft or horse-stealing or violence or harboring fugitives or attempting suicide or anything else, it was pro forma to inquire when he or she had last gone to confession—and, in the case of an unsatisfactory answer, to send his or her (offenders were overwhelmingly, though not universally, male) case to the consistory.[33]

An absolutely typical early consistory case is that of the house serf Merkul Ksenofontov Kondrat′ev from the district of Sviiazhsk in the diocese of Kazan. In the summer of 1819, Kondrat′ev escaped from the estate of the court counselor Mikhail Emel′ianov and was arrested for flight and for having false identity papers. For those offenses, he was lashed thirty times. For not remembering the last time he had gone to confession and communion, he was sent to the Kazan Consistory to be assigned his penance. On completing that penance, he was to be returned to Emel′ianov.

The penance was set at half a year (given that Kondrat′ev could not remember when he had last gone to confession, the rationale was that it might have been ten years ago or more), and Kondrat′ev was sent to the Theophany monastery in Sviiazhsk. Archimandrite Izrail, in his report, informed the consistory that, under the supervision of the hieromonk Leonid, Kondrat′ev had satisfactorily completed his penance, had shown good conduct, and, after appropriate preparation, had gone to confession and Holy Communion. Kondrat′ev was then released.[34] This pattern—being arrested for something else, questioned routinely about confession, assigned a church penance for not having gone to confession (culminating in confession and communion) along with one's secular punishment for one's secular crime, and exhorted to continue to partake of these sacraments "without fail"—applied throughout the Russian Empire, before and after the emancipation of the serfs.[35]

But penances were assigned not only to arrested individuals who had not gone to confession. *Through the beginning of the twentieth century, civil criminal sentences automatically carried church penances along with them.* The Kazan Consistory, covering territory in present-day Tatarstan, went the furthest in this respect. The Kazan District Court had standard forms for every criminal offense earmarked for the consistory, specifically so that a church penance could be assigned. The relationship of jail sentence and penance was directly proportional. For the shortest term of arrest—seven days—the penance was left to the discretion of the authorities.[36] Most interesting, though, is the automatic reduction (halving) of the penance in the case of a prison sentence. The law, cited in full on each form, spelled out this relationship:

Although [name of person sentenced by the Court], for the crime he or she committed of [type of crime] should be subject to a church penance for a term of [*n*] years, but, bearing in mind that he or she has been sentenced by the civil court for the aforementioned crime [type and duration of sentence], then according to established practice the accused's penance is reduced by half to [*n* divided by 2] under the supervision and guidance of the parish priest, granting the latter the right, on the basis of the 102nd canon of the Sixth Ecumenical Council, in cases of the criminal's despair, risk of death, or sincere repentance, to reduce the term of penance according to his own discretion.[37]

Even in cases where someone received only a "stern reprimand/warning" from the court instead of a jail sentence, if the offense had warranted a penance of five years, the church penance was reduced to two and a half years, not to a warning. When a group of male peasants were sentenced to three months in prison each, their penance was reduced from the stipulated ten years to five. In general, by the early twentieth century, penances ranged from two and a half to five and a half years.[38] Church penances continued to be applied as a routine component of criminal sentences through the February Revolution of 1917.[39] There could be little better illustration of the interweaving of old regime church and state agencies in imperial Russia as regards confession.

My argument, then, seems to exemplify the hoary Foucauldian (European) categories of surveillance, discipline, internalization, and control as components of the modern state. But it is not quite so simple. Paradoxically, the increased role of the state and the increased politicization of confession in Russia did not make people mistrust the sacrament. In fact, they may have invested confession with more importance than it might otherwise have had and brought it closer to the forefront of people's religious lives—certainly to a more prominent role than it had occupied in earlier periods.[40] Perhaps precisely because the state (indeed, sometimes the ruler personally, whether Elizabeth with Dolgorukova or Nicholas I with the killer of the poet Mikhail Lermontov) was so interested in one's inner life, and because the ruler and his or her family were incorporated into public religious observance (the Great Entrance, the commemoration at intercessory and thanksgiving services (*litya* and *molebny*), private piety became much more closely linked to civic responsibility. At a time of perhaps the greatest social stratification in the Russian Empire, the annual confession introduced at the beginning of the eighteenth century was the greatest legal equalizer to which Orthodox Christians of both sexes and all classes were subject. Going to confession became as much a part of civil religion as commemorating the empress's birthday. Not only did rulers assume spiritual responsibility for their people, but the populace too began to identify their own spiritual lives with the state. By the end of the eighteenth century, confession had become accepted as a litmus test—and the point of intersection for—individual piety and state control. Precisely its being a government requirement made confession *more* successful, more widespread as a practice, more privately sought-after in the lands of the Russian Empire, even after it stopped being compulsory, than it did in other Orthodox nations, whether Greece, Bulgaria, Romania, or Serbia.

Indeed, as regards confession, *imperial Russia has more in common with its contemporary Western European neighbors than with its Orthodox coreligionists*. In France alone, the "secular" and the "religious" were inextricable in the old regime. In 1750, for example, a group of zealous bishops began systematically refusing the sacraments to anyone who would not produce a *billet de confession*, a written attestation that one had been confessed by an approved priest. This actually sparked an assassination attempt on Louis XV. The "secular" and the "religious" remained intertwined in France during the period of the Concordat, from 1801 to 1905. During the Restoration (1815–30), the alliance of throne and altar produced a famous piece of legislation—a law of 1825 banning sacrilege that included, among other things, amputation of the hand followed by the death penalty for those who attacked the Eucharist. (This punishment, the same as for patricide, was applied because God-killing was considered analogous to father-killing.) True, this part of the law was never enforced, but it was on the books, and it had disastrous political consequences. In the Papal States, almost all criminal actions had theological implications; one could, for example, be brought up before an inquisitorial tribunal for theft in the nineteenth century. Complicating the picture further yet, cases from the nineteenth century onward show that confession was not only a tool used by the authorities to control their subjects. Instead, confession was also something individuals sought out themselves, and they became indignant when denied their right to go to confession when they wished, particularly during and after the revolution of 1905. Confession could also be a means of settling scores with authorities, whether landlords, employers, or priests.

Thus, as regards religious and state control over confession from the mid-seventeenth century through 1917, and particularly in the eighteenth and nineteenth centuries, imperial Russia was within the spectrum of broad European patterns. The attempts by Russian tsars, emperors, ober-procurators, and archbishops to control subjects through sacramental confession—and of Orthodox believers to turn these attempts to their own purposes—do not make Russia or Orthodoxy a freak Other; they make them part of the modern world.

Church and State versus Church and People

The Two Social Orders of the Russian Orthodox Church

Kristina Stoeckl

The ways in which Russian Orthodox religion has negotiated its relationship with secular state power are as diverse as they are fascinating.[1] In this book about the multifaceted engagement of Russian Orthodoxy with the secular order, two particular modes of engagement or, as I call them in this chapter, two "social orders" stand out: Russian Orthodoxy as a state church and Russian Orthodoxy as a people's church. Drawing on two different theoretical perspectives on religion-state relations—the Byzantine concept of *symphonia* and the modern concept of public religion—this chapter sketches these two orders throughout Russian history. With reference to secondary literature about the Byzantine Orthodox concept of *symphonia*, church-state relations during the Russian Empire, and debates over the state and secularism by Russian religious philosophers, and using works about the Soviet and post-Soviet Russian Orthodox Church and official declarations made by the Moscow Patriarchate, the chapter offers a genealogy of how these two social orders developed within the Russian Church since the eighteenth century.

Symphonia and Public Religion: Two Theoretical Perspectives on Religion and the Secular State

In any discussion about the relationship between Russian Orthodoxy and secularism, one cannot avoid the doctrine and teaching of *symphonia*. In the *Eisagoge* (also referred to as *Epanagoge*), a law codex promulgated by the Byzantine emperor Basil the Great in the second half of the ninth century, the doctrine is described as follows: "The temporal power and the priesthood relate to each other as body and soul; they are necessary for state order just as body and soul are necessary in a living man. It is in their linkage and harmony that the well-being of a state lies."[2] *Symphonia* is the outward sign of a regulated state order based on two sources of authority: the worldly order displayed in the emperor, on the one hand, and the church (that is, the spiritual order) represented by the patriarch, on the other. Both institutions depend on the cooperation of the other for the system to work, since both serve one and the same Christian community.

In practical terms, in the condition of *symphonia*, the Byzantine Church saw itself not as rivaling or standing against the emperor, but as part of a relationship in which both sides worked together to serve the interest of the people. The concept of *symphonia* was, in essence, not much different from Western Christian models of the time—Augustine's doctrine of "two cities" or the Gelasian theory of "two swords"—but unlike in the West, where these models were challenged in the course of the Middle Ages and eventually replaced by secularism as a statecraft doctrine, in the Orthodox world the tension between church and state over the right balance of power remained unresolved.[3] The emperor, as head of state, was subordinated to the true spiritual ruler—Christ Pantocrator. Patriarchs were assigned the task of constantly reminding worldly rulers of this fact and of their obligations toward God and to the people. Thus, the Orthodox Church was permanently torn between the demands of a "high" church in direct proximity to the sovereign and the demands of the people's church serving the community.[4]

Public religion is a modern concept that tries to capture the political role of religion. We generally assume that the modern secularization process divorces political thinking and religious beliefs from each other, with religion becoming a matter of private conscience. Seen from a secular perspective, religion can thus become a valid and justifiable engine to drive active civic commitment.[5] However, apart from the indirect political role of religion via personal religious beliefs that drive social attitudes and behavior, religion can also have a direct political impact through institutionalized relations between churches and faith communities and state institutions. This is the second meaning of *public religions*, and, at least in Europe, we find diverse models of institutionalized public religions.[6] Thus, strictly speaking, the secularization process brings forth two forms of public religion: religious persuasions in private that motivate public engagement and public religious institutions that interact with the political sphere.

The ancient concept of *symphonia* and the modern notion of public religion share one aspect; they both express the dual role that religion plays in the order of state and society. Just as for the proper historical and theological understanding of *symphonia*, for the concept of public religion the distinction between a "state" and a "people's" perspective on religion is central; religion can be understood as an independent source of motivation or a sense of belonging for citizens or as an institution that functions as a partner of the state. In this chapter, I explore in depth these two social orders of religion in the context of Russia and the Russian Orthodox Church. Focusing on the difference between a state church and a people's church, one recognizes that the two phenomena exist parallel to each other inside Russian Orthodoxy: the church as a recognized partner institution of the state and as a people's church. My thesis is that, against a background of totalitarianism, persecution, and emigration in the twentieth century, the two distinct social orders of Russian Orthodoxy have clearly emerged. With hindsight, we can trace a parallel development of a state-centered and a people-centered perspective on the church in history. In very broad strokes, I argue that the latter is the work of Russian monasticism, the Russian religious philosophical tradition, émigré theology, and religious dissidents in the Soviet Union; the former, by contrast, belongs to the Moscow Patriarchate, which has firmly held on to a state-centered perspective, from prerevolutionary tsarism on through Soviet domination and into present-day Russia. Both social orders of the Russian Orthodox Church play an important role in present-day Russia; both are, in principle, compatible with a secular state and democracy, and the two are in competition with each other, with the state-centered order insisting on formal establishment inside the Russian state and the people-centered order affirming the church's independence from the state.

Historical Sketch of the Two Social Orders of the Russian Orthodox Church

Following the Byzantine state-church model, *symphonia* was to be the determining factor in the development of relationships between the tsars and the Orthodox Church in Russia, since the Muscovite Rus' saw itself as the direct successor to the Byzantine Empire, which had ceased to exist in 1453. However, in the context of the emerging Russian Empire, the equilibrium between worldly and spiritual power gradually but constantly shifted in favor of the tsars and led to the church losing its equal share of power playing a subordinate role.[7] This in turn meant that the church that had hitherto been traditionally regarded as representing the people was now seen as representing and being legitimized by the state. While the contrast between a church of the people and the church as a hierarchical institution may be a constant for all Christian churches, I would argue that, in the case of the Russian Orthodox Church, the gap between these two "social orders" of Russian Orthodoxy acquired a particular significance. Dualistic models are necessarily reductive of a more complex social reality, but they nonetheless have explanatory power. In this chapter, I speak of this division as state church versus church of the people; other scholars have used (and transcended) different distinctions—church and believers, high and low church, elite and peasant church, authority and lived religion—to make a similar argument.[8]

Church, State, and People

The church reform of the eighteenth century is widely regarded as marking the subordination of the Russian Orthodox Church to the tsarist state regime and its role as state church within that regime.[9] In 1721, Peter I abolished the patriarchate and replaced it with a board of bishops called the Holy Synod. The Synod was supervised by a lay official, the chief procurator, and church-state relations were hitherto determined by the *Spiritual Regulation* (*Dukhovny reglament*, 1721), which oversaw religious and church life in numerous ways.[10] This is perhaps best illustrated by the fact that clerics were regarded as state civil servants who were answerable to the police. Peter's refashioning of the church as subordinate to the state constituted a break with the Byzantine symphonic model.

While the Byzantine model had been one of balance between church and state, Peter's reforms introduced an Erastianism more commonly associated with Protestant churches in the West. The reform was fashioned mainly on Western models and influenced both the administrative machinery of the church and the structure and syllabus in schools of theological study. Russia was no exception to a general trend in Europe in the eighteenth century when, one after another, "the official churches . . . were subjected to royal absolutist control" and "became more and more ingratiated to the rising bourgeois classes."[11]

The Petrine reforms brought the Moscow Patriarchate into the position of a "handmaiden of the state," as Gregory L. Freeze terms it.[12] The role of the church as absolute and an unrestricted ally of the state was intensified when, in the course of the nineteenth century, Orthodoxy came to be seen as a leading factor in preserving Russian and pan-Orthodox unity. One significant architectural landmark expressing this "national" unity between church and state is the Cathedral of Christ the Savior in the center of Moscow, commissioned by Tsar Alexander I to commemorate the defeat of Napoleon in 1812. The fate of this cathedral symbolizes the twists and turns of the Russian Orthodox Church's history as state church, and I will return to it in this chapter.

At the turn of the nineteenth to the twentieth century, the church hierarchy was under pressure, both from clergy within and from intellectuals outside the church, to reform. The desire for reform was also due to the political institutional situation of the church, still under the control of the state. The Petrine reforms, as pointed out by Randall A. Poole, had produced two very different responses in Russian society. One was irreligion or indifference, the other religious revival and call for reform.[13] On the question of irreligion and atheism, it is important to note that, in the period leading up to the Bolshevik Revolution, the chasm between religious and social issues had become increasingly unbridgeable. The plight and poverty of the Russian people had been exacerbated by the abolition of serfdom in 1861 and the spread of industrialization. The church had done little to prevent class conflict, since the hierarchy had become increasingly out of touch with its traditional role as advocate of the people before the tsar. The church could not be brought to support the demands of the people against the tsar.

Whereas the hierarchy appeared out of touch with the grievances of believers, simple priests did react. A striking example of the ambivalent mood in which the church found itself, and which reigned on the eve of the revolution, are the events of Bloody Sunday in 1905. Tsar Nicholas II had a peaceful demonstration of workers fired on as they were marching toward the Winter Palace, led by the Russian Orthodox priest Georgij Gapon. The Holy Synod supported the cause of the tsar and condemned the demonstration. Another and less well-known conflict between "state" and "people's" church at that time is also worth mentioning: the dispute between the Holy Synod and the *imiaslavtsi* [name-glorifiers], a group of monastics who sought to revive the principles of ancient Eastern Orthodoxy on Mount Athos. The mystical approach and ascetic values defining their theological doctrine were rejected by the Moscow Patriarchate, which, aided by the tsarist military forces, had a number of Russian monks arrested on Mount Athos in 1913.[14] This conflict illustrates the deep rift between official theology and practiced spiritual life within the Russian Orthodox Church before the revolution.

The balance changed during the interim months between the abdication of Tsar Nicholas II and the October Revolution of 1917. This short period became a window of opportunity for the Russian Orthodox Church, and the self-image gained during this time would continue to be of relevance up until today, more than a hundred years later.[15] The hurriedly convoked All-Russian Orthodox Council of 1917 marked the end of the Holy Synod and the reintroduction of the Muscovite patriarchal system. Central issues at the council included questions such as how far and to what extent the laity should be allowed to play an active role in the church leadership and whether parishes should be given greater independence. The council thus strengthened the "people's" perspective on the church. At the same time, the council expressed an approach to ecclesiastical law that, although envisaging a division of state and church powers, stipulated the hegemony of the Orthodox Church within the Russian state government system, thus upholding its ambition to play a special role inside the Russian state.[16] However, any hopes of either the one or the other model being implemented were quickly dashed when the Bolsheviks seized power.

In the period that followed, the Russian Orthodox Church became the subject of massive persecution and repression by the Soviet state, which meant either that the governing bodies of the church had to submit to the Communist regime to survive or, as was often the case, that antiestablishment believers were forced to work underground. In retrospect, we can distinguish a clear division between state-centered and people-centered values within the Russian Orthodox Church in Soviet Russia. The Moscow Patriarchate and its dignitaries, who did in part collaborate with the Soviet State Security Committee (KGB), upheld a state-centered vision of the church; many ordinary believers and religious dissidents stood for a people-centered vision of the church.

The state order of Russian Orthodoxy was in part purposefully instigated by the Soviet government, first during World War II when it was a matter of drumming up public support for defense policy and then again in the 1980s when, in the throes of glasnost (openness), the church once again began to play a key role in public everyday life. The 1988 millennium celebrations commemorating the advent of Christianity in Russia were attended by the Soviet leader Mikhail Gorbachev and broadcast on state television. Orthodoxy took center stage as a national hallmark everyone could relate to and identify with in some way. Today, more than thirty years on, the Russian Orthodox Church's status as an emblematic state institution appears to have been upheld. The Cathedral of Christ the Savior, destroyed by the Soviets in 1931 and painstakingly rebuilt during the 1990s, vividly symbolizes this process of restoration.

Monasticism, People's Church, Diaspora

Parallel to the growth of a state church, one can also trace a line from the fifteenth to the twentieth century showing Russian Orthodoxy becoming a church of the people. We could consider as a starting point for this parallel development the opposition to the reform of the monasteries under Joseph of Volokolamsk in the fifteenth century. Joseph was an advocate of monasteries as landowners to secure for the church political clout and leverage. His attempts to reform were met by strong opposition notably from those monks who lived by the teachings of Nilus of Sora the Athonite, who demanded a monastic life of contemplation in poverty and asceticism. This particular dispute ended in favor of Joseph's school of thought, even if modern-day historians concur on the judgment that the Josephites in the end failed to fulfill their key concern, namely, to establish an autonomous church.[17]

In the nineteenth century, the church dwelt under the conditions of the Petrine reforms and was increasingly criticized by reform-minded clergy, anticlerical intellectuals, and Orthodox Slavophiles alike for having become a mere instrument of the secular state.[18] One typical example of the critical mood at the time is found in Fyodor Dostoyevsky's 1880 novel *The Brothers Karamazov*, in the character Starets Zosima, who evokes a tradition of monastic life that had been eclipsed under the pressures of Joseph's reforms: the monastery as a place of asceticism and spirituality and in which the monk is regarded as mentor and counselor by the common people. The main accusation of the time was that a monk served no useful social purpose, and in the novel one finds both accusation and defense:

> For it is not we, but they, who are in isolation, though they don't see that. Of old, leaders of the people came from among us, and why should they not again? The same meek and humble ascetics will rise up and go out to work for the great cause. The salvation of Russia comes from the people. And the Russian monk has always been on the side of the people. We are isolated only if the people are isolated. The people believe as we do, and an unbelieving reformer will never do anything in Russia, even if he is sincere in heart and a genius. Remember that! The people will meet the atheist and overcome him, and Russia will be one and orthodox. Take care of the peasant and guard his heart. Go on educating him quietly. That's your duty as monks, for the peasant has God in his heart.[19]

In this passage, Dostoyevsky voiced a socially centered perspective within the tradition of Orthodoxy that built on completely different principles than those governing the church of his time. It was exactly this spiritual self-understanding of church—far-removed from any clerical hierarchical understanding—that became the defining principle of the religious intelligentsia of the nineteenth century.[20] The years immediately preceding the Russian Revolution in 1917 represented the zenith of theological and philosophical debate pertaining to the way the church perceived itself and the way others saw it. The Religious-Philosophical Society of St. Petersburg is perhaps the best example reflecting the socially centered approach to the Orthodox tradition.[21] Key protagonists in this movement for renewal, who were moreover inclined to be moderately liberal in their political ideology, included Sergei Bulgakov, Nikolai Berdiaev, Semyon Frank, and Peter Struve. In *Vekhi* (*Landmarks*), a collection of essays published in 1909, they vehemently attacked revolutionist thinking as propounded by Vladimir Lenin and followers and instead advocated a return to a more Christian-Socialist school of thought, which they saw the Russian Orthodox Church as embodying. Their line of thinking was additionally inspired by Marxism, which demanded social justice and equality. It was against this backdrop that Bulgakov and Berdiaev voiced their opinions in the conflict between the church and the *imiaslavtsi*. They sympathized with the ideology embraced by the monks and rejected the authoritarian attitude of the church and government.[22]

The religio-philosophical and sociopolitical debates ended abruptly with the Bolshevik takeover. Many of the religious intelligentsia, including Bulgakov and Berdiaev, took their ideas and views with them when they emigrated in the early 1920s. While the diaspora of Russian religious life was characterized by institutional dispute and conflict over the right approach to the Moscow Patriarchate back in the Soviet Union, at the same time it voiced its views in theological debate, listing the many faults and weaknesses of Russian Orthodoxy that it wanted to see remedied by new theological approaches. Migration and the way events in the Soviet Union were assessed resulted in the traditional state-centered understanding of the church being questioned in its entirety. Which state was the church based on anyway? Was not the traditional church-state relationship ludicrous in that it had even submitted to recognizing Soviet sovereignty? The answers were as varied as their émigré advocates; the synod of Karlovac—which regarded itself as the new official home of the Russian Orthodox Church outside of Russia—remained loyal to a tsarist Russia that no longer existed; the Russian Orthodox community in Paris under the leadership of Bishop Evlogii broke away from Moscow and turned instead to the ecumenical patriarchs of Constantinople; the Russian Orthodox community in Great Britain chose to remain within the jurisdiction of the Moscow patriarchy.[23]

Even more significant than these developments in institutional church-state relations was the theological redefinition of the role of the church in society. There were two decisive views in this regard: the first, led by Bulgakov, stressed the social role and duties of the church and was keen on drawing up new codes of practice in Orthodox social teaching; and the second, headed by Georges Florovsky, envisaged a theological reform rooted in the patristic tradition.[24] For Florovsky and his students (including John Meyendorff), monastic life and particularly the practice of "hesychasm" were the backbone of the Orthodox faith.[25] By contrast, Christian Orthodoxy was kept alive outside of monastery walls and indeed outside of Russia by émigrés who carried out social and charitable work. One well-known example is that of the Orthodox nun Maria Skobtsova (Saint Maria of Paris), who during World War II worked with the French Resistance to help Jews and other refugees to escape a Nazi-controlled France and paid with her own life in the gas chambers of the Ravensbrück concentration camp.[26] What both schools of thought had in common were their efforts to keep the church a community or "congregation" of believers and their underscoring of the importance of human freedom in the Christian understanding of salvation. The state as such no longer assumed the dominant role it had previously played. In the diaspora, the Russian Orthodox Church was/became—at least in the eyes of this particular spiritual elite—a church for and of the people.[27]

Inside the Soviet Union, at the same time, another type of "emigration" was taking place, namely, an "inner emigration" of those religious individuals who remained in the Soviet Union but chose to reject the Soviet system and the restricted space it had allotted to the church. As they challenged the delicate compromise between the government and the church, they not only had run-ins with the Soviet regime authorities but also met the ire of the Moscow Patriarchate. The dissident priest Gleb Yakunin, for example, who repeatedly condemned the church for having been corrupted by the state and attacked the limits on freedom of worship in the Soviet Union, was sentenced to a labor camp in 1979. Another outspoken dissident, Zoja Krachmalnikova, was arrested in 1975 for setting up a literary religious journal.[28]

Monastery, people's church, diaspora—any of these three definitions could describe the "social order" of the Orthodox Church beyond the clutches of the state and its clinging on to the same. But they also describe the limits of the attempt to construct a viable public religious identity solely through reference to religious community. Modern-day observers tend to judge the role of the monastery much more critically than has been put forward here so far. The Russian sociologist Oleg Kharkhordin, for example, interprets the regulated world of monastic life as a model for Soviet *collectivization*.[29] I should add, however, that Kharkhordin has overlooked the fact that monastic life as propounded by Joseph of Volokolamsk, on whose writings he draws, was in contrast with the model of asceticism and mystic spirituality implied in my use of the term.

Vera Shevzov has critically pointed out that the distinction between the two religious subcultures, one represented by "the church" and the other by "the people," is a simplification and risks repeating the errors of the Soviet ethnographic tradition, which, combined with a methodology influenced by Marxist-Leninist principles, resulted in the study of a peasant or popular (*narodnoe*) Orthodoxy that was treated as if it had little connection to the institutional church.[30] Taking into due account such critical views on Russian Orthodoxy, one can nonetheless conclude that both a socially centered perspective and a state-centered perspective had at least a century-long historical lineage by the time of the Russian Revolution and continued throughout the Soviet period. And also, today, the two "social orders"—state church, on the one hand, and people's church, on the other—play an important role in defining Russian Orthodoxy.

The Two Orders of Public Religion in the Present-Day Russian Orthodox Church

I have distinguished two forms of public religion: religious persuasions in private that motivate public engagement and religious institutions that cooperate with the political sphere. Throughout the history of the Russian Orthodox Church, these two orders of public religion have been realized as religious dissidence in opposition to both church and state and as church partnership with the state. Both orders of public religion play an important role today. The Russian Orthodox Church of modern-day Russia continues to be linked to its traditional role as a state church. At the same time, Orthodox faith continues to be an engine for antiestablishment public engagement inside Russia.

The Church as Civil-Society Stakeholder

With the collapse of the Soviet Union and the founding of the Russian Federation, the Moscow Patriarchate entered a new phase of its history in seeking to consolidate its position of privilege as partner of the state. If the law on freedom of religions in 1990 had envisaged equality of all religious organizations in the Soviet Union, the amended law in 1997 foresaw a two-tier religious system in Russia whereby "traditional" and "foreign" religious communities were distinguished.[31] This move represented a revival of the objectives of the 1917 Church Council under changed auguries.[32]

In the document *Bases of the Social Concept of the Russian Orthodox Church*, adopted by the Bishops' Council of the Russian Orthodox Church in 2000, we also find clear indications for the self-acclaimed special status of Orthodoxy in the Russian state.[33] Chapters 2–5 of the document—"Church and Nation," "Church and State," "Christian Ethics and Secular Law," and "Church and Politics"—are devoted to the balance between the religious and political orders. The statements on nation, state, and politics contained in "Social Concept" present the Russian Orthodox Church as a fundamental authority in Russian society that encourages not only moral but also patriotic values and principles.[34] The church appears to be pinning its hopes on a unique relationship to the state to achieve its social, charitable, educational, and other social programs. The architects of the "Social Concept" adhere to the traditional model of *symphonia* as the ideal church-state relationship but acknowledge that this model has historically never been fully realized and, regarding modern-day needs and circumstances, is not feasible.[35]

Chapter 3 of "Social Concept," titled "Church and State," contains a critical reflection on the domination of the state over the church throughout Russian history. The chapter places a strong emphasis on non-subordination and church independence. The precise definition can be found in Chapter 3, section 5, of the official English translation on the website of the Moscow Patriarchate: "The Church remains loyal to the state, but God's commandment to fulfil the task of salvation in any situation and under any circumstances is above this loyalty. If the authority forces Orthodox believers to apostatize from Christ and His Church and to commit sinful and spiritually harmful actions, the Church should refuse to obey the state."[36]

This emphasis on non-subordination constitutes a break with the overarching logic of the entire document, which suggests that the public role of the Russian Orthodox Church is something to be negotiated with the state. At the same time, it is, as I have pointed out elsewhere, not necessarily of a liberal nature.[37] Judging from the agendas of different institutions that manifest the church's status as a civil-society stakeholder, the independent role of the Russian Orthodox Church vis-à-vis the Russian state appears that of a conservative nationalist actor intent on preventing liberal reforms. The World Russian People's Council (Vsemirnyi Russkii Narodnyi Sobor), for example, has become a center for Orthodox nationalist ideas and ideologically covers the right wing of both the government and the church.[38]

People's Church and Civil Society

For the opposite, people's perspective on Russian Orthodoxy, the legacy of monastic life and the diaspora continues to play an important role. Those Russian Orthodox communities in emigration that developed independently outside of Russia throughout the Cold War have become living examples for another model of Orthodox church life. In particular, they have provided lay members a greater and more active part in the church. Orthodox intellectuals who learned about this reality after the end of the Cold War were impressed.[39] When the Soviet Union came to an end and the Moscow Patriarchate tried to renew its influence on its diaspora communities, conflict was destined to ensue. The most memorable example of conflict between the Moscow Central Church and satellite congregations was the schism inside the Russian Orthodox Church in the United Kingdom in 2006, when the incumbent bishop deemed it better to leave the jurisdiction of the Moscow Patriarchate and set up a new diocese of Great Britain and Ireland under the jurisdiction of the Ecumenical Patriarchate of Constantinople. Viewed by many Moscow-friendly observers as a drastic step triggered by personal animosities, those directly involved spoke of an untenable conflict between conservative and liberal views of the church, which manifested in attitudes toward the liturgy being conducted in English rather than Russian and other ecumenical activities.[40]

In 2013, Moscow's Cathedral of Christ the Savior, the symbol of the Russian Orthodox Church–state bond, became the site of a protest performance by the punk group Pussy Riot. The performance itself was politically motivated, but the court trial exemplified the division between a state- and a people's-centered perspective on the church. One member of the punk group said before the court that the performance was intended to lead "intelligent people to the thought that Orthodox culture belongs not only to the Russian Orthodox Church, the Patriarch, and Putin, but it can also be on the side of civil insurrection and the oppositional mood within Russia."[41]

A socially centered approach that continues an age-old tradition of people's church is a component part of present-day Russian Orthodoxy. Although it may only be expressed in confined spaces by small church communities, in academic institutions, and in artistic circles, its impact should not be underestimated. It interrupts the state-centered point of view that dominates the church. The religious dimension of a civil society is no longer dominated by a Moscow Patriarchate, but could potentially be the seedbed of religious initiatives.

The question I posed at the outset of the chapter was whether the Russian Orthodox Church today is orientated more toward the state or toward the people and what conditions and quantifiers determined each side of the issue. This historical overview has shown that the Russian Orthodox Church is, both institutionally and politically, very much anchored in its role as "state" church. At the same time, however, it become clear that if we take a wider perspective on Russian Orthodoxy, including non-church arenas and Russian Orthodoxy outside of the Russian territory, this picture changes. Against a history of totalitarian rule, persecution, and forced emigration throughout the twentieth century, both the state-centered order and the socially centered establishment define the character of Russian Orthodoxy. Both sides must be considered when discussing the relationship between Russian Orthodoxy and secular state power, since both represent phenomena running parallel to each other and demonstrate the duality of public religion.

PART TWO

Intellectuals between Religion and the Secular

CHAPTER 3

Russian Religious Thought and the Christian Justification of the Nation

Kåre Johan Mjør

In 1926, Carlton J. H. Hayes, the academic and diplomat, described nationalism as a modern, political religion. This idea was taken up by the historian Reinhard Wittram, who in 1949 published a collection of lectures titled *Nationalism and Secularization*, in which he argued that the modern ideology of nationalism was inconceivable without secularization. The decline in belief from the eighteenth century onward had been the intellectual premise (*geistesgeschichtliche Voraussetzung*) for the rise of nationalism in Europe. Wittram also stressed that secularization did not imply that belief as such disappeared; rather, the belief in God was gradually replaced by a belief in the nation.[1]

That nationalism is a modern, secular ideology was maintained in Elie Kedourie's classic study, *Nationalism*, of 1960 and has remained a keystone of the study of nationalism to this day.[2] Eric Hobsbawm claims that "the basic characteristic of the modern nation and everything connected with it is its modernity."[3] Similarly, Adrian Hastings, while acknowledging the existence of nationhood in late medieval Europe, regards the political theory of nationalism as a construct of the nineteenth century.[4] For Hastings, categories such as "people" and "nation" came to occupy a hierarchical position above God and the church. Since the late twentieth century, scholars have questioned the simple understanding of nationalism as a replacement for religion (known as the "substitution hypothesis"). Anthony D. Smith's *Chosen Peoples* (2003), for example, explores the ways in which nineteenth-century nationalism often drew on religious discourses. Smith discusses modern nations as "sacred communities," meaning that they regard themselves as "chosen" in relation to a specific territory and that they have a "sacred foundation." According to Smith, religion has not been replaced by nationalism; rather, these two worldviews have informed each other in the modern age, creating a variety of "religions of the people."[5]

This chapter looks at the interaction between religion and nationalism in Russia by focusing on a collection of Russian religious thinkers of the late nineteenth and early twentieth centuries who defended the nation, but who attempted to do so using traditional Christian concepts. Vladimir Solov'ev (1853–1900), arguably the most important religious philosopher in late imperial Russia, took up the issues of nation and nationality from a religious-philosophical point of view. Two thinkers of the next generation then explicitly sought to develop Solov'ev's project: Sergei Bulgakov (1871–1944) and Evgenii Trubetskoi (1863–1920). Bulgakov and Trubetskoi followed Solov'ev in rejecting particularistic nationalism, or what they simply called "nationalism" (*natsionalizm*), on ethical grounds. At the same time, they all eagerly defended "nationality" (*natsional'nost'* or *narodnost'*), which they held to be a universal, Christian idea supported by various New Testament writings.[6]

By implication, Solov'ev, Bulgakov, and Trubetskoi all developed their conceptions of the nation in dialogue with secular modernity, including the ideology of secular nationalism and the belief in the need for peaceful coexistence between modern national groups with strongly felt identities. As such, their novel approaches to the nation did not use traditional religious concepts uncritically, but situated them in the discourse of modernity, creatively combining religious and secular ideas, including Kantian ethics.

Their critique of "nationalism" notwithstanding, the intense preoccupation of these thinkers with the nation must nevertheless be characterized as nationalist. Some scholars have found similarities in their ideas with what is often described as "liberal nationalism." Traditionally associated with the names of Johann Gottfried von Herder and Giuseppe Mazzini, liberal nationalism can be defined as a celebration of "the particularity of culture together with the universality of human rights, the social and cultural embeddedness of individuals together with their personal autonomy."[7] Solov'ev, Bulgakov, and Trubetskoi shared with these liberals the belief that all nations are equal, that they are constitutive parts of humanity, and that they provide an indispensable framework for individual creativity.[8]

However, scholars of Russian religious thought have debated to what extent the label "liberal" applies to these thinkers.[9] Therefore, a more precise description of their worldview may be found in Ernest Gellner's definition of such nationalism as "ethical, universalistic." According to Gellner, these are "nationalists-in-the-abstract, unbiased in favor of any special nationality of their own, and generously preaching the doctrine for all the nations alike." Although Gellner admits that there are "no formal contradictions in asserting such non-egoistic nationalism," he believes that the idea is impossible to put into practice, since nationalism for Gellner means the congruence between the political and national unit, and the number of nations is, in principle, unlimited.[10] Ethical, universalistic nationalism is, in other words, "utopian," a fact that is neatly demonstrated by the future mode in which the discussions of nationality by Solov'ev, Bulgakov, and Trubetskoi are cast.

Certainly, the goal of such nationalists was not a world of independent nation-states in the way Woodrow Wilson would later model it, nor were they particularly concerned with the congruence between national and political units—which was otherwise what the "nationality principle" first and foremost came to mean in the late nineteenth century.[11] None of them actually wanted to dissolve the Russian Empire, and as for its non-Russian nationalities, they defended their rights to cultural self-determination, while arguing that this was best achieved within the multinational and multi-confessional Russian Empire under the supervision of a Christian tsar.[12] They saw empire not as an obstacle to nationality, but rather as the most relevant political framework for uniting different nationalities. Moreover, the main interest of Solov'ev, Bulgakov, and Trubetskoi with regard to nationality lay in the creation of a new Christian world order. They focused mainly on issues such as "national cultural creativity" and conceived of nationality as the expression of collective, "positive energies."[13]

As noted, Haynes, Wittram, and the huge body of literature on nationalism that has appeared since have mostly regarded nineteenth-century nationalism as a secular project, formulated in opposition to the traditional religious claims of authority characteristic of the absolute states. Nationalism bases its legitimacy on the secular principle of the *people*. However extensively religion or religious symbolism has been invoked in nationalist discourses, it is primarily an ideology compatible with the secular order.[14] By contrast, Russian religious thought, especially toward the end of the nineteenth century, sought to religiously reconceptualize the modern, secular vision of the world as divided into nations as a potentially Christian world order. In their embracing of a universalist outlook, Russian Christian thinkers were nevertheless deeply indebted to nineteenth-century discourses on the nation. They were not willing to do without the nation, but wished to reconcile it with a Christian worldview, believing that a genuine Christian had to be what Gellner has termed an "ethical, universalistic nationalist." They accepted, at least partially, a key premise of nationalism as a secular category and secularizing ideology, namely, the privileging of human autonomy over divine control, while at the same time seeing religion as an "ally" with nationalism.[15] Christianity also provided the ethical ideal for national coexistence.

Solov'ev: What Is a Nation?

In the 1880s, having written a series of comprehensive philosophical works, at times with a Slavophile flavor, on issues such as "all-unity" and "Godmanhood," Solov'ev emerged as a harsh critic of nationalism, including Russian nationalism.[16] His main publications on this issue include *The National Question in Russia* (two parts, 1888–91), which consisted of articles published in the press from 1883 onward; the pamphlet *The Russian Idea* (1888, first published in French); and the chapter on the national question in his magnum opus on ethics, *The Justification of the Good* (1897). In these texts, Solov'ev accused nationalists of fostering hostility between peoples. At the same time, Solov'ev wanted to defend nations as indispensable to the realization of the highest task of humanity creating a "universalism without cosmopolitanism."[17]

"What is a nation?" Ernest Renan had asked just a few years earlier.[18] In the foreword to *The National Question in Russia* (dated 1888), Solov'ev referred to Russia's "historical position, national character, and worldview," which should contribute to the integration of the world's nations into one humanity.[19] For the most part, he refrained from elaborating more specifically on these concepts. In his writings on nationalism and nationality, the existence of the nation as a distinct phenomenon is taken for granted, wholeheartedly defended, but rarely defined in positive terms.[20] In fact, a significant part of *The National Question in Russia* is devoted to the critique and even ridicule of other attempts to define the Russian nation according to its past achievements or inherent traits. Regarding the claim that there exists such a thing as a "Russian philosophy," for instance, he wrote that "all that is philosophical in these works is not Russian, and that which is Russian does in no way resemble philosophy, at times it resembles nothing at all."[21]

In Solov'ev's view, nations are great when they manage to "raise themselves above the soil" and contribute to a reintegration of the family of Christian nations. And in doing so, "nationality ceases to be a simple ethnographic and historical fact."[22] Solov'ev is first and foremost concerned with the future: "By Russian nationality I understand not only the ethnographic unity with its natural characteristics and material interests, but a people that feels that above its peculiarities and interests there exists a common universal task of God—a people that is ready to devote itself to this task, a *theocratic* people according to its calling and duty."[23] Solov'ev detects in the Russian past a few moments of "national self-denial," which are widely celebrated in his writings on Russia. These were the invitation of the Varangians, the Christianization of Russia, and the reforms of Peter the Great. The significance of these events can be observed in their results—in their "fruits" (*plody*); Russian nineteenth-century literature, for instance, was inconceivable without Peter's Europeanization of Russian culture.[24]

These few moments of national self-denial are presented by Solov'ev not as inherent Russian traits, but as exceptional moments characterized by the will to act. These moments, according to Solov'ev, should be seen as key points in Russia's cultural memory. Solov'ev's approach thus parallels Renan's voluntaristic and anti-genealogical definition of the nation as a series of endeavors, sacrifice, and devotion. For Renan, memories of past national accomplishments were indeed important, but primarily as sources for new, collective actions. He rejected the determinism of ethnic nationalism; for Renan, nationality was a question not of identity but of active identification.[25] Solov'ev, in a similar fashion, argued that great achievements are accomplished when the focus is on the task, and the nation forgets about itself. Nationality is an "energy" that operates by itself, not one that should be actively stimulated. "People and nations are unique, but no one can make themselves unique."[26]

However, in the subsequent essay of *The National Question in Russia*, "Love to the People and the Russian National Ideal (Open Letter to Ivan Aksakov)," Solov'ev goes on to suggest that the Russian past has offered not only these few moments of exemplary self-denial, but also a continual historical development that represents a confirmation of Russia's specific tasks at present. The highest ideal of the Russian people, Solov'ev claims, has been "holiness," an ideal that has come to expression in the idea of "Holy Russia," which more concretely has involved the "creation and continual preservation of the Russian state" and has "prevented us from chaos and self-destruction."[27] An important aspect of Solov'ev's utopian thinking in this period was the unification of the Christian churches through Russia—he firmly believed that this would become the "word that Russia proclaims to the world." This unification project has to be Russia's initiative, due, seemingly, to its history of successful state building. The tradition of statehood—in which two acts of national self-denial have been decisive: its establishment by the Varangians and its reformation by Peter the Great—is the foundation for ascribing Russia the future task of creating a new, Christian world order. In *The Russian Idea*, Solov'ev suggests that the existence of a mighty Russian empire must indicate that it has a crucial role to play: "When you look at how this huge empire with greater or smaller splendor during two centuries has appeared on the world stage . . . , when you see this historical *fact*, then you ask yourself: what is the *idea* [*mysl'*] that it hides for itself or reveals to us; what is the *ideal* principle animating this huge body or the new word that this people will utter to the humanity; what will it *accomplish* in world history?"[28]

As we have seen, Solov'ev described Russia as a "theocratic people," but what were the grounds for this claim? In Andrzej Walicki's interpretation, Russia's "capacity for self-denial" was for Solov'ev itself "an argument in favor of the conception of Russia as a nation with a universal mission, destined to serve the spiritual unification of mankind."[29] However, despite his severe critique of his contemporaries' attempts to demonstrate the greatness of Russia, Solov'ev, too, celebrated Russian might. Apparently, it was its imperial legacy that provided it with a unique theocratic task. Still, Walicki is right to point out that Solov'ev for the most part emphasized the need for self-denial, and this idea occupied a far greater place in this part of his oeuvre than state building.

Solov'ev's Ethics for Nations

The first essay of *The National Question in Russia*, originally published in 1883, bears the title "Morality and Politics: Russia's Historical Duties," a formulation that clearly signals the ethical approach that Solov'ev now wanted to take in relation to the issues of nation and nationality. And in the "Russia and Europe" essay of 1886, we find the following ethical principle, which seems to extend Kant's categorical imperative to the national level: "Every nationality has the right to live and freely develop their energies [*sily*], without destroying this same right of other nationalities."[30] (The context of the statement is a defense of small, oppressed nations, hence the stress on rights rather than duty.) Solov'ev understands nations as analogous to individual human beings, so that Kantian deontological (duty) ethics as formulated for human beings apply also to nations. This is not without foundation in Immanuel Kant's writings. Kant also made in his treatise *Perpetual Peace* (1795) a comparison between nations and "moral persons," but he did not apply the categorical imperative as actively to nations and states as Solov'ev did.[31] Throughout his writings on the "national question," Solov'ev's conceptualization of the nation and other collective entities is founded on this analogy: "Just as Christian morality aims at realizing the kingdom of God within the separate human being, Christian politics should prepare for the coming of God's kingdom for all humanity as a whole, as consisting of larger parts: peoples, tribes and states."[32]

Moreover, Solov'ev's texts of the 1880s are also dominated by the imagery of nations as the constitutive parts of the universal whole—as a member of the universal body (*telo*). In Solov'ev, the body as consisting of members refers not to the nation itself—this is how the "nationalists" mistakenly had understood it—but to the *humanity as made up of nations*. This image, too, figures in the opening of his *National Question in Russia*—"A people should recognize itself as what it really [*poistine*] is, that is only a part of the universal whole"—but plays an even more prominent role in *The Russian Idea* and its attacks on contemporary Russian nationalists, who had failed to recognize that Russia was a member of the universal body (humanity). Humanity as a whole, Solov'ev wrote, should be conceived of "as a great collective essence or social organism, whose living members are separate nations."[33] The important implication of this for Solov'ev was that no nation existed independently, only as a part of a larger whole, but also that humanity could not do without nations.

Thus, Solov'ev's conception was ambiguous. He described nations both as "moral beings"—as analogous to individuals—and as members of a body. In addition to being a part of a human being (or organism), the nation was also compared to one. This understanding of the nation was, on the one hand, functionalistic; on the other hand, it assigned human beings with moral responsibility, granting the nation thereby a certain, if relative, autonomy. The overlapping of these two models in Solov'ev's concept of a nation amounts to the following paradox, as aptly formulated by Judith Deutsch Kornblatt: "You must give yourself to the whole in order to be an independent part. . . . [Solov'ev] demands at once an active embrace of self-renunciation and self-affirmation."[34]

One might ask why Solov'ev insists on defending the nation when nationalism has caused so much hatred. The answer that emerges from his own texts is that the idea of humanity as made up of nations is a Christian idea. According to Solov'ev, Christianity is a religion that recognizes the nations while condemning "nationalism"—it is a transnational but not anti-national religion. Solov'ev extensively quotes the Bible in order to justify his philosophy of nations, most centrally the "Great Commission": "Go therefore and make disciples of all nations" (Matt. 28:19). This is mentioned in *The National Question in Russia* and figures even more prominently in *The Russian Idea*. Christ, in Solov'ev's interpretation, did not himself address and did not send his disciples to a particular nation, since to Him they existed only in their moral and organic union, as living members of one spiritual and real body. Thus, the Christian truth confirms the immutable existence of *nations* and of the right to *nationality*, condemning at the same time *nationalism*, which for a people represents the same thing as egoism for the individual: a bad principle that seeks to isolate the individual entity by turning difference into separation, and separations into antagonism.[35]

Self-denial is for Solov'ev likewise a Christian principle, as grounded in Luke 9:23–24: "If any man would come after me, let him deny himself and take up his cross daily and follow me. For whoever would save his life will lose it; and whoever loses his life for my sake, he will save it."[36] The notion of "fruits" (*plody*) encountered above has also strong New Testament connotations (cf. Matt. 7:16 or Gal. 5:22). These biblical sources make up one discursive context evoked by Solov'ev in his discussion of the national question.

Another important philosophical context for Solov'ev's justification of the nation is, as noted, Kantian ethics. In *The Justification of the Good*, Solov'ev returns to Kant in the chapter "The National Question from a Moral Point of View." According to Kantian ethics, human beings are to be seen not as a means to an end but as ends in themselves, and Solov'ev applies this principle to the relationship between nations. However, since nations are (also) members of humanity, they cannot be seen as ends in themselves throughout; they serve first and foremost an overall end, outside themselves. Thus, they are in one respect means, but not to other nations (this would be "nationalism"). They are means to a common, universal end. History has shown, Solov'ev writes, that "nations prospered and were great only so long as they did not make themselves their final end, but served the higher, the *universal* ideal ends."[37]

Nationality in History

In *The Justification of the Good*, the Kantian starting point is followed by an account of the historical development of the idea of nationality, or rather of its gradual recognition in history. Solov'ev is a perennialist (but not primordialist) who sees nationality as an idea that has existed from time immemorial. In *The Russian Idea*, he wrote that "the idea of a nation is not what it conceives of itself in time but what God conceives of it in eternity."[38] Still, the recognition of this idea is a gradual achievement of the historical process—a belief that resonates more generally with Solov'ev's conception of "Godmanhood." As Kornblatt has pointed out, to provide a review of human history was one of Solov'ev's favorite practices, and the nationality chapter of *The Justification of the Good* takes us back to the ancient world, where the understanding of nationality was still weakly developed;[39] the "other" was defined here not as one of a different nation, but as belonging to a different city or as one of the "barbarians." Before Christianity only the Jews had developed a "firm national consciousness," but it was an exclusive one.

Christianity, however, represents the central event in this history. It replaced Roman universalism and its indifference to nationality with a new universal-

ism: the Christian idea of all-humanity, according to which every human being may become "formed in Christ" (Gal. 4:16) in a way that accounts for
differences. And just as Christianity, according to Solov'ev, does not wipe out
the individual differences, it cannot extinguish cultural differences either:

> According to the well-known saying of St. Paul, the peculiarities of struc-
> ture and of function which distinguish a given bodily organ from outer
> organs do not separate it from them and from the rest of the body, but
> on the contrary are the basis of its definite positive participation in the
> life of the organism and make it of unique value to all other organs and
> the body as a whole. Likewise, in the "body of Christ" individual pecu-
> liarities do not separate one person from others, but unite each with all,
> being the ground of his special significance for all and of his positive in-
> teraction with them. Now this obviously applies to nationality as well.
> The *all-embracing humanity* (or the Church which the Apostle preached)
> is not an abstract idea but is a *harmonious union of all the concrete positive
> characteristics of the new or the regenerated creation*. It therefore includes
> the *national* as well as the *personal* characteristics.[40]

Since the body of Christ is perfect, Solov'ev goes on, it cannot consist only
of "simple cells," but must also contain more "complex organs," which are
the nations. Again, we observe Solov'ev's use of analogy in order to apply New
Testament ideas to nations. His projection from individuals to groups is not
without basis in the Bible. In Paul's first letter to the Corinthians, to which
Solov'ev here refers (1 Cor. 12:12–14), the unity of the congregation is visual-
ized by a comparison of its individuals, who are even of different nationalities, to the members of a body: "By one Spirit we were all baptized into one
body—Jews or Greeks, slaves or free." Still, Solov'ev's approach must nevertheless be regarded as a creative and modern interpretation of Paul. He uses
Paul's portrayal of the ideal congregation (or the universal church) as a model
for the ideal coexistence of nationalities.

In fact, Solov'ev argues that there is no principal difference between the nation and the individual, only one of "greater stability and wider range" in the
case of nations. And he goes on:

> Since Christianity does not demand absence of individual character [*be-
> zlichnost'*], it cannot demand absence of national character [*beznarod-
> nost'*]. The spiritual regeneration it demands both of individuals and of
> nations does not mean a loss of the natural qualities and powers; it means
> that these qualities are transformed, that a new direction and a new con-
> tent are given them. When Peter and John were regenerated by the

spirit of Christ, they did not lose any of their positive peculiarities and distinct characteristic features. So far from losing their individuality, they developed and strengthened it. This is how it must be with entire nations converted to Christianity.[41]

Solov'ev firmly maintains that the positive understanding of nationality is a Christian idea, evoking also in *The Justification of the Good* the Great Commission. The rejection of abstract, empty cosmopolitanism is likewise provided a biblical foundation; Paul, according to Solov'ev, was deeply concerned also with his own "nation"—the Jews. He was "not a cosmopolitan."[42]

Despite its Christian basis, the idea of nationality was, in Solov'ev's account, not the main preoccupation of the first Christians, but one that only gradually gained foothold in Europe, by way of a "free human realization of the divine idea in this world," as Randall A. Poole defines "Godmanhood" according to Solov'ev.[43] Its first significant manifestations can be found in late medieval Italy (in Dante, for instance), and Solov'ev provides a rich overview of the universal significance of national contributions in literature and art: contributions that, because they are significant, are always also expressions of nationality. Italy and others "took the greatness and the value of their nationality to lie not in itself taken in the abstract, but in something universal, *supernational* that they believed in."[44] A significant creative act emanates from a national source—with universal results. It is not possible to make significant contributions without expressing one's nationality, Solov'ev argues. "Cosmopolitanism," while correct in its critique of "nationalism," is unacceptable from a moral and Christian point of view, since it rejects nationality—a principle sanctioned by the Bible and Christian ethics as understood by Solov'ev.

As I have shown, Solov'ev used the device of analogue on two levels: nations as members of the human body and as individual human beings. In the final part of the chapter on the "national question" in *The Justification of the Good*, Solov'ev argues that there is an even deeper connection between the nation and the individual human being than the analogical one. Nationality, according to Solov'ev, is an inseparable *part* of the human personality, "an inner, inseparable property of the person."[45] And since the individual is always part of the nation, it expresses this nation. An ethical relation to a human being also requires a recognition of his or her nationality; if not, we do not recognize the whole person, only the person "abstractly." Persons do not exist apart from their nationalities, and if we love a person—which we should—we must also love his or her nationality. And Solov'ev concludes his chapter by combining the biblical and Kantian discourses in the following way: "Love all other nations as your own."

To what extent were these ideas unique to Solov'ev, writing at the end of the nineteenth century? Ethical universalistic (or liberal) nationalism, as such, was *not* unique to Solov'ev; the idea that nations form the component parts of humanity had already been formulated by Herder and Mazzini, who also provided a similar critique of cosmopolitanism.[46] And although Herder is likely to have found Solov'ev's at times quite negative comments on non-Christian, "barbaric" peoples unacceptable, Herder, too, regarded Christianity to be the only truly universal religion. It contains a universalist ethics while being the only religion that addresses all nations. Herder identified Christianity with the moral ideal of humanity (*Humanität*), believing that all nations belong to the Kingdom of God.[47] A difference between Solov'ev and Herder lies in the latter's broad interest in the past (language, folk culture, mores, and so forth), which we do not find in Solov'ev. The most original contribution of Solov'ev in this respect, however, appears to be his consistent and systematic biblical justification of nations and nationality. This was a Providentialist view that the concert of nations would be a realization of a Divine plan.[48]

Solov'ev's attempt to ground the nation in Christianity was both a response to processes of secularization and an attempt to bring religion and politics together (again). In this perspective, Solov'ev represents a reaction to modernity. In justifying nations religiously, he sought to sacralize the secular spheres of politics.[49] This confirms, in turn, that he was a post-secular thinker.[50] However, this implies that his project was not merely a reaction to modernity but also an expression of it, which incorporates several of its features.

Solov'ev's discourse on nations and nationality is characterized by a combined appeal to reason and revelation, the latter as conveyed by authoritative texts whose source lies beyond what Kant called "mere reason." Or to use Charles Taylor's distinction, it evokes both the immanent frame and the transcendent order.[51] Reason figures most evidently in Solov'ev's application of the moral law. But also his treatment of the biblical sources, which he reinterprets theologically and philosophically by means of analogies ("this must also apply to . . ."), suggests that scripture for Solov'ev was, while authoritative, subject to continual reinterpretation, and not a text with a final, given meaning.[52] Solov'ev's writings on nations, nationality, and nationalism are therefore expressions of reason, understood as the ability of rational analysis, on the one hand, and as practical reason, the ability of self-determination, on the other.[53] And yet, reason is not entirely self-sufficient, but has a transcendent reference in that its statements, in this case about the nation, are aided by revelation (scripture), which makes the transcendent present in this world. Thus, Solov'ev's biblical references testify to a theist and Providentialist worldview where the transcendent and the immanent are seen as "working together."[54]

Bulgakov's National Universalism

The issues of "nation" and "nationality" figure prominently in Bulgakov's works after the turn of the twentieth century. In these, the impact of Solov'ev, who had passed away in 1900, is evident.[55] In his comprehensive essay "What Does Vladimir Solov'ev's Philosophy Offer the Contemporary Consciousness?" (1903), Bulgakov described Solov'ev's discussion of—and solution for—the "national question" within the framework of Christian ethics as one of the most important achievements of his public activities.[56] In the "idea of nationality" (*ideia natsional'nosti*), Solov'ev had managed to find a middle way between "cosmopolitanism" and "nationalism" (or "zoological patriotism"). Referring to Solov'ev's maxim that we should "love all other peoples as we love our own" as a Christian commandment, Bulgakov argues that Solov'ev's synthesis managed to overcome the limitations of previous positions "in the spirit of a positive, Christian universalism."[57]

Thus, what Solov'ev "offered the contemporary consciousness" was *synthesis*. More specifically, nationality as a universal idea was, in Bulgakov's interpretation, Solov'ev's "synthesis of Westernism and Slavophilism," under the inspiration of Fyodor Dostoyevsky's vision of Russia as characterized by a unique universalism and openness toward other nations. This idea recognizes the "rights of every nationality" and proclaims the "highest norm of international relations" to be love among the peoples and not hatred. True, Bulgakov argued, there were problematic elements of classical Slavophilism from which Solov'ev had not managed to free himself entirely, and the task now was therefore to purify Solov'ev's ideas as well. Nationality does not consist in "historical remnants," that is, some ancient national heritage, as classical Slavophilism, Dostoyevsky, and to some extent Solov'ev himself, had believed; it is a "positive spiritual force, which requires that these [remnants] are removed in order for it to be fully and freely realized." More specifically, Bulgakov promoted a synthesis of the Slavophile philosophical rejection of cosmopolitanism with an acceptance of the "political credo of Russian Westernism": the importance of juridical rights.[58]

This synthesis is described by Bulgakov not only as "reformed Slavophilism" (by means of a synthesis with Westernism) but also as *national universalism*. Bulgakov is therefore ambiguous in that he, on the one hand, clearly addresses his own, Russian society, which should embrace this philosophy of nationality. On the other hand, "reformed Slavophilism" is also presented as a universal philosophy—a contribution of the Russian nationality that is of universal significance. It is Russia's task not only to express its own nationality as one of many contributions to humanity but also to provide the true version of the universal principle itself. Thus, Bulgakov's text contains (moderate) messianic visions of Russia's contribution to world history, features that would become even more prominent in his writings after the 1905 revolution.

"Messianism" was a topic that Bulgakov briefly touched on in his contribution to the *Landmarks* collection of 1909, "Heroism and Humility." Toward the end of the essay, Bulgakov makes an explicit connection between nationality and religion: "The foundations of the national idea are not merely ethnographic and historical, they are primarily religious and cultural; it is based on religio-cultural messianism, into which all conscious national feeling is necessarily cast. So, it was for the greatest bearer of the religio-messianic idea, ancient Israel, and so it remains for every great historical people."[59] Bulgakov's main purpose in this passage was to criticize the cosmopolitanism of the (positivist, Marxist) intelligentsia, which had ignored the importance of the national idea, a critique that resonated more generally with the overall aims of *Landmarks*.[60] In denigrating spiritual life and individual creativity, the intelligentsia had also missed the positive potential of nationality, which in Bulgakov's understanding was closely related to the domain of spirituality. But Bulgakov's mention of the topic of messianism in this context inevitably suggests that Russia has the potential to become a "great historical people." He devoted more attention to this issue in another article published not long after the *Landmarks* collection, "Reflections on Nationality" (1910).

"Reflections on Nationality" sets out to analyze the nation as a "metaphysical problem." Distinguishing at the outset between a "nominalist" and "realist" approach to the nation, Bulgakov gradually sides with the realist one, later in the text also described as "mystical realism." In opposition to the nominalist position held by positivists, empiricists, and "idealists" (whereby he means neo-Kantians rather than religious idealists like himself), according to whom the nation is merely the "sum" of "national facts and features," the realists regard the nation as a "transcendental reality" and "substantial being." It exists "not as a collective concept or a logical abstraction, but as a creative living principle, as a spiritual organism, with which its members exist in an inner living connection." But how can we really know that the nation in this sense exists? Bulgakov's idealist answer is that our feelings tell us so and that we are therefore deeply related to it. "We *recognize* ourselves as members of the nation, because we *in reality belong* to it as a living spiritual organism."[61] Making use of Kantian terminology, Bulgakov conceptualizes the nation not as a "phenomenon," but as a "noumen," a "thing-in-itself." It is accessible to us first and foremost via intuitive or mystical perception, as based on its occurrences ("phenomena"). The nation's existence is not dependent on our consciousness but exists independently of our reflections upon it. By contrast, the subject does not exist independently of the object: "In order to exist, a conscious and volitional life presupposes a personality whose core is rooted in being (*bytiistvennoe iadro lichnosti*) as a nourishing, organic environment."[62] Bulgakov distinguishes this "personality" (*lichnost'*) from the "empirical self," and it is the former that makes up the point where the subject (human being) and object (external world) meet. Bulgakov's thinking here is clearly influenced by Friedrich Schelling, as Schelling was also cited in his main philosophical work of this period, *Philosophy of Economy* (1912).[63]

Humanity is made up of nations; nations, not "abstract cosmopolitan all-humans," make true universality possible. And nations represent the main framework for the creative being of the human personality. "We participate in the common cultural work of humanity as members of a nation."[64] As we have seen, Bulgakov also understands the nation as a reality continually created and acted out by human beings, whose personalities are part of the nation. The reflection on the past is nevertheless important in order to stimulate the national instinct further and bring about "new national creativity." National self-awareness leads, in turn, to a recognition of the "national calling," which Bulgakov equates with "national messianism." Examples of Russian national messianism for Bulgakov include the "Russian Christ," that is, the distinct understanding of Christ among the Russian people, and the "Russian socialism" of Aleksandr Herzen, that is, socialism in accordance with ancient Russian peasant ideals. These are discoveries of and by the national spirit, which because of their significance should be announced to the rest of the world. The belief in universal significance is what allows Bulgakov to introduce the concept of "messianism" here: "This messianism emerges in all epochs and in all peoples in periods of national revival; this is the general form of the consciousness of national individuality."[65]

Bulgakov's concept of messianism does not mean that there is only one chosen nation, and he discusses at length the danger that the feeling of exclusiveness as the outcome of such callings may create. Messianism must be "ascetic." And yet, separate nations—not all of them, but those that in the *Landmarks* article are referred to as "historical"—have their particular periods of revival, and there is no doubt that Bulgakov saw his own period as one of a national revival of Russia. The idea that particular nations tend to dominate in particular periods was in this period taken up also by Nikolai Berdiaev, who likewise foresaw an imminent Russian ascendancy.[66]

In "Reflections on Nationality," Bulgakov argues philosophically for the existence of nations as a reality that exists beyond its empirical manifestations and as an inseparable part of the human being. The human being is a "living, concrete personality, styled in national-historical flesh and blood."[67] Bulgakov follows Solov'ev in defining nationality as a "force," an expression of the nation, without which significant contributions in literature and art are inconceivable. Johann Goethe's *Faust* is a "universal achievement that at the same time could be born from the depths of the individual and national spirit only." It could never have been written in Esperanto, Bulgakov proclaims. Bulgakov conceptualizes the relationship of nation and personality metonymically. Although we find some analogical comparisons of nations to human beings and an extensive use of personified descriptions of nation in his text, Bulgakov by and large abandons the functionalistic vocabulary that characterized Solov'ev's writings on the nation. To Bulgakov, nations exist independently even of active human creativity and continue to exist also in periods when the national self-awareness is hibernating. Thus, in comparison to Solov'ev, Bulgakov's metaphysics of the nation represents a shift toward viewing nations as more independent and self-sustained component parts of humanity. This development is part of a broader preoccupation with the nation among Russian intellectuals, including the "religious intelligentsia," after the 1905 revolution.[68]

Bulgakov's "realism" and belief in the transcendental reality of nations, which is styled in a philosophical language of Kant and Schelling, is in turn grounded also in Christianity. Throughout the article, Bulgakov refers to the Bible in order to justify his idea of the nation and nationality. The nation as a "real, vital unity" is evident in the personified descriptions in the Bible of various peoples, Bulgakov claims, emphasizing that this is not merely a rhetorical device, but rather the proof of a "religious-metaphysical idea." The Old Testament prophets have likewise confirmed that nations exist not in an ethnographic sense, but in terms of faithfulness to their calling and serving and of their righteousness. Most importantly, Bulgakov also evokes the Great Commission, in order to show that Christianity is the only religion that addresses "all peoples" (*vse iazyki*). It is universal, but not anti-national; it appeals not to human beings in an "abstract" sense, but to *personalities*, and nationality is an integral part of the personality. A defining feature of Christianity is that it has been "nationally realized," and, according to Bulgakov, it is therefore also the only "supranational, truly catholic religion."[69]

Trubetskoi: Nationalism against Nationalism?

In 1912, Trubetskoi published an article called "The Old and the New National Messianism," in which he subjected the Russian messianist ideas of the past and present to a severe critique. He attacked his contemporaries, Bulgakov and

Berdiaev (the article was partly a response to their latest publications), as well as Russian messianist visions throughout history, including the early sixteenth-century idea of Moscow as the "Third Rome," the visions of the Slavophiles and Dostoyevsky, and Solov'ev's utopian, theocratic ideas. According to Trubetskoi, Solov'ev, while having exposed the "old messianism" of the Slavophiles, remained in his theocratic writings of the 1880s a Slavophile messianist, since he believed that Russia would and should play a leading role in the transition to a new, theocratic world order. Solov'ev saw the Russian people as a "theocratic and tsarist" people, the "salt of the earth."[70] Trubetskoi, however, rejected both the belief that Russia had an exclusive mission in accomplishing this theocracy and the very utopian idea of theocracy itself.

As we have seen, both Bulgakov and (in particular) Solov'ev were critics of nationalism. According to Trubetskoi, however, they did not go far enough; they remained nationalists since they believed that Russia had a unique mission in the world. Even Bulgakov's "subdued [*smiagchennyi*] messianism" was dismissed by Trubetskoi, who saw it as a contradiction in terms; a nation is either chosen or not.[71] Besides, Trubetskoi felt that Bulgakov, when conceptualizing a "Russian Christ" as the aspects of Christ discovered by the Russian people and left unnoticed by others, turned this difference into a *norm*.

However, Trubetskoi was a wholehearted defender of the nationality idea and hence, in keeping with the vocabulary introduced at the outset of this chapter, an ethical universalistic nationalist. According to Trubetskoi, national perspectives are indispensable; it is not possible to receive Christ without a particular, cultural perspective and without focusing on one of his particular aspects, but he stressed at the same time that such perspectives always also imply a *limitation*. The full recognition of all aspects of Christ is a collective task of all the Christian nations together, while to "localize Christ," as Russian thinkers from the Slavophiles to Bulgakov have tended to do, means to limit Christ himself.[72]

More specifically, Trubetskoi distinguished between the Christianity of Paul (Protestantism), Peter (Catholicism), and John (Orthodoxy). He drew this typology from Solov'ev's final work, *Three Conversations*, in which, according to Trubetskoi, he finally abandoned his utopianism in favor of a pluralistic understanding of Christianity.[73] The synthesis of these understandings, in turn, should be a common, universal task and not the task of one particular nation.

By implication, Trubetskoi also believed that every nation has a task or a calling: to reveal not the truth of Christianity as such, but an aspect of it. No nation is chosen, according to him; they are all equally important. "Messianism" must therefore be replaced by "missionism": "Every people has its service, its calling and its mission in the Kingdom of God. There cannot be any other solution from the point of view of a universal religion, which insists that in the Heavenly Father's house there are many rooms," Trubetskoi writes, referring to the Gospel according to John (14:2).[74] His text is filled with biblical quotations and references to an even greater extent than those of Solov'ev and Bulgakov. He promotes what he calls the "Christian doctrine on nationality, as inherited from Christ, his disciples, and Paul.[75] Trubetskoi, too, draws fundamentally on the Great Commission, which he reads not only as a confirmation and sanction of the existence of a manifold of nations but also as a text that provides all of them with a task, emphasizing the verse "teaching them to observe all that I have commanded you" (Matt. 28:20). In addition, Trubetskoi evokes the Pentecost story, construed here as the story of both the unification of all the peoples of the earth and the sanctification of their national differences, as symbolized by the languages. "Every people found in this revelation of the universal Messiah its particular *fiery* tongue [*ognennyi iazyk*]."[76] The confusion caused by the building of the Tower of Babel was hereby eliminated, without, however, national differences being erased. All nations are boughs on the Christian tree, Trubetskoi writes, referring to Paul's "if the root is holy, so are the branches" (Rom. 11:16), but the messianists have mistaken the boughs themselves for trees. The Pentecost event, by contrast, did not separate; it united the nations; it "confirmed national particularities and at the same time surmounted national borders."[77]

If Trubetskoi used the Bible as the main, explicit, authoritative source for this idea of national coexistence, he appears to have been led to this understanding by the philosophy of Solov'ev. He particularly praises the Solov'ev who eventually abandoned utopianism and messianism, the Solov'ev of the *Three Conversations*. In his comprehensive *Vladimir Solov'ev's Worldview* (1913), Trubetskoi also emphasizes the chapter on the "national question" in *The Justification of the Good* as the "best pages" of this work. "The value of nationality lies not in itself, but in something universal, in the contribution it makes to the universal culture. And in these universal principles lies the source of strength and greatness for every singular nation."[78] Trubetskoi, like Bulgakov, endorses Solov'ev's positive definition of nationality, as opposed to both "nationalism" and "cosmopolitanism." Trubetskoi is a perennialist who sees nationality as an "eternal principle": "Like the personality it is according to its idea a repository of the Unconditional, Divine life."[79] Repeated references to "task" and "calling" point toward the future, and yet the essence of this task is given at the outset—in Russia's case, to represent and maintain within the family of Christian nations the mystical interpretation of Christianity of Saint John. This means that Russia indeed has a calling, or what he refers to as the "Russian national" or "religious idea." The main difference between him and

Bulgakov or Solov'ev, none of whom actually believed that there was only one chosen nation, appears to be that Trubetskoi rejects the idea of a cultural and religious hegemony of certain "historical nations" in particular periods.

During World War I, however, Trubetskoi's harmonious vision of a Christian world made up of equal nationalities would be replaced by an increasing belief in Russia's ability to liberate other nationalities from German hegemony and, more generally, in the coincidence between Russia's national interests (or their "calling") and Christian ends. Thus, views that he consistently should have regarded as "messianist" were now also emerging in his own thinking, and his Providentialist interpretation of the war and of Russia's role brought him again closer to Bulgakov.[80]

Since the late twentieth century, scholarship on European nationalism has emphasized that the modern discourse on the nation is not as purely secular as previously thought.[81] Many nations, as articulated by their national strategists (politicians, public intellectuals and academics, artists), have seen themselves as "chosen peoples" (Anthony D. Smith). The religious justification of the nation as discussed in this chapter is therefore by no means an exclusively Russian phenomenon. By the same token, Russian thinkers have been inclined to apply messianist perspectives to their own nation. While Trubetskoi criticized both Solov'ev and Bulgakov for being too nationalist and even messianist, Trubetskoi himself, as we have seen, was hardly opposed to messianist ideas on behalf of Russia. And yet it is important to emphasize that the Russian religious philosophy of the nation, or what I here call the Christian justification of the nation, was not about Russia only—it had a universalistic ambition.

This raises in turn the question as to whether the Russian thinkers were unique in grounding the principles of nation and nationality in Christianity, that is, in regarding Herderian "liberal" or "ethical universalistic" nationalism as a specifically Christian idea. The material analyzed in this chapter does not permit us to draw any decisive conclusions in this respect. However, so far research on the combination of nationalist and religious discourse in the nineteenth century has mostly revealed that the construction of a modern national identity has made active use of a people's religious traditions, be it Catholicism in Ireland, Protestantism in Germany, or Orthodoxy in Russia (in particular from 1881 on). The thinkers analyzed in this chapter, still, proclaimed the equality of *all* nations, while maintaining the nation's crucial importance for both the individual human being and the entire humanity.

In the early nineteenth century, some representatives of German protestant thought, who have been described as "Christian nationalists," saw the separation of humanity into nations as "God's plan for humankind."[82] During the Napoleonic Wars, Ernst Arndt imagined that God had wanted a plurality of nations and religions. "Diversity is the motto of my world," Arndt's God exclaimed. Friedrich Schleiermacher likewise wrote that "each nation was designed to illustrate a special aspect of the image of God, in its own peculiar setting and by its own specially determined position in the world."[83] These views seem to differ from the Hegelian perspective, according to which only some nations were called to play a "historical role," though G. W. F. Hegel too, in keeping with his own reading of Christianity, accorded for a plurality of nations. For all of them, a sound sense of nationality was more truly Christian than "cosmopolitanism." Meanwhile, the idea of a "unity in national diversity" would in the period leading up to World War I yield to increasing proclamations of German superiority, not unlike what happened in Russia. As A. J. Hoover has commented on the development in Germany, "Maintaining the balance between human unity and diversity is a delicate walk on a tightrope." This comment applies to Russian thought before and during World War I as well.[84]

And yet the attempts by Russian thinkers to ground pluralistic ideas about nation and nationality in scripture have, to my knowledge, few clear parallels in West-European thought. What is remarkable about the material examined in this chapter is the extensive striving for justifying the plurality of nations with reference to the Bible. Is there anything that might explain the Russian interest in nationality as a distinctly Christian idea, apart from the fact that they lived and operated in the formative age of nations and nationalism that the nineteenth century was, after all?

Although Solov'ev, Bulgakov, and Trubetskoi rejected "nationalism" and would not have accepted this term for their own projects, all of them nevertheless promoted a nationalism that was universalist in its intentions. They demonstrated a point made by Shmuel N. Eisenstadt, that universalist projects are inevitably shaped by the settings in which they are formulated.[85] The universalisms discussed in this chapter are projects that, implicitly or explicitly (in particular in the case of Trubetskoi), *include* Russia on equal footing with the West, contesting Western hegemony. And although they mainly addressed Russian society, a general quest for *recognition* is clearly present within their projects. Their epistemological situation can therefore be described as postcolonial.[86] They formulated a dream of true universality in a context where it was experienced as absent. At the same time, these universalisms, when compared for instance to that of Herder, are also exclusionary in their undeniably Christian-Providentialist understanding of world history.

It may seem problematic to regard Russian religious ethical universalistic (or liberal) nationalism as a specifically Orthodox (and not merely a Christian) response to modernity, although Bulgakov himself argued that his own philosophy of "national universalism" grew out of an Orthodox understanding of the world. The thinkers as they appear in the texts discussed in this chapter are too indebted to Kantian ethics for them to be regarded as "Eastern thinkers" exclusively. And while they all may be said to reject a strong separation of the religious and secular dimension, they do this by combining (Orthodox) biblical justification with a modern philosophical discourse in the tradition from Kant.

Still, I would argue that Orthodoxy represents a context that has significantly shaped the worldview of these thinkers and their positive vision of nationality. In the Orthodox context, national differences matter religiously. Commentators have claimed that "it remains one of the great paradoxes of modern Orthodoxy that a faith with such universalist theological claims could have its ecclesiastical structure fracture so severely along political and ethnic lines in the past century and a half."[87] The nationalization of Orthodox churches was a process that was particularly significant in the former territory of the Ottoman Empire in the nineteenth century.[88] In imperial Russia, the situation was different.[89] Still, as we have seen, Solov'ev's writings on the "national question" were precisely a response to the growing *Russian* nationalism that emerged in post-reform Russia, where Solov'ev sought to redefine the nation—a Western nineteenth-century construct—in a positive way for Christian purposes, while preserving the empire.[90]

And yet, the belief in a close affinity between religious confessions and national or ethnic groups represents in the Orthodox context a legacy, I would suggest, that extends beyond nineteenth-century state- and nation-building projects, which in turn means that the modern Orthodox preoccupation with the nation is not as paradoxical as suggested in this chapter. As argued by Adrian Hastings, the "development of autocephalous state churches, primarily within the Orthodox tradition, . . . is one of the strongest and most enduring factors in the encouragement of nationalism."[91] In my view, this Orthodox background—a church of one faith separated nationally—may explain why a Christian world order with universalist aims was for the thinkers discussed in this chapter unthinkable without the nations, and why they could not accept universality without nationality. As Bulgakov wrote in 1910, "The connection between religion and nationality has not been sufficiently appreciated."[92]

CHAPTER 4

"Dark" Intellectuals

Engaging with Modernity through *Kruzhok* Culture

PETER A. SAFRONOV

Writing the intellectual history of the Soviet Union is not a straightforward enterprise. The usual source base, such as books, artworks, or other material evidence of the creative process, including highly circumscribed by the censorship regime. Yet it is essential for intellectuals to have a means of communication to express ideas and gain recognition. Institutional and material infrastructures, including independent media, publishing houses, and universities, help to maintain human or textual relationships.[1] In this chapter, I examine how Soviet intellectuals created their own "dark" infrastructure to substitute for missing or censored public and civil institutions. I highlight *kruzhki* (circles)—informal gatherings of relatively small groups of friends and colleagues to discuss various topics of common interest, political, cultural, or philosophical—as the core element of this homegrown "dark" infrastructure of intellectual life. My focus is on one *kruzhok* in the USSR of the 1950s and onward. Through a rereading of its (hi)story, I highlight a specific mode of engaging with secular modernity in the late Soviet context that evolved around personalities and circles.

Kruzhki were a rather peculiar form of social interaction. Deliberately eschewing influence on society as a whole and having no means of open communication with the broader public, *kruzhok* members communicated one with another in a self-enclosed, hermetic manner often supported by occasionally invented private language.[2] Deprived of the possibility of transforming the social order, they turned to self-transformation, using an implicit set of norms, standards, and habits imposed by the *kruzhok*. Successful personal transformation often led to group recognition and the feeling of being "in demand." Numerous circles of intellectuals became a substitute public sphere, an arena for social and political debate not necessarily opposing official ideology. It is difficult to define the outcomes of circle activities of members in terms of distinct professional outcomes. *Kruzhok* members had the much greater ambition of creating a new self. This new self, however, required the products of the inner *kruzhok*'s linguistic operations, the constant naming and renaming of philosophical concepts and social realities.

By looking specifically at the Moscow Methodological Circle (MMC), I demonstrate that this *kruzhok* functioned less as a typical philosophical discussion group and more as a secular "congregation" or even dissident cult. The MMC required that its members engage in the circle emotionally and that they dedicate themselves to what was seen as, in effect, a "chosen" people. Initiation into the methodological movement demanded the complete reordering of the moral and intellectual priorities of the new member, and it is not surprising that many members spoke of a kind of conversion to the MMC, which involved a "second birth," a total reassembling of a personality from scratch. Of central importance was the fact the MMC demanded a kind of mystical union with the organizer of the circle, who became a "teacher" with devoted disciples who came together in a space of contemplation and communication.

In essence, this chapter argues that the MMC became yet another example of "secular religion," a term used as early as the 1930s and 1940s to describe totalitarian political movements (Nazism and Stalinism), which seemed to incorporate religious ritual and systems of belief minus a belief in a deity or the transcendent. In time, however, *secular religion* has become a term that is a means of understanding, as Emilio Gentile has written: "The conferring of sacred status upon a secular political entity takes place in such a way as explicitly to transform this entity into the principal controller of collective existence, and into an object of cult status and an object of dedication though the creation of celebratory rituals in which participate not occasional crowds, but a liturgical mass."[3]

I also demonstrate that, when MMC members borrowed from cultic and religious practice, they did so in part because of the Soviet context in which they were embedded; in a sense, they mirrored the prevailing ideological culture, in which the power to appropriate reality came through changing nomenclature, demanding strict obedience to a fearless leader, and insisting on collective participation in ideological self-transformation. As such, they borrowed from the secular religious qualities of Soviet Communism as a whole.

Yuri Slezkine has made the argument for a Bolshevik "millenarianism" that demanded "conversion" and "transformation" of its adherents.[4] More interestingly, Victoria Smolkin has convincingly detailed how, especially during the Nikita Khrushchev era, the Soviet Communist Party explicitly copied religious ritual to create "atheist" experiences for baptisms, weddings, and funerals. The MMC, then, operated in an environment of Soviet secular religion, and paradoxically appropriated elements of it, even as members sought to separate themselves from officialdom and to create their own secular-religious space.

"*Kruzhok* culture" blossomed in imperial Russia in the early nineteenth century.[5] It was substantially suppressed, but not exterminated, after the October Revolution and then reinvigorated in the mid-1950s. The activities of various artistic and literary circles were, in part, organized within a patronage system. Their organizers thus acted like patrons, providing emotional comfort and limited social recognition for *kruzhok* members, becoming "charismatic fathers, disciplinarians and mentors."[6] In the Soviet context, the moral authority of the circle organizers was seen as quite distinct from the financial sponsorship monopolized by state authorities.[7]

Throughout the nineteenth and twentieth centuries, Russian literary and philosophical circles were tightly connected with various educational institutions at the postsecondary and graduate levels. Beginning in the 1920s, rapidly proletarianized universities played a leading part in the formation of new Soviet intelligentsia. Soviet educational policy has long been researched in the context of Soviet social and political history. Of great influence is Sheila Fitzpatrick's work dedicated to the relationship between education and social mobility.[8] Over decades, the educational system was persistently used as the chief mechanism for implementing the Soviet egalitarian ideology. Starting in 1917, revolutionary events became the catalyst for dramatic migration within the borders of the former Russian Empire and brought considerable numbers of former peasants to the cities and to the institutions of higher education.[9] Nonetheless, even by the end of the 1950s, Soviet universities still did not provide equal access to higher education for all social groups. Party and state officials who repeatedly claimed the necessity for higher education "to stand closer to life" ironically advertised the extent of the educational gap.[10] Therefore, some caution must be exercised in labeling universities in the USSR as fully "Soviet," by distinguishing external performative uniformity and internal substantial diversity within the institutions of higher education. Especially the oldest and most prestigious universities in Moscow, Leningrad, and Kiev were able to produce sophisticated self-enclosed forms of elitist sociality, while maintaining and reproducing all of the rituals of the Soviet social context.[11]

The Soviet state thus failed to complete the radical egalitarian transformation of the educational system and ended up providing much better educational opportunities for the children of intelligentsia and party elite than for any other classes in the Soviet state.

As the political climate in the USSR changed after Joseph Stalin's death, the issue of where to employ the increasing number of "specialists" with university diplomas came to be more and more pressing. Further clarification of this problem by the government was postponed due to the emerging realization that, were the real condition of industry in the USSR revealed, it would have demonstrated a persistent need for low-skilled workers without higher education. In other words, there was the very real possibility of large-scale intelligentsia unemployment.

The late 1940s and early 1950s saw the generation born and raised under Stalin graduating from universities. The atmosphere of ferocious totalitarianism was obviously intolerant toward any kind of public, grassroots intellectual initiatives. Unrestrained intellectual communication existed only in small groups of friends who could fully trust each other. Conditioned by performative involvement in the practices of the socialist regime and the simultaneous intellectual and emotional detachment from it, a generation of intellectuals regarded themselves as aliens in their own country.[12]

The partial relaxation of totalitarianism after 1953 had a decisive impact on *kruzhok* culture. Young intellectuals fully committed to the collectivist ideals of Soviet society got a unique historical chance to step out of the shadows of pervasive fear. The Khrushchev era was the golden age of the Soviet intelligentsia, which could now enjoy its elitist position in a still undereducated country. The vagueness of the egalitarian foundations of the Soviet educational policy was extremely important for assigning special status to certain universities and disciplines, objectively contributing to the growth of social inequality in the Soviet society. The struggle for greater instructional and financial autonomy among the most prestigious educational institutions contributed significantly to the imbalances in the educational system and social stratification.

In contrast with the bright engineers and physicists whose talents were almost immediately absorbed by rocket or nuclear science, those educated in the humanities and social sciences were under much tougher ideological control. There were obviously no vast state funded enclaves of freedom and prosperity like nuclear cities for philosophers, economists, or would-be sociologists, although they were readily recruited by the party and state apparatus.[13] The network of *kruzhki* continued to mediate communication in philosophy, sociology, economics, and other ideologically sensitive fields of scientific research well after Stalin's death, until the era of perestroika.[14]

Focus, Sources, and Methodology

Against the background of intellectual circles of the "thaw" era, one group stands out due to its long-lasting influence. In 1952, the so-called Moscow Logical Circle originated in the scientific seminars at the faculty of philosophy at Moscow State University.[15] Created by several alumni and postgraduates from the university's faculty of philosophy, this circle was headed by an energetic war veteran, Alexander Zinov'ev, and soon established itself as a center of unprecedented intellectual activity, attracting younger generations of students from many other university departments. The meetings of the Moscow Logical Circle unfortunately were not carefully documented, but, according to personal memoirs, it was focused on a detailed reconstruction of Marxist philosophical logic as outlined by Karl Marx himself in his works.[16] In the mid-1950s, the Moscow Logical Circle was transformed into the Moscow Methodological Circle (MMC), chaired by Georgii Shchedrovitskii, who studied physics and philosophy at Moscow State University. The members of MMC, including Shchedrovitskii and his disciples and friends, founded circles and seminars in Moscow, Krasnoyarsk, Novosibirsk, Kiev, and other Soviet cities, most of which remained very active until the collapse of the Soviet Union. These activities are usually grouped together as part of the "methodological movement."[17] The preservation of Shchedrovitskii's legacy and further development of the methodological movement is now supported by the nonprofit foundation Shchedrovitskii Institute of Development (SID). The SID website hosts the collection of around 250 memoirs and biographies of the participants of the methodological movement from the 1950s onward. These documents were also published in 2006–7 in two volumes titled *MMK v litsakh (The Faces of MMC)*.[18] This collection was augmented by the study of the materials of the International Biography Initiative website, maintained by the University of Nevada, Las Vegas, professors Boris Doktorov and Dmitri Shalin and hosting the documentation of the work of many Soviet intellectuals, including a lengthy interview with the well-known Soviet émigré sociologist Vladimir Shlapentokh, who had a close connection with some methodologists at one time.[19]

Given the shortage of the usual sources for intellectual history in the case of the Soviet Union, the SID collection seems to be a valuable source as it is. The reading of memoirs, diaries, letters, and autobiographies as "life stories" is almost de rigueur in the humanities. No less than active face-to-face interviews, written accounts are improvisations.[20] Yet despite the power of intentional and unintentional retrospective transformations, memories tend to align with certain patterns. Therefore, an analytical lens adopted toward narrative inquiry might help to discern hitherto unseen practices of refined intellectual communication that developed in the twilight zone of the *kruzhok* culture. A narrated life story is a result of an iterative process of selection and composition of "relevant" facts as well as silencing others.[21] Common strategies of highlighting a certain event while omitting another equally testify to some shared meaningful experience in the lives of narrators. As a whole, the (auto) biographies of the circle's participants provide a window into the core elements of a peculiar communicative culture able to sustain itself across multiple upheavals and to shape strikingly similar identities and worldviews. Examination of postwar Soviet intellectual history thus finds its way through the dialectics of inclusion and exclusion.

A Privatized Public: *Kruzhok* Interactions

Among the different circles that were established or flourished during the Khrushchev era, the MMC proved to be extremely influential and durable. Inspired by the study of Marxist philosophy at the informal meetings of the Moscow Logical Circle, Shchedrovitskiy proclaimed that the circle should not limit itself to a self-enclosed collection of canonical great texts. Abstract philosophical speculations were taken into consideration as a practical plan for the rearrangement of the whole array of human intellectual capacities. The social world was, in turn, analyzed as a "system" of objectified results of mental activity.[22] That explicitly idealist account was completely unacceptable for orthodox Marxist pundits at the faculty of philosophy. Shchedrovitskiy was expelled from Moscow State University, forbidden from defending his candidate dissertation. In the late 1950s, he searched for alternate careers, unusual for a Soviet philosopher.

Even after Khrushchev's critique of Stalin's cult in 1956, the Communist Party monopoly of the interpretation of social reality remained basically unchallenged. There were no opportunities to openly address current political or social events in academic research. Overall, conformism penetrated the behavioral strategies of all social groups, including the intelligentsia. A common intelligentsia strategy for those unwilling to collaborate with party and state apparatchiks was to "run away" to the fields of research detached from modern social issues, such as ancient or medieval studies, mathematics, logic, and the history of science.[23]

For those who still wished to discuss contemporary issues in a forum free from state control, the *kruzhok* was the only option. Therefore, the fact that Shchedrovitskiy himself was not permitted to teach at the faculty of philosophy at Moscow State University on a regular basis, due to his unorthodox views, made it perfectly logical for him to found the MMC.

The personal memoirs of the rank-and-file members of the methodological movement from the 1950s to the 1980s have many recurrent themes in their portrayal of regular circle meetings. There are few mentions of discussions of philosophical problems or of any sophisticated conceptual arguments produced by a *kruzhok* leader. Instead, most informants readily share their vivid memories of the kinds of emotions that their *kruzhok* inspired—describing the *kruzhok* as "the single most intense existential experience" or "the happiest time in my whole life."[24] The MMC, it appears, was not a network for the exchange of ideas but rather an emotional community of people sharing common feelings.[25] These affective bonds had a certain spiritual flavor. The life stories of the participants of the methodological movement often contain references to religious terminology.[26] For instance, *kruzhok* members would repeatedly describe the contents of the circle meetings as a "revelation" and Shchedrovitskiy himself as "the Teacher in Action."[27]

It is worth noting that, despite the geographical expansion of the methodological movement, the leader's home seminar in Moscow remained central in the network. In the tradition of *kruzhok* culture, the regional circles copied the structure of the central circle, and even tried to reproduce the leader himself. Indeed, though *kruzhok* members were consciously rejecting the authoritarian quality of Soviet authority, they paradoxically still held to a kind of centralized authoritarian leadership in the person of the *kruzhok* leader, who was expected to provide an inspiring example of complete self-transformation under unfavorable conditions. The circle leader was usually excluded from a wider range of social and professional activities, and this, in turn, validated his or her position as founder and leader of a *kruzhok*.

Kruzhok intellectuals attempted to "recycle" the concept of collectivity at the core of Communist ideology. Collectivity seemed to them to be essential to any act of thought. Thinking always meant thinking *together*, apart from any authorship claims.[28] Despite their growing alienation from Soviet reality, circle members never envisioned outright individualism as a mode of intellectual production.[29] The Kantian understanding of Enlightenment as rooted in individual responsibility for one's own thoughts and propositions and the Husserlian notion of the spiritual solitude (*Einsamkeit*) of the researcher were both completely alien to the MMC. People kept attending circle meetings for years or even decades, simply because they might otherwise have nothing to do with their lives.[30] According to the majority of the memoirs, *kruzhok* activities did not provide any psychological comfort for individual participants.

On the contrary, the circle was violently "reforged into a working collective from a crowd."[31] Personal intellectual autonomy was by no means regarded as a natural prerequisite for freethinking. In fact, the circle leader was the only one who fully preserved an individual personality. What resulted was the "hypertrophy of a lone creator" in the circle, which sometimes evoked protests against an authoritarian style of leadership, though no one ever seriously challenged the paramount dominance of Shchedrovitskiy in the circle.[32]

"Chosen" People: *Kruzhok* as Destiny

In the eyes of *kruzhok* members, the insularity of the movement did not imply a rejection of the public good. Shlapentokh, a prominent representative of the *kruzhok* culture in the USSR in the 1950s, recalls: "We felt ourselves like a band of brothers, chosen to improve life in the whole country."[33] Again, though it rejected official ideology, here *kruzhok* culture seemed to borrow from the intensively propagated Soviet moral value of feeling responsibility before the "people," and before the Soviet nation as a whole. Moreover, these values were considered their own reward, and moral satisfaction in the methodological movement was placed far above any material gain.

The message of the MMC was selective and targeted. Participation in the methodological movement required a sort of sublime affinity, a shared sense of intellectual and moral superiority, which established a sense of belonging to a very special group of "chosen" people. The methodological movement was not open to the public. Those who were kicked out of their universities and who were unable to publish their manuscripts saw themselves as a distinct elite that could not tolerate any challenge to their intellectual supremacy from outside.[34] In contrast with the Central European intellectuals willing to disseminate values of Enlightenment to a general public, members of Soviet *kruzhki* preferred to keep their community limited to representatives of Soviet elites (such as alumni of the most prestigious universities and former party activists).[35] Since the public sphere seemed to be corrupted by its purely performative requirements, intellectuals invented their own uncompromised "true" public. Every communication to this "true" public was mediated by a "filter" of close friends and admirers, who each declared their exceptional ability to understand and disseminate the "exact" words of their leader.

Circle members tended to equate the needs and hopes of their own *kruzhok* with the needs and hopes of Soviet society in general, apart from any gender, ethnic, or religious differences.[36] This does not contradict Shlapentokh's words on the desire of circle members to "improve life in the whole country." The "country" was considered a passive population awaiting an original creative impetus from *kruzhok* members. In contrast to Alexei Yurchak's account of Soviet everyday life in late socialism, the MMC was not deterritorialized from Soviet reality.[37] On the contrary, it considered the (Soviet) world as its natural territory. It is important to carefully distinguish between the performative uniformity of *kruzhok* members as Soviet citizens and their inner identity as the guardians of a certain communicative and intellectual ethos. Informal circles operating throughout the whole country at the scale of the methodological movement (apparently displaced from Soviet reality) produced sophisticated self-enclosed forms of sociality, but they had as their aim the reconstruction of the broader social context. Following Michel Foucault, this could be labeled as a heterotopia.[38] The heterotopian nature of intellectual circles in Soviet society by no means provides a universal explanation for various kinds of *kruzhok* culture.

Critics sometimes suggest that Shchedrovitskiy and his circle were a nonphilosophical, straightforward, progressivist enterprise due to his authoritarian, top-down style of leadership, which suppressed individual freedom for a would-be common good.[39] This account accurately represents the arrogant elitism of the MMC leader, but it fails to capture one crucial element of the methodological movement as a whole; participation in the *kruzhok* was an ongoing act of the "creation" of one's own self *ex nihilo* or, more precisely, out of heavily constrained linguistic experimentation.[40] Conversion to the methodological movement was like a "second birth," a total reassembling of a personality from scratch.[41] Initiation in the methodological movement abruptly changed all moral and intellectual orientations of the newcomer. Unlike modern scientific reasoning that presupposes the distinction between subjective and objective, the "methodological" movement put forward the paradoxically idealist premise that there is nothing purely subjective or objective in the field of intellectual activity. Free-floating, formal, intellectual effort, which mainly took the form of constant renaming of philosophical *trivia*, was regarded as a universal power that could crack whatever problem may come up.[42] The doctrine of "thought-in-action" (*mysledeiatel'nost'*) expressed the sense of belonging to some shared space of "ideal" practice. Up until now, former members of the methodological circle easily preserved recognizable psychological habits, like drawing up so-called schemes while explaining conceptual relations.[43] Speculation on a specific issue performed through "schemes" was seriously regarded as the path of transformation of thought into practice.

Spectral Intellectualism

Any discussion of the Soviet *kruzhok* culture cannot and should not be taken out of the context of the general political, economic, and social problems of Soviet society, which can offer a critical evaluation of the analytical usefulness of the category of "Soviet." It is important to acknowledge the heterogeneity of the communicative framework of Soviet intellectual culture. Postwar Soviet society was not a unified entity but rather a multitude of lifeworlds, whose existence in many ways followed the premises of Soviet ideological and social order.

Individualism, both in terms of mental habits and social patterns, was equally unacceptable for party apparatchiks and members of unofficial *kruzhki*. The style of communication and type of interaction that prevailed in the methodological circle reveals the fundamental problem of Soviet *kruzhok* culture. It cherished the ideal of free intellectual development in a rather impersonal if not downright abusive manner. Speaking their own language and keeping a distance from any official institutions, "methodologists" consciously remained amateurs with respect to any given field of professional expertise. There was no point being a professional in a community based primarily on cherishing the affective ties of its members. Developing one's own personal autonomy let alone intellectual standing was paradoxically both promoted and heavily suppressed by inclusion into a specific community speaking "the same language."

In the *kruzhok*, value was placed on the practice of thinking. Yet the act of thinking was not regarded as the autonomous enterprise of a rational individual. *Kruzhok* members had to conform to the "teacher's" expectations, which were never explicitly articulated, but had to be inferred from "schemes" and from the atmosphere of the *kruzhok* meeting as a whole. Shchedrovitskiy did not dominate the discussions of the circle. Yet his mere presence, and the tacit signs of his esteem, subtly directed the conversation of the *kruzhok*. In fact, the leader was the only absolutely free participant of *kruzhok* activities since he was the one to establish the rules of communication and could change them without warning.

To an extent, the methodological circle acted like a congregation—in which conversion experiences were prized, adoration of the leader was encouraged, and faith in the values and ideas of the group was essential. That cast the flavor of *crypto* philosophy on the representations of the MMC and its members. Circle members still vividly remember their first encounter with a circle leader. So deep was this transformative event that they desired to relive it repeatedly. The alchemy of Stalin's grand cult shriveled up to a much smaller affective cult of

Shchedrovitskiy.[44] The dialectics of physical absence and affective presence was and is extremely important for *kruzhok* culture. The legacy of the MMC was (and partially—in the memories and actual practices of its bearers—is) constituted by an ongoing conversation with an absent or even late teacher, supported by a very strong emotional memory of the existential shock experienced at the first encounter.[45] This emotional fixation represents a quasi-religious *unio mystico* of teacher and disciple in the ideal space of contemplation and communication. Affective bonds in the circle could be regarded as a specific form of spiritual patronage, irreducible to the ongoing exchange of ideas between the living.[46]

Striving to transcend socialist reality, the *kruzhok* could inspire intense spiritual experiences. Truth and decency for Soviet intellectuals were supposed to stand apart from official state institutions and conformist public life. *Kruzhok* membership often proved to be a single powerful substitute for corrupted ideological values disseminated by state-controlled media. Ties of friendship formed in the circle were the only personally legitimate source of moral evaluation and authority. Yet, within the circle, participants constantly had to submit to the undisputed intellectual and moral supremacy of the circle organizer and leader.

Soviet ideology had always exploited the future to legitimize the present. This turned out to be true of the methodological movement as well. It established an ideal of thought-in-action, not in the form of a transient horizon of social history, but as a true accomplishment of intellectual work. Consequently, it underwent a shift in orientation toward the interaction between thought and action; the action in question here, unendingly stretched between the present and the future, allowed circle members to experience mental activity as an ongoing experience of personal transformation *hic et nunc*. This meant that there was no clear distinction between thought acts as such and affective experiences, which in turn further obfuscated *kruzhok* culture for outsiders who often perceived the methodological movement as esoteric and nontransparent.[47]

The affective dimension of circle membership served the comprehensive objective of creating a new type of personality. The modern tendency to encourage intellectual autonomy, to develop critical thinking in all social groups, and to strengthen the connection between creativity and application was not entirely alien to Soviet society and culture. Intellectual life depends on infrastructure: libraries, media, publishers, and so on. If an intellectual has none of these at his or her disposal, it is hard to see how he or she could act as a public intellectual in a proper sense of the word. Soviet intellectuals produced alternate means of communication to substitute for the missing official institutions and organizations. Since the exchange of ideas itself happened in a dangerous twilight zone between ideological lip service and outright dissidence, its setting took a rather specific form. Individualism was never embraced as a core part of the public sphere. *Kruzhok* culture from the very start encouraged communicative and infrastructural collectivism, thus contributing to decay of the possibility of thinking as a stand-alone activity in Russia.

Father Aleksandr Men' and Jewish-Christian Identities under Soviet Secularism

APRIL L. FRENCH

In 1975, a Jewish man traveled to a church in Novaia Derevnia, a village north of Moscow, and asked the parish priest, Father Aleksandr Men' (1935–1990), questions about Jews and Christianity, in light of "the recent influx of Jews . . . into the Russian Orthodox Church."[1] The priest offered "private reflections in response to private questions," but the stranger asked whether he could share Men''s answers with friends. Men' gave permission, but the "friends" turned out to be readers of the Jewish self-published (samizdat) journal *Evrei v SSSR*. With the subsequent republication of this "so-called interview" in the Paris-based émigré journal *Vestnik Russkogo khristianskogo dvizheniia* (*VRKhD*), Men''s private conversation with a Jewish visitor soon spread to Russian-speaking readers around the world.[2]

Men', who was born to Jewish parents and baptized as an infant with his convert mother, told the visitor he had never experienced antisemitism in the church. The publication of the "interview," however, exposed him to a swell of antisemitic diatribe.[3] Although underground Jewish groups had already been discussing the conversion of Soviet Jews to Russian Orthodox Christianity, the interview brought this issue to the attention of Russian nationalists, who looked to the Russian Orthodox Church (ROC) as a source of *their* national heritage. They thus viewed Men' as the alleged ringleader of a pernicious "Judeo-Christianity." This publication and its fallout highlight the way Men' lived at the uneasy intersection of two late Soviet ethno-religious communities:

Russian nationalists who identified with the ROC and Soviet Jewry in the midst of a self-conscious cultural awakening.

Few scholars have addressed Men''s Jewish identity or his thoughts on Jews/ Judaism and Christianity. Those who have discussed his Jewish origins have not considered the full breadth of his written and spoken ideas on the subject.[4] Within his life was woven a complex tapestry of Christian, Jewish, and secular experience and thought, and his own identity was forged at their intersection. This chapter examines the way Men' understood his and others' Jewish identity through the lens of his Christian theology in engagement with a secularist Soviet Union.

Indeed, as this chapter will demonstrate, Men''s very life and thought— including his discussions with Soviet Jews about Christianity and his arguments against antisemitic Russian nationalists—counter the simplistic binary between the religious and the secular; instead, Men''s thought reflects a complex interaction of the sacred and the secular while sitting comfortably within Charles Taylor's portrayal of religion as a vital aspect of modernity, which is a space where faith "is one human possibility among others."[5] Men''s theological and philosophical discussions were infused with certain secular concepts such as freedom of conscience (which had been enshrined in the Soviet Constitution but was infringed on regularly by leaders of Soviet forced secularization). He sometimes reappropriated Soviet secular terminology in his discussion of modern Jewish realities, but he melded this with a Christian theology of radical equality and universality. He believed that equality and universality were rooted in the teachings and mission of ancient Israel and that they must also be central tenets in any truly secular government (the Soviet Union and modern Israel both falling short of this ideal, in his opinion). From this complex perspective, Men' espoused an explicitly Christian theology concerning the People of Israel and Judaism, entered into the "Who is a Jew?" debate, reflected on the identity of Jewish converts to Christianity, and stood against chauvinism and for freedom of conscience. Father Men', who played a unique role in the public sphere as a rather popular religious figure in the late Soviet period, navigated resistance from representatives of religious, secular, and ethno-religious spaces and engaged questions of Jewish identity through an explicitly Christian grid, engaging with secular concepts in the process. Men''s story complicates two simplistic moves commonly made by scholars in different camps. On the one hand, it obviously challenges the secularization thesis and its attempts to place the religious and the secular in a static binary. On the other hand, it also reveals that it is incorrect, as scholars of civil religion seem to suggest, to conflate the religious and the secular such that they each effectively lose their meaning.[6]

Jewish Roots, Christian Upbringing

Alexander Agadjanian notes that Men''s Jewish background "deserves special exploration," in order to understand how his ethnic "identity influence[d his] worldview and work."[7] In his ministry, Men' focused his energy predominantly on his priestly duties and theological writing, so he wrote and spoke comparatively little about his Jewish origins. Yet, an examination of his family roots and early experience reveals the context for his thought concerning Jews/Judaism and Christianity.

Men''s brief description of his ancestry featured his maternal great-grandmother, Anna Osipovna Vasilevskaia, whose husband died early, leaving her to raise seven children.[8] In 1890, Anna fell ill with a growth in her abdomen. When no doctor or medicine could remedy her situation, she went to see the famous priest Father John of Kronstadt, when he visited Kharkov. The story goes that, despite the crowds, Anna's friend helped her to reach the priest, who told her, "I know you are a Jewish woman, but I see in you a deep faith in God. Let us pray to the Lord, and He will heal you of your illness." He blessed her, and the swelling subsided within a month.[9] This event held deep spiritual significance to Men' and his mother, despite the reported connections of Father John with the antisemitic Black Hundreds.[10] Anna's faithful Judaic practice continued until her death in 1936. Her grandchildren recounted that she instilled in them the importance of prayer and "a sense of national pride and . . . great, personal, moral responsibility . . . [that they were from] the Jewish people, who had 'revealed' the One True God . . . to the rest of the world."[11]

As a young child, Men''s mother, Elena Semenovna Tsuperfein (1908–1979), acquired a self-professed love for Jesus Christ in a required Russian Orthodox *Zakon Bozhii* (God's Law) class at her school in Kharkov.[12] In her memoir, Elena describes several moments when her mother (and occasionally her father) reacted violently to her attraction to both Russian Orthodox and Baptist Christianity. This included a "scandal" when eighteen-year-old Elena sustained cuts on her face from her mother's beating. Despite parental opposition, Elena's spiritual search continued until September 1935, when she and her infant son, Aleksandr (Alik), were baptized by Archimandrite Serafim (Sergei Mikhailovich Batiukov, 1880–1942), the head of an underground Orthodox group.[13]

Elena married Vladimir Grigor'evich Men' (Vol'f Gershleibovich Men', 1902–1969) in Moscow in 1934.[14] Vladimir wanted his sons to receive the sign of belonging to the Jewish people. In late January 1935, therefore, baby Alik was circumcised on the eighth day in the presence of his devout paternal grandfather, Gersh-Leib Men'.[15] Aleksandr described his father as "a patient, good, and cheerful man, [who] lived in fear."[16] According to Pavel Men' (b. 1938), their father wanted them "to understand Judaic tradition," so he invited them separately to accompany him to the Moscow Choral Synagogue on Jewish holidays.[17] The synagogue in the "Black Years" of postwar Stalinist antisemitism (1948–53) was a place to discuss the fate of the Jewish nationality in the Soviet Union, yet the holidays were rich in religious significance. "But Papa was an agnostic," explains Pavel. "For him, it was a matter of national identity."[18]

Vladimir's use of the synagogue for traditional instruction reflects the role the synagogue played as a cultural and sociopolitical institution, and Pavel's assessment reveals the extent to which the family's Jewish self-identification was influenced by the Soviet discourse of a clear separation of "religion" from "nationality."[19] Scholars who have long examined the circuitous but ultimately successful secularizing transformation from the Russian imperial state have used the terms *evrei* (Hebrew/Jew) and *iudei* (practicing Jew) as confessional (religious) designations, to the exclusive Soviet use of the term *evrei* (ethnic Jew) as a secular (national) term devoid of religious significance (and the resultant negative connotation of the term *iudei* for secularist officials). Some have observed that "religious" and "national" are thoroughly modern distinctions.[20] In the Soviet Union, this intensive transition took place over the course of the 1920s and 1930s, as the Bolsheviks experimented with the incorporation of all nationalities (stripped of their ethno-confessional baggage) into their state-building efforts.[21]

While Vladimir wanted his sons to appreciate their Jewish roots, his wife, Elena, and her cousin, "Aunt Vera," gave the boys a Christian upbringing. They regularly attended Russian Orthodox services, and, at the age of twelve, Alik attended an underground catechism class.[22] At around this same age, Alik felt called to ministry. He recounted this as a process culminating in an encounter with Jesus Christ and a decision to become a priest and pursue a theological writing career.[23] Since his death, however, another version of the story has emerged. Father Mikhail Meerson claims that Men', whose family celebrated the state of Israel's creation in 1948, decided to become a priest "to serve the Zionist cause." According to Meerson:

Men' thought that if Jesus is the Messiah of Israel, the time for the people of Israel to acknowledge Him as such will eventually come. The emergence of the Jewish state was a sign. Living in diaspora, the Jews had to preserve their identity. The walls of uncompromising rabbinical Judaism were absolutely necessary for the preservation of the people's existence. With the restoration of the Jewish state, the danger of assimilation would eventually disappear. The people, liberated internally from the fear of losing their national identity, would become ready to look at what Men' considered the earliest Jewish legacy—the New Testament. At this point the need for Jewish priests and preachers of the Gospel would be felt.[24]

Several questions arise from Meerson's account. First, the term Zionist—typically a political designation—should be defined well and used advisedly. Although Men' maintained a special concern for Israel, he avoided the self-characterization of "Zionist" as an adult and was never active in Soviet Zionist circles.[25] It is further doubtful that Men' would have claimed the New Testament, rather than the Old Testament (Hebrew Bible), as "the earliest Jewish legacy." Finally, Men' understood his call being to all Soviet citizens, not solely to Jews, as is implied in this excerpt. Nevertheless, the formation of modern Israel may have factored into his decision to become a priest. Pavel Men' recalls their father asking teenaged Aleksandr one day whether he realized that Christianity "is not for us [Jews]." Aleksandr replied, "I will prove otherwise!" He became an altar server at age fifteen (1950) and, unbeknownst to his father, was ordained a deacon at age twenty-three (1958) and a priest at age twenty-five (1960).[26]

Men''s Theological Framework

As a young deacon and priest, Aleksandr Men' began writing in earnest. By the end of his life, his works included a life of Christ, a six-volume history of religions, multiple works of catechetical instruction and biblical scholarship, and scores of journal articles—a remarkable output given the strict censorship of religious works in the Soviet Union.[27] His discussion of Judaism and the People of Israel spanned the length of his ministry and reflected his theo-historical interpretation that Jesus of Nazareth was the Messiah and that the Jewish people retain their election and are, therefore, crucial to the Christian story.

In Men''s most well-known works—a life of Christ, *Syn Chelovecheskii* (The Son of Man), and a multivolume history of religions, *V poiskakh Puti, Istiny i Zhizni* (In search of the Way, the Truth, and the Life)—one sees a historical understanding of Christianity's roots in Second Temple Judaism and an insistence that the covenant between God and the People of Israel was intended to bless all people on earth. These works began as popular samizdat manuscripts in the late 1950s and 1960s before being published pseudonymously in Europe and smuggled to the Soviet Union.[28] Men''s historical and theological writings express a Christian message of radical equality and universality, as grounded in his understanding of Jesus of Nazareth's life and ancient Israel's history. In his multivolume work, Men' wanted his readers to see the history of religions "not [as] a throng of confusion, but [as] streams of creeks and rivers carrying their water to the ocean of the New Testament."[29] He considered ancient Israel a major tributary; three of the six volumes explicate its history. In *Syn Chelovecheskii*, Men' portrayed Jesus of Nazareth as the long-awaited Jewish Messiah, seen as a rabbi by his earliest followers. Citing Galatians 3:28, he wrote that this Messiah's message "destroyed obstacles that had separated people since ancient times. . . . To Jews and to foreigners, to men and to women, to everyone it opened the road to the Kingdom of Christ, where one's affiliation with a nation, class, gender, or age became secondary."[30]

In a series of letters to Mikhail Galperin, a Jewish convert whom Men' baptized, the priest explained his views concerning the Old and New Covenants while exhorting the young man to stay true to his chosen faith of Christianity. Two themes emerge in these letters: (1) the Law (Torah) as instructive and essential, but now secondary, and (2) the New Covenant, established through Jesus the Messiah, as the source of salvation, and now primary. He encouraged Galperin to learn from the Tanakh (Hebrew Bible): "Its spirit stands over the temporal, the particular, the tribal, the ethnic. . . . The foundation of everything is Micah 6:6–8 [that is, above religious ritual, one must act justly, love mercy, and walk humbly with God]."[31] Men' warned against Galperin's perceived need to start living by Judaic Law:

> We are not saved by the Law, for the Law is a sign of . . . belonging to a people, [which] is not enough. . . . Many rabbis understood that God could make a people out of stone. Christ showed that there is a Law of love for God and humanity. The Apostle Paul showed that only faith in the God who reveals Himself in Jesus of Nazareth truly saves. . . . In Him, we discover who God is and what humanity should be. Yet in light of union with Jesus, the Law also acquires meaning [for Jewish Christians] as a second consecration to God (according to the flesh) due to the responsibility of being a member of the People of God.[32]

Men' explained that when the Messiah states, "'[You have heard that it was said, . . .] but *I* say to you . . . ,' He places His teaching on equal footing with the Tanakh."[33] In January 1980, he wrote, "The 'filling up' of the Law by Christ gives it a new perspective and meaning. It is already something new—'The Messiah's Torah.' This new Torah preserves the Old Testament rites, but as secondary in comparison with faith and ethics. And this [secondary] Law is preserved only for *Yehudim*. Our tradition is the Bible in its entirety and in its basic *meaning*. . . . We need the spirit and not the letter."[34]

Thus, while Men' did not advocate a supersessionist view of the church, he did argue that faith in Jesus Christ, rather than adherence to Judaic Law, was the source of salvation for all peoples, including Jews. Jewish Christians could choose to continue in the Law, but only if they considered it secondary to faith in Jesus as Messiah.

In Men''s commentary on Romans 11, he explained, "Israel, the seed of Abraham, is the blessed root from which the salvation of the world has grown," whose descendants can freely choose to acknowledge Jesus as Messiah, thereby "entering into the New Covenant" and becoming part of the "remnant." This remnant is "the guarantee of the restoration of the chosen people." Those who have not entered in are sanctified by those who have, "just as the whole batch of dough is sanctified in the offering of the first fruits (Num. 15:19–21 [Rom. 11:17])."[35] Serge Ruzer observes that Men' exhibited a "low-key eschatology," since he saw the history of Christianity as just beginning.[36] Men' seems to have believed the "full sanctification of Israel" (Isa. 27) would occur in the distant future, connected to the eventual purification of individuals in the "New Jerusalem" (the consummation of the kingdom of God) within a world transformed via *theosis*. As evidenced by Men''s ministry, he may have believed that continued mission (that is, counseling Jews who are considering conversion to Christianity) also contributes to this sanctification.[37]

For some, Men''s view that Jews who believe in Jesus as Messiah sanctify those who do not may resemble the thought of Jewish convert Edith Stein (1891–1942), though she focused more on the unbelief of the Jewish people than he did.[38] Zev Garber, in his critique of Stein, claims, "To identify with the Jewish people (*guf* = body) and not practice the Jewish religion (*neshama* = soul) is not grounds for group or self-excommunication. However, to proclaim Jewish ethnicity and to practice voluntarily another religious sanctum (e.g., Christianity) is grounds for self and group removal from Jewish identity."[39] Judging from statements Men' made in 1975, he would have disagreed with Garber. For example, he was perplexed by modern Israel's acceptance of atheist Jews but exclusion of Christian Jews as citizens. As he saw it, both practicing Jews and Christian Jews believed in the God of Israel and shared a "common religious ethic," whereas atheist Jews denied God altogether.[40]

"Who Is a Jew?": Soviet *Evrei-Khristiane* and Their Critics

Ruzer claims that Men''s works exhibited such a thorough understanding of "the historical and cultural context of Jesus' life . . . and biblical archaeology" that they evoked "a clear biblical and Israeli emphasis" for his readers who were *evrei-khristiane* (literally, Jews-Christians or Jewish Christians).[41] Among those readers were many secularized Soviet Jews who, in the process of a voluntary search for religious meaning, found their way to Men''s parish. He had a noticeable influence on the Jewish intelligentsia from the 1960s until his death. Men' plays a significant role in Judith Deutsch Kornblatt's study of the phenomenon of Jews becoming Orthodox Christians in the late Soviet period.[42] He was a spiritual mentor to a number of well-known Jewish figures, including Mikhail Agursky, Nadezhda Mandelshtam, and Aleksandr Galich. Those Jews who knew Men' and converted to Russian Orthodoxy see him in a favorable light. Of those studied by Kornblatt, some compare him to a Jewish rabbi in appearance, in wisdom, and in his "feeling for Israel"; one compares him to Aleksandr Solzhenitsyn in terms of his "charisma"; and another calls him the "Soviet Billy Graham."[43]

Some Jewish scholars and commentators have likewise acknowledged Men''s significance, though others have dismissed him as insignificant, ignored him altogether, or decried his purported methods.[44] Among the latter, Natan Feingold—a Soviet Jewish emigrant to Israel—denounced the "dialogical" and seductive methods allegedly practiced by *"vykrest* Aleksandr M."[45] Inter alia, Feingold suggested that Men' wrote the final pseudonymous article of the 1972 samizdat collection "Dva Zaveta" (Two Testaments), in which the author adheres to the "Third Rome" principle of Russian messianism and insists that millions of Jews paid with their lives for their centuries-long stubborn refusal to embrace Christianity.[46] These positions, however, are antithetical to Men''s views. In fact, when Men' spoke of his "fellow kinsmen [*edinoplemenniki*]" resisting Christianity, he called it "just another step in the drama taking place between God and the world, [which] . . . is also ongoing among other peoples."[47] Furthermore, Men' (whose paternal great-uncle was murdered with his family at Babi Yar in September 1941) referred to the Shoah (Holocaust) as an "unparalleled massacre" that took the lives of "millions of absolutely innocent people."[48] Nevertheless, Men''s spiritual guidance of Jewish converts inadvertently provoked Soviet Jews like Feingold into holding views similar to those of ultraconservative Russian nationalists, who insinuated that Men' was creating a dangerous "Judeo-Christian" church.

The "Who is a Jew?" debate was central to the questions asked of Men' by the visitor in 1975, reflecting three themes that Jewish converts were discussing in secret meetings and samizdat: the phenomenon of Soviet Jews becoming Christians and their spiritual praxis and identity; potential obstacles facing newly converted Jews; and possibilities for a "Jewish Christian Church."[49] Men''s responses to these questions drew sharp criticism from Russian nationalist readers, including two anti-Judaic samizdat pieces: an anonymous letter (1976) and a collection of articles (1978) aiming to compel the purported proponents of "the new Jewish enthusiasm . . . called 'Judeo-Christianity'" to repent.[50] The pivotal nature of this "interview" warrants an exploration of the dialectic of Men''s responses and his critics' reactions.

Men' drew particular criticism on the subject of the vocation and identity of Jewish converts, especially in his assertion that the People of Israel are still chosen and that *evrei-khristiane* should consider it "a great honor" to be related by blood to Christ and the apostles.[51] Feliks Karelin (1925–1992), in a collection of articles titled *Invitation to a Dialogue* (distributed via samizdat in 1978), claimed that when *"iudo-khristiane"* assert an ethnic chosenness, they exhibit "religious Nazism" and "nationalistic selfishness exaggerated to the point of messianic claims."[52] Karelin, whose work betrays an idealized *Russian* messianism, echoed the antisemitic, apocalyptic interpretation of Sergei Nilus (1862–1929): "Baptized Jews, who are prone to consider their ancestry 'a great honor,' should also agree with the corresponding dishonor. For if they are related to the Prophets and the Apostles, then they are also related to those who killed the Prophets and persecuted the Apostles. It is indisputable that the Mother of God and Christ Himself are from the Jews. But is it not also true that Judas the betrayer and the coming Antichrist are from the Jews?"[53]

Men' also provoked controversy through his comments regarding the Jewish saints, Gabriel of Bialystok (d. 1690) and Eustratius of the Kyiv Caves (d. 1097), who were allegedly killed by Jews, and regarding the liturgical texts containing "severe attacks on Jews." Men' had registered a general hope that antisemitic portions of the liturgy (later specified as the Good Friday liturgy), "remnants from medieval times," would be removed and that saints whose hagiographies perpetuate the blood libel myth (that Jews murder Christians to use their blood to perform rituals) would be decanonized.[54] In a letter to the editor of *VRKhD*, Igor Shafarevich (1923–2017) expressed "painful disappointment" that a priest would discuss decanonization and the removal of liturgical texts without specifying criteria for such dire actions. Men''s response to Shafarevich explicated historical precedents for liturgical revision and decanonization in the wider Christian tradition, but did not mention Jews or Judaism.[55] This was likely to avoid provoking *VRKhD* readers further, yet it did not prevent Gennadii Shimanov (1937–2013) from writing a satirical piece in the 1978 collection "praising" Men' for expounding his "extraordinary theological erudition" to ignorant readers.[56] L. Ibragimov (Vladimir Prilutskii) focused his ire on the issue of decanonization and called Men' "an enabler of Judaizers [*potakovnik iudaistov*], who persistently oppose Christ."[57]

Finally, Men''s views on the combining of "Christian observances with Jewish rituals (the Sabbath, the Passover, and so on)" came under attack. He stated that it would not be a contradiction for converted Jews to celebrate Hanukkah, just as other Christians continue to celebrate their national holidays.[58] Responding to questions concerning the possibility of creating "a Jewish Christian Church with divine services in Hebrew," Men' said that such a church already existed in Israel under Catholic jurisdiction—the community of St. James near Haifa, led by Jewish convert "Brother Daniel" (Oswald Rufeisen, 1922–1998)—and that any Jewish church "must have apostolic succession, wherein no autonomous action be allowed." To an additional question about jurisdiction over various Jewish Christian groups, he replied hypothetically about distant-future possibilities in Israel, not in the Soviet Union.[59]

No attack on Men' was as vicious as an anonymous letter penned in 1976 and widely circulated in samizdat.[60] The letter parroted the inflammatory forgery *The Protocols of the Elders of Zion*, which some saw as proof of a Jewish-Masonic conspiracy to rule the world through infiltrating of Christian nations.[61] The writer thereby misconstrued thirteen of Men''s seventeen "interview" responses, calling him a deceptive Zionist "guard" who leads people astray from Orthodoxy and "preaches lies disguised as truth." He accused Men' of planning to establish his own independent Jewish church to destroy the ROC, of conducting "secret Satan worship" (clearly implying Men' was capable of ritual murder), and of making the ROC into a lifeless puppet for Zionism to establish the Antichrist's "spiritual and political reign in the world."[62] Considering such malevolent accusations, Sergei Bychkov claims that this letter constituted "the ideological justification" for Men''s brutal murder fourteen years later.[63]

Men' refused to publicly reply to the anonymous author, but he did send an explanatory note in December 1984 to his dean, Archpriest Zinovii Anisimov (1930–2008), who had received a copy of the letter. Arguing that he was "the victim of malicious slander," Men' took issue with the "ludicrous accusations" written in "the spirit of inquisition and 'witch hunts.'" He rejected all allegations and stated that he never planned "to create an independent Judeo-Christian community in the heart of the Orthodox Church."[64]

By the mid-1970s, a Jewish movement to emigrate from the USSR had been underway for nearly a decade, in the wake of the Soviet Union's denunciation of Israel after the Six-Day War.[65] Many of Men''s Jewish friends and spiritual children made *liyah* to Israel or emigrated to North America. He admitted wistfully that this wave of emigration dramatically shifted his circle of intellectual engagement, but his opinion on the advisability of his friends leaving differed according to each person's personality and circumstances.[66] A Jewish cultural awakening accompanied this movement toward emigration, with various underground groups forming in Moscow, including some that studied Hebrew.[67]

Men''s brother, Pavel, actively participated in Jewish underground groups, where he encountered questions about why a Jew would ever become a Christian and whether there was really such a thing as "Judeo-Christianity."[68] Pavel asked Aleksandr to formulate a response, recorded it, and took the recording to share with several Jews at a secret meeting, which likely occurred on March 3, 1977.[69] Given the nature of the questions, the fifty-minute recording had a decided tone of Jewish Christian apologetics.[70] Aleksandr Men' began by stating he had thought deeply about the relationship between Judaism and Christianity. He asserted that David Flusser (1917–2000), an expert on the Second Temple period, "was both right and wrong" when he claimed, "Judaism and Christianity is one faith."[71] Yes, Jesus was a practicing Jew, but if, as Flusser asserted, Jesus were *merely* a practicing Jew (*iudei*) who lived in and died for Judaism, then why did Christianity exist at all?[72] Men' addressed this question by exploring such concepts as the Incarnation, the New Covenant, the establishment of grace, and even the Jewish roots of the complex Christian doctrine of the Trinity (Chochmah (wisdom in Hebrew, for the Father), Memra (word in Aramaic, for the Son), and Ruach (spirit in Hebrew, for the Holy Spirit)).[73] Curiously, he avoided discussing the Crucifixion or the Resurrection. As evidenced by the high Christology in his writings, this was not due to theological heterodoxy.[74] Rather, it was likely a deliberate choice. The audience was all too familiar with accusations of Jews as "Christ killers," so any conversations on these topics were best held privately. One can only imagine the discussion that ensued among those who listened to the recording that evening. Pavel Men' recounts that although those present had varying perspectives about Jewish conversion to Christianity, "the overall atmosphere was friendly, because our animosity was directed toward the authorities . . . who would not allow Jews to [emigrate to] Israel."[75]

An examination of Aleksandr Men''s spoken output in the 1970s indicates that he saw both the "religious" and the "national" playing a role in the "Who is a Jew?" debate, but in a way that would seem foreign to Jews outside the Soviet Union. On the one hand, he acknowledged the importance of Israel's religion: "Israel came forth not as a nation but as a religious community . . . and perceived itself thereafter as a 'church' rather than a race." This "church," he claimed, had a "religious mission," which took on a new life when "Christianity expanded [this church's] borders, embracing all peoples and thereby fulfilling the prophets' expectations."[76] Men' likewise stated, "God conceived of Judaism as a *world* religion, which cannot remain within the borders of Israel.

What was placed within the framework of our people should be and was carried out *for the whole world.*"[77] His conception of the universal appeal of Christianity was, therefore, grounded in his interpretation of his universal Judaic heritage. Judaism, he maintained, was "a dynamic religion [with] a hope for the future," fulfilled *not* in the modern state of Israel with its "ordinary parliament, ordinary sins, and ordinary restaurants," but in Jesus Christ, who came to the world as Prophet, High Priest, and King.[78]

On the other hand, Men' used strong language against the "mixing" of religious and national questions evident in the Israeli press: "Not long ago in the Israeli newspaper *Menorah*, a certain Bar-Sela, while foaming at the mouth, wrote that Jewish Christians are trying to poison Israelis' national consciousness by bringing the heresy of Christ into their heads. According to him, a Jew who has adopted another faith has become an apostate from his own people. For me, of course, *such pogrom-like speech is our national form of Black Hundredism.*"[79] Men' insisted that a Jew remains a Jew, whether an unbeliever (like Leon Trotsky), a theosoph (like Rudolf Steiner), or a perceived heretic (like Baruch Spinoza). Claiming that an "automatic equation of 'nation' and 'religion' in the twentieth century is absurd," he discussed a crucial historical shift: "In the ancient world, 'nation,' 'society,' and 'religion' were almost always identical. Closed civilizations required such, and it was partially maintained in later societies. 'Russian' and 'Orthodox [Christian]' were also considered identical terms. Yet now we know that a Russian can be a militant atheist, an Orthodox believer, or a Baptist, and he does not stop being a Russian. . . . We have entered an era when life unavoidably forces us to separate 'faith' and 'nation.'"[80] Men''s embrace of the modern decoupling of faith from nation brings his thinking close to the rabbinical halakhic tradition that anyone with a Jewish mother is still a Jew, even if the mother has converted to Christianity (as Elena Men' had).

Taking an implicit stance against Israel's non-halakhic interpretation of the Law of Return—and likely against the case of Jewish convert "Brother Daniel," with whom he corresponded—Men' argued that modern Israel should be a secular state that refrains from claiming an "official state religion," thereby allowing genuine "freedom of choice" for all its citizens. He argued that just as it would be acceptable for secular Israelis to "return to Judaism" or to "look for other alternatives," if they were to "come to Christianity, they [would] not stop being Jews as a result, but [would] only more firmly get in touch with their own tradition, . . . not in an archaic, exclusively national sense, but in a wide, universal, powerful sense, as the very foundation of the Church."[81] Men' thus utilized the strict definition of a Jew as a member of a nationality in order to formulate his vision of ethnic Jews tapping into their Judaic heritage by choosing to follow Jesus of Nazareth, thereby entering into a wider religious community.

Given this understanding that Jews should have the freedom to choose to follow Jesus as Messiah, how did he understand the frequently discussed, but rarely defined, notion of "Judeo-Christianity?" Men' began the 1977 recording by defining "Judeo-Christianity" as "a certain synthesis between Old Testament customs and New Testament faith," which was currently a "myth," though it had existed in some form in the first five centuries of Christian history. The present reality, he explained, was different; Jewish people can adopt Christianity and retain their nationality, just as Russian or English or Japanese people can.[82]

Men' thought Jewish converts to Christianity had every right to retain and value their Jewish heritage. In fact, as a Soviet Jew, he would have considered the question of whether to retain one's Jewish identity absurd, since being a Jew in the Soviet Union was an ethnic reality that one could not lose merely by changing religious persuasions. Yet, this ethnic identity was charged with biblical significance for Men': "I view my belonging to the People of God as an undeserved gift and a sign of added responsibility before God. . . . I am happy that I can serve the God of Israel and His Church with my weak powers."[83] Likewise, he suggested that *evrei-khristiane* should consider their "kinship to the prophets, the apostles, the Virgin Mary and Christ himself . . . a sign of dual responsibility as a member of both the Church and the People of God." In this, they realize their people's "spiritual vocation" to be a light to the nations.[84]

Several of Men''s Jewish spiritual children espoused a view that *evrei-khristiane* are "doubly chosen."[85] This concept caused discontent in Soviet Jewish circles, as evidenced by an émigré memoir, which likely depicts one of Men''s spiritual children: "[Anatoly Shteynfeld's] claim to fame was his closeness to a Moscow Russian Orthodox priest of Jewish origin, Father M., who made it his life's work to convert to Christianity as many Jewish intellectuals and artists as there were crenellations on all the Kremlin walls. Under Father M.'s influence, Shteynfeld was baptized sometime in the late 1970s; later he began to spread among refuseniks the message that Jewish Christians were 'doubly chosen' and supposedly fulfilled a double mission."[86]

This is a distorted portrayal of Men''s ministry; he did not seek out Jewish converts, but they found him.[87] Men''s comments about a "spiritual vocation" tied to "dual" or "added" responsibility thanks to the People of Israel's continued "chosenness" may contain the seeds of the "doubly chosen" conception perpetuated by Shteynfeld and others. Yet, in none of Men''s extant writings or statements does he use the phrase "doubly chosen." Those of his Jewish spiritual children who amplified his concept of "dual responsibility" would have done well to heed a warning from his recording: "[We Jews] should not be obsessed with our own chosenness. This looks very obtrusive and unattractive, and we must be sure to say so among ourselves."[88] This caution carries an implicit acknowledgment of the threat of antisemitism.

Genealogy of Authority: Confronting Chauvinisms

Jean-Paul Sartre wrote, "It is the anti-Semite who creates the Jew," thereby suggesting that the experience of antisemitism reinforces Jewish self-identification.[89] Although Men''s encounters with antisemitism from the mid-1970s onward probably heightened his Jewish identity, he had been proud of his Jewish heritage since childhood, when he was largely sheltered from such encounters. Nonetheless, from a 1962 article against Nazi racist theories until an interview he gave soon before his death in 1990, Men' took on the role of an anti-chauvinist, anti-racist, and anti-antisemitic apologist. He thus assumed a "genealogy of authority," much like Jewish converts Aleksandr Alekseev (1820–1895), who defended Jews against blood libel charges in late imperial Russia, and Cardinal Jean-Marie (Aaron) Lustiger (1926–2007), who stood against Jean-Marie Le Pen, leader of the National Front in post-Holocaust France.[90] Men' once told an acquaintance, "As a Christian, and simply by my nature, I have a deep aversion to any chauvinism. I value and love the culture in which I grew up. . . . Yet not for a minute do I forget the responsibility and call that my belonging to Israel has placed on me."[91]

From 1959 to 1962, Men' wrote twenty articles for the official ROC periodical, *Zhurnal Moskovskoi Patriarkhii*.[92] One of his final contributions to the journal, "Rasizm pered sudom khristianstva," constituted his first public attempt to articulate views against chauvinism.[93] The article is an indictment of the pseudoscientific racism espoused by the Nazis. Men' explicates four themes: the biblical teachings concerning "the brotherhood and equal rights of all peoples"; the thinkers who espoused "anti-Christian" and modern "scientistic" views about a hierarchy of races; Nazi racism and its "cannibalistic practice"; and scientific evidence refuting "teachings on the inequality of races."[94]

Men''s views on the final three themes were likely partially informed by Soviet ethnographic studies, conducted in the 1930s to debunk Nazi theories of race and to set forth an ideology of multinational unity. In Men''s discussion of the first theme, his frequent use of the phrase *bratstvo narodov* (brotherhood of the peoples) could be interpreted as "Soviet-speak," derived from the clarion call of Soviet nationalities policy: "friendship of the peoples!"[95] Since this article appeared in a highly censored journal, such an interpretation is conceivable.[96] Yet Men' deliberately employed this secular construct to marshal scriptural justifications for human equality. For example, the Hebrew prophets "understood the election of their people as an idea of service to all humanity, . . . in which there must be no place for national exaltation," and the books of Ruth and Jonah demonstrate that "God's all-encompassing love and mercy [extend] to all humanity . . . without exception."[97]

A state-driven, anti-Zionist campaign arose in the late 1970s, in response to the continued emigration of Soviet Jews from the USSR.[98] A wave of antisemitism hit Soviet society, including the wide distribution of samizdat copies of *The Protocols of the Elders of Zion*.[99] By the summer of 1979, Men' concluded it was "necessary to combat antisemitic propaganda with serious scholarly research."[100] Convinced that Norman Cohn's *Warrant for Genocide* had "removed the detonating device from [the] dangerous and heinous weapon [of *The Protocols*]," Men' obtained a copy of Cohn's work, commissioned Sergei Bychkov to translate the text, removed chapters that did not discuss Russia or Germany, and wrote a foreword and an appendix.[101] The translation first circulated via samizdat and was finally published in 1990 (without Men''s contributions) and in 2000.[102]

Men' held a consistent line against chauvinism, which he called a perversion of a "healthy love for one's homeland."[103] He did not reserve his anti-chauvinistic passion for *Russian* nationalists: "Any chauvinism—whether Russian, Jewish, or Chinese—has always disgusted me, but it is especially shameful when Christians espouse it."[104] Since Men' traced the historical roots of racism and antisemitism to the pre-Christian period, one might read his historical analyses as attempts to exonerate Christians of these practices.[105] Yet a closer reading reveals a more subtle argument. In his 1962 anti-racist article, Men' did not deny that the Roman Catholic conquistadors perpetrated violence against those they deemed lower. He stated in his appendix to the Cohn translation that "ancient, pagan antisemitism firmly took root in the Christian milieu," leading to violence and pernicious rumors directed against the Jews of Europe (including the tenacious blood libel myth, which continued into twentieth-century Russia with the trial of Mendel Beilis).[106] But he argued that, just as the behavior of the ancient Israelites, who exhibited hostility toward other ancient peoples, should not be conflated with the "religion announced to Israel, [which] declared the equality of all peoples," chauvinistic Christians such as "Russian Orthodox believers who call themselves *pochvenniki* [that is, supporters of the "native soil movement"]" should not conflate their antisemitic beliefs with their church's teaching, which actually calls for people "to relate in love to everyone, regardless of their faith and ethnicity."[107]

One theme Men' reiterated frequently was the collective instinct to blame others. For example, in his appendix to the Cohn translation, he wrote, "Any era of crisis gives rise to myths used to indoctrinate the masses with the idea that the source of their misfortunes and miseries has been found." In such instances, "the role of the 'scapegoat'" could fall on any group—including "'saboteurs' and 'vile priests' ['*vrediteli*' i '*popy*'], Communists and Catholics, Jews and 'colored people,' Masons and sectarians."[108]

A motivating factor in Men''s struggle against antisemitism and racism was his conviction that every Christian should oppose chauvinism.[109] In 1962, he challenged Christians of all affiliations and backgrounds to "fight without hesitation against [racism,] this ideology of human hatred."[110] Men' made an idealistic claim that the church has always "raised a voice in defense of the unity of the human race and the equality of all people before God."[111] His aforementioned separation of the behavior of chauvinistic Christians from the Universal Church's teachings allowed him to assert this as a reflection of his ideal of radical equality.

Since Men' opposed belief systems that dehumanized "outsiders" by restricting choice, he also took an uncompromising stance in favor of *svoboda sovesti* (freedom of conscience). He made critical statements regarding the limited choice available in the modern state of Israel, as noted. He also implicitly critiqued both secularist authorities and Russian ultranationalists in the Soviet Union by calling *svoboda sovesti* "the holy of holies within humanity," which must be protected by "the honest and consistent application of the principle of a secular state . . . that serves the interests of its citizens regardless of their religious affiliations."[112]

"Time of Troubles": Men''s Final Decade

Despite Men''s efforts to counter chauvinism, antisemitism became a regular feature in his parish at Novaia Derevnia. In early 1980, Father Stefan Serednii, the parish's head priest, who circulated *The Protocols* and "a collection of articles against Father Aleksandr," encouraged two parishioners to collect signatures on a petition accusing Men' of creating "a half-Greek, half-Jewish church."[113] At a service in 1981, Father Stefan preached a sermon in Men''s presence, accusing him of inspiring the "black guard" of Yids, Masons, and Zionists, who were setting out to destroy the church. Men' later admitted that conducting the Divine Liturgy with Father Stefan was "perhaps the most difficult ordeal" of his entire ministry.[114]

In 1982, A. A. Trushin, a provincial commissioner of the Council for Religious Affairs, reported that Men' was "deliberately conspiring to commit illegal actions," including gathering youth in his parish, most of whom were "of Jewish nationality." Trushin recounted a complaint by "believers" expressing "concern for the fate of [their] nation," due to Men' receiving a "large number of Jews . . . with fat briefcases" during and after services. The commissioner also cited a March 1982 report from Father Stefan, who linked an increase in Jewish baptisms at Novaia Derevnia with three robberies at the church.[115] For the next four years, the Soviet State Security Committee (KGB) and the Council for Religious Affairs regularly summoned Men' for questioning, under various pretexts.[116]

In 1986, Mikhail Gorbachev spoke of a need for glasnost (openness) in the public sphere. Coupled with the state's concession permitting the ROC to celebrate its millennium in 1988, this facilitated an outpouring of spiritual interest within the Soviet Union. Men' played an important role in the subsequent public "desecularization." In May 1988, he gave the first of nearly two hundred lectures in Moscow, and his radio and television appearances reached millions.[117] Yet, he observed, "when Gorbachev opened the floodgates, reaction as well as democracy poured in. But reaction is always more aggressive."[118] In the late 1980s, antisemitism gained further steam with the ultranationalist organization Pamiat'; one branch associated itself with the ROC, though the church claimed no such connection.[119] During perestroika, Men' received a growing number of threatening letters, faced inquiries at his lectures about what he, a Jew, was doing in "our" church, and experienced an increase in discriminatory behavior toward him in church circles.[120]

In July 1990, Vladimir Sychev, a KGB official whom Men' knew from years of "prophylactic" questioning, spoke with him near the altar after a service. Men' told friends that Sychev had advised him to "be on guard, [for] a Time of Troubles" was coming.[121] Whether this was a threat or a warning, Sychev was aware that Men' was being threatened in certain official circles. Men''s wife told an interviewer that representatives of Pamiat' also visited him in the summer of 1990.[122] Before these encounters, Men' had spoken of his time being short, but such statements became more pointed by the end of July. "I must hurry," he told one parishioner, "I have very little time left."[123]

Four days before his death, Men' gave an interview to the Spanish journalist Pilar Bonet. Despite various threats, he did not refrain from confronting the ideas inspiring those in the midst of a noticeable rightward shift.[124] In fact, his language intensified from his 1975 charge of "chauvinism" to a more provocative accusation of "Russian fascism." He observed a direct link between Russian fascism and some of the Russian clergy who wanted to "restore the church just as it was before the revolution . . . [forgetting] that it is precisely because the pre-revolutionary church was the way it was that the catastrophe happened." Acknowledging that "Zionistophobia" had become a feature of the ROC, he said such thinking had become more noticeable after his 1975 interview but had "mushroomed" in the preceding five years. He then reasserted his frequent theme that antisemitism is a cowardly manifestation in a society of people who blame anyone but themselves for the tragedies that have befallen them.[125]

In the early morning of September 9, 1990, Men' left his house and walked along a forest path to the train station, on his way to church. Someone struck him from behind with a sharp object, mortally wounding him.[126] He died a few minutes later at the gate to his house, having managed to stumble back home. His funeral was held on September 11, the day in the Orthodox calendar commemorating John the Baptist's beheading. The significance of this concurrence was not lost on his spiritual children, who indicated that Men' resembled the forerunner who pointed people to the Messiah.[127]

Men''s murder remains unsolved, due in part to the incompetence and obstruction of various investigators.[128] In 1992, the investigator Ivan Leshchenkov distributed a questionnaire to Men''s former parishioners asking whether the parish was Orthodox or "Judeo-Christian," whether Men' preferred Jewish parishioners over others, and whether he had ever encouraged parishioners to continue the rituals of Judaism while in the Orthodox faith.[129] Not only do such questions demonstrate the long and distorted memory of Men''s 1975 "interview"—and that the *religious* presumption of a Judaizing heresy had influenced *secular* officials—but they also reveal a clear bias against the deceased and an unwillingness to investigate his murder with due diligence. Several theories exist concerning who could have been behind Men''s death; although these all remain conjecture, the theory of an antisemitic perpetrator is plausible.[130]

Father Aleksandr Men''s pride in his Jewish heritage was heightened by his Christian theology, which he saw as rooted in the teachings of ancient Israel. His concomitant positions of the radical equality espoused in Christian theology and the continued election (that is, uniqueness) of the Jewish people may seem paradoxical. Yet he resolved this universalist-particularist tension via an uncompromising anti-chauvinistic stance and an understanding that the Jewish election was a call to extend salvation to *everyone* through the Jewish Messiah.

Men''s views pose a challenge for scholars of Russian religious thought, since they seem to defy categorization. For example, he exhibited continuities with Vladimir Solov'ev in his understanding of the Jewish foundation of the universal Christian Church, but he had a clear disagreement with the enigmatic eschatology in Solov'ev's later work.[131] Dominic Rubin suggests (*a*) that Men''s views were "illiberal," reflecting Sergei Bulgakov and Lev Karsavin in insisting that Jesus Christ came to complete the Law, and (*b*) that Men' was "Bulgakovian" when discussing the honor of Jews being related to Christ.[132] Men' differed from these thinkers in that he himself was an ethnic Jew who ministered and wrote in the post-Holocaust moment. And although he actively disseminated the work of Silver Age thinkers via samizdat, he was not uncritical of their thought. If some of his theological views were "illiberal," he was decidedly "liberal" in his stance on individual and collective freedom and in his insistence on the need for a genuinely secular state in the Soviet Union and Israel—a critique of anti-religious Soviet secularists and of ethno-religious ultraconservatives in both countries, all of whom, in his estimation, sought to diminish true *svoboda sovesti*.[133]

Despite challenges in categorization, one thing is certain. From the 1960s to 1990, thousands of individuals from a variety of backgrounds found their way to Men' and his writings while searching for spiritual grounding in a state with a secularist ideology. The influence this noteworthy catechist had on spiritual seekers and new converts within the ROC, especially in the Moscow province, reflects a shift from a "pre-modern" confessional view of the church to a more modern, voluntarist notion. As for the Jewish converts in his parish, the modern paradox is that the successful secularization of Jews that took place during the late imperial and early Soviet periods opened a window for Jews who were seeking to reconnect with their religious roots to find their spiritual home in the ROC during the late Soviet period. And Men'—with his attractive theology of radical equality and universality, his deep understanding of ancient Israel, his encouragement of Jewish converts to value their ethnic (secular) identity, and his uncompromising anti-chauvinistic stance—was happy to accompany several of them on this journey. In the intersection of these aspects of Men''s thought, one finds an "elective affinity" of religious thought and secular concepts such as freedom of individual choice, a phenomenon that the anthropologist Sonja Luehrmann found has been rather common among religious believers in the Soviet and post-Soviet periods.[134] In his theological writings and teachings, Men' was one whose affinity toward and critique of certain secular realities and concepts did not fit easily within either the secular-sacred binary or the equation of the sacred and the secular.

Religion and Russian Art and Literature

CHAPTER 6

Zinaida Gippius and "Christian Infatuation"

ANA SILJAK

For scholars studying the work of Zinaida Gippius, sexuality is paramount. Her vast literary output, including plays, short stories, and poems, has been combed through to tease out her views on androgyny, homosexuality, bisexuality, and chastity. Her own memoirs, and those of her contemporaries (mostly men), have been used to reconstruct the complicated nature of her relationships to men and women. Descriptions of her appearance and even photographs and portraits have been analyzed in great detail, all in the service of elucidating her relationship to her own gender and sexuality. She did, of course, write about many other things, but for scholars, even feminist scholars, she is primarily an object of sexual analysis.[1]

Unfortunately, despite all the emphasis on the topic, I believe that Gippius's philosophy of sexuality has been entirely misunderstood. The best-known scholar on Gippius, Olga Matich, has categorized her as a misguided champion of a kind of erotic apocalypse, in which a new sexuality would bring about the end of the world. Dazzled by the seemingly transgressive and revolutionary nature of her views on the subject, feminist scholars have sought in her a proto-feminist critic of traditional concepts of gender. In all cases, she has been seen as a theorist of a kind of "sublimation"—repressing sexual impulses and then transforming them into higher spiritual or metaphysical acts of art and love.[2]

Gippius's views on sexuality were, indeed, nontraditional and perhaps (to the contemporary scholar) rather odd. But there is a central, methodological problem at the heart of all of this scholarship on Gippius: the incomplete, and sometimes entirely absent, conception of the fundamental philosophical and theological underpinnings of Gippius's approach to love and sex. Most striking is the lack of consideration given to Gippius's particular interpretation of Orthodox Christian theology, an interpretation widely shared by her symbolist and Silver Age contemporaries. This pointed absence in the literature is in part the result of a common modern methodological problem, one that originates in a particular approach to historical and literary material that ignores or dismisses the speech and writing of the subject of study, in the name of "revealing" the "actual" sources of their ideas and actions. Indeed, one of the foremost contemporary scholars on Gippius wrote explicitly that she would not read Gippius and other symbolists "primarily through the lens of their own philosophical writings on gender and sexuality." The rather perplexing implication of this approach is that Gippius herself did not really understand her own views on sexuality—at least not as well as a scholar of her work.[3]

In the case of Gippius and sexuality, this methodological problem is reinforced by a broader assumption about the relationship between religion and sexuality, in which religion is believed to insist on strict limits on sexuality and to encourage individual self-denial, repression, and sublimation, and in which the toleration and liberation of sexuality belongs exclusively to the secular. This binary dominates the scholarship on sexuality in Russia. Religion is often equated with the official Orthodox Church and its explicit moral code, and the assumption is that, by definition, religion stands for the control and regulation of sexuality and for the view that sex is "evil, unhealthy, and abnormal." The history of sexuality in Russia, by extension, is told as part of a larger narrative of secularization; the advent of modernity in Russia led to an increasing religious/secular divide, where "the moral interests of the church in reinforcing sacred values . . . competed with the aspirations of a trained professional class eager to fashion a modern polity based on secular values" in which individual pleasure and autonomy could reign.[4] This scholarship ignores the complicated nature of both religious and secular approaches to sexuality in Russia, especially at the end of the nineteenth century, when Russian writers and activists were openly discussing the questions of sex, not only agitating against a "traditional," ascetic, religious worldview but also questioning the modern secular view of sexuality that reduced human relationships to innate, predictable, biological drives.[5]

My own approach is to take very seriously the theological and philosophical base on which Gippius built her theory of sex and to demonstrate that Gippius's idiosyncratic views on sexuality precisely participated in the challenging of conventional religious and secular attitudes toward the subject. In particular, I use the insightful work of Steven Cassedy and Irina Paperno, which carefully delineates the Orthodox Christian response to modernity that the Silver Age developed through philosophical discussion and creative rendering. Gippius's understanding of sexuality is rooted in the overall Silver Age response to the prevalence of the secular philosophical positivism and materialism that viewed human beings as biological creatures subject to the laws of "science."[6] As such, her work represents a creative Christian engagement with the secular view of sexuality, one whose complexity has something to say even in the present age.

The Silver Age as a movement began as a revolt against the scientism and utilitarianism of modernity—the European celebration of technological progress and scientific discovery to the exclusion of all other human endeavors. Dmitrii Merezhkovskii, the husband of Gippius, first expressed his desire to revolt against the sterility of the modern world, against the "suffocating, deadly positivism, which lies like a stone on our hearts." In his well-known 1892 speech and essay "On the Reasons for the Decline and on the New Currents in Contemporary Literature," he sought a new, symbolic approach to reality that could "express the limitless side of thought" and reveal "new, still undiscovered worlds of sensitivity."[7]

The challenge was taken up by not just the symbolist poets, but by the artists, philosophers, and theologians of the Silver Age. For many of them, modern materialism could only be overcome through a new approach to religion—in the Russian case, a new Orthodox Christianity—one whose theology would directly engage with a Russian intelligentsia enthralled with the modern, secular, scientific approach to human life. Gippius herself wrote that one of the major tasks of the journal she and her husband founded together, *Novyi put'*, was committed to a fight "against materialism, and one of its tasks was to prove that 'religion' and 'reaction' were not always synonymous."[8]

For Gippius, in order for religion to respond to secular materialism and positivism more effectively, it needed to jettison its emphasis on asceticism—on the denial of the worldly cares in the service of the "otherworldly."[9] Some moderns who professed to follow traditional Christianity looked on their bodies with hatred, as on a "useless," "harmful" thing, and were forced to view all worldly things with contempt, including "science, art, culture, society, and money." But the fundamental problem with this sort of religious attitude lay in the fact that human beings simply could not despise their earthly lives in such a fashion, since "a person is still alive and loves that he is alive." That person is then forced to continually make "compromises," to tend to the earthly cares that ascetic religion dismisses: "I believe that my daily concerns about my food, my wife, my pleasures, my appreciation of art, my work, and my service are necessary, true, and good; if I do not believe it, then I can neither serve, nor eat, nor have pleasure. In the meantime, I am told to repent of my daily concerns, my pleasures, and my food. But after repenting, I once again must go work and live, as if I have repented of repenting."[10] For Gippius, modern religion could no longer simply offer a denial of the worldly but had to embrace a sanctification of the earthly and temporal. There should be nothing alien to faith—"We love 'trifles' with our God-created heart, and we terribly need them to be sanctified precisely because we love them."[11]

As can be seen in the quoted passage, Gippius, like other Silver Age poets, artists, and philosophers, wanted to resist the encroaching materialism of the age, but also wished to avoid a lapse into a dualist insistence on the superiority of the spiritual over the material, or into a romantic preference for the otherworldly at the expense of this world. Instead, Gippius and others sought to overcome the binaries of material/spiritual, flesh/soul, real/ideal. To do so, as Paperno has elucidated, they relied on two specifically Orthodox Christian ideas: "materialization of the spirit (incarnation) and the spiritualization of matter (transfiguration)." The theology of Vladimir Solov'ev figured heavily in their understanding of these terms.[12] As Cassedy explains, "Solov'ev had placed great primacy in the significance of Christ in the history of humanity— as the 'God-Man.'" When, through the miracle of the Incarnation, God became man, this event pointed to the reconciliation of the divine and the human—not just in the relationship between God and human beings, but between the divine potential and the human reality present within each person, like Christ, who achieved this through "divinizing his humanity and humanizing his divinity."[13] Transfiguration was a closely related concept for Solov'ev; it was part of his insistence on the role of art for achieving the higher synthesis of the material and spiritual. The purpose of true art was both "internally transfiguring, spiritualizing matter" and "the transformation of physical life into its spiritual counterpart."[14]

For Silver Age poets and writers, "symbolism" was thus an aesthetic theory that incorporated theological principles, based on the writings of Solov'ev. A symbol, for poets such as Gippius, was the means to achieve the merging of the spiritual and material in artistic form. In one sense, symbolists envisioned a similarity between the "symbol" and the Christian conception of Logos (Christ) as "Word become flesh"—the incarnation of the divine into the real, the eternal into the temporal. In another sense, however, as Cassedy eloquently notes, the symbol was thus also an "icon"—a kind of window, made of this-worldly materials and concepts, which allowed people to see into the eternal and spiritual beyond. In Cassedy's words: "The physical object, the piece of wood adorned with colors and lacquers forming a picture of the Mother of God, is understood as a mere facade for the grace that stands behind it. One has to look *through* the wood and paint into the invisible and immaterial. . . . It allows the worshiper a limited contact with the immeasurable through the intermediary of sensible matter."[15] In both the icon and the symbol, the unity of spirit and matter is such that the material and real becomes transformed, allowing it to reveal the divine and the eternal.

For the Silver Age, and for the symbolist poets and writers in particular, art, if attuned to the symbolic, was the route to true beauty, and thus to the divine. As Clemena Antonova has noted, beauty, through art, was thought to "save the world," by giving human beings contact with the divine and limitless side of existence.[16] But they did not stop there. Art, for the symbolists, was not a mere activity or profession or even calling. True art was linked to life itself—and a symbolist poet and writer was called on to merge his or her art and life into one. As Paperno explains, "For the artist no separation existed between the 'man' and the 'poet,' between personal life (*zhizn'*) and artistic (creative) activity (*tvorchestvo*)."[17] Thence came the Silver Age concept of *zhiznetvorchestvo*—life creation—where artists sought to turn their biographies into works of art, both by writing about their own experiences and by allowing their beliefs to transform their lives. As the poet Valerii Briusov later wrote: "The abyss between the artist's 'words' and 'deeds' disappeared for us when it turned out that creation is merely a reflection of life and nothing more. . . . Whoever accepts Verlaine's verses must accept his life; whoever rejects him as a person, let him reject his poetry; it is inseparable from his person. . . . Let the poet create, not his books, but his own life."[18]

It is this Silver Age symbolism—the struggle against materialism and positivism, the desire to reconcile the spiritual and the material, the fascination with the concepts of incarnation and transfiguration, and the desire to merge art with life—that provides the true basis for understanding Gippius's views on love and Eros. For Gippius, love, like art, was the key to infusing the material with the divine and, moreover, a central part of what she called the "process of ascending [*voskhozhdenie*]" toward God-manhood, the creation of a divine humanity.[19] This symbolic, religious understanding of love would, in fact, prove a liberation from the sterility of the modern, scientific, secular approach to sexuality that pervaded the European fin de siècle.

The question of love, and its relationship to sexuality, was a burning question in Russia at the turn of the century. A particularly fierce debate erupted over the Christian approach to sexuality, marked by the two extremes of Leo Tolstoy, with his full renunciation of sexuality, on the one hand, and of Vasilii Rozanov, with his desire for a full Christian embrace of sexuality, on the other. Tolstoy's most influential statement on the subject came in the form of a short story, "The Kreutzer Sonata," which depicted, in brutal detail, the evil consequences of what Tolstoy saw as the oversexualization of society. The men and women of his day, Tolstoy first suggested in the story and then later explicitly delineated in a series of "explanations" of the text, were transformed into brutish, animalistic figures subject only to their lusts, which led to divorce, despair, and even murder. Lust was an evil desire that used deception to lure its victims—those who felt the pangs of lust were deceived by swirling romantic images of the beloved that disguised the evil nature of the original base sentiment. Tolstoy particularly shocked Russian society with his claim that all sex, even that taking place within marriage, was adulterous. He advocated, instead, abstinence as the only route to a true Christian love. "The Kreutzer Sonata" sparked wide-ranging public discussion.[20]

On the opposite side of the debate stood Rozanov, who saw the stigma and shame attached to sexuality as a product of a misguided, Christian ascetic hatred of the flesh. At times, he even used the attitude toward sexuality to denounce Christianity as a "sodomite" religion—one denying the beauty of heterosexual sex and the resulting procreation of children. (Oddly, Rozanov was not a critic of homosexuality in general and even sometimes wrote about homosexual fantasies.) His explicit writings on sexuality and the biology of intercourse, and his desire that the Orthodox Church completely revise its stance on sexuality, led to the championing of a number of ecclesiastical reforms: accepting illegitimate children, abolishing consanguinity rules, and, perhaps most radically, consecrating marital consummation by allowing couples to remain in the church after the marriage until the act had been accomplished (though this last was, most likely, offered tongue in cheek).[21]

The role of Tolstoy and Rozanov in sparking the long-standing Silver Age debate over sexuality is revealed in the discussions of the Religious-Philosophical Meetings of 1901–3, which were established by Merezhkovskii and Gippius and attended by many of the artists and philosophers of the Silver Age, including Nikolai Berdiaev, Alexandre Benois, Dmitrii Filosofov, and Briusov. Five of the twenty-one panels were devoted to the topic of "marriage," the most of any other subject. It was here Rozanov and Tolstoy were mentioned as the instigators of what Merezhkovskii called the "painful" question of sexuality, and Rozanov actively participated in the discussions by speaking and commenting on the question.[22]

Most Silver Age thinkers wanted a third approach to the question—one that avoided the asceticism of Tolstoy and the overly biological emphasis of Rozanov. In a sense, Tolstoy and Rozanov became representatives of the kind of dualism between spirit and matter that the Silver Age wished to overcome. Gippius, along with Merezhkovskii, Berdiaev, Viacheslav Ivanov, Pavel Florenskii, and others, sought to find a modern Christian response to the question of love, especially sexual love, which would expose the poverty of materialist philosophy but also reject the perceived religious hatred of the "flesh" that characterized many Christian approaches to sexuality, including Tolstoy's. Love, like art, could serve the Silver Age ideal of infusing the material with the spiritual in the manner of incarnation and transfiguration.[23]

For both Gippius and Merezhkovskii, the writings of Solov'ev pointed the way to a fuller understanding of human sexuality. Solov'ev himself sought explicitly to respond to Tolstoy's "Kreutzer Sonata" and its views on love, and he expressed his understanding of the subject in the "The Meaning of Love," an essay first published in 1892.[24] Solov'ev echoed Tolstoy's critique of nineteenth-century Russian approaches to sexuality; viewing sex as a purely biological act was indeed "shameful." Solov'ev compared the desire for a woman's body with the then much discussed abnormality of "fetishism"—as the unnatural desire for a part of a human being as opposed to the whole. Prostitution catered to a fetish: the desire for the dead flesh of the prostitute, and not for her entire person, body and soul. The modern world, Solov'ev believed, placed primacy on the material aspect of human life and saw sexuality as originating in the physiological—but this had things the wrong way around. Indeed, the modern argument for marriage was little more than an insistence that the law should regulate biological desire. As such, then, marriage became a trivial thing, unworthy of a whole human person.[25]

By contrast, Solov'ev also dismissed purely spiritual or Platonic love as nonsensical; purely spiritual love was also impotent, because it was impossible to love someone as pure spirit—their body was as crucial to their personality as their soul or mind.[26] Instead, the beloved had to be loved as both empirical and fleshly, and also in all of his or her divine potential—"in God." For Solov'ev, love had a twofold nature: "We love, in the first place, the ideal being . . . the being whom we ought to install in our ideal world. And in the second place, we love the natural human being, who furnishes the living personal material for the realization of the former, and who is idealized by means of it . . . in the sense of its actual objective transformation or regeneration."[27]

Eros, then, was a perfect route to achieving the very theological aims that Cassedy outlines—incarnation and transfiguration. Solov'ev himself directly noted this: "In sexual love, truly understood and truly realized, this Divine essence receives the means for its definitive, ultimate incarnation in the individual life of a human. . . . Hence come those beams of an unearthly bliss, of a breath of gladness not of this world, by which love even when imperfect is accompanied." And in love, for Solov'ev, "true spirituality is the regeneration of the flesh, its salvation, its resurrection from the dead."[28]

In one form or another, the symbolists and philosophers of the Silver Age echoed and modified Solov'ev's understanding of Eros and its potential and specifically linked it to aesthetic expression. Art and love both aspired to the union of fleshly and spiritual, to the true higher beauty. "Love is the absolute limit of our existence," Briusov wrote, "and the beginning of a new existence, a bridge of golden stars, over which a person crosses to that which is 'not man,' or even 'not yet man'—to God or beast." Ivanov explicitly thought art was erotic: "When the aesthetic is experienced erotically, artistic creation becomes symbolic. The enjoyment of beauty is similar to the enamorment of beautiful flesh and proves to be the initial step in erotic ascent."[29] And Berdiaev wrote, "Love is the way to revealing the secret of the person, to a comprehension of the person in the depth of his being. . . . In God the lover meets the beloved; in God he sees the beloved person. . . . Erotic energy is the eternal source of creativity. . . . The erotic shock is the way of revealing beauty in the world."[30] As I have noted elsewhere, *Leonardo da Vinci*, the second volume of Merezhkovskii's trilogy of historical novels, *Christ and Antichrist*, modeled the idea of Eros as the source of transfigurative and symbolic art, making Leonardo the exemplar of Silver Age "life creation." For Merezhkovskii, Eros was central to the story of Leonardo—both of his scientific research and of his artistic work. Indeed, like Sigmund Freud after him, Merezhkovskii believed that Leonardo's scientific genius and creativity were founded on Eros.[31]

For Gippius, as for Merezhkovskii, the questions of love and sex were indeed the "cursed" questions. The problem, as Gippius delineated in her essay "Infatuation" ("Vliublennost'"), was that no existing social form could capture the true meaning of love and sex. Anyone considering the question was left only with erratic impressions connected to sex: "Not that! not like that! shameful! or vulgar! or a sin! or painful! or silly! And *not* castration! And *not* 'anything goes.' And *not* marriage." Most people were simply unable to define the proper place for sexuality in love, at least not in all its fullness: "We do not know what is true, do not know where to find the truth for our *whole* being, for our *entire* nature."[32]

Developing ideas borrowed from Solov'ev, Gippius articulated her own vision of a new form of sexuality—a form of "Christian infatuation." In "Infatuation," she begins with an analysis of the conventional view that marriage was the pinnacle of earthly Eros. According to her, most ordinary people believe that marriage is the summit of the mountain of love—and most people desire to reach that summit. Once there, however, they find themselves dissatisfied; a part of every married person wants something more. "Even in the happiest marriage, full of love and family tenderness, the soul and body sometimes dimly dream and yearn: surely there is something better?" Beyond the peak, it seems, there is nothing, and yet people still want to go "higher. . . . Not to climb, but to fly."[33]

To explain this yearning for something "higher," Gippius uses the term *vliublennost'*, the quality of being "in love," often translated as "amorousness" or (better, in my view) as "infatuation." Gippius argues that people mistakenly use the phrase "in love," or *infatuation*, to describe a desire for possession, the yearning for someone to be "theirs"—through marriage or even through the simple sexual act. For Gippius, a better word for this kind of attraction is simply *desire*; it is an impulse that wishes to be satisfied, that has a very specific goal in mind, and, once achieved, the impulse will vanish, at least temporarily. And even if this "desire" is never satisfied, in most people it is still destined, in time, to gradually fade away.[34]

For Gippius, the state of being "in love," however, has a very different quality. In the first place, it has no concrete end in mind; the person in love seeks neither marriage nor sexual consummation as some kind of logical fulfillment. Indeed—and this is where Gippius's thoughts on sexuality become complicated—infatuation "does not seek, and even rejects all forms of bodily union—even as it rejects the very rejection of the body." Sexuality, for Gippius, can paradoxically include a desire specifically not to have sex, not to possess the other.[35]

In privileging celibacy, Gippius was not alone among the Silver Age poets. Some, like Berdiaev and the poet Alexander Blok, justified this by observing that procreative love was marred by death (since the outcome was the birth of those destined to die). Others, however, emphasized more strongly that the rejection of physical lust constituted the rejection of a poor substitute for the true aim of Eros, which was divine ascent. Since transfiguration was the aim of Eros, sexual consummation was a trivial thing, often degrading true erotic love. Berdiaev, for example, celebrated the ability of erotic desire to achieve human transformation, if the temptation of lust was avoided. Berdiaev put it most simply: "Sex energy contains the source of creative ecstasy and the prophetic vision of genius . . . sex life is possible, even much more intense, without the sexual act."[36] The complicated nature of this question has caused some confusion in the literature, leading some scholars to talk of Freudian "sublimation," which is not the same thing (though Freud's own thinking on sublimation was, in part, formulated after reading Merezhkovskii, which I have discussed elsewhere).[37] It is important to delineate precisely what Gippius means by a sexuality without sex.

She begins with a telling example, asking the reader to imagine an "innocent" young boy, "burning" with his first love, informed that his "beloved" would come to him that very night, and she would allow him to "possess" her. "Not only would he not want this," Gippius suggests, the infatuated, innocent boy "would be offended, he would weep and shudder." And would he even accept marriage as the "consummation of his feelings for his beloved"? Neither sex nor marriage, in this instance, would satisfy his longing. Here, Gippius might be describing a typical innocent, romantic, "Platonic" love, which idealizes its object as unattainable. But Gippius is very careful to make clear that she is not talking about a purely "spiritual" love. Following Solov'ev, and in keeping with her contemporaries in the Silver Age, she denies any kind of material/spiritual dualism. She wishes to make clear that her idea of infatuation is not based on an ascetic impulse; she wants no rejection of sexuality or the "flesh" as sinful or shameful. "That very same lover," she writes, regarding this particular example, "least of all rejects the body of his beloved: he loves it, it is dear to him, in it there is no 'sin' for him."[38]

Gippius acknowledges the central conundrum of her vision of love and predicts that her reader might ask how one can love the body of another and still reject sexual union. For her, the solution lies (as Cassedy and Paperno might suggest) in the fact that love does not repress the desire of the flesh (as it does in Freud's theory of sublimation), but rather transfigures the flesh of the beloved, and seeks Christ in the body of the one who is loved. "The flesh is not rejected, not repressed, in truth, because it is already accepted as the flesh that Christ sanctified . . . in the non-rejection of the flesh, infatuation presses closer to Christ."[39] Indeed, Christ himself never rejected the body, and he never rejected sexuality. The New Testament is quite sexual in its connotations, according to Gippius, especially when it directly refers to Christ erotically as the "Bridegroom" who sometimes appears "in the middle of the night." Infatuation, then, especially Christian infatuation, is a taste of this very Christian sexuality, which is a "new feeling, heady, like flight, unquenchable, like a thirst for God."[40]

"Sexuality needs to be transfigured," writes Gippius, echoing Merezhkovskii. It needs to be seen as a "mystery" that cannot be reduced to any existing forms of physical union—neither marital union, nor homosexual desire, nor even asceticism. Again, she anticipates her readers' objections: What other possible forms of "sexual expression and satisfaction" could there be?[41] The one form of physical union she is willing to wholeheartedly accept is the "kiss." In the kiss, she claims, there is a union of equals, a joining that still allows each to remain individual. Moreover, she is adamant that, though a kiss can be lustful, lust has "stolen" the kiss from its proper place. The kiss, she writes, is after all, in both the New and Old Testaments, an entirely acceptable greeting and expression of affection.[42]

In the end, however, Gippius does not pretend that she has an answer that will satisfy everyone. Here, she claims she departs from her husband; the "mystery" cannot be "solved," or it will no longer be a "mystery." Like "peace,

God, truth, and life," sexuality cannot be "found." It can be sought after, one can begin on the path toward it, but it will never be achieved or resolved or discovered. "In the search for truth, happiness, justice, God draws people forward, and people do not tire in their quest, though truth is only better understood, happiness is only recognized, God is only drawing nearer."[43] Here also, chastity is seen not as limiting, but as opening up possibility, bringing people of all kinds closer to one another.

Gippius expressed her quest for a new kind of sexuality not only in her essays, but also in her private letters and diaries, as well as her art. Perhaps most telling are two sets of personal records: her "Love Stories," an intimate journal she kept about her quest for true love among a variety of relationships with men and women, and her letters to Dmitrii Filosofov, the man she often lived and traveled with in the early 1900s, and with whom she had a tumultuous and confused relationship and correspondence. These sources reveal that, for Gippius, infatuation was indeed a personal quest, one that often led her to question herself and her ideals, but one to which she was deeply committed.[44]

In "Love Stories," Gippius writes of a series of "love affairs," which seem to avoid, for the most part, sexual union. It is a scathingly honest account of her relationships, and she includes many details unfavorable to herself: showing, and in many cases admitting, where she was manipulative, vain, or desiring power and control over the men and women in her life. Despite all the contradictory elements within her diary, however, it is clear that Gippius was seeking a different kind of love, one that could consume her with passionate longing, but without limiting her to any physical consummation.

At times, especially in the early years of the diary, she is adamant that a purely chaste love is her aim, one free from all taint of sexual desire. In the case of her affair with the poet Nikolai Minskii, her attraction to him is self-directed; she was filled with "a burning fire of infatuation" with herself through him. But this passionate attraction is coupled with a strong distaste for any physical touch; indeed, she declares that she feels "agony" at the thought of him "even touching her dress." In other cases, she finds herself falling in love with "ascetic" or homosexual men because of the impossibility of physical intimacy. Her long, epistolary affair with Akim Flekser (known as Akim Volynskii), the critic and essayist, began because Gippius was drawn to the fact that he had lived ascetically for ten years: "He promised to be pure all his life, like me. I will not hide the fact that this won me over." She similarly confesses her attraction to homosexual men because of the sense of something "deceptively possible."[45]

In other places, she admits, she is capable of the kind of lust that "hides within me and which I do not understand." Nonetheless, she adds, "despite my desires and my senses, *I don't want* that specific form of love, that, silly one, about which I know." Instead, she desires something else, something higher and intangible, which can be revealed through love: "I will accept and can accept love and lustful desire *in this world*, only in the name of a possibility of transforming them into another, new love, a new, limitless lust: the fire of it in my blood." As in her essay "Infatuation," the true form of physical union she completely accepts is the "kiss," that physical union that is "equality, individuality, the union of two." And, she writes, "the whole point of my kiss—that it is not the step to that form of love . . . a hint at possibility. It is a thought, or feeling, for which there are as yet no words . . . but there will be. It is possible. To the heavens. To God. To Christ."[46]

The same quest for a new kind of love, free of desire, is found in her letters to Filosofov. Their relationship was long and complicated, and in her letters she expresses many thoughts and ideas identical to those found in her diary. She references a discussion that she had with him and Merezhkovskii, regarding the sexual act, in which both men agreed that, if procreation were abolished, a new "act" would have to replace sex—in which a couple would have a strong sense of physical and spiritual union. She agreed that in the present, the sexual act was "one and the same for all couples" and was therefore, at heart, anti-individual and impersonal. In any case, it was not the essence of the "mystery of two"—the kind of love that unites and yet preserves the individuality of each member of the couple.

For Gippius, modern, secular approaches to sexuality were just as constraining as the traditional ascetic attitudes, reducing sexuality to mere biological lust. It was simply wrong to believe that sex was the goal of sexuality—that one person could desire another, possess them physically, and then feel that their desire was fulfilled. Lust is cold; the "coldest" individuals are the most "lustful." Lust is the seeking of salvation only for the flesh, in the "grimace of love," in an "as-if" kind of love.[47] Finally, lust treats others as objects; it demands that one "satisfy one's sexuality *by means of* another human being." Indeed, the scientific approach to human sexuality that was growing in importance toward the end of the nineteenth century was highly limiting and constraining in this respect; it envisioned all aspects of human love as reducible to an inner, predictable, biological drive that sees others as mere means to an end. For Gippius, this was an illusion, a "danger," and she implied it was a kind of trap—the belief that the physical union of two people was the proper and fitting end of love. Sexual acts would continue to exist, because "until the end of life our bodies remain incompletely transfigured." But the ideal was a new, future love that did not inevitably demand physical union for its satisfaction.[48]

Gippius, like other Silver Age writers and poets, believed in *zhiznetvorchestvo*, the merging of art and life. As a result, Gippius poeticized her own quest for love—and created characters that embarked on journeys very similar to her own. The poem "The Kiss," analyzed in detail by Presto in *Beyond the Flesh*, is a poem in which the narrator tells his "Agnes" that he is about to kiss her and speaks of his "knowing the joy of drawing closer," of "the moment of promise," of the fact that it is "uncertainty" he loves, "not fulfillment, but possibility." Presto misinterprets the narrator as disdainful, looking down on his victim, in awe of his power over her. But within Gippius's philosophy, the description of the "kiss" is the same as in her diary and in her essays. It is the closeness of the unknown, "not fulfillment, but possibility"—"touching the edge" of some unknown passion. Presto is right—"nothing happens"—but for Gippius, it is precisely because "nothing happens" that everything is possible.[49]

In Gippius's short story "Apple Trees Blossom," "nothing happens" as well. Volodia, a reclusive musician deeply attached to his mother, finds himself suddenly attracted to a mysterious woman, Marta, who appears in an apple orchard near their house in the south of Russia. He is struck by everything about her—the white of her dress, the red of her belt, the sound of the train of her dress as it sweeps the ground behind her, the grayish color of her hair, and the transparent color of her eyes. She claims that she is one with the natural world and that she has a sense of when the apple trees will bloom, and, indeed, her dress seems to turn slightly pink as the blossoming approaches. In this manner, she is of the natural and physical world, but she also seems to point to higher things; she is "beautiful, like the sky through the trees." He falls in love with her, but bristles with indignation when his controlling mother accuses him of wishing to "marry" Marta: "I want to marry Marta? I—marry? No, either one of us was crazy, or we were all crazy." The mother forbids him to see Marta again, but he disobeys, finding his one moment of true, untainted happiness in simply sitting next to Marta in the orchard, silently waiting for the trees to blossom: "I wanted nothing more than what happened. I think that that indeed is happiness."[50]

The mother dies shortly thereafter, and the young man believes it is because he betrayed her. The mother, in a sense, represents the controlling, this-worldly idea of love, which reduces love to marriage and physicality. Its end is death. But for Gippius, it was the young man and Marta who understood the true happiness of eternal love, one that could not be bound by time or convention.

Finally, in the short story "Miss May," Gippius uses the woman of the title to express the fullness of her erotic vision. In this story, Andrei, who is engaged to another woman, falls deeply in love with May. For him, she is both alive and more than alive, and he realizes: "There was no miracle there . . . she was simply a real girl, and all the same she seemed a miracle, because she did not seem real and ordinary. To touch her required only a few steps, but it seemed that for this it was necessary to cross the heavenly and cloud-strewn abysses, and that it was even better not to touch her at all." In a moment of misunderstanding, he decides to leave his fiancée and ask Miss May to marry him. But she gently tells him she is not a "wife." They have love, and it is enough. She explains later: "I only know that love is one thing, marriage another. . . . Why is it that whenever there is talk about love there is always a need to arrange something, like a marriage? . . . as if you wish to hammer love down with tiny nails." And she chides Andrei for mixing up heavenly and earthly love: "You reduced a God-given love to a wedding, a mechanical combination, a habit."[51]

Though I began this chapter by suggesting that Gippius was not a writer who exclusively wrote about sex, it is nonetheless true that she spent a good deal of her philosophical and creative energies on the subject. She, along with many of her Silver Age contemporaries, thought that the question of love was an important one, because it linked together so many of the other religious, spiritual, and artistic questions of the modern age. It touched on the question of the human personality, and whether people were determined or constrained by biology—for Gippius and others, it was imperative that human freedom be preserved from biological determinism. It touched on human relationships, and whether these could be reduced to their material substrata, and, here again, Gippius wanted to create space for the spiritual, unique, and free. Her vision of love was that of liberation—not because it freed people to have sex with whomever they chose, but just the opposite.

Chaste love freed people to love one another without seeking to solve the problem of love, whether by reducing it to the desire for sex or for marriage. For Gippius, chastity was liberation in that it allowed people to create their own relationships, unfettered from gender norms and social expectations. Moreover, chaste love allowed everyone to personally experience the concepts of incarnation and transfiguration—not as the denial of the fleshly and earthly, but as its incorporation into the higher, unearthly, and immaterial.

Gippius, Merezhkovskii, and other writers of the Silver Age reveal that the relationship between religion and sexuality in the late nineteenth century in Russia was far more complicated than traditional accounts would suggest, involving a complete reconsideration of the body, human relationships, and sexuality. The Silver Age challenged both the secular materialist accounts of sexuality of the day and religious calls for self-denial, trying to find a new, more holistic account of sexuality for the entirety of the human person.[52]

CHAPTER 7

Disbelief and Piety

The Irony of Maxim Gorky's Secular Religion

ERICH LIPPMAN

The Russian formalist critic Viktor Shklovskii once observed that Maxim Gorky was "made of disbelief and piety, with irony for cement."[1] Despite his atheism, Gorky was in a certain sense religious, and that religiosity operated within a Christian and even specifically Orthodox context.[2] The pinnacle of his religious expression came in his "God-building" period in which he sought to combine what he considered true Christianity with socialism, seeing the latter as a natural evolution from the vital forces of the former. Gorky's is thus a particularly interesting case of the tension between religion and modernity in late imperial Russia. Steeped in the Orthodox tradition from his childhood but well-read in eighteenth- and nineteenth-century secular humanist thought, a friend of Vladimir Lenin and A. A. Bogdanov, and an avid reader of the religious intelligentsia, Gorky embodied the paradox of the age. If we accept José Casanova's suggestion that "we should think of processes of secularization, of religious transformations and revivals, and of processes of sacralization as ongoing mutually constituted global processes, rather than as mutually exclusive developments," it also becomes possible to reimagine Gorky's God-building differently from the traditional dichotomous terms that label it an atheistic counterpoint to the burgeoning "religious renaissance" of the intelligentsia.[3] Rather, God-building and "God-seeking," as the latter phenomenon came to be called, can be seen as alternative processes, often drawing on the same sources of inspiration, which ranged from traditional

Russian religiosity to Western secular modernity. As such, God-building and God-seeking contain elements from both ends, but inhabit a space between those seemingly contradictory poles.

Gorky's case, in many ways, epitomizes Russia's experience of secularization. Casanova points out that "the secular . . . emerged first as a theological category of Western Christendom that has no equivalent in other religious traditions *or even in Eastern Christianity*" (italics added).[4] In theory, then, one might be tempted to include Russia's engagement with Western secularism in the category of those (such as colonized populations) who confronted Western secular modernity as "the other" and were consequently "more likely to recognize the European process of secularization for what it truly was, namely, a particular Christian and post-Christian historical process, and not . . . a general or universal process of human or societal development."[5] However, Russia's religious history included considerable political, cultural, and theological interaction with the West, as is evident from the frequent, decontextualized application of Western anticlericalism to the Russian Church by its critics, including Gorky. Thus, if we are to see the West as an "other" from Russian eyes, it is at best a "proximate other." The Russian émigré theologian Alexander Schmemann preferred to broaden secularism to a "Christian heresy," seeing its roots in the core theological content of Christianity itself.[6]

Charles Taylor writes that, despite the Western European origins of secularism, we should not fall into the trap of assuming that secularism must therefore remain in Western Europe. Rather, he suggests that the concept could "travel across borders in an inventive and imaginative way."[7] Taylor claims that most secular Europeans adhere to what he calls "subtraction theory," which implies that there is "no epistemic loss" in the transition from a religious to a secular worldview—that "we have just shucked off some false beliefs, baseless fears, and imagined objects."[8] While Lenin, and the burgeoning Soviet state after him, certainly adhered to this approach to religion officially, Gorky, who would later become one of the dominant symbols of that state, is a more ambiguous case.

Paragon of Proletarian Literature or Nietzschean Marxist?

Gorky scholarship has waned significantly in the years since the collapse of the Soviet Union. Likewise, in the United States, there is but a handful of scholars who continue to take Gorky seriously. In both cases, the reason for the demise of Gorky's literary and intellectual legacy is specifically the way it played itself out in the Soviet Union and abroad. His defense of the Soviet experiment and canonization as the ideal proletarian writer, willing to collaborate with Joseph Stalin, colored his legacy forever. His identification with Bolshevism forever linked his fate to the fate of the system to which his name was attached. As Donald Fanger has written, that association made him "not simply too productive but too familiar, too much praised by the wrong people, too compromised. More dead than alive."[9]

It is significant to note, however, that many of Gorky's contemporaries held a much more complex view of the man. Writers such as Shklovskii, Victor Serge, Kornei Chukovskii, and Nina Berberova portray a much more colorful personality than can be gleaned from the official hagiographies. Each of these portrayals has one specific point in common—the highly conflicted nature of Gorky's personality. Perhaps the most famous analysis of Gorky's split personality was Chukovskii's *The Two Souls of M. Gorky*, in which he posited a Gorky torn between consciousness and creativity.[10] In Bertram D. Wolfe's *The Bridge and the Abyss*, this conflict is defined as "the quest for truth and justice and the longing to believe in the salutary lie."[11] Finally, Berberova mused that "it is strange, given his rejection of mysticism, that he thought that if you believe wholeheartedly in an illusion it can cease to be an illusion and become real: man is God and there is no limit to what he can achieve."[12]

In an attempt to develop a more nuanced understanding of Gorky and his milieu, George L. Kline posited the term "Nietzschean Marxist," which has held considerable sway among American scholars for the past fifty years.[13] "Nietzschean Marxist" effectively addressed the dichotomy in Gorky's mind between creativity and consciousness, but Kline did not originally use the term in reference to Gorky. Kline's 1960 article "Changing Attitudes toward the Individual" mentioned two groups of deviant Marxist thinkers in the early twentieth century—the Kantians and the Nietzscheans.[14] This article focused on four major Nietzscheans within the Marxist camp—A. V. Lunacharsky, Stanislav Volsky, A. A. Bogdanov, and V. A. Bazarov—but did not mention Gorky.

The actual term "Nietzschean Marxists," although implied in "Changing Attitudes toward the Individual," did not appear until later in the aptly named article "'Nietzschean Marxism' in Russia."[15] Here Kline again turned to Volsky, Lunacharsky, Bogdanov, and Bazarov, but this time briefly mentioned that "Maxim Gorky . . . was for a time closely associated with this group."[16] Only in 1968, in his famous book *Religious and Anti-religious Thought in Russia*, did Kline unequivocally apply the term to Gorky. In his chapter on the God-builders, he referred to Gorky and Lunacharsky as the movement's two major spokesmen, and Bogdanov and Bazarov as its minor spokesmen, stating that "all of them may properly be called Nietzschean Marxists with respect to their ethics, social philosophy, and general theory of man."[17] Thus, in this text and in reference to the concept of God-building, Gorky simply replaced Volsky as one of the four representatives of Nietzschean Marxism.

Bernice Glatzer Rosenthal reinforced Gorky's association with "Nietzschean Marxism" in her 1986 publication of *Nietzsche in Russia*, for which Kline provided the introduction. This edited volume devoted one section to dealing with "Nietzsche's influence on Russian Marxism," in which three articles address Gorky, Lunacharsky, and Bogdanov, respectively.[18] In Rosenthal's 2002 monograph *New Myth, New World* (dedicated to Kline), Rosenthal set aside one section for "Nietzschean Marxists," among whom she includes Bogdanov, Lunacharsky, Gorky, Bazarov, Volsky, and Aleksandra Kollontai (her own addition).[19] The label continues to be applied to Gorky in contemporary scholarship on God-building.[20]

Whereas the term "Nietzschean Marxist" works relatively well for Bogdanov, Lunacharsky, Volsky, and Bazarov, scholars who focus on Gorky have been less comfortable with it. It is well known that Gorky read Friedrich Nietzsche and that the characters of his early short stories had distinctly Nietzschean characteristics. As such, various authors have allowed themselves to overlook Gorky's personal rejection of Nietzsche's thought in favor of seeing his ongoing creative impulse in Nietzschean terms. However, by the time Gorky settled on Capri and had begun his God-building experiment, his "Nietzscheanism" was mitigated by a variety of plausible competing, and often contradictory, impulses. Thus, the term "Nietzschean" is less wrong than misleading. It reduces aspects of Gorky's aesthetic and religious vision to a generic category that fails to encompass it. While it has provided a useful framework for interpreting aspects of Gorky's creative output, it suffers from the same malady as any category; it obscures other currents in Gorky's thought.

Contrary to what might be assumed from the many statues and images around Moscow, the term "Marxist," as applied to Gorky during his God-building period, could be less accurate than "Nietzschean." Gorky was in no way a systematic thinker, preferring to reject all systems of thought as antivital. Kline writes that, "by 1900, he had become a Marxist and joined the party."[21] However, contemporary academic consensus suggests that Gorky may never have joined the Bolsheviks, or at least that the question is still open.[22] Gorky often vacillated between populism and Marxism.[23] Describing Gorky's political disposition around the turn of the century, V. A. Posse wrote that "Gorky had no sympathy at this time for Marxism, which demeaned the human personality, in his view."[24] If he eventually opted for Marxism, it is not necessarily because of the merits of the idea, but because his experience with one of the populist education programs contributed to a lifelong distrust of peasants, who often formed the target audience of the populists.[25] He was also powerfully attracted to the particular personalities associated with Marxism—first Lenin, then Bogdanov.[26] However, Gorky's transition from populism to Marxism did not represent a complete break from his past. Vera Zasulich, the populist assassin of the governor of Petersburg, wrote that after her conversion to atheism, Christ remained with her "as if [she] were more tied to him than ever."[27] The populist tendency to draw parallels between their political ideology and Christianity suggests that the "subtraction theory," so common among the Marxists, was not a universal approach to revolutionary secularization. Gorky's God-building certainly comes closer to the populist than the Bolshevik model on this point. Perhaps this is why Shklovskii wrote that "only in his last things . . . was Gorky able to write for someone other than Mikhailovsky."[28]

Above all, Gorky may have avoided the Marxist label in the name of vitalism, which he frequently touted as an antidote to charges of ideological inconsistency. In a 1917 article titled "On Polemics," Gorky claimed that he considered himself a "heretic everywhere" because resolving the contradictions in his thought would cause him, he wrote, to "murder precisely that part of my soul that so ardently and painfully loves the living, sinning, and—forgive me—the pitiful little Russian."[29] This artistic and humanistic adherence to inconsistency is one of Gorky's hallmark characteristics and is echoed throughout his letters and creative works. Gorky also valued action above ideological purity. In words that would later come to haunt him, he proclaimed in the same article that "a person should do everything possible that is good and needed, although the 'thing' may not completely harmonize with his basic beliefs."[30] Perhaps this disposition explains not only his willingness to collaborate with the Bolsheviks but also his willingness to make future compromises in the 1920s and 1930s. Chukovskii writes that, while working on behalf of the new Bolshevik state in 1919, Gorky always referred to the Bolsheviks as "they." "He never said we. He always speaks of them as enemies."[31] However, Chukovskii also observed Gorky's pragmatism in action. Accused of talking one way to the writers under his charge and another way to the Bolsheviks in power, Gorky confessed to Chukovskii: "I realize I'm often duplicitous. Never before have I dissembled, but with our regime I have to dissemble, lie, and pretend. I know there's no other way."[32]

If a heretical Bolshevik or Marxist at best, Gorky was clearly a socialist, who employed Marxist rhetoric and terminology (as did virtually all socialists of the day), but usually in a less-than-coherent manner. His concept of socialism as the "religion of the workers" tormented his more orthodox Marxist comrades to no end.[33] The "Nietzschean Marxist" label made more sense as a type of synthesis during the dialectical days of the Cold War than it did before 1917 or after 1991. In the twenty-first century—a time in which religion and modernity are constantly reimagined in relation to each other—it makes more sense to leave it to its time and place.

God-Building as Secular Religion in a Russian Context

Gorky's relationship to religion has long been neglected. Perhaps unsurprisingly, the most promising work done on this topic has been by Russian scholars. If the official Gorky rose and fell with the USSR, then the unofficial Gorky provides the most abundant opportunity for the exploration of this topic. To this end, scholars associated with the Institute of World Literature and Art have produced some impressive analyses of the religious and philosophical dispositions of Gorky. Salient works in this genre include E. N. Nikitin's *"Ispoved'"* *M. Gor'kogo*, L. Spiridonova's *M. Gor'kii: Novyi vzgliad*, and the collection *Kontseptsiia mira i cheloveka v tvorchestve M. Gor'kogo*, to name a few.[34] Even the Russian Orthodox Church has involved itself in the process of interpreting Gorky anew.[35] Rather than see Gorky's God-building as a revolutionary socialist contrast to the so-called God-seeking occurring among the Petersburg intelligentsia at the time, it is more helpful to see him in terms of the overall climate of religious questioning and grappling with materialism that was so common in the Silver Age. In other words, he fits better into a narrative of Russia's particular path(s) of modernity and secularization.

In order to add Gorky to this spectrum of thought, which is typically reserved for his ideological adversaries, it is necessary to understand that the thinkers of what Nicholas Zernov has called the "Russian Religious Renaissance" were nothing like a homogenous group and, consequently, their God-seeking often took very specific and personal turns.[36] Perhaps because of that powerful interest in the individual, these thinkers seldom fell into easy agreement with the official spokespeople of the Russian Orthodox Church. Commenting on this tendency years later, Siniavskii stated to a largely émigré audience in Paris, "Their religious project [*stroitel'stvo*] is quite often connected with quests for their own inner, personal God, as if unlike any other gods, unique, existing as though in a single number, 'my' number."[37] For present purposes, the important parts to remember about this quotation are, first, that God-seeking was indeed a process of myth-creation, that is, a religious "construction" (*stroitel'stvo*), as was Gorky's *"bogostroitel'stvo,"* [God-building] and, second, that the internally derived individuality and uniqueness of the God (or gods) of the God-seekers allowed for an endless number of derivations. It is impossible to assert a consensus point of view for this group, as their competing concepts of God ranged widely.

Irina Gutkin, in her 1999 book *The Cultural Origins of the Socialist Realist Aesthetic*, maintains the distinction between Marxism and what she calls the "theurgic transformationism" of the idealists (that is, God-seekers). However, even in positing this dialectic, she moves to synthesize it, stating that "the materialist and idealist schemes, paradoxically, were not as far apart as their proponents saw them in the heat of the political moment" and that ultimately "the history of the revolutionary artistic avant-gardes in Russia unfolded as a gradual rapprochement between the two utopian schemes that can be measured in terms of the degree of their removal from traditional Christian metaphysical authority."[38] It is this emphasis on seeing these seemingly competing concepts as part of a continuum of ideas wrestling with the inherent tensions of religion and modernity and differing primarily in their *degree* of removal from traditional Christian metaphysical authority that forms the crux of my argument.

If dialogue is context, it is clear by all accounts that Gorky considered himself to be in conversation with the religious intelligentsia during his God-building period. From his voluminous correspondence, one can easily glean that he read the articles of the God-seekers frequently, although often with disdain. It is also during his God-building period that he corresponded directly with Vasilii Rozanov, one of the preeminent God-seekers. Bogdanov and his followers had already responded to the God-seeker symposium *Problems of Idealism* with their own symposium, *Essays on a Realistic Worldview*. In 1910, Gorky joined Bogdanov's symposium response to the *Landmarks* symposium, titled *Essays on the Philosophy of Collectivism*.

In this latter collection, Gorky contributed one of his most controversial articles, "The Disintegration of Personality" ("Razrushenie lichnosti"), which in its own right is significant evidence that Gorky saw himself in dialogue with the religious philosophers.[39] In the very title, he temporarily departs from his traditional term for personality—*chelovek*—and instead uses the religious intelligentsia term—*lichnost'*—complete with all of its religious connotations.[40] This would be evidence enough if he did not go on to challenge specific religious thinkers in the article and attempt a conflation of socialist collectivism with the Orthodox concept of *sobornost'* [conciliarity] and Solov'evan supra-individualism.[41] This effort to co-opt religious verbiage to make an atheistic point was not Gorky's own innovation. Bogdanov had employed religious terminology in his 1905 article "Sobiranie cheloveka," while Kline highlights Bazarov's intentional conflation of the term *sobornost'* with the collectivist ideal in his 1910 book *Na dva fronta*.[42]

More importantly, however, "The Destruction of Personality" has to be seen in the context of the recent publication of Gorky's God-building novel *Confession*. This novel employs powerful Christian imagery in order to posit socialism as the true vital religion of the people from which traditional Christianity had emerged as warped by power. Christ, according to Gorky, was the God of the people, created by the people as the culmination of all of the potential good within them. However, as with so many other efforts of the people, power-seeking individuals (that is, the institutional church) had made Him subservient to the interests of power. Only when Christ is returned to the people through the revolutionary process of throwing off power can people be transformed from atomized power-seeking individuals to true supra-individual persons.[43] For example, this quotation, in which the novel's hero Matvei finds transcendence among the working people, illustrates Gorky's supra-individualism: "I stood in their circle, and they were my body, and I was their soul and their will, and my speech was their voice. And at times it was I that was a part of the body, and I heard the cry of my own soul from other mouths, and it sounded good when I heard it. In my relationship with people, I did not lose myself; instead, I grew larger, taller, and the strength of my soul increased manyfold."[44]

To those familiar with traditional Slavophile concepts of *sobornost'* and Solov'evan *vseedinstvo*, [all-unity] this should all sound quite familiar. However, even this moment does not achieve the full "union with the whole" in which "happiness and the origin of the greatest pleasures of the soul are found," as Gorky described the "thesis" of his novel to his legal wife, E. P. Peshkova.[45] That would only be accomplished during an icon procession in which a young girl is healed of her infirmities by the collective will of the faithful and Gorky's protagonist finds his true spiritual union with the human collective, all in the context of an icon procession for the Virgin of Kazan.[46]

Gorky between Lenin and the Religious-Philosophical Society

As Gorky was a literary superstar in 1908, but also quite clearly allied with the Bolsheviks, *Confession* caused considerable confusion in both Bolshevik and religio-philosophical circles. Lenin's allies immediately began attacking Gorky's foray into mysticism, while a hopeful Petersburg intelligentsia scrambled to find a positive change in Gorky's direction.[47] For about five months, the halls of the Petersburg Religious-Philosophical Society were abuzz with talk of God-building and the "religion of Gorky."[48] Barry P. Scherr, in his 2000 article

"God-Building or God-Seeking? Gorky's *Confession* as Confession," writes that "nearly all the early critics, whether positively or negatively inclined toward the novel, in fact saw it as a work about seeking—seeking God, and through God a sense of connectedness to the world and to humanity."[49] Many, like Alexander Blok, hoped that this signaled a departure from Bolshevism, while others, like Dmitrii Filosofov, were guardedly optimistic that God-building and God-seeking could find some common ground.[50] While critical of Gorky's turn, Rozanov saw *Confession* as evidence that Gorky was following the same path as Fyodor Dostoyevsky's character Shatov from *Demons*, implying that he was deifying the people.[51] It is significant that Rozanov chooses to identify Gorky with the Slavophile Shatov, who desperately wants to believe in God, rather than the religiously atheistic Kirillov, whose own beliefs would seem to have much more in common with Gorky's.

Eventually, V. A. Rudnev (pseudonym Bazarov) came from Gorky's villa on Capri with a small delegation of Bolsheviks to present reports at the Petersburg Religious-Philosophical Society. The session began with a presentation by Filosofov titled "God-Building and God-Seeking," which was followed by Bazarov's presentation titled "God-Seeking and 'God-Building.'"[52] In his presentation, Filosofov concludes with the conciliatory comment that "on the question, are the God-builders friends or foes, God-seekers can answer thus: we believe that they will become friends."[53] Bazarov responds by proposing Gorky's God-building as an answer to the God-seeking of the religious intelligentsia—an end to the incessant religious quests of the philosophers.[54] Not all of the religious *intelligenty* were impressed by this "flirtation" with the Marxists. Rozanov remarked that after Filosofov's presentation, "it would follow to do a curtsey, but he sat and so he couldn't do it. It is true, however, that under the table he shuffled a leg."[55] Rozanov recoiled at the God-seekers' pandering to the Marxists, parodying the attitude of Dmitrii Merezhkovskii and Filosofov: "Knight me, future king. I want to be a knight of the proletariat."[56] The Bolsheviks, in Rozanov's words "not so much anthropological as zoological," were unimpressed by their bourgeois flatterers.[57] On a more sober note, Rozanov does move to synthesize the two sides, however, noting a similar tendency in each to relegate religion to an abstraction, while "talking incessantly about God without actually thinking of Him." On this point, "between Filosofov and Nevedomskii, Bazarov and Merezhkovskii, *there is full confluence and no difference whatsoever.*"[58] Ironically, much of the God-builders' purpose was to inspire that religious vitality that Rozanov could not feel in this discussion of it.

Gorky took seriously his role as respondent, and it was in that capacity that he wrote his articles "O Karamazovshchine" and "Eshche o Karamazovshchine" and attended meetings of the Religious-Philosophical Society after his return to Russia in 1913. The first article, "O Karamazovshchine," argued against a staging of Dostoyevsky's *Demons* in Moscow.[59] The strength of his invectives carried over into his second article, "Eshche o Karamazovshchine," in which he famously preached to the religious philosophers of his day: "You have no God, you have not yet created him. Gods are not sought—they are created!"[60] Having restrained himself to some extent after the publication of *Confession* and having hoped that political pressure had forced Gorky to give up on his God-building, Lenin could no longer contain his ire upon reading this article and immediately penned a furious letter to Gorky, claiming that "god-seeking differs from god-building or god-creating or god-making, etc., no more than a yellow devil differs from a blue devil."[61] Lenin does not stop there, however, continuing that "the Catholic priest corrupting young girls . . . is much *less* dangerous . . . than a priest without his cassock, a priest without crude religion, an ideological and democratic priest preaching the creation and invention of a god."[62] The last paragraph of "Eshche o Karamazovshchine" engendered such a powerful response from Lenin equating God-seeking and God-building that the paragraph has been excluded from most Soviet-era collections of Gorky's work.[63]

Given Gorky's attempt to create a myth that could elevate socialism to the status of religion utilizing traditional Christian imagery, one might wonder how exactly he was able to manipulate that imagery to reach his conclusions. Following in the footsteps of Leo Tolstoy, Gorky imagined himself a heretic. Because Gorky saw the church as a bastardization of the true religion by official, ossified institutions, heresy was the only way to rediscover vitality and truth. In other words, if the traditional church interpreted scriptures in ways that supported its power base, only the heretics could discover the true, vital faith. For this reason, Pavel Basinskii, one of Gorky's later Russian biographers, referred to him as a "Russian Luther."[64] He appreciated religious schismatics and maintained strong contacts among Old Believer communities.[65] One example of his manipulation of Scripture comes from a letter to Rozanov, praising the latter's recent book *Solitaria*. Here Gorky writes that his favorite book of the Bible is Job, especially in chapter 40 when, according to Gorky, God calls man to stand by his side as an equal.[66] Elsewhere, Gorky writes that parts of chapter 42 (Job's repentance) were added later to misdirect the significance of the Job story.[67]

One of Gorky's letters to Rozanov illustrates many of these trends. For this excerpt, it is important to remember that Rozanov had written an article about *Confession* titled "O 'narodo'-bozhii kak novoi idee Maksima Gor'kogo," which derived from discussions at the religious-philosophical society. Gorky wrote to Rozanov:

Everything is from the people: both the church and social democracy, from there also comes every heretic—including you. "And even—who knows—maybe"—social democracy is an external expression of the presently chaotic, universal, creative work directed toward the erection of a new church. House spirits, wood-goblins, mermaids—will not be excluded in the future; we will always live in miracles and mysteries, from them is the most miraculous and mysterious essence—man, the people, the mighty people.

Here I like even the word itself and it intoxicates me—the people [*narod*]—a clan upon a clan [*rod na rod*]—it is the construction of the Tower of Babel, every rebellion, a variety of tongues, animal egoism and a great revelation of one licentious, Italian, old woman.[68]

Although these are only a few lines, they are extremely dense with literary, philosophical, and biblical imagery. First, Gorky announces his basic idea that everything stems from the creative imagination of humanity (*chelovek*), including the church and social democracy. However, here he posits social democracy as an imperfect next stage of development along the same path traveled by the church. This time, however, as a party of the people, it has the ability to go beyond what the church represents today even while subsuming all of the good it may have to offer. Thus, Gorky's commentary on social democracy here anticipates the role of the soldiers in Blok's 1918 poem, "The Twelve."[69]

Gorky implies that Rozanov will appreciate what he has written, as he and Rozanov share the kinship of heresy. In the second paragraph, Gorky plays with the Russian word for the people (*narod*) to illustrate the fact that it is the all-inclusive experience of humanity. The *"rod na rod"* section is a play on the Russian Synodal translation of Mark 13:8: "Vosstanet narod na narod" (Nation shall rise up against nation). The pun plays on a double meaning of the preposition *na* as "against" and "on top of," thus correlating this seemingly destructive verse phenomenon to the ultimately human construct of the Tower of Babel. Steeped in cultural-philosophical references, this short passage holds considerable meaning for Gorky's view of religion. The conflation of rebellion and construction at least resonates very strongly with the Solov'evan/Dostoyevskian view of rebellion as necessary for the process of building the Kingdom of Heaven.[70] Thus, all of the revolutionary chaos present in these political movements of the day will ultimately reveal themselves to serve a divine purpose. To all of this, Rozanov would reply slyly, "This is perhaps 'another church' and certainly a Tower of Babel."[71]

The significance of this example for my argument is specifically Gorky's attempt to conflate his own revolutionary aspirations with the Slavophile and

Solov'evan concepts of *sobornost'* and *vseedinstvo*. It is yet another illustration of the degree to which Gorky read and interacted with the religious philosophy that so dominated the Russian intellectual culture of the day and attempted to articulate his own views in its terms. Thus, we are led to the question of what, if anything, distinguishes Gorky from the crowd. What makes him something other than a radical revolutionary and atheistic version of Nikolai Berdiaev, Sergei Bulgakov, Merezhkovskii, or Rozanov?

Differentiation and Integration

The answer to this question again refers back to Gorky's experience with Tolstoy—the internality of God in Gorky's worldview. Here he has abundant recourse to the Russian religious-philosophical tradition, as theologians and philosophers since Aleksei Khomiakov had railed against the West specifically for its desire to externalize God.[72] However, for these thinkers, to use one of Solov'ev's favorite catchphrases, the relationship between God and man was "undivided, yet unmerged."[73] This paradox breaks down in Gorky's monistic cosmology. God is real for Gorky but only as potential, only as the culmination of human creative imagination. He is within the people and theirs to actualize, although such an actualization would only be a self-actualization for humanity. Thus, Gorky is distinguishable from the majority of religious *intelligenty* at the time by his unwillingness to acknowledge any fundamental distinction between God and man.

But this does not exclude him from the religious-philosophical milieu entirely. After all, was it not Rozanov who wrote, "My God is particular. He is only my God, and nobody else's. If He is somebody else's, then I do not know Him, and am not interested in knowing Him"?[74] An internal God is not Gorky's claim alone, which returns us to Siniavskii's point above—that the God-seeking project was about finding an "inner, personal God, as if unlike any other gods."[75] This diversity of perspectives creates a broad-enough umbrella to at least include Gorky in the dialogue. Rather than try to parse out the particular aspects of Gorky's God-building that separated him from the God-seekers, which has already been thoroughly accomplished, it now seems appropriate to balance the narrative with a corresponding look at how Gorky fit into the broader tensions between religion and modernity in late imperial Russia. The contemporary debates about the various world processes of secularization allow the greatest opportunity for synthesis on this point. In José Casanova's terms, we should "enter into a much more open analysis of non-Western civilizational dynamics and be more critical of our Western Christian secular categories, in order to expand our understandings of the secular and secularisms."[76]

Gorky, in many ways, embodies the complex nature of Russia's encounter with modernity. Even Chukovskii, who considered himself quite close to Gorky, admits that he "often did not understand Alexei Maksimovich."[77] Gorky intentionally operated within the context of—and borrowed the terminology of—the religious philosophy of the day, albeit in a way that reflected the highly conflicted nature of his mentality and his particular political leanings. His articulation of these tensions was, however, in Gutkin's terms, simply another degree of removal from "traditional Christian metaphysical authority."[78] Perhaps this quotation will do more than any to exemplify the paradoxical relationship of Gorky to the religious questions of his day:

> The basic contradiction in my opinion about social life is connected to the combination in me of two elements—an aristocratic understanding of personality, freedom, and creativity, and a socialistic demand for the assertion of the dignity of every man, of even the lowest of men, and for a guarantee of his rights in life.[79]

Although this quotation has a "Nietzschean Marxist" ring and could easily be attributed to Gorky, it was actually written in Paris, France, three years after Gorky's death by one of the ideological antagonists—Berdiaev, the herald of Personalism and, according to Zernov, one of the four benchmark personalities of the Russian Religious Renaissance.[80] These types of resonances, of which there are many, allow us the opportunity to reimagine God-building and God-seeking as "mutually constituted . . . processes, rather than as mutually exclusive developments" in the Russian process of grappling with modernity and secularization, as well as positing the Russian case study as "an inventive and imaginative way" that secularism "travel[s] across borders."[81] After all, according to Shklovskii, "irony . . . can tie everything together."[82]

CHAPTER 8

The Dazzling Darkness of *Black Square*
Malevich's Religious Metaphysics

Tatiana Levina

Kazimir Malevich is usually perceived as a revolutionary and iconoclast and is rarely seen as a worshipper of the divine.[1] However, these are two interconnected sides of his intellectual output—his way of glorifying God demanded a revolutionary form. In this chapter, I discuss Malevich not only as an artist and art theorist, as he is best known, but as a metaphysician, and even a religious metaphysician. It can be said that Malevich's theoretical legacy has yet to be fully understood, and, indeed, multiple, contradictory scholarly interpretations of his work have been published. As Aleksandra Shatskikh, a prominent scholar of Malevich's legacy, points out: "Scholars contradict one another even regarding his epistemological principles; some declare him a mystically oriented, irrational thinker, who discovered his truth in the depths of his own intuition, while others call him a confirmed rationalist and a cerebral analyst."[2] In part, this is because only fifteen years have passed since the publication of the most complete collected edition of Malevich's works, compiled by Shatskikh. Before this publication, some scholars thought that Malevich's main texts were inevitably lost, so they felt it necessary to extrapolate his ideas from the limited texts available. Sometimes, scholarly interpretations were focused only on a partial translation of a particular text, leaving out the rest of the material. And sometimes scholars relied on a simplification of Malevich's ideas as found in works such as Malevich's "Cult of Lenin." This is true of Nina Tumarkin's book *Lenin Lives! The Lenin*

Cult in Soviet Russia as well as Boris Groys's *The Total Art of Stalinism: Avant-Garde, Aesthetic Dictatorship, and Beyond*, both of which suggest that Malevich praised Vladimir Lenin and Joseph Stalin.[3] Alexei Kurbanovsky similarly argues that Malevich's "new theology" developed from glorifying God into extolling Lenin.[4] All of these scholars ignore Malevich's explicit statements on the subject. As he wrote, "Communism is nothing but constant hostility and lack of peace, because it strives to subjugate any ideas and suppress them. No other type of slavery was as harsh as Communism is now, because everyone's life depends on the elder [the Communist leader]."[5]

As Shatskikh points out, Malevich was an unappreciated genius, not only in his day but in the present as well. There were followers of his suprematist method, but his suprematist theoretical literary legacy remains unknown.[6] In this field he was solitary, mostly because he criticized everything: the arts, the church, Communism, the West, and totalitarianism.[7] My discussion begins with contemporary scholarship and analysis of the Russian avant-garde in general, and Malevich in particular. Because these topics are closely linked with the contemporary attitude toward religion in the arts, I then discuss Malevich's own perspective on religion. Finally, because his thoughts on religion were intimately related to his metaphysical writings, it will be important to elucidate the philosophical principles behind these writings.

The Avant-Garde, Religion, and Contemporary Art

Ana Siljak, in her introduction to this book, refers to Charles Taylor's definition of secularism as the insistence on immanent reality as the only obvious worldview. Transcendence, in the secular frame, is considered lacking traits of existence and is understood as "otherworldly." Malevich was often portrayed as a radical secular artist, who kept pace with the secularism of the revolution of 1917. However, avant-garde art was not necessarily secular. Indeed, I argue that it was post-secular; in the Russian case, it often returned to Orthodox Christian symbols that had been marginalized during the secularization process that had begun in the early eighteenth century. The Soviet regime obstructed this interpretation of avant-garde as a post-secular phenomenon because of its commitment to state-sponsored atheism and attacks on the Orthodox Church and other religions.[8] Only after the fall of the USSR did it become possible to talk about the religious roots of the avant-garde, and not just its constructivist and Communist ideals. Still, the subject continued to be ignored with the beginning of the postmodern era, with its ironic stance toward the sublime and transcendent. For example, the Russian philosopher Valery Podoroga declared that "to be sublime is to be out of fashion."[9] The art critic Yekaterina Dyogot' expressed it best, on visiting Mark Rothko's exhibition at the Tate Gallery in London in 2008: "A long string of dark-gray walls with abstract paintings absolutely identical both in size and color, emanating inconceivable and *unfounded spiritual pretension*. . . . after all, one cannot forget that abstract art [was] initially designed as a grandiose trickery."[10]

Thus, art critics in the 2000s were blind when it came to art that pointed to the sublime and to spiritual experience. James Elkins considers this problem in his book *On the Strange Place of Religion in Contemporary Art*. Elkins claims that art journals accept articles with discussion on a religious topic if, and only if, they include a critique of religion. Moreover, critics will explicitly deny the presence of religious themes in art, even when artists themselves have clearly included them. For instance, Rothko himself admitted that he was saddened by such interpretations.[11] The American minimalist Donald Judd, who was interested in Malevich's forms and colors in the mid-1960s, believed that the metaphysical elements of European art were out of date: "All that art is based on . . . *a priori* systems; they express a certain type of thinking and logic that is pretty much discredited now as a way of finding out what the world's like."[12]

In part, contemporary art critics are resistant to religious interpretation in art because contemporary artists are often explicitly atheistic and even antireligious. Take, for instance, Avdey Ter-Oganyan's performance *Young Atheist* (1998), in which he chopped up icons in public.[13] The artist asserted that this action was performed to speak against the stranglehold of the church on society. To vindicate his performance, colleagues of Ter-Oganyan claimed that the icons were not originals, but "photo reproductions" bought in the church shop very cheaply.[14] They were missing the point—an icon, to an Orthodox believer, has intense symbolic significance, whether as an original or as a cheap reproduction.[15] As Pavel Florenskii explained in his seminal work on icons, "Iconostasis," an icon is not a painting, so a reproduction of an icon is still a holy image, indeed *is the saint himself or herself*, symbolically represented on it.[16] Both the artist and the art critics who defended him failed to understand the basic precepts of a religion they claimed to criticize.

In the Russian case, this attitude toward church symbols is a product of Soviet Communism. Lenin and the Bolsheviks decided to recontextualize religious objects when building their new culture.[17] Church antiquities were removed from monasteries and churches and placed in recently nationalized art galleries and museums. The Soviet state preserved icons behind museum glass as valuable artistic artifacts. As Lenin told A. V. Lunacharsky, it was necessary to catalog "those ancestors of Socialism or its theoreticians and fighters, but also outstanding names in philosophy, science, art, etc., who even without having a direct relationship to Socialism, were genuine heroes of culture."[18] In effect, the mindset of Ter-Oganyan and his supporters is a legacy of Leninism—reinterpreting religious, sacred art in secular terms. The Russian avant-garde, by contrast, was historically and theologically connected to Russian iconography, and, as this chapter will demonstrate, we can only understand Malevich now in a way that we could not before.[19]

Black Square: Malevich's Metaphysics

Malevich's revolution began in 1915 with *Black Square*. In part, the work was the utmost expression of primitivism, a movement that inspired Russian avant-garde artists such as Mikhail Larionov and Natalia Goncharova.[20] More importantly, this painting was a crucial part of the process of artistic exploration that led Malevich to the theory of objectlessness.[21] In his manifesto "From Cubism and Futurism to Suprematism: The New Realism in Painting" (1915), Malevich proclaims objectlessness as a new order, changing "the world of meat and bone." In this, he seeks to distance art from "illusionism," from attempts to copy or imitate life.[22] As "suprematists," then, Malevich and his associates asserted that imitation was about consuming illusion and not about the discovery of natural laws. He radically insisted on the refusal of all traditional forms of painting.

Malevich traced the artistic development from cubism and futurism to the purification of form. Cubism, from Malevich's point of view, was only the preparation for a higher form of painting. Cubism, unlike realism, saw nature differently—it deconstructed nature into its component parts. Like futurism, however, it could not overcome nature. Malevich was radical, stating that "the artist can be a creator only when the forms in his picture have nothing in common with nature." He proclaimed that art is the ability to build not on the interrelation of form and color, or on the aesthetic foundation of beauty in composition, *but on the basis of the weight, speed, and direction of movement.*" Malevich concluded: "If for thousands of years past the artist has tried to approach the depiction of an object as closely as possible, to present its essence and meaning, then in our era of Cubism the artist has destroyed objects together with their meaning, essence, and purpose."[23]

Criticizing all forms of "practical realism," Malevich refused to see visible reality as true. He saw the world as something consisting not of elements, or of anything that could be broken: "no dishes, no palaces, no chairs. Man possesses all those things, and that's why they break, and his life is a heap of crockery, scrap."[24] Science explores reality by analyzing its parts and breaking things down to their fragments. What should be done with all those countless fragments, Malevich asked, and what do they mean? Investigating reality thus "means investigating what does not exist and is incomprehensible; but for man, what is incomprehensible is non-existent—hence it is something non-existent that is being examined."[25] He continues to build his suprematist theory: "Therefore what we call reality is infinity without weight, measure, time or space, absolute or relative, never traced in a form." Reality, as it is, cannot be comprehended. Reality is an inconceivable, "eternal nothing," and objects perceived by us have a completely different nature.[26]

Kurbanovsky, an art historian, compared Malevich's theory of art with Edmund Husserl's phenomenology. According to Kurbanovsky, the central philosophical project of phenomenology is to elucidate structures of experience and propositions that cannot be doubted or questioned even by the most skeptical reasoning. This reminds Kurbanovsky of Malevich's statement on suprematism as "the construction of planes liberated from interrelations of both color and form," which Kurbanovsky describes as "pure, structural—essentially transcendental—principles/ideas defined as the 'preservation of the sign.'"[27] On closer examination, however, the ideas of Husserl and Malevich diverge. Husserl proposes "go[ing] back to the things themselves," whereas Malevich rejects those things. He appeals, instead, to the eternal and abstract Nothing. This is particularly revealed in Malevich's analysis of Dziga Vertov's texts. Malevich "enthusiastically criticize[d]" Vertov as he moved toward objectlessness. Malevich concluded that the world, in fact, is nothing, and "whoever wants to express the wholeness of the world must come only to this 'nothing,' for 'the something' of the world does not exist."[28]

Malevich opposes the world of ideas to the world of things, but "ideas" are not found in consciousness. The world and its manifestations are not the result of the activity of consciousness, as consciousness does not exist. Only abstract ideas exist, in the Platonic sense: "Only thanks to the evolving organization of man, did man realize 'something' from this 'nothing-world,' whose force destroyed the world and did this in the name of the 'real,' which was born in his consciousness as an appearance of one form or another. But this was no longer the world, this was its destruction, division, therefore the emerging technology which arose has two purposes: the first purpose is the destruction and the reorganization of immutable destruction, and the second purpose is the reorganization of destruction in the immutable."[29] Malevich concludes that things are just constructions in human consciousness, and pure experience, cleansed of the content of consciousness, will lead to the "nothing" of things, and not to "things as they are" or to "structures of experience and consciousness." For this reason, religion, art, and science are directed toward the cognition of the world, which is an abstract world. Then a question arises: How can this true abstract world be known, if mankind is part of a material, sensual world? And Malevich answers: "But if the world is abstract, then it can be cognized through the abstract, as the body is cognized through the body."[30] Consequently, Malevich's core ideas are far from phenomenology.

The complexity of Malevich's theory of objectlessness has long been underestimated. Eager to find a theoretical basis for his artistic experience, Malevich escaped from the traditional confines of art and explored theoretical and philosophical ideas generally not associated with painting or sculpture. Malevich stood apart from the academic community, revolutionized art, and subverted academism. Traditional standards were not perceived as barriers for him. For Malevich, most significantly, objectlessness was a path to the divine: "Jesus Christ as the son of God is an empty name, absolute silence . . . Jesus Christ, as also God, is a non-objective, empty, silent space, so to speak, in which the human brain, diseased by apparitions, is seeing, hearing and even feeling objects."[31] In this manner, by declaring the opposition between the world of objects and the world of objectlessness, Malevich proposed a metaphysics that traces its roots back to a Platonic world of ideas.[32]

Dazzling Darkness: Malevich's Religious Metaphysics

Much of the theory of suprematism, as expressed by Malevich, does not seem to be related directly to traditional aesthetics. For example, when discussing color, Malevich explains: "The devil is a dark spot and God a light one."[33] This interpretation of colors is not an isolated case; Malevich saw himself as much a metaphysician as an artist, claiming, on the one hand, to be "the last philosopher," who discovered the absolute falsehood of everything that existed before, and, on the other hand, to be "the first philosopher" who was able to see the world open-mindedly.[34] Shatskikh writes on the ambivalent character of the *Black Square*; it is not the end or beginning, it is the "end/beginning." Malevich applies this duality in his theory: "Christ, according to the church's interpretation, came from God in the beginning; and his return to Him *through the Resurrection was the future advent to Him. If all our aims have come from nature in the beginning, then they will return to it in the future. The Future is the beginning,* which, having completed a certain path, has come to back itself. *In the advent of this future, faith and hope await their justification*, all aims must be justified by their future return to the starting point."[35] Malevich found evidence for his aesthetic theories by turning to the Gospels. He wrote in his notebook in 1924: "According to St. John the Divine: God is Light in which there is no darkness."[36] He also cited the Epistle of St. Paul to the Ephesians: "But all things that are reproved are made manifest by the light: for whatsoever doth make manifest is light."[37]

Malevich's concentration on the Divine Light could have been influenced by the ideas of Saint Gregory Palamas, a Byzantine theologian of the fourteenth century, who taught hesychasm, and whose influence in Russia was felt after the revival of monasticism in the nineteenth century.[38] Malevich most likely never read Palamas directly, but his ideas were part of the nineteenth-century intellectual landscape. Even prominent writers on the icon, such as Pavel Florenskii, wrote on iconography using Palamite ideas, without explicitly engaging with Palamas in a sustained fashion.[39]

Palamas sought to explain the non-created nature of the Divine Light and the associated inability of the intellect to comprehend God. He argued that the Divine Light is perceptible neither by senses nor by the intellect. Contemplating the idea of light, Palamas refers to the theology of Dionysius the Areopagite. As God is beyond all seeing and knowledge, the way to perceive his divine nature is only through light, such as that seen by Christ's disciples on Mount Tabor. The glory of God bedazzled them. This light is "invisible because of a superabundant clarity, [and] it cannot be approached because of the outpouring of its transcendent gift of light." Moreover, Dionysius adds: "The divine darkness is that 'unapproachable light' where God is said to live."[40] As Palamas explains, "Though indeed a darkness, it is yet beyond radiance, and, as the great Denys says, it is in this dazzling darkness that the divine things are given to the saints."[41]

In Dionysius's text, we can observe the same ambivalence mentioned by Shatskikh. The eyes of saints are benighted, as the light is simultaneously darkness. Because of the "superabundant outpouring of light," even the saints, who are the only witnesses of the glory of God, cannot perceive the Divine Light in its wholeness. Instead, they are dazzled by it. They, who are so close to God, see only darkness. Dionysius explains that the Divine Light is light as such, but for those who attempt to intelligibly understand or perceive it, it becomes darkness, as it becomes invisible.

If *Black Square* is made in accordance with this great theological tradition, could it symbolize "dazzling darkness"? Evidence for this can be found in the story of how the black square was painted. According to Shatskikh, it was unintentionally created on June 8, 1915. Malevich first painted a polychromatic abstract canvas, then had no time to clean that canvas or prepare another one, so the black figure was painted over an existing geometrical composition. Later, Malevich described this moment of creation as ecstatic illumination to Ivan Kliun, who noted in his memoirs: "When he was drawing *Black Square* 'fiery lightning bolts' were constantly crossing the canvas in front of him."[42]

After *Black Square* Malevich produced *Black Cross* (1915) and *Black Circle* (1920). The mystical significance of this series can be found in part in Malevich's interest in traditional culture and Christian symbols, as explained by Kurbanovsky: the square was the traditional symbol of the earth in medieval iconography, designating all earthly things; the circle represented the skies or God; and the cross signified the church as the union of the earth and the heavens. The choice of a Greek-style cross pointed toward the Orthodox tradition.[43]

Kurbanovsky further suggests that *White Square* (*White on White*, 1918) was Malevich's most radical painting. It is a symbol of the end of representation, where there was nothing left to see: "Visuality was transcended by the artist's quest for immaterial transcendence."[44] Kurbanovsky uses Malevich's own words: "The universe is the senselessness of God liberated and concealing himself in rest."[45] In his opinion, Malevich's *Black Square* is connected with a negative theological path, and *White on White* resembles the Divine Light (or "rest").[46] The painting may also reference "hesychasm," a word that originates in ἡσυχία, *hesychia*, which means "stillness, rest, quiet, silence." Disciples of hesychasm must conduct spiritual discipline, practicing "inner prayer" as a path toward God, who is inaccessible and incomprehensible and can be perceived only in a form of supernatural light.

Alain Besançon characterizes Malevich's theoretical writings as a kind of negative theology, citing Malevich's statement that "God is not sense, but senselessness."[47] Besançon sees Malevich's God as radically separated from all things, compared only with nothingness: "This God beyond God, in whose nature the artist's soul participates, is intuited as a perfect void, as nothingness, as being/nonbeing, and all figuration—of objects and of the absolute itself—appears in that dark light as an idol."[48] Interpreting God as "God beyond God," Besançon concludes that Malevich could be named an iconoclast. Here, Besançon goes too far. Malevich has not abandoned the possibility of making an image of God, as the iconoclasts did. Rather, he represented symbols of God and of Christianity within secular painting. In his later works, he painted figurative peasants with crosses (*Running Man*, 1932); nonfigurative crosses, inscribed onto an oval (*Black Cross on the Red Oval*, 1927); and a cross made from two intersecting rectangles (*Suprematism*, 1921–27). Of particular interest are the four peasants depicted in Malevich's suprematist-style painting, *Sportsmen* (1930–31), which probably refers to the Pskov icon of the Four Saints, of the late fourteenth or early fifteenth century, which represented saints especially venerated in the Russian city of Pskov: Parasceve Piatnitsa, Gregory the Theologian, John Chrysostom, and Basil the Great.

Malevich was not the only avant-garde artist to turn to icons. Natalia Goncharova painted *The Evangelists* and *Virgin and Child*; Vassily Kandinsky painted his *All Saints*, *Saint George*, and *The Last Judgment*. One could include Pavel Filonov and many others. In general, avant-garde painters were absolutely amazed by the colors and geometry of "old-style icons," which made a great impact on their art. The artistic experiments of neo-primitivists, cubo-futurists, and suprematists were inspired by icons, but specific ones—"old icons" in the style of the fifteenth through sixteenth centuries. Under Peter I (1682–1725), those icons of "old style" were banned, as they became associated with the sect of the Old Believers.[49] The process of cleaning icons in search of "old images" started at the beginning of the twentieth century, when, in 1905, Nicholas II signed an act of religious freedom and an interest in the Old Believer heritage arose.[50] As Alexander Rodchenko wrote in 1919, "Russian art has its origin in the icon."[51]

Avant-garde artists are often judged as iconoclasts in popular and academic culture. In fact, Malevich and other avant-garde painters worked to save "old icons" in the twentieth century, even as they used ascetic abstract versions of them in their own art. In 1920, the avant-garde painter Mikhail Larionov wrote the following about icons in a short article, explaining the inspiration icons had for the avant-garde:

> There are two artistic principles. The first: to copy nature on the basis of acquired knowledge and to use naturalistic forms in various ways for the composition. . . . The second: to study life in itself, regardless of the manifestations of the surrounding world and, based on these always moving and changeable forms, to render only the most expressive aspect of the object or situation. Russian icon painters were inspired by the second principle and were strongly drawn towards abstraction. This abstraction manifested itself in the use of schemas and formulas related to a predetermined style through which they expressed the mystical and abstract sense of life.[52]

Therefore, we can see that Russian avant-garde artists, including Malevich, honored icons and were inspired by them precisely because they opposed the naturalistic and representational "Westernized style" that has spread through Russia since the seventeenth century.

Russian Religious Philosophy: The Source of Malevich's Metaphysics

From the beginning, Malevich was judged as an artist who subverted holiness because of his revolutionary rhetoric. As the artist and art critic Alexandre Benois lamented: "It is no longer futurism that we have before us at present, but the new icon of the square. Everything holy and sacred we possessed, everything we loved, and which was our reason for living, has disappeared."[53] Benois was not the only one concerned about the crisis of the arts; in 1918, the philosopher Nikolai Berdiaev characterized the crisis as a blow to art in its "millennial foundations."[54] He thought that this shock would not allow for the preservation or revival of classical ideals, which were formed in ancient culture. Acknowledging the "dematerialization [and] excarnation of painting" and the artist's urge to "enter through the material shell of the world," Berdiaev acknowledged that this was a historical process.[55] Berdiaev's words did not mean that the art was irretrievably lost. He, on the contrary, was optimistic about this new art and its attempt to free itself from the prison of material reality. This was what he saw in suprematism: "In those newest movements such as *suprematism*, a long overdue task is sharply defined—the final liberation of the pure creative act from the realm of the natural and material. Painting in pure color must reconstruct a new world. . . . In it, there should be neither nature, in all of its variations, nor man. This is not simply an emancipation of art from narrative, it is an emancipation from the whole created world, relying on creation from nothing."[56]

Berdiaev's thoughts on suprematism were likely developed after he visited various exhibitions where friends of his niece, Natalia Davydova, were showing their work. Shatskikh supposes that the contact between two opposite circles of the Moscow intelligentsia—Silver Age philosophers and radical avant-gardists—may have been made through Davydova. The strongest connection in the two groups was between Malevich and Mikhail Gershenzon, a scholar and editor.[57] The *Black Square* and other abstract paintings were exhibited in Moscow toward the end of 1916, at the exhibition of the Jack of Diamonds group. For Gershenzon, as Shatskikh explains, the *Black Square* became the symbol of nihilistic liberation from an oppressive cultural heritage. Gershenzon's ecclesiastical tiredness made it possible for him to see Malevich as a "barbarian with fresh blood," who had not been poisoned by a dying culture. Malevich's mystical views had little in common with those of the Silver Age. Malevich's theory had no room for the psychological aspect of personality; it made space neither for love nor for grace. Philosophical suprematism broke from the tradition of Russian religious philosophy, which implicitly embodied the concept of grace—God's love for men and their dialogical interconnection. "The love that begot the religious conception of Sophia—Holy Wisdom—in Russian philosophy was profoundly alien to suprematist ontology, which instead strove for universal monistic objectlessness."[58]

Nevertheless, Shatskikh notes, Malevich's philosophy borrowed from the main principles of Russian philosophy: synthetism, universalism, prophetic pathos, and eschatological messianism. Moreover, as with other Russian philosophers, disciplined thought and systematization were eschewed in favor of the "purely intrinsic, intuitive, and mystical knowledge of being, its secret depths, which could be comprehended only by the power of imagination and the vitality of one's inner life."[59]

Malevich and Classical Metaphysics

Shatskikh notes that Malevich wanted to appear as a distinctive thinker, but he had little systematic training in philosophy. Shatskikh found some philosophical notes and comments in Malevich's notebooks, but his longest excerpts were from the Gospels. Despite Malevich's disinterest in reading philosophical writings, later scholars have tried to interpret his work through various philosophical lenses.[60] Besançon, for example, assesses Malevich's writings as an elaboration of Baruch Spinoza's aphorism *Omnis determinatio est negatio*, contributing to the formulation of a notion of reality that is infinite and exists apart from material objects.[61] Besançon also finds the Kantian *noumenon* in metaphorical form in the following statement: "What we call reality is infinity without weight, measure, time or space, absolute or relative, never traced in a form. It can be neither conceived nor comprehended."[62] But my question is whether Malevich was a transcendentalist.

Generally, Malevich could be said to follow Immanuel Kant: "All things come from the amalgamation of the psychic and physical, they impart a completely different form to that given by existence." Things, therefore, are the products of perception. Malevich goes further; every existing thing is not the thing in its being, as we perceive only the accidental form of it. Being, as Malevich writes in "World as Non-objectivity," is abstruse and incomprehensible as a form, and being exists regardless of time and space. The visible world is not being as it is, from Malevich's point of view; it is only reasoning about being. [63]

In the 1922 manifesto "God Is Not Cast Down," Malevich proclaims the comprehension of God as his prime goal.[64] Here, he departs from Kant. For Kant, we cannot know things in themselves, because all possible knowledge is limited to knowledge of appearances.[65] Kant limits the ambitions of speculative reason regarding transcendent knowledge, "because in order to attain to such insights, speculative reason would have to help itself to principles that in fact reach only to objects of possible experience, and which, if they were to be applied to what cannot be an object of experience, then they would always actually transform it into an appearance, and thus declare all *practical extension* of pure reason to be impossible."[66] Therefore, Kant concludes, by eliminating God and soul from the realm of knowable objects, he preserves a place for faith.

Malevich, on the contrary, endeavors to speak about unknowable being. The main problem, for Malevich, is that we cannot describe the world completely because we cannot see many aspects of it. Objective thinking builds a mirror for itself. "Striving to make itself master of the world," he writes, "the factory at the same time says that in order to achieve the latter one must *know, learn, understand, investigate and 'scientifically base' 'everything'*: for you can only become master and rule the earth when you know everything. . . . How can one collect and contain this 'everything' in order to examine and study it?"[67] Those objects of objective investigation are scattered in space, not wishing to be objects, and "our will, wisdom, experience and visual comprehension are smashed to pieces on their non-objective truth or simply non-objectivity without any truth."[68]

In 1922, Malevich finished writing his treatise "Suprematism: World as Objectlessness, or Eternal Peace," which appeared after Gershenzon encouraged Malevich to write down all of his philosophical ideas. The second chapter of the treatise is dedicated to Gershenzon.[69] "Suprematism" was first published in 1922 as the manifesto "God Is Not Cast Down." The publisher omitted fragments of the text that looked like anti-materialistic content, and only thirty-three of the original forty-four paragraphs remained. In this treatise, Malevich describes the man-made world and juxtaposes it to the objectless world of absolute divine peace. In this work, nature appears as infinite, multifaceted, and unknowable. "The miracle of nature is that it all is contained in a small seed, and yet this 'all' cannot be embraced. Man, holding a seed, holds a universe and yet cannot examine it."[70] For him, the way of knowledge is like that of Nicholas of Cusa—a way of development and moving to perfection. Faced with the unknowable quality of nature, man has discovered that *"everything that is clear in nature tells him* by the power of its perfection that the universe, as perfection, is God."[71]

Malevich's ontology includes God as the creator of the world, resting in peace. God pantheistically resides in all things, as he created everything, but at the same time he is transcendent. The great drama for man, as Malevich writes, is in returning to God. As the main characteristic of God is perfection, man craves unity in God. Malevich sees man as a "part of the absolute thought" of God.[72] Malevich poeticizes this movement in avant-garde terms, seeing it as a history of technical achievements, beginning with the invention of wheels, then the inventing of wings of airplanes, and finally breaking the bounds of the earth's atmosphere. Man makes efforts to become a part of infinity, which is the universe. He walks the path to God as perfection. What can one do to reach God as perfection? "Not a great deal: guide the starry space of suns and the universal systems."[73] Not surprisingly, this phrase reveals Malevich's ultimately Platonic idea of beauty as upward ascent from things to ideas: "From beautiful things and using them like rising stairs: from one body to two and from two to all beautiful bodies, then from beautiful bodies to beautiful customs, and from customs to learning beautiful things, and from these lessons he arrives in the end at this lesson, which is learning of this very Beauty, so that in the end he comes to know just what it is to be beautiful."[74] This is what Malevich also thinks about God as perfection. Hoping to attain a lost relationship with God, man forced himself to turn to humanity, to technical production, striving for perfection, which is God. As with Plato, a path to knowing intelligible truth is through cognition of general terms.

Malevich, revolutionary and subverter of art, has been credited with the annihilation of the forms of art associated with the representation of reality. Benois accused him of an outrage upon the sacred. Malevich could have responded that if his revolution were the subversion of painterly realism, it was a return to metaphysical realism.[75] As my investigation has shown, while criticizing representation, Malevich nevertheless applied classical philosophical and aesthetic concepts to his aesthetic theory, which he separated from his religious metaphysics. I argue that Malevich rehabilitated classical philosophical and theological arguments in the terms of his time. Malevich continued the tradition of metaphysical realism in the theory and practice of suprematism. Moreover, he sought to reinvigorate religion in this new approach to the transcendent: "Perhaps the 'Black Square' is the image of God, as the essence of his perfection, on the new path of today's fresh beginning."[76]

CHAPTER 9

Magnitogorsk as Jerusalem

Bolshevik Revolution and Jewish Messianism

VASSILI SCHEDRIN

> And, behold, the Lord passed by, and a great and
> strong wind rent the mountains, and broke in pieces
> the rocks before the Lord; but the Lord was not in the
> wind; and after the wind an earthquake; but the Lord
> was not in the earthquake; and after the earthquake a
> fire; but the Lord was not in the fire; and after the fire
> a still small voice. And it was so, when Elijah heard it,
> that he wrapped his face in his mantle, and went out,
> and stood in the entrance of the cave. And, behold,
> there came a voice unto him, and said: What doest
> thou here, Elijah?
>
> —1 Kings 19:11–13

Solomon Mikhoels (1890–1948), one of the
founders and the greatest star of the Soviet Yiddish theater, wrote in 1919, as
if echoing these biblical verses, "Fierce raged the tempest of revolution on the
street. . . . And human eyes and overly human thoughts flounced in fear and
confusion among the chaos of destruction and haste of new construction. . . .
And at this very time, when entire worlds were cracking, dying and being replaced with new worlds, it happened; it may seem something very small [to
others], but for us, Jews, it was a great miracle—Jewish theater was born."[1] In
this picture, as in the biblical verses, natural cataclysmic disasters (wind, earth-
quake, or revolution) and chaos serve as a mere background for the true manifestation of the Divine power, a miracle. However, in 1947 Mikhoels seemed
to change his mind, arguing that human-made revolution created Jewish theater directly: "Soviet power [established by the Bolshevik Revolution] created
the opportunity to build the first state Jewish theater in the thousand-year history of the people."[2]

In fact, the 1917 Russian Revolution dramatically changed Jewish life in Russia. On the one hand, the revolution emancipated Russian Jews, granting

them full citizenship. On the other hand, it deeply affected the lifestyle and religion of Russian Jews, undermining traditional communal bonds and eradicating Judaism. These changes shaped a unique Jewish identity and culture in the USSR. Some contemporary observers and subsequent scholars believed that Jewish culture could not exist in a secular framework, and hence, in their opinion, Soviet Yiddish culture was essentially Soviet culture, not Jewish, translated into Yiddish (Bolshevik ideologues deemed Yiddish the language of the Jewish proletariat to be officially supported by the Soviet state). However, other contemporaries and many later scholars have created a more nuanced picture of Soviet Yiddish culture in which Soviet themes intertwined with identifiably Jewish motifs and strong Jewish nationalist sentiments coexisted with religious ones.[3]

During his career, Mikhoels himself, according to Jeffrey Veidlinger, a historian of Soviet Yiddish theater, while keeping a copy of the Bible on his desk and referring to it in his speeches, maintained a "Janus-faced attitude toward [religion] . . . he could prate anti-religious platitudes, but his subsequent words and deeds betrayed him."[4] These "deeds" are the focus of this chapter. First, Mikhoels's one-act play *The Builder* (*Stroitel'*), written in 1919 for the debut performances of the Petrograd Yiddish theatrical studio, will be analyzed as a creative synthesis of biblical text, its traditional Jewish interpretation, and modern European and Russian drama.[5] Second, the Soviet-made movie *The Return of Nathan Becker* (*Vozvrashchenie Neitana Bekkera*) (1932), to which Mikhoels contributed as a supporting actor and, most likely, as co-screenwriter and co-director, will be analyzed as a fusion of the Soviet style of socialist realism and Jewish religious motifs that utterly underpin the secular ideological import of the movie.

Using the examples of Soviet Yiddish theater and film, this chapter will demonstrate that in Soviet Russia, traditional Judaism and, in particular, its messianic doctrine intertwined with the secular ideology of the Bolshevik regime and its revolutionary anti-religious messianism. Paradoxically, in the context of the Russian Revolution, these two messianic ideologies—religious and secular—were not mutually exclusive. They not only were able to coexist but also complemented, justified, and reinforced each other.

Jewish Messianism, Politics, and Culture at the Turn of the Twentieth Century

According to traditional Jewish sources, including the Talmud and kabbalah, the *geula* (the final Redemption of the Jewish people) will unfold in two distinct phases linked to two messiahs: Mashiach ben Yosef (Messiah the son of Joseph) and Mashiach ben David (Messiah the son of David). Mashiach ben Yosef will do the groundwork and put in place the material conditions for the Redemption. Once finished, this messiah will "die" and be replaced by Mashiach ben David, whose goal is to create the spiritual conditions for the Redemption and thus bring the process to completion.

In 1904, in his article "The Lamentation in Jerusalem" ("Misped ba-Yerushalaim"), Rabbi Abraham Isaac Kook (best known as Rav Kook, the first chief rabbi of interwar Mandate Palestine) established a connection between the emerging Zionist movement and the messianic process, identifying Theodor Herzl, the founder of Zionism, as Mashiach ben Yosef. According to the Basel Declaration adopted by the First Zionist Congress in 1897, "The aim of Zionism is to create for the Jewish people a home in Palestine secured by public law."[6] In Rav Kook's opinion, the main goals of Zionism—to normalize the Jewish people (that is, make the Jews a sovereign nation like other nations) and to protect them—resonated with the vision of the Hebrew Bible: "That we also may be like all the nations; and that our king may judge us, and go out before us, and fight our battles."[7]

In the words of Rav Kook, "The Zionist vision manifest in our generation might best be symbolized as the 'footstep of the Messiah son of Joseph.' Zionism tends to universalism as opposed to Jewish particularism."[8] Hence, Rav Kook argued, Zionism is the secular means for the realization of the religious mission of Judaism in the global arena: "The prerequisite for the generation of Messiah is the ability to utilize all forces, even the most coarse [that is, Zionism, because of its blatant secularism], for the sake of good and the singular sanctity with which Israel were crowned."[9] Thus, based on this theological premise, Rav Kook's ideology made possible the practical political alliance between religious and secular Jews and eventually led to the emergence of the Religious Zionist movement.

Ahad Ha-Am, another important Zionist thinker, called the "agnostic rabbi" by the historian of Zionism Arthur Hertzberg, argued that the religious framework of Jewish life (including both institutions and traditions) would eventually disintegrate, so the Judaism of the future should be a collective Jewish identity framed by the secular spirit of the nation. At the heart of Ahad Ha-Am's doctrine of Cultural Zionism is the concept of secular Jewish culture built on inherent Jewish values, that is, the core ethics of Judaism.[10]

Kenneth Moss, in his study on Jewish literature and art in revolutionary Russia, demonstrates that the search for a modern Jewish culture was a central and self-sustaining development in modern Jewish life at the turn of the twentieth century. According to Moss, in Eastern Europe, where most Jews lived then, modern Jewish culture "took shape in dialectical tension with a still-potent religious tradition that permeated the everyday life of East European Jews far more pervasively than did the religions of their urban neighbors; many of its creators were themselves renegades from the traditional elite steeped in Judaism's most abstruse texts."[11] However, Moss argues that "the champions of Jewish culture sought more than the overthrow of tradition . . . [they wanted] to forge a 'new Jewish culture.' This culture was to be secular, 'modern,' and high. It was to be modeled on Europe's leading national cultural spheres, and seek to become their equal. It was supposed to serve as a wellspring of a more general revolution in Jewish identity, psychology, and social life. And it was also intended to be an end in itself, indeed the highest end for modern Jews: the locus of all further Jewish creativity in a postreligious age" (15, 281).

From the outset, as Moss points out, Jewish cultural producers—writers, critics, artists, actors, and public intellectuals—conceived their secular project in messianic terms, as a means of redemption of the modern Jewish nation. For example, Natan Grinblat, the Hebrew literary critic, asserted that the very act of writing good poetry in Hebrew directly contributed to national revival: "Literary revival in its true meaning means the renewal and elevation of creativity, and each one who has enriched the literature . . . , each who has plowed the earth, renewed form and content . . . behold, it is he who has revived the literature, the spirit of the people, and prepared hearts for redemption" (22). Some promoters of secular Jewish culture welcomed the 1917 Russian Revolution. They perceived it as the dawn of the messianic era, a turning point in the realization of their project. After February 1917, the Zionist journalist Moshe Kleinman wrote that "all those questions which in the years before the war and the Russian Revolution seemed for the most part 'matters undecidable until the days of the Messiah' have now become questions of the moment that brook no delay" (23). After October 1917, the Yiddish literary critic Shmuel Niger enthusiastically greeted the Bolshevik Revolution, arguing that what made Bolshevism attractive to the Jews was "its laying bare the roots of culture—its forcing us to begin everything anew; its wake-and-push-power, its giving to us a taste of the birth pangs of the messianic age" (217).

In 1919, in the midst of the Russian civil war, Beynush Steiman, a young revolutionary Yiddish writer, attempted to explain the current violent turmoil in Russia in terms of traditional Jewish eschatology. His play, a "dramatic poem" called *Messiah the Son of Joseph* (*Meshiekh ben Yoysef*) is set in the dark "frozen world," the "thousand-year realm" of Lilith (a female demon in Jewish mysticism and folklore), where people "lost God's image in them" and turned into Lilith's slaves. A silent stranger suddenly appears. People welcome him as Messiah the son of David. He brings sun, lots of light, and hope. But it turns out that only the future generation would be redeemed, while the current one was doomed. The frustrated and infuriated people, instigated by Lilith, stone the messiah to death. In the end, night and darkness return, and the stars, dying out, utter a prophecy: "He will return."[12] Thus Steiman's play—a metaphor of revolution and civil war, a violent yet inevitable prelude to a bright future—alluded to the traditional Jewish view that the Messiah, the son of Joseph, was coming to do the groundwork and die, and the Messiah the son of David was coming after him to complete the Redemption.

Capsule History of Yiddish Theater

One of many Jewish cultural start-ups that proliferated in revolutionary Russia, the modest Yiddish theatrical studio (the future State Yiddish theater—GOSET after its Russian acronym) founded in January 1919 in Petrograd by the modernist director Aleksei Granovskii, held the mythical status from the beginning as "the first state Jewish theater in the thousand-year history of the people."[13] In the expression of the art critic Abram Efros, one of the founders of GOSET, Soviet Yiddish theater had no roots in history. Created from scratch and being its own grandfather, father, and son all at once, the theater had to make its own history, including past, present, and future.[14] Granovskii and the studio cofounders—Lev Levidov, Mark Rivesman, and Solomon Mikhoels—immediately got on the task. Even before the studio opened its doors to the public, it published, in both Russian and Yiddish, a booklet called *Jewish Theater: To Its Opening*. The publication included a short capsule history of Yiddish theater, accounts of current work in the studio, and programmatic statements about future goals. It is remarkable that this secular revolutionary manifesto was framed by biblical symbolism and messianic tropes.

According to the booklet, the mythical history of Yiddish theater was as old as that of the Jewish people and its lot was even more unfortunate:

> The sphere of Jewish theatrical art is as flat and dull as a desert, where Moses has never appeared, where the "pillar of fire" has never illuminated the way of wanderers roaming the wilderness . . . , where these wanderers could not even cry out: "Oh! Take us back to Egypt." "Pharaoh"—the bitter lot [of Yiddish theater]—has never loosened its tight grip on the Yiddish actor.
>
> Having no thought about tomorrow, [Abraham] Goldfaden, the "creator" of Yiddish theater, lay the first crumbly stone and started to build Yiddish theater using rotten material.

Yiddish actors were sinking lower and lower. They made J[acob] Gordin their god and were conscientiously offering him sacrifices while the altar of Yiddish stage remained defiled. . . . The immortal genius [Yitskhok Leybush] Peretz had a dream—to become [as strong as] Samson to break chains and set free Yiddish theatrical art. . . . Young, sickly and sensitive [Peretz] Hirschbein who desired to establish new Yiddish art theater and hoped to write a new cheerful page in "jeremiad" about Yiddish theater . . . lonely and miserable . . . desperate and angry he had to flee [abroad].[15]

The "biblical period" in the mythical history of Yiddish theater was followed by the era of *galut* (exile), full of misery and longing for future redemption:

The whole life of the old Yiddish theater and Jews [in general] was [a mixture of grim] anecdote and agony.[16]

Yiddish theater never existed and the existing circus [*balagan* in original Russian] served as perpetual memento—build [the real] Yiddish theater![17]

We . . . sat dispersed, nestling in individual corners. . . . The frost of "golus"—dispersion—made us bow low and bend to earth. . . . Each of us felt and acknowledged the need of Yiddish Theater-cum-Temple, some comrades have already attempted (to build it) in the past, but . . . all such attempts failed as miserably as many other initiatives on the Jewish street. . . . Stepmother-history mocked all such serious efforts and brutally extinguished every spark of hope.[18]

Finally, the endless night of the dark era faded away:

Where thick darkness used to reign supreme, there appeared first flashes of light . . . the fact that the Yiddish theater-studio exists refreshed and multiplied our energy threefold, tenfold.[19]

The revolutionary destruction and chaos that followed ushered in the era of redemption:

Theater saw the light . . . it was born amid the agony of the old regime.[20]

Fierce raged the tempest of revolution on the street. . . . And human eyes and overly human thoughts flounced in fear and confusion among the chaos of destruction and haste of new construction. . . . And at this very time, when entire worlds were cracking, dying and being replaced with new worlds, it happened; it may seem something very small [to others], but for us, Jews, it was a great miracle—Jewish theater was born.[21]

The new era was also ushered in by new leaders—creators able to lead and educate the people:

> Paradoxically, the same stepmother-history, nurtured and brought up the right person, who was able to find the right word, to create. . . . He called us, he became our leader. . . . We answered the call of a new builder.[22]
>
> "You should give the stage a human [*cheloveka* in original Russian]." Thus said the leader. . . . But we . . . we could only give ourselves. . . . But to give a human in general, a human with capital H—became our goal. We learned to control our voices pretty soon; however, our hands continued to be the hands of Jacob—tightly bound to prevent any movement and action.[23]

The new generation living in the new era understood their work as that of laying down the foundation for a brighter future. In traditional messianic terms, they were the generation of Messiah the son of Joseph preparing the soil and souls for the final redemption in the era of the coming Messiah son of David to be welcomed only by future generations:

> We are working. Our work is a prayer. We are praying to gods about whom we know that they are great, bright and attentive to sincere prayers.
>
> We approach our work with utmost piety and humility. We know that we are playing the humble role of the first experimental material. Nonetheless, our hearts are overwhelmed with joy—we are partaking in the creation of Yiddish theater.[24]

The authors of the 1919 booklet envisioned the future in traditional Jewish terms. Thus, when redeemed by Messiah son of David, the Jews would return to the Holy Land and rebuild the Jerusalem Temple to be the focus of a universal religion, then the Petrograd Yiddish theatrical studio would build the Theater-Temple as the focus of universal art:

> Jewish Theater is a [universal] Theater, first and foremost, it's a Temple of Bright Beauty and Joyful Creation in which the prayer is sung in the Jewish language. . . . What kind of theater will it be? Which gods will it worship? We do not know our gods yet . . . we are searching for them . . . maybe we would be making gods only to throw them off their pedestals . . . our only excuse would be our strong desire to find the right way to true gods.[25]
>
> Come on you, writers, artists, musicians, actors! Answer our call and courageously help to build a new edifice of Jewish theater. Do not just

stand by watching, bring mortar and bricks, proudly raise the tower, let the language of its builders be understood by all, let the top of the tower reach the bright Sun of beauty.[26]

In sum, the 1919 booklet devised a history of Soviet Yiddish theater, including its past, present, and future, seen in the traditional Jewish perspective and, in fact, parallel to the history of the Jewish people—from wandering in the desert, to the exile, to the redemption. However, the booklet conveys the past and present of the theater through elaborate myth, while, besides the imperative to build the new Yiddish theater, the future is charted imprecisely. Efros noted that, according to the booklet, the main goal of the new Yiddish theater was, ironically, to build a new Yiddish theater. And construction began.

Two "Builders"

In reality, in contrast to this mythical capsule history of Yiddish theater, Granovskii's Petrograd Yiddish studio did not build in the void, or on sand. There were forty years of experience and current live examples of professional Yiddish theater (referred to as "old" in the 1919 booklet), despised as *shund* (Yiddish: "trash") and *balagan* (Russian: "kitschy street show") by Jewish intellectuals while enjoyed and admired by Jewish crowds in Eastern Europe and America. There were cutting-edge developments in European and Russian theater. To be sure, Granovskii and his studio did use all of these as their building material. However, the newly born Soviet Yiddish theater approached this material critically and used it on a selective basis. To use Granovskii's expression, sometimes they "made gods" out of this material "only to throw them off their pedestals."[27] Such was the case of the father of theatrical modernism, Henrik Ibsen.

Ibsen's influence on modern Russian and international art is hard to underestimate. In his dramas, Ibsen established the absolute freedom of the creative individual as a universal cultural value. Nikolai Minskii, a Russian symbolist poet of Jewish descent, in his biography of Ibsen argued that he was able to harmonize his national character with contemporary European philosophy and literature "by focusing all his dramas on the absolute primacy of the human will, and on the struggle between the individual and society."[28] Ibsen's ideas obviously resonated with the creators of modern Jewish culture based on secularity and individual autonomy. Russian educated society at large enthusiastically welcomed Ibsen's dramas and eagerly grasped his liberating philosophy that introduced European modernism to Russian culture. Russian symbolist writers and poets, including Alexander Blok, Konstantin Balmont, Andrei Belyi, and Minskii himself, deeply revered Ibsen as their patriarch. Ibsen's ideas and dramas greatly inspired such influential and diverse phenomena of the Russian stage as the theater of psychological realism of Konstantin Stanislavsky, the symbolist theater of Vera Komissarzhevskaia, and the avant-garde theater of Vsevolod Meyerhold.

In 1917, the Russian political and social revolution coincided with a revolution in Russian art. Supported by the revolutionary Bolshevik regime, the champions of avant-garde art forcibly imposed their universalistic ideals and iconoclast agenda (*bogoborchestvo*) onto Russian art, effectively pushing out the individualism and God-seeking (*bogoiskatel'stvo*) of Russian symbolism. While symbolism aestheticized physical death as a prerequisite for individual spiritual regeneration, the avant-garde sought the death and destruction of bourgeois individualism seen as the main obstacle for the spiritual regeneration of the masses.[29]

It is hardly surprising, then, that Russian avant-garde theater, especially after 1917, declared Ibsen's dramas obsolete as too individualistic and essentially bourgeois. In Meyerhold's words, theatrical art must sweep the "psychological mysticism" of symbolism off the stage. The new avant-garde theater should be essentially a political theater based on sharp conflicts, intense movement, and strong rhythms.[30]

The Petrograd Yiddish theatrical studio joined the avant-garde revolution as its founders—Granovskii and Mikhoels—brought to the stage the symbol of Ibsen in order to publicly rebut his ideas and to proclaim their own path in art. Ibsen's play *The Master Builder* (*Bygmester Solness*, 1892) was the carefully considered choice of the means for this undertaking, since, as many critics and scholars believe, this play was the author's confession, summing up his own life and work.[31] According to Minskii, "When young, [Halvard] Solness built church towers, similar to Ibsen's own writing of moralistic and religious works; then Solness abandoned churches for human dwellings—a hint at Ibsen's social and family dramas; finally, Solness sought to build an air castle on a solid basis—the symbol of Ibsen's mysticism based on science."[32]

In the play's finale, Solness climbs the scaffold of a newly built tower to reach the skies and listen to the eternal harp music of the high spheres; suddenly, he falls down and dies. Hence, Mikhoels's own *The Builder* (*Stroitel'*, 1919) could be both a sequel and a prequel to Ibsen's *The Master Builder*. One could argue that *The Builder* begins immediately after Solness's fatal fall; however, Mikhoels set it "thousands and thousands" of years ago in the land of Babylon, where people started to build a tower touching the heavens. They wanted to reach the heavens, where the gods of beauty and truth were hiding since they had left the untruthful earth. . . . The curtain opens. The new Builder is onstage watching the construction. He is full of energy and joy listening to his brother-builders singing while they work on the top of the tower. Suddenly he gets the feeling that he is not alone. A couple of strangers are watching him: they are Yesterday, a crooked figure in black, and Tomorrow, a blurred figure in shining blue. Yesterday says that there is nothing new under the sun, new builders come and go every day, but the tower has never grown beyond certain limits. Eventually, the day comes to an end and at dusk the builders start to fall from the top of the tower totally exhausted. Night falls. "Your day is expired . . . still the tower is the same as left by yesterday's builder," says Yesterday.[33] The exhausted Builder lies on the earth, dying. Yesterday laughs. His laugh is interrupted by the loud voice of Tomorrow, who is trying to encourage the desperate Builder.

> Your brothers are dead, and you will follow them soon. But new builders are coming. They will speak a new language. They will envision a new reality, which the old liar Yesterday could never see with his weak eyes. Their souls will enable them to get to the highest realm of truth and beauty. They won't build the walls with bricks and clay—they will build with the power of their vision. They will tell Yesterday, the old liar, that his reality is a cemetery for the dead. The tower must not be built the way peoples' dwellings are built; the new builders won't build it with stones. It's not a stone but our spirit that will bring the light and dispel the darkness that hides heaven.[34]

The Builder dies. The song of emerging new builders is growing stronger from behind the scene. Curtain.

Using a form of symbolist drama, Mikhoels and Granovskii advanced their anti-symbolist agenda. Avant-garde Yiddish theater reenacted on its stage the death of Ibsen's Solness, shown as a symbol of the death of Ibsen's individualism.[35] Therefore, it is not a coincidence that in the play's finale the exhausted and dying single builder of the present is being replaced by the many coming builders of the future. While the single builder of the present is destined only to continue building, it is the collective of future builders that could successfully bring this work to completion.

Mikhoels's *The Builder* opened one of the Petrograd studio's debut performances in July 1919. Two other one-act plays by the classic Yiddish writer Sholem Asch—*Amnon and Tamar* (*Amnon un Tomor*, 1909) and *In Winter* (*Um vinter*, 1906)—were presented the same night following *The Builder*. According to Efros, this repertoire was "a whole long decade late." Efros believed that the studio's evident "strong determination to being" should be counted as the most important result of the debut. At the same time, he argued that the choice of repertoire and goals declared by the studio should be discounted as immature.[36] In contrast, Vladislav Ivanov, a historian of Jewish theater in Russia, argued that the repertoire was well thought and well chosen by Granovskii. According to Ivanov, Granovskii planned "to include all Asch's plays in one performance. . . . This plan was based on careful calculation and made perfect sense. The show would open with *Amnon and Tamar*, a biblical story—a reference to the historical roots of the Jewish people; it should be followed by a dramatic episode from the bleak contemporary life of the Jewish shtetl (*In Winter*). . . . Granovskii's grand scheme used these small pieces by Asch as building blocks of a great eschatological cycle encompassing the past, present and transcendental future of the Jewish people."[37] However, Granovskii changed his initial plan, so the "theme of the past, present, and future of the Jewish people was superseded by the theme of the utter futility of life of . . . erring humanity."[38] As a result, the show opened with Mikhoels's *The Builder*—"a home-baked symbolist piece"— followed by *Amnon and Tamar* and *In Winter*. Thus, Ivanov argues, "Granovskii's direction was based on a single idea. Exploring it, the director was going from general to specific. Seeking universalism, Granovskii's style fused symbolism, myth, and naturalism."[39]

On the one hand, from a secular perspective, the controversial arguments of Efros and Ivanov about the style, conception, and overall relevance of Granovskii's studio repertoire make perfect sense. On the other hand, the Jewish religious perspective reveals a deeper layer of meaning in Granovskii's choice of plays and in their sequence on stage. Seen in this light, *The Builder*, *Amnon and Tamar*, and *In Winter* represent major aspects of the Jewish messianic future.

Mikhoels's *The Builder* is based on the biblical story of the Tower of Babel.[40] According to midrash, traditional Jewish exegesis, the Tower's builders were hell-bent on completion of their project. They grieved for the loss of every single brick fallen from the scaffold, crying, "How difficult it will be to replace it!" However, when one of the builders fell and died, the others did not even notice.[41] In Mikhoels's play the Tower's builders were falling from the scaffolds at dusk, while the Builder, the main character of the play, watched, frightened. Unlike his biblical counterparts, the Builder is really concerned with the lives of other builders because they are his "brothers." Thus Mikhoels offers his own commentary on the biblical story. In his interpretation, the unfinished Tower of Babel that divided humanity in the beginning of its history, has the potential of becoming the foundation of the Jerusalem Temple that would make people brothers and unite all of humanity at the end of history with the coming of the messiah.

Asch's *Amnon and Tamar* is based on another biblical story, about King David's son Amnon, who raped his half-sister Tamar.[42] Similar to the story of the Tower of Babel, it is not to be understood literally and taken at face value. Jewish tradition regards this story as a parable emphasizing the significance of love and unity. The Talmud says: "Any love that is dependent on something, when that thing perishes, the love perishes. But [a love] that is not dependent on something, does not ever perish. What's [an example of] a love that is dependent on something? That's the love of Amnon and Tamar."[43] An example of a love that is not dependent on something is God's love for his chosen people and for all humanity. According to the medieval Talmudic authority Maharal of Prague (Rabbi Judah Loew ben Bezalel), such love "that is not dependent on something does not ever perish because it strengthens unity."[44]

Finally, Asch's *In Winter*, in contrast to *Amnon and Tamar*, exemplifies love "that is not dependent on something." In addition, this play could be seen as a symbolical scenario of the Redemption. Roma, the older sister gave up a prospective groom (Roma's long-awaited match) to Ulka, the youngest sister, just because Roma unconditionally loves Ulka. Symbolically, in the same way, based on unconditional love, the older generation of the Jewish people would prepare the coming of the messiah to be welcomed only by the younger generation.[45] This symbolism is further reinforced by such details as the harsh winter in the background and the sisters' two-thousand-ruble dowry left by their late father, hinting at the two-thousand-year-long harsh Jewish experience in exile.

Thus, in the traditional Jewish perspective, together, the three plays represented the whole picture of Jewish life and complete history of the Jewish people—from its biblical past to its messianic future.[46] While the traditional Jewish perspective is implied here, very different, explicitly stated ideas guided the practical steps of Granovskii's studio taken in order to overcome the "chaos of destruction." In the opinion of Efros and Moshe Litvakov—Jewish communists who, in 1921 moved Granovskii's studio from Petrograd to Moscow and conferred on it the prestigious status of state theater—only the revolutionary Bolshevik regime was able to bring order to the chaos, fulfilling both its atheistic and messianic task: to replace, in the expression of the Russian philosopher Nikolai Berdiaev, the coming heavenly kingdom of God with the earthly kingdom of Communism.[47]

Chaos and Order

In 1925, Litvakov—Yiddish literary critic, member of the Moscow Yiddish theater's governing board, leading member of the Jewish section of the Bolshevik party, and chief editor of the major Soviet Yiddish newspaper *Emes*—published a book called *Five Years of the State Yiddish Theater*. In addition to a long list of the theater's achievements, analysis of the performances, and profiles of actors, set designers, and musical composers, Litvakov's book discussed Jewish revolutionary art, focusing on Soviet Yiddish theater as an exemplary revolutionary institution.

Litvakov's discussion echoed programmatic statements explicitly made in the Petrograd Yiddish studio manifesto booklet of 1919 and implicitly present in Mikhoels's *The Builder*. In particular, Litvakov emphasized the difference between the individualism of bourgeois art and its "severe asceticism and hermit's alienation from the world" collectivism of revolutionary art based on the explosive "ecstasy of the masses."[48] Litvakov explained that this ecstasy was a "service to art with joy and spontaneity," adding that spontaneity of the masses should be "controlled by the collective genius mind—the vanguard of the working class, the Communist party" (11). According to Litvakov, the rationality of revolutionary Jewish art is to be grounded in Marxist theories, while its spontaneity is linked to Jewish religious sentiment. Rationality and spontaneity are dialectically related. Litvakov explained the rationality of revolutionary art through the interpretation of Friedrich Engels, arguing that "the leap from the kingdom of necessity to the kingdom of freedom means that in the future our lives will be controlled by reason and not by spontaneous feelings—on the condition, that [in the future] reason would become as sensitive [as feelings]. . . . Marxism and Communism are nothing more than [an apparatus] enabling our consciousness to put restraint on our emotions" (32–33, 54). Litvakov explained spontaneity by using, in a positive way, a Hebraism—*avoydo misimcho*—in his Yiddish text (11). Depending on the context, the Hebrew word *avoydo* (*avodah* in modern Hebrew pronunciation) could mean "work" or "religious service," or "prayer," while together with *misimcho* (*misimcha* in modern Hebrew pronunciation) it is a religious term—"prayer with joy"—referring to the ecstatic prayer style practiced by Hasidic Jews. As if to illustrate the dialectic relationship between rationality and spontaneity throughout the text, Litvakov also used the Yiddish *arbet* ("work," "labor") in addition to *avoydo*. He wrote that the Soviet Yiddish theater practices "the cult of labor . . . blissful gestures, movement, . . . music and song are permeated with sublime ecstasy of labor, [industrial] production . . . [with] the youth of the [working] class and of its ancient element—labor" (73–74).

In Litvakov's opinion, the primordial folk element of Jewishness was confined within the shell of Jewish religious tradition. Hence the goal of Jewish revolutionary art—to break the shell and free the folk spirit: "[In terms of music, Soviet Yiddish] theater set Jewish motifs and melodies free from the dictates of the synagogue" (78). In addition, "Hasidism contains many precious elements of Jewish folk aesthetics to be freed from their mystical wrappings" (107). In a word, the revolution should release the elemental Jewish folk spirit from the bonds of Judaism and Jewish tradition; the revolutionary rationality of Bolsheviks would overcome the resulting chaos and build a new just world order.

It is hardly a coincidence that Litvakov's iconoclast theory remarkably resembles Jewish religious mysticism—kabbalah—the foundation of traditional Jewish perceptions of a messianic future. One of the key kabbalistic ideas is *tikkun olam* (repair or ordering of the world)—a mission assigned to humans by God. Work on realization of this mission makes humans God's partners in creation. An important part of this work is seeking and releasing sparks (*nitsotsot*, symbolizing dispersed pieces of Divine wisdom) of Divine light (*or ein-sof*) seized and constrained by the shell (*klipah*, symbolizing confusing or wrong theories, ideas, and beliefs). In this way, humans could restore the broken harmony of the universe, hence the Jews and the rest of humanity would be finally redeemed.

Paradoxically, Jewish religious messianism continued to be a leitmotif in the art of Soviet Yiddish theater and of its new leader Solomon Mikhoels despite the increasing party control of the country and the institution of ideological censorship.[49] Moreover, religious messianic motifs and symbols became an integral part of the emerging secular art of socialist realism. In particular, the party-sponsored propaganda movie portrayed 1930s socialist industrialization as a messianic redemption of the Soviet Jews.

Redemption

In 1932, celebrating the fifteenth anniversary of the Bolshevik Revolution, the Leningrad production facility of the Belgoskino studio released the movie *The Return of Nathan Becker*, starring David Gutman, Boris Babochkin, and Mikhoels.[50] According to the movie's codirectors, Boris Shpis and Rakhel Milman, they "simultaneously produced two different movies [under the same title]—one in Yiddish, another in Russian."[51] Shpis and Milman also admitted that the movie's essential dualism created many difficulties, especially for the cast: "Some actors knew no Yiddish, others—no Russian."[52]

The movie is set in the late 1920s. Nathan Becker (played by Gutman), a bricklayer, who emigrated to America twenty-eight years ago, returns to his native shtetl (small Jewish town), where his father, Tsale (played by Mikhoels), still lives. Nathan joins the other shtetl Jews getting a job at the construction site of Magnitogorsk, an emblematic metal plant successfully completed during the first Soviet five-year plan (1928–32). As a skilled worker, Nathan is assigned to train novice builders; however, he struggles to grasp the socialist labor system and develops the wrong attitude. For example, he sees the socialist competition as his coworkers' attempt to gain attention and the favor of superiors. To show off his American attitude and superior work method, Nathan challenges other builders to a bricklaying competition. One young worker accepts the challenge, and he and Nathan lay bricks in front of a cheering crowd. Defeated and broken, Nathan believes that he will be fired and sent back to the America. His father convinces him that it is impossible in the Soviet Union, where "workers are their own bosses." To his great surprise, Nathan is promoted and receives encouragement from the local party boss Mikulich (played by Babochkin). The movie ends as Nathan, Tsale, and their Jewish coworkers enthusiastically lay bricks using the best Soviet and American techniques.[53]

The first critics of the movie noted its dualism revealed in the shaky balance between Yiddish and Russian, Jewish and Soviet. The *New York Times* reviewer of the Yiddish-language version of *The Return of Nathan Becker* wrote: "In the screen telling of this simple tale the directors have presented many highly entertaining incidents of Jewish life in the Russia of today and have refrained from dwelling too much upon the building activities."[54] Soviet reviewers of the movie's Russian-language version were more critical, arguing that socialist competition is shown as a caricature and that instead of showing a new Jewish shtetl "transformed by the revolution," the directors portrayed it as "the old ghetto."[55]

A few decades later, the movie's dualism was still evident to Miron Chernenko, a historian of Soviet Jewish cinema: "While watching the movie and especially when thinking about it after watching I cannot stop sensing a dualism [implicit] in the picture. Its ideological focus and propaganda import was evident. . . . At the same time, it seemed to be made 'for fun,' not seriously, as if the moviemakers, trying to keep up with [the ideology of] the epoch and to be loyal [to the regime], could not restrain their Judaic subconscious, which inadvertently added a certain oddity to the movie, . . . and discounted the [message of] the original heroic script."[56]

The dualism of the movie could reflect the dualism of the epoch. *The Return of Nathan Becker* was made around 1929, the "great turning point year" (*god velikogo pereloma*). The preceding decade, the 1920s, immediately followed the Russian civil war that wiped out many traditional Jewish shtetls in the former Pale of Jewish Settlement (sixteen provinces along Russia's western border) and caused the mass migration of Jews to the largest cities of Soviet

Ukraine and central Russia. As a result, the traditional Jewish world of the shtetl, the Jewish past, was dying, while the world of socialism and Soviet society, the Jewish future, was not yet built. Therefore, the makers of *The Return of Nathan Becker* captured the Jewish present—a transitional period bearing features of both past and future, when Soviet Jews were still wandering toward their final destination. The Bolshevik messiah, the Soviet party-state was leading them.

The party launched an unprecedented program aimed at the social transformation—that is, Sovietization—of Russian Jews. Both exploited and exploiters—"paupers," "petit bourgeois," "clerical," and other "former" segments of traditional Jewish society—were to be "recast" (*perekovany*) into "toiling masses"—workers and peasants—enjoying free socialist labor. As a whole, Russian Jews, the former imperial minority, were supposed to become the Jewish people, equal members in the brotherhood of the other Soviet peoples. The Jewish agricultural colonization of Crimea and the establishment of the autonomous Jewish socialist republic in far eastern Russia were the key strategic initiatives in the field. Then why was *The Return of Nathan Becker*, a visual propaganda of "recasting" (*perekovka*), set in the Urals and not in Crimea or Birobidzhan? Why was the movie's plot based on a story about mythical Jewish bricklayers and not on the real Jewish collective farmers and frontier explorers? Why is it about Magnitogorsk?

A study by Yuri Slezkine identifies the Bolsheviks as "millenarian sectarians preparing for the apocalypse."[57] Slezkine discusses literary works that were meant to interpret and mythologize the quasi-religious Bolshevik ideology. The literary genre of "production novels" (*proizvodstvennye romany*) originated and proliferated in the USSR in 1929–32, around the "great turning point year." Penned by top Soviet authors Valentin Kataev, Fedor Gladkov, Boris Pilniak, Leonid Leonov, and others, the settings of these novels were the great constructions sites—colossal steel mills, river dams, and canals—of the First Five-Year Plan of the Bolshevik industrialization of Soviet Russia; all these texts were also stories of the "recasting." Slezkine argues that none of these "production novels" is about actual production. They are really "construction-cum-conversion stories" about human souls, told in a religious idiom mixing Bolshevik politics with Christian millenarianism rhetoric (364). In some of these stories, as in Mikhoels's *The Builder*, biblical themes such as the Tower of Babel were reimagined and reversed—"from dispersion to unity" (364). According to Slezkine, they were all essentially "stories of creation," in which new worlds emerge from chaos, in the wilderness. The authors of these "production novels" often identified the imaginary wilderness with Asia (Siberia, Central Asia, the Far East), so in their texts "the departure from Europe is marked as a prologue to genesis" (365). In addition to the physical departure from the old world, "production novels" also anticipated a painful and even violent generational change—the dying out or purging of the older generation "not fit for the Promised Land," as a prelude to a bright future, as in Steiman's *Messiah the Son of Joseph* (369). The general themes and poetics of "production novels" are found in *The Return of Nathan Becker*, framed by the unique Jewish perception of the "Bolshevik prophecy."

The focus of the movie is not the real Magnitogorsk but a mythical city built around Magnetic Mountain—both the real mountain in the Urals actually so called and a symbolic peak serving as a spiritual beacon to the peoples of the world, like the biblical Mount Zion.[58] Accordingly, *The Return of Nathan Becker* focuses on the specifically Jewish spiritual aspects of the Soviet "recasting" manifest in four main themes of the movie—return, people's unity, messiah, and the Promised Land.

Return is the central theme of the movie. The New York bricklayer and Russian Jew Nathan Becker, in his words, is "coming home," returning to Soviet Russia from capitalist America. Twenty-eight years ago (most likely, during the epidemic of anti-Jewish violence in Russia—the pogroms of 1903–5), Nathan left his native shtetl, emigrated to America, learned masonry, and, laying brick after brick, "built New York." Now, in the wake of the Great Depression, obviously jobless, Nathan and his wife, Meike, and his friend and coworker, an African American named Jim, were going to the USSR. In 1929, when the American economy was in a deep crisis, Soviet Russia launched the First Five-Year Plan—an ambitious program aimed at the industrialization of the economy and the modernization of society. Hence, skilled and experienced workers, like Nathan, were in high demand. Nathan looked forward to starting a new job and new life in Russia. While on the ship heading toward Europe, the excited Nathan examined his newly issued Soviet visa. He also raised his strong hands of a laborer and looked at them as a visa supplement, his "party [membership] card," as he put it. From a historical perspective, both of Nathan's journeys—from East to West in the early 1900s and from West to East in the late 1920s—seem to be migration for political and economic reasons. However, from the perspective of the movie, only the first journey was a mere migration, while the second one—from West to East—was a return, symbolizing aliyah (ascent) to the Promised Land. Therefore, the return of Nathan Becker signified the end of the exile and beginning of the Redemption.

The destinations and routes of Nathan's journeys are an important aspect of the theme of return. In many cultures and literatures, including Jewish and Russian, journeys traditionally symbolized people's life trajectories framed by spatial, temporal, and spiritual dimensions.[59] Thus, on a pilgrimage to holy places in the East, Western believers obtained holiness. Medieval Russian defectors to the West were considered not only traitors but also heretics, betraying true Eastern Orthodox faith to embrace godless Western Catholicism. Former Jewish slaves left Egypt in the West to become, in forty years, God's chosen people in the eastern land of Canaan. Often, such journeys blazed the path to the future. In 1799, Nikolai Karamzin, who traveled to Western Europe seeking true enlightenment, published the account of his journey, called *Letters of a Russian Traveler*. According to Karamzin's contemporaries, his book was read as an account of Russia's future.[60] In the Jewish tradition, the future of the Jewish people is firmly linked to the lost Promised Land in the East. Hence, the Jewish future is a restoration of the Jewish past, and the return to the past is a way to the future. Therefore, the return of Nathan Becker to the USSR—the journey to the East and the resulting spiritual improvement, the "recasting"—symbolizes the dawn of the Redemption.

Jewish tradition views a reunion of the dispersed Jewish people returning to the Promised Land as an important integral component of the messianic era's scenario. In the movie, the theme of the people's unity is represented by the family reunion. Nathan's return to his father, Tsale, is a symbol of the Jewish future attainable by a return to the Jewish past. Thus, the modernized and Americanized Nathan and his traditional shtetl father are reunited. Moreover, the reunion could be seen as a resolution of the old conflict between fathers and sons and a reversal of the trend of the disintegration of the traditional Jewish family described by the classic Yiddish writer Sholom Aleichem in a series of short stories about Tevye the Milkman. Tevye's family was disintegrating as his daughters were leaving their father's home: Hodl married a revolutionary and was exiled to Siberia; Beilke married an entrepreneur and emigrated to America; Chave converted to the Russian Orthodox faith to marry a Christian peasant. Leaving home, all of Tevye's daughters built their own families and homes and hoped for their own future.[61] Echoing this motif, the moviemakers exaggerated it to the utmost, showing the fully disintegrated Jewish family without any future. On his return, Nathan received such a warning, listening to the following song sung by the street musicians in his native shtetl:

> Four brothers, four of us lived together,
> We used to sell biscuits.
> When one of us deceased,
> Three of us remained.
> Three brothers, three of us lived together,
> We used to sell firewood.

When one of us deceased,
Two of us remained.
Two brothers, two of us lived together,
We used to sell kerosene.
When one of us deceased,
One of us remained.
One brother I was,
I started to sell whatever I got.
When one of us deceased,
None of us remained.[62]

Nathan's reunion with his father reversed the imminent disintegration. The family reunion symbolizes the restoration of the people's unity. In the USSR, Jews once again became one people, with one goal and one future shared with other Soviet peoples.

Returning to his father's home, Nathan returns to his childhood to be re-educated (through "recasting") and to grow up to become a new kind of adult. Therefore, Nathan throws baby-like tantrums just because he dislikes physical education; like a teenager, he is extremely vulnerable and overly emotional when confronted with tough life situations. In contrast, Tsale, his father, patiently and gently pushes his son in the right direction, only rarely complaining about Nathan's stubbornness in embracing new Soviet "family" values: "You always argue with us, Nathan!" In the first half of the movie, Tsale obsessively "measures" Nathan's spiritual growth with a folding ruler that he keeps in his breast-pocket (that is, closer to his heart).[63] In the second half of the movie, when Tsale sees that Nathan embraces his new family and thus comes of age, he stops measuring his son's progress.

If the return of Nathan Becker ushered in the messianic era, then who is the messiah? The echo of this question and a possible answer could be found in the short story "Shifs-karta" (1922) by Ilya Ehrenburg, the prominent Soviet writer of Jewish descent, another tale about the Russian Jewish family—a Berdichev watchmaker, Girsh Ikhenson, and his son living in America—divided by the Atlantic and by destiny. Girsh believes that America is the Promised Land, as he receives an infrequent correspondence from his son, who "might forget the [native] language or might be using words in God's language, incomprehensible and frightening[.] [These words] sound as a promise of happiness to Girsh. . . . Especially one of them, the strange and enigmatic 'Shifs-karta' [literally, "ship ticket" in Yiddish]. Please wait a bit more [his son writes]. [Everything] will be alright. 'Shifs-karta' will come to you. Year after year. And in times of trouble, this word . . . becomes for Girsh a consolation, an unpronounceable name [of God], a God's smile."[64] However, instead of the anticipated "Shifs-karta," civil war, fear, and death come to Berdichev and Girsh perishes in a pogrom. Obviously, "Shifs-karta" is Ehrenburg's metaphor of the false messiah, who enticed the sons of Girsh Ikhenson and Tsale Becker to America, the false Promised Land. This is why in "Shifs-karta," the false messiah did not come to redeem Russian Jews from the turmoil of the civil war, nor did it make Russian Jewish immigrants happy in America, such as Nathan Becker. It is also obvious that the Bolshevik Revolution symbolizes the true messiah in the movie. Its coming is invisible but is revealed in fateful and profound changes shown in the movie. The revolution was the turning point of Jewish history, dividing it into the exilic past and the messianic future. The world of exile is orderly and essentially material: time goes by, measured by hours, days, and religious holidays, such as the Sabbath. Meike, Nathan's wife, remembers their last Sabbath in America, when they saw jobless people quarreling in a long line to a soup kitchen in New York. The messianic world is metaphysical; there is no time in the normal sense. In Magnitogorsk, Meike struggles to understand how to measure time in the USSR. How to differentiate between weekdays and holidays? What is the "day-off" (*vykhodnoi*)? And when, after all, does the Sabbath begin?!

In addition to changing time, the Promised land—the last theme of the movie under consideration—reshaped space and affected people's lives. Nathan's entire shtetl seemed to instantly move from the former Pale of Settlement to Magnitogorsk, as if space shrunk and there was no more 2,500-kilometer distance. On arrival in Magnitogorsk, people immediately started to build. What did they build? According to Jewish tradition, on return to the Promised Land, Jews would rebuild the Temple on the Temple Mount in the city of Jerusalem. The movie hints that former shtetl Jews would build "a factory," where everyone gets a job, near Magnetic Mountain in the city of Magnitogorsk. Panoramic shots from the movie show not actual buildings, but a vast construction site with colossal, towering, scaffolded structures.

During his first day of work at this enormous job site, Nathan, who used to simply lay bricks in America, learned that Soviet bricklayers should approach their work with an attitude similar to the traditional Jewish attitude toward prayer, called a "holy work" (*avodat kodesh*) in Hebrew. Soviet builders' rituals include rites unheard of in exile such as the socialist competition and physical education. Initially, Nathan mocked this ritual as "theater," but in the end he wholeheartedly embraced it. Thus the "holy work" in the Promised Land forever changed Nathan. In the final scene of the movie, he excitedly acknowledges that Soviet builders build with their souls, literally referring to the words of Tomorrow in Mikhoels's *Builder*: "The new, mighty, brave builders will be coming. . . . Neither brick nor mortar, neither hammer nor sword will they use building the tower. With their bare souls will they ascend and enter the palace of eternal truth and beauty."[65] In Magnitogorsk, atop the scaffolded tower, Tsale-Mikhoels nods approvingly to Nathan and starts singing a *nign*, a Hasidic prayer without words.

Soviet messianic ideology and Jewish messianic tradition peacefully and even harmoniously coexist in *The Return of Nathan Becker*. The movie, like other contemporary Soviet pictures such as *Chapaev* (1934) and *Tsirk* (1936), was framed by the stylistic canon of socialist realism, showing the transformation of an ordinary human into the ideal Soviet citizen and thus mythologizing the reality, portraying it in the way it should be, not in the way it was. In terms of the Soviet formula of a socialist national art—socialist contents in national form—on the one hand, *The Return of Nathan Becker* seems to fulfill the ideological imperative, to infuse Jewish art with the spirit of builders of Magnitogorsk.[66] On the other hand, in the case of *The Return of Nathan Becker*, it is hard to differentiate between contents and form. Whether, for example, Mikhoels's *nign* at the end of the movie represents Jewish form. Or, whether the idea of the USSR as the Promised Land is the socialist content. In the words of Miron Chernenko: "The poetics of the movie, which has very little in common with realism, . . . allows one to conclude that *The Return of Nathan Becker* could be seen as a traditional [Jewish] parable, a theatrical metaphor of Jewish existence, an exalted utopia set in the 'period of reconstruction' . . . showing how a meager shtetl Ahasverus becomes master of the new life along with those who already become such masters."[67]

As Solomon Mikhoels's contribution to Soviet Yiddish theater and film shows, in the first decade following the 1917 Bolshevik Revolution, the creators and champions of modern secular Jewish culture perceived revolutionary changes in Jewish terms with religious underpinnings. Some, including Mikhoels, wholeheartedly embraced the revolution for Jewish reasons framed by Jewish messianic tradition.

Such religious perceptions of political changes echoed Western European Jewish responses to emancipation in the first half of the nineteenth century. The 1806 Assembly of French Jewish Notables answering the inquiry of Napoleon stated: "At the present time . . . the Jews no longer form a separate people, but enjoy the advantage of being incorporated with the Great Nation [that is, France] (a privilege which they consider as a kind of political redemption)."[68] The 1845 Frankfurt Program, the foundational manifesto of Reform Judaism, maintained: "Messianic hope, truly understood, is religious . . . our [German Jews'] newly gained status as citizens constitutes a partial fulfillment of our messianic hopes."[69] Giving up the hope of political restoration of a Jewish state in the land of Israel, French and German Jews kept the idea of messianic redemption, believing that it was realized in France and Germany, their new Promised Lands. As an embodiment of this idea, in the nineteenth century, many Western European Jews renamed their synagogues "temples."

In revolutionary Russia, many secular Jewish intellectuals supported and even participated in anti-religious campaigns launched by the Soviet state, targeting traditional institutes of Judaism including the rabbinate, synagogues, religious law, ritual, and holidays. However, paradoxically, these intellectuals did not deny or reject their own Jewishness, which they proudly acknowledged as a primordial folk spirit (*narodnost'*).[70] Like Moshe Litvakov, they did not aim at eliminating Judaism altogether, but rather sought to release the folk spirit that animated Judaism from the ossified shell of religion.

Producers of secular Jewish culture in Soviet Russia, such as Mikhoels, welcomed revolutionary changes. In their eyes, the revolutionary politics of the Bolshevik regime supported Jewish aspirations promising redemption to a living generation of Soviet Jews. Hence, as a messiah, the Russian Revolution warranted the Jewish future. Supporting the messianic revolution, by means of Soviet Yiddish theater and film, Mikhoels and like-minded Jewish cultural producers created a modernist art that was as Soviet as it was thoroughly Jewish. From this perspective, *The Return of Nathan Becker* was meant to be not a historical document of Soviet industrialization, or outright propaganda of "recasting," but rather a multilayered image of Jerusalem, a rich metaphor of the Jewish future.

PART FOUR

Religion and Modernity in Cross-Cultural Dialogue

CHAPTER 10

"Holy Russia" and British Conservatism at the Turn of the Twentieth Century

ALEXANDER POLUNOV

The perception of late imperial Russian religious institutions and practices are found in the writings of two British contemporaries, William John Birkbeck (1859–1916) and Stephen Graham (1884–1975). Of particular interest is the contact that these two figures made with Russians, their representations of Russian religious life, and the role that these figures played in the religious and cultural rapprochement between Russia and Britain. The encounter between the turn-of-century Britons and the life and habits of an ostensibly alien culture gave birth to a number of different insights, many of which reveal the key European concerns of the time, namely, the relationship between traditional churches and political democracy, the church and mass education, the church and religious pluralism, and the role of the traditional confession in the era of mass politics and public opinion. The observations of Birkbeck and Graham reveal a fascinating paradox at the heart of turn-of-the-century Russian religious life: the British conservatives desired to discover, in an ostensibly traditional Russia, a haven from industrial modernity, but what they found turned out to be more modern invention and less Orthodox tradition than what appeared on the surface.[1]

Late nineteenth- and early twentieth-century modernity took the form of increasing urbanization and industrial growth, social mobility, and the unsettling of the traditional social hierarchies. Traditionally, it has been assumed that this modernity was increasingly secular, as manifested in the declining importance of religion as an ideology and a social institution. Indeed, sociological theories of the 1960s argued that the process continued well into the twentieth century and predicted that religion would increasingly become privatized and displaced from the center to the margins of public life.[2]

The period of modernization is also known as a time when the all-encompassing political ideologies of liberalism, socialism, and nationalism reached their maturity, exerting powerful influence on different aspects of social and political development. The growth and transformation of modern ideologies were inseparably linked with the emergence of utopian projects, which became an important part of the political and spiritual landscape of the modern epoch. Finally, the second half of the nineteenth and the early twentieth centuries (the period of "early globalization") were marked by the growing interrelation of the different parts of the world, which is viewed most often as a rise of Western influence on non-Western countries.[3]

Many of these theories are currently the subject of scrupulous scholarly attention, and their traditional treatment is now often criticized and revised. In particular, the classic theory of secularization, which treats this phenomenon as an inevitable result of worldwide modernization, has undergone an especially far-reaching reconsideration in the twenty-first century. It has become clear that the traditional notions of the "decline" and "privatization" of religion in the modern age reflect the specific (in fact, unique) experience of European Latin Christendom and that other world regions have experienced the encounter with secularism in significantly different ways. Instead of treating secularism as a natural consequence of modern society, José Casanova argues that scholars should attend to a critical comparative analysis of the different types of secularisms that have emerged in the process of modern state formation.[4]

Even in Western Europe, where the processes of "decline" and "privatization" of religion allegedly occurred in their classical form, the impact of modernization on the social and cultural evolution of society was much more ambiguous than has been asserted. Thus, many works emphasize the relative vitality of European Christendom in the nineteenth century, which not only reflected the durability of old beliefs and practices but also stemmed from the ability of Christian churches to adapt and innovate.[5] It goes without saying that the period of modernization was a hard time for the big confessional organizations, which lost a significant portion of their traditional flock and had to yield to the influential secularist tendencies in various areas of social and ideological life. But, in any case, these organizations were not the helpless and silent victims of secular attacks; they fought back vigorously and sometimes successfully.

The experience of Russia, as one of the largest non-Western countries, should be considered when discussing modernization and secularization. Russian encounter with modernity, rather than leading to a marginalization of religion, spurred the emergence of a "modern Russian Orthodoxy," which, despite serious hardships, was able to adapt itself to the new circumstances.[6] This "new Orthodoxy" revealed itself in such phenomena as the rise of priestly social activism, increased lay participation in church affairs, the emergence of new forms of religious veneration, and the influence of traditional religious ideas and values in secular spheres.[7]

A comparative look at the experiences of various cultures can be done by exploring the work of travelers and their observations of cultures and traditions different from their own. One interesting perspective is provided by Britons' conservative views of Russia as expressed through what they saw of Russian religious traditions in the second half of the nineteenth century. Their observations expose a paradox; what the British travelers saw as the unchanging traditions of the Orthodox Church were actually innovative responses to modernity. Indeed, what they observed was modernity in the guise of tradition, carefully crafted to respond to the challenges of secularism at the turn of the century.

Ex oriente lux: British Russophiles at the Turn of the Century

In 1888, the *Guardian*, the weekly newspaper associated with the Catholic wing of the Anglican Church, published a series of articles written by William John Birkbeck, a prominent member of the High Church movement. The articles were devoted to the Russian celebrations of the nine-hundred-year anniversary of the Russian conversion to Christianity, which took place in Kiev and in other cities of the Russian Empire. It was unusual for a member of English high society to visit Russia for the purpose of observing religious ceremonies, especially in the period when the relations between the two countries were highly strained given tensions over Afghanistan. Even more surprising was the feeling of deep sympathy toward Russian religiosity that appeared in the pages of Birkbeck's articles. "Words cannot describe the beauty of the scene," wrote the English traveler, "the officiant surrounded by the other clergy, amidst numerous burning tapers and clouds of fragrant incense, raising the Cross on high and blessing the people. . . . It was plain, that they [believers] had come together not for the sake of witnessing a pageant, or from the motives of curiosity, but in order religiously to take part in the rejoicing on the occasion of this great festival of their Church and Nation."[8]

The admiration for the Russian religiosity expressed by Birkbeck was by no means common in Britain, as the British public, for the most part, perceived the Russian Church as "backward" and "absorbed into the rite-belief."[9] Mass events such as the celebration in Kiev, which stressed the world importance of Russian Orthodoxy, were treated as manifestations of the "traditional expansionism" of Russia. "A Panslavist current at that time moved the Russian ship of state," wrote Arthur H. Hardinge, the second secretary of the British embassy in St. Petersburg and Birkbeck's childhood friend, who first alerted him to the celebrations of 1888. "The Kieff ceremonies . . . were intended to be not merely a religious but a masked political demonstration."[10] Despite such statements, Birkbeck continued to insist that events in Russia had a predominantly spiritual meaning, that the Church of Russia should be seen as a depository of dogmatic truth and of the unbroken ancient Christian tradition, and that the Church of England had to establish closer ties with Russian Orthodoxy in order to restore the ecclesiastical unity that had been lost centuries ago. For Birkbeck, it was the "duty of the Church of England, as well as her interest, not only to get to know more of the Easterns, but to allow herself really to be influenced by them."[11]

In the 1890s and 1900s, Birkbeck became a prominent propagandist of the Anglo-Russian ecclesiastical rapprochement, publishing numerous articles and delivering public lectures on this topic. Traveling to Russia more than thirty times, Birkbeck visited not just Kiev, Moscow, and St. Petersburg, but also ancient towns around Moscow (Sergiev Posad, Vladimir, Suzdal, and Rostov), the Volga area, the Urals, the Baltic provinces, Pskov, and the Russian North. As an influential Anglo-Catholic, Viscount Halifax put it, Birkbeck "knew Russia better than many Russians."[12] According to the notes of Russian contemporaries who visited Birkbeck's manor in Norfolk, Birkbeck introduced into his parish "almost Orthodox rites," and his home reminded the Russian travelers of a "Church-archeological museum" full of Orthodox icons, books, and vestments.[13]

One of Birkbeck's most important initiatives was organizing the visits of Anglican and American Episcopal senior clerics to Russia, in order to strengthen the personal and institutional ties between the two churches. In 1896, the bishop of Peterborough, Mandell Creighton, attended the coronation of Nicholas II as an official representative of the Church of England. In the following year, the archbishop of York, W. D. Maclagan, traveled to Russia, as did the bishop of Fond du Lac (Wisconsin), Charles Grafton, in 1903.[14] In 1912, four Anglican bishops came to Russia as members of the British official delegation, and Birkbeck even tried to persuade the archbishop of Canterbury to participate in this program.[15] Though these visits had few concrete results, they nevertheless helped to create a more sympathetic impression of the Russian Church in Britain. As Birkbeck reported, the Anglican prelates during their trips were profoundly impressed by the piety of the flock and the beauty of the church services in Russia, and Bishop Creighton even said that Britons might learn "a lesson from a nation which so evidently put the worship of God, whether in the streets, or in their houses, or in their churches, before everything else."[16]

In response to the visits of Anglican clerics to Russia, the Russian archbishop of Finland, Antonii (Vadkovskii), undertook a trip to Britain in 1897 to attend the celebrations for Queen Victoria's Diamond Jubilee. Accompanied by Birkbeck, he met high clerical and lay dignitaries (such as the archbishop of Canterbury, the Prince of Wales, and Viscount Halifax), received a *honoris causa* doctorate from Cambridge University, and was warmly accepted by both ordinary believers and members of the High Anglican Church circles.[17] The visit of Archbishop Antonii was one of the pinnacles of the rapprochement between the Russian Church and the Church of England. "If things will go on in the same manner, the points of contact between Orthodoxy and the Anglican Church will become more and more numerous," Antonii enthusiastically reported after his visit to St. Petersburg.[18]

Birkbeck's sympathy for Russian religious life was shared in the late nineteenth and early twentieth centuries by other Britons, including Stephen Graham, a journalist and novelist who lived for several years in Russia and authored a number of sketches and travelogues. Birkbeck was familiar with the works of his younger compatriot and recommended them enthusiastically to Russian readers.[19] The two men may have met personally and collaborated, most likely through the intermediation of Olga Novikoff (Novikova), a Slavophile journalist who lived in London and contributed extensively to the Russian and British press. Novikoff, in turn, introduced Birkbeck to many influential Russians. Graham collaborated with Novikoff and wrote the preface to her 1916 book *Russian Memories*.[20]

In a manner very similar to that of Birkbeck, the young British journalist depicted Russia "as a reservoir of spiritual richness," as a kind of "sacred space where the traditions and rituals of everyday life embodied in their very substance a set of deeper spiritual truths," where "the material and spiritual worlds came together in a way that made 'Holy Russia' a country fundamentally different in character from any other," especially compared to the countries of the West.[21] Strongly influenced by the works of Fyodor Dostoyevsky, and, later, by the writings of the fin de siècle Russian religious philosophers, Graham stressed that the whole character of Russia was shaped by the spirit of

Orthodoxy and that the church constituted one of the most important institutions of Russia.

Of special interest was Graham's book *With Russian Pilgrims to Jerusalem* (1913), in which he contrasted the sincere piety of the ordinary Russian spiritual travelers with the more tourist-style curiosity of Westerners and rich Europeanized Russians. Ordinary Russians perceived the whole Holy Land as a living sacred reality, experiencing the direct connection between the geographical objects of Palestine and the concrete events in biblical history. It is interesting that many Western travelers at that time wrote about Russian pilgrims in the same manner, depicting their "simple faith, the deep reverence, the heartfelt love and sorrow," their "devotion and enthusiasm."[22] Their sympathy for Russian religiosity thus became a visible tendency within British intellectual and spiritual life, and the views of Birkbeck and Graham were simply the clearest example of this trend. But why were these authors so interested in Russia? How did their sympathy for Russia reflect the European ideological evolution at the turn of the century?

Conservative Romanticism in Britain

Graham was a typical representative of conservative romanticism, inspired by the works of Thomas Carlyle, German romantics, and British poets of the Lake School. Graham condemned the destructive effects of urban and industrial civilization, looking for a quiet shelter where the traditional values and institutions usually associated with a rural way of life could be safely protected. A relatively backward Russia, allegedly remote from the harmful influences of Western industrialism and commercialism, was perceived as such a shelter. An important source for Graham's views were the writings of his father, the journalist and writer Peter Alexander Graham, who edited the journal *Country Life* for a quarter century, providing readers with pastoral and exotic pictures of the rural world remote from the prosaic rhythms of big cities.[23]

Traveling extensively across Russia, Stephen Graham visited big cities, such as Rostov-on-Don and Novorossiisk, where the capitalist evolution of the country was presented in its most obvious form. This evolution, however, was seen by the British journalist as a sign of the degradation of Russia, which was about to lose its unique vocation as a sacred place. Some of the most vitriolic passages the British writer reserved for the Russian bourgeoisie, who wanted "to know the price of everything" and who knew nothing "of things which are independent of price." For Graham, the bourgeoisie was the ugliest and most abnormal product of the new epoch.[24]

The true guardian of Russian spirituality was, for Graham, the ordinary people, members of the *narod* who allegedly "were not interested in abstruse questions of doctrine," but "lived in a God-saturated world in which a sense of the divine permeated every aspect of their daily life." Russia's greatness, Graham stressed, "starts from the peasant soul, that draws out of all the store of national tradition and belief and experience."[25] During his numerous travels Graham visited prominent Russian monasteries (New Athos, Trinity-Sergius), provincial towns (Arkhangel'sk), and the historical centers of Russian Orthodoxy such as Moscow. He was convinced that the true spirit of religiosity in Russia could be found among the rank-and-file provincial-dwellers, peasants, monks, and townspeople, who had an intuitive faith and a sense of the importance of tradition and therefore led far richer spiritual lives than the inhabitants of big Russian cities and their counterparts in Western countries.

Graham's views had much in common with those of the Russian Slavophiles, who also praised the spiritual qualities of the ordinary people who preserved traditional customs, kept the patriarchal family, and remained faithful to religion. These ordinary people were contrasted to the corrupt Russian high society, allegedly torn away from its popular roots by harmful European influences. But, as Andrzej Walicki argues, even while criticizing the West, Russian Slavophilism remained a typically modern and undoubtedly European phenomenon, which had striking affinities with the views of Western conservative romantics such as Friedrich Schelling, Friedrich Schlegel, and Franz von Baader. Slavophiles found it impossible to isolate themselves from the influences of modernity and Western culture, even while protesting against them. Walicki has called the Slavophiles conservative utopians, seeking to create a utopia out of elements of the past.[26] This utopian strain was also found in Graham, whose search for a "patriarchal shelter" expressed his sense of alienation and deprivation engendered by the dark sides of European urban civilization.

Elements of a utopianism based on conservative romantic feelings were also visible in the worldview of Birkbeck, who, just like the Slavophiles and Graham, tended to idealize the *narod*, the rural and provincial life of Russia, and contrasted it to "rootless" high society and the life of urban centers. Describing Russian religious ceremonies, he readily depicted the crowds of ordinary believers who often "walked from the furtherest parts of the empire" in order to visit the shrines of the traditional centers of Russian Orthodoxy and who "bathed in tears" during the church services.[27] Being, like Graham, convinced that true spirituality was found outside the big cities, Birkbeck strove during his numerous visits to Russia to reach small towns and remote ancient monasteries. He lived in monastic cells and even in the homes of rural priests, peering, as one of his Russian friends noted, "eagerly and with living interest into Russian life as it revealed itself in monasteries and parishes."[28] On many occasions the British writer insisted that the foreigners who wanted to obtain a true knowledge of Russia should venture beyond the confines of the capitals. His typically romantic aesthetic led him to a fascination with the beauty of church music and icons, and architecture was also of great importance to Birkbeck. At the same time, there was at least one serious factor that made Birkbeck different from his younger contemporary and played a very important role in the set of reasons that encouraged Birkbeck's sympathy for Russia.

British Political Conservatism and the Russian Church

Birkbeck's admiration of the Russian Church was not purely limited to aesthetic matters. A scion of a prosperous gentry family and a graduate of Eton and Oxford with strong Tory instincts, this British Anglo-Catholic was highly concerned about Britain's contemporary political situation. He was sure that the elite British democracy of his time was beginning to wane, descending into an "uncontrolled form of popular government," mostly due to the rise of secularism, atheism, and religious pluralism in Europe as a whole.[29] The close ties between church and state that existed in Russia were perceived as a positive phenomenon, one that was, to some extent, worthy of emulation. "Englishmen, whatever the political difficulties which they may have with her [Russia]," Birkbeck wrote, "have no reason whatever to wish to see Russia under an infidel Government, or that her Church should lose its influence in directing her destinies, or that her internal affairs should be directed according to foreign ideas."[30]

The system of church-state relations in imperial Russia, which had been conventionally portrayed as an "enslavement" of the spiritual realm by bureaucracy, was represented by Birkbeck as a harmonious combination of secular and clerical elements, "neither that of tyrant and slave, nor that of cat and dog, but that of a *mens sana in corpore sano*."[31] The Church of England, Birkbeck wrote, should form with the Russian Church a common front against nonbelief, especially since all of Europe faced a struggle "between Christianity and materialistic paganism." The introduction of religious freedom in Russia proposed by Russian and European liberals was fiercely rejected by Birkbeck, who was sure that such a measure would inevitably foster religious indifference and secularization. Such a measure, the British conservative asserted, would mean permission "for every grotesque ignoramus, every silly self-appointed apostle to enter Russia and experiment upon the simple-minded Russian peasantry."[32]

An important factor in Birkbeck's gravitation toward Russian spirituality was the position of British Anglo-Catholics, who were looking for a rapprochement with the Orthodox churches in order to establish the position of the Anglican Church as an integral part of universal ecclesiastical unity, stressing its Episcopal and basically non-Protestant character.[33] Such support was especially needed after 1896, when Pope Leo XIII published a papal bull denying the validity of Anglican orders.[34] Birkbeck emphasized the traditional character of Orthodox teaching and the adherence of the Russian Church to the doctrines of church fathers and ecumenical councils, in order to bolster the position of the Anglican Church within the international ecclesiastical commonwealth and even to reverse the centuries-old schism in Christianity. These motives, however, were combined in Birkbeck's writings with some contrasting tendencies, which demonstrated how profoundly the spirit of modernity influenced the thinking of this conservative and sometimes overtly anti-modernist author.

While depicting the Russian Church as an essentially traditional institution, Birkbeck was well aware that the archaic traits of ecclesiastical organization would not gain wide popularity among the Western audience. The Orthodox Church appears therefore in his writings not just as a conservative institution, but as one that was adapting itself successfully to the challenges of modernity. Disputing the widespread impressions of the total ignorance of the Russian Orthodox laypeople and clergy, Birkbeck wrote about rural priests who preached regularly and were able to discuss with the British traveler complicated theological issues and the most recent events in the life of Western and foreign Orthodox churches.[35]

Birkbeck admitted that the average Russian believer was receiving less formal schooling than his Western counterpart, but he was sure it did not lead to any kind of religious ignorance. Contradicting, to some extent, Graham's assertions of Russian peasants' indifference to the religious doctrine, Birkbeck claimed that the majority of ordinary believers were very familiar with church teaching due to the features of the Orthodox liturgy. "In the Eastern Church," wrote Birkbeck, "all the dogmas of the Church are set forth in the clearest way in the everyday services of the Church" and had become therefore "a part of the life of the people to an extent which is difficult to realize in the West."[36] Birkbeck claimed he heard more biblical citations among Russian peasantry than he had ever heard among the farmers in his native Norfolk County.

The formal school education of the parishioners was not neglected in Russia either. The last decades of the nineteenth century witnessed a number of important educational initiatives related to the church, such as the founding of parish schools launched by the chief procurator of the Holy Synod, Konstantin

Pobedonostsev (1827–1907), and the initiative of the prominent missionary and orientalist Nikolai Ilminskii (1822–1891), who strove to educate the non-Russian Christians of the eastern regions of Russia in their native languages.[37] The Russian Church did not oppose education as such, stressed Birkbeck. "What it does desire is that it should begin with reading, writing, and arithmetic, and Christianity," and not with Henry Buckle, Herbert Spencer, or other representatives of modern secularism. The Ilminskii school movement, the British conservative was careful to emphasize, started not as a bureaucratic endeavor, but as an independent initiative of "devout and enthusiastic laymen of which the Russian Church, perhaps more than any other Church in Christendom, has such good cause to be proud."[38]

Traveling regularly to Russia, Birkbeck, as Michael Hughes contends, "developed an astonishing range of contacts," which "were probably more extensive than those of any other Briton."[39] It is necessary to note that an important place among these contacts was occupied by the figures who represented the reformist and renovationist tendencies in the Russian Church, such as Archbishop Antonii, the future church reformer, and Protopresbyter Ioann Ianyshev, a prominent theologian and the proponent of the rapprochement between Russian and Western churches.[40] Birkbeck was familiar with many professors of Russian theological academies. He met with the famous spiritual elder John of Kronstadt and the abbess Ekaterina (Efimovskaia) of the Lesna convent, both of whom were active in organizing church social services in impoverished urban and rural areas. While traveling to the Kazan Province in 1894, Birkbeck visited the parish schools, accompanied by Vasilii Timofeev, the Kriashen (Baptized Tatar) priest, one of the disciples and main collaborators of Ilminskii.[41]

While in St. Petersburg, Birkbeck participated in laying the foundation stone of a church in a poor proletarian area, funded by money collected by local workers. He repeatedly visited St. Vladimir's teachers' school, which prepared pedagogues for elementary schools within the framework of Pobedonostsev's program.[42] Writing on these and other similar phenomena, Birkbeck strove to represent the Russian Church as a living institution, quite able to adapt itself to the changing conditions of modernity.

Modernity in the Guise of Tradition

Birkbeck, and to some extent Graham, failed to notice that the numerous phenomena of Russian religious life that impressed foreigners as authentic representations of traditional religiosity were in fact of recent origin, engendered by an encounter with modernity. For example, the demonstrations of popular piety that struck Birkbeck so powerfully during the Kiev celebrations of 1888 were, in fact, the product of a relatively new phenomenon—the mass religious festival. The Kiev festivities, in particular, were part of a massive campaign launched by Pobedonostsev, appointed to the post of chief procurator in 1880, and aimed at increasing the influence of the conservative monarchist ideology in Russian society.[43] There were seventeen mass religious celebrations in the 1880s and early 1890s marking important events in Russian religious history, such as the commemoration of the thousandth anniversary of the death of Saint Methodius in St. Petersburg in 1886, the commemoration of the five hundredth anniversary of the death of Saint Sergius of Radonezh in Moscow in 1892, and others. All commemorative events were accompanied by measures deliberately aimed at the involvement of the masses in the process of celebration, such as immense processions of crosses, mass distributions of small icons, leaflets and brochures, and inexpensive perceptive books for ordinary people.[44]

It is possible to assume that if Birkbeck had first visited Russia not in the 1880s but ten to fifteen years earlier, he would not have perceived it as a repository of eternal religious truth, since the whole picture of Russian spiritual life that the British conservative witnessed was strongly influenced by the measures undertaken by Pobedonostsev. This is not to say that the chief procurator and other Russian conservative politicians "forged" or "invented" popular piety. It existed and developed irrespective of the policy of the authorities.[45] But without the measures launched by the chief procurator, many important elements of this piety could not find a stage for their expression, as they had been confined to the narrow framework of the parish.

Striving to strengthen the societal foundations of Russian monarchy, Pobedonostsev took measures aimed at increasing the social role of the Orthodox Church, which were also quite modern in their nature. He stimulated the growth of the number of clergy, parish churches, and monasteries and encouraged the monasteries' charitable and educational efforts. A number of new religious fraternal organizations (*bratstva*) were formed that supported churches, hospitals, and poorhouses. At the same time, the activities of the church typographers and publishers were significantly expanded, and the ordinary believers were provided with numerous publications that included saints' lives, patriotic stories and histories of the Russian past, scriptures, gospels, and psalters. The mass-circulation press was also widely used, especially for covering mass religious events.[46]

Being fully aware of the importance of public opinion in Western countries, Pobedonostsev did his best to influence it and to create a favorable image of Russia in Europe. The high-placed conservative collaborated closely with Western journalists working in Russia and encouraged those who wrote positively about the country. The chief procurator was very familiar with the works of contemporary European political thinkers (mostly conservative) and used them widely in his writings.[47] For Birkbeck, Pobedonostsev became one of his most important Russian contacts, introducing the British conservative to high-placed ecclesiastical and lay Russian dignitaries and helping him to obtain firsthand information on Russian religious life. As Hughes puts it, the relationship between Pobedonostsev and Birkbeck was not one of purely pragmatic collaboration but was "marked by a real degree of mutual sympathy and shared interests in theological and ecclesiastical questions."[48]

All these tendencies, important as they were, did not mean, of course, that the Russian Church and conservative religious circles faced no problems in the late imperial period. Such problems were tremendous and numerous, and, as is well known, they contributed in the long run to the collapse of tsarist Russia. Thus, Pobedonostsev, despite of all his energy and sensitivity to the issues of public opinion, was very often extremely intolerant of both the Orthodox clergy and non-Orthodox confessions and used heavy-handed and even despotic methods in his church policy.[49] The poverty and submissive status of the Russian parish clergy hampered the implementation of the broad plans designed by the church authorities and aimed at the elevation of the church's social role. Against this backdrop, the picture of traditional Russian piety presented by Birkbeck and Graham must be treated as seriously idealized. "There was in truth something profoundly inadequate" and "deeply naïve" in it, as Hughes notes.[50] Keeping all of this in mind, we should still recognize that the evolution toward secularism in late imperial Russia was not a straight and predetermined process. Rather, as elsewhere in Europe, it was "a contest, in which adherents of rival world-views battled it out."[51]

Many phenomena of Russian spiritual and cultural life that may have been perceived by the foreign travelers as authentic elements of historical heritage represented, in fact, the recent innovations started as a response to the challenges of modernity. Thus, important elements of traditional icon painting and church singing were restored in the late nineteenth century as a part of the policy of church and lay authorities aimed at the revival of the old Muscovite traditions.[52] The beauty of the ancient temples and monasteries that adorned for centuries the historical centers of Russian Orthodoxy was complemented in the late nineteenth and early twentieth centuries by the construction of new churches in the "Muscovite" or "neo-Russian" style, which had to symbolize the natural bond between the tsar, the people, and Orthodoxy rooted in the remote past.[53] The 1880s and 1890s also witnessed the restoration of a number of ancient architectural monuments, such as the cathedrals of Dormition in Moscow and Vladimir, the St. Sophia cathedral in Novgorod, and the Rostov Kremlin. But possibly the most striking example of the modern phenomenon represented in the guise of tradition was the Russian pilgrimage to Palestine, which so impressed Graham and other Western contemporaries.

Russian spiritual travels to the Holy Land, which represented the seemingly most traditional form of popular piety, were, like many other phenomena of Russian religious life, strongly influenced by the tendencies of the modern epoch. Relatively weak and sporadic over most of its history, the Russian pilgrimage started to acquire a massive dimension only in the second half of the nineteenth century, especially since the early 1880s, when it was supported by the Orthodox Palestine Society (later the Imperial Orthodox Palestine Society, IOPS). Modeled after analogous Western structures (the Deutsches Palaestina-Verein, British Palestine Exploration Fund, and French Société de l'Orient Latin), the IOPS represented a typical example of the societal organization characteristic of the modern epoch. Its founding was attributable to the independent initiative of a lay activist, Vasilii Khitrovo (1834–1903), who had to overcome the stubborn resistance of the official structures and received during the first period of its existence neither financial nor administrative support for its activities. As Theofanis G. Stavrou points out, the founders of the IOPS strove "to draft the constitution and formulate the objectives of their organization as they saw fit, with the least possible supervision from the government or the Holy Synod [the supreme governing body of the church]."[54]

Striving to attract the attention of Russian society to the Holy Land, the IOPS launched numerous initiatives funding scholarly research in Palestine: organizing geographical, ethnographical, and archeological expeditions; and publishing academic bulletins, books, and journals. Of special importance, as noted, was the support of Russian pilgrimage. The most up-to-date logistical and financial technologies were used in this sphere. The Palestine Society negotiated with the railroad and steamship companies and secured reduced-priced tickets for passengers going on pilgrimage. In various cities of the empire, special pilgrims' booklets or coupons (*palomnicheskie knigi*) were sold that gave holders the right to use both train and steamship on the way to Palestine. The IOPS and its departments in various cities in the empire sponsored the publication of brochures and delivery of lectures with instructions to pilgrims and disseminated tour guides with detailed descriptions of the Holy Land.[55]

Special monastic-like shelters were established in Odessa, the main pilgrimage hub of the empire, in order to protect unsuspecting and inexperienced spiritual travelers (mostly peasants) from the dangers and temptations of the big cosmopolitan city. Church services, edifying public reading, and a monastic-like organization of life were used to maintain and develop the spiritual exaltation of pilgrims.[56] The abundance of Russian travelers in Palestine on the eve of World War I, which so strongly impressed Graham and other Western contemporaries, was therefore the result not just of the natural religiosity of the common people but also of the skillful application of the sophisticated financial and organizational techniques used by the IOPS.

It is interesting that the shelters for pilgrims were organized on the territory of the dependencies (*podvor'ia*) that the Russian monasteries of Mount Athos (an international center of Orthodox monasticism in Greece) had in Odessa.[57] The monks of the *podvor'ia* helped spiritual travelers to secure Turkish visas, buy return tickets, and resolve other organizational issues. As Nikolaos Chrissidis has shown, the civil authorities assumed a role only insofar as they processed passports and checked the necessary documentation regarding permission to travel abroad. In this sense, the Athonite monastic dependencies were the IOPS's allies, functioning in a fully complementary manner to the aims of the IOPS.[58] The history of pilgrimage from the Russian Empire to Palestine thus demonstrates that the church bodies and societal organizations were able to function as de facto independent and active structures.

The religious life of Russia represented, at the turn of the century, a peculiar mixture of archaic and up-to-date elements, and the British conservatives who expected to find in Russia a secure shelter against the perils of industrialization and modernization very often faced quite modern phenomena in the guise of tradition. It is instructive to reiterate in this regard the conclusions of José Casanova, who has criticized "the dominant theories of secularization, which have postulated a progressive decline of religious beliefs and practices with increasing modernization, so that the more modern a society is, the more secular, the less 'religious,' it is supposed to become."[59] As an analysis of the views of British conservatives and of their relationship with Russian religious institutes reveals, even those confessional organizations that were conventionally treated as "backward" and "immovable" could find an important place within the processes of modernization.

The writings of Birkbeck and Graham on Russian religious life demonstrate how the non-Western country could become in the age of "early globalization" an object of fascination and even of inspiration for Western contemporaries. Of course, the approaches of the two Britons, as noted, were based to a large extent on a utopian vision. But this utopianism, being an integral part of the modern mode of thinking, helped the British Russophiles to notice important features of Russian religious life that were not seen by many of their contemporaries. Some conclusions of Birkbeck and Graham are corroborated by the findings of current scholarship. It is necessary to stress again that the traditional notions of the church's role in late imperial Russia are being reconsidered now by scholars who reveal the church's ability to adapt itself to the realities of modernity. The monarchy's downfall in 1917 and the subsequent establishment of the militant anti-religious Bolshevik regime were, from this point of view, just one possible outcome of the evolution of tsarist Russia. The notes and arguments represented in the writings of British Russophiles give valuable material for the analysis of the unrealized alternatives of Russian history. The further investigation of this and related topics will reveal all the complexity and ambiguity of Russian modernity within the framework of which the religious and secular tendencies interrelated and fought each other in a very contradictory and sometimes unpredictable manner.

CHAPTER 11

Power, Freedom, and Modernity

Spiritual Christian Molokans in Russia and the United States in the Early Twentieth Century

J. EUGENE CLAY

Power and freedom are both important elements of the fiercely contested category of "modernity."[1] On the one hand, social theorists such as W. W. (Walt) Rostow have imagined modernity as a complex of measurable processes that offered unprecedented *power* to the societies transformed by them: industrialization, urbanization, mass education, capitalist production, and advancements in transportation, communication, and electrical power. In the Darwinian geopolitical struggles of the early twentieth century, science and technology offered important advantages to societies (nation-states) caught in the vagaries of international competition. As Stephen Kotkin starkly put it in his biography of Joseph Stalin, modernity is a "a geopolitical process: a matter of acquiring what it took to join the great powers or fall victim to them." Mark Elvin, a historian of China, likewise stressed in his working definition of modernity the ability of "modern" Europe "to create power" over other human beings and over nature. "What went wrong" with the Muslim world?, the Islamicist Bernard Lewis famously asked on the eve of the attacks of September 11, 2001. His answer: Muslim societies had failed to modernize, to adopt the features of Western civilization, including the secular state and civil society, that had led to European domination of the globe.[2]

On the other hand, liberal political philosophers from John Stuart Mill to Stephen Eric Bronner emphasize *freedom* as the essential characteristic of modernity: the autonomy of the self, parliamentary democracy, private property, individual liberty, free scientific inquiry, art for art's sake, human rights, freedom of conscience, and equality under law. The German political philosopher Jürgen Habermas envisioned modernity as an incomplete project marked by ever-increasing freedom, which included the autonomy of art, science, and morality. Laura Engelstein, in her study of sexuality in the late Russian Empire, also stressed the liberal aspirations of a growing professional class that sought the "keys to happiness" and personal autonomy as the promise of modernity. For Bronner, modernity is the opposite of bigotry; it is a space of both pluralism and individualism where science can flourish, and authority is freely questioned.[3]

In these grand narratives about modernity, religious minorities and the process of secularization play an outsized role. Analyzing the origins of capitalist *power*, Max Weber argued that classical Protestant soteriology, which emphasized God's sovereign and inscrutable grace, had paradoxically led to the rationalization and instrumentalization of every aspect of life—the spirit of capitalism—which in its turn "disenchanted" and secularized the modern world. In Weber's view, the Protestant Reformation, with its this-worldly asceticism, had produced both the modern capitalist system, with all of its power to transform the world, and a secularized, disenchanted worldview. For liberals like Mill, who emphasized the *freedom* that modernity brings, secularization liberates the state and its subjects from religious constraints. As Kristina Stoeckl argues, the religious schisms in both the West (the Reformation) and Russia (the seventeenth-century schism that split the Orthodox Church) were traumatic experiences of modernization, for they created long-lasting dissenting communities that pushed their respective societies toward pluralism. By offering alternative spiritual paths, a different vision of society, and a repertoire of techniques for personal transformation, minority religions often act as agents of modernization. Yet religious minorities can also resist the homogenizing modernization programs (such as the imposition of standardized national educational curricula or compulsory military service).[4]

Russia's rich history of religious dissent included the Spiritual Christians, who broke with the state church because they refused to venerate icons (for them, an idolatrous practice). In the first decade of the twentieth century, thousands of these iconoclastic Spiritual Christians left Russia, a modernizing empire committed to social inequality, for the United States, a liberal democracy that nevertheless discriminated on the basis of race. Fleeing from their status as a persecuted religious minority in Russia, the Spiritual Christians found that the United States challenged their pacifist convictions. The experience of these Spiritual Christians illuminates the varieties of modernization in the early twentieth century. As Shmuel N. Eisenstadt has argued, modernity and modernization are not monolithic; historians and ethnographers can distinguish varieties of modernity in different societies. Although modernity has often been identified with the doctrines of popular sovereignty, the equality of all citizens, and patriotic loyalty to the nation-state, it is also true that monarchies, which place sovereignty in the ruler alone, have often undertaken projects of modernization. As Valerie A. Kivelson and Ronald Grigor Suny have pointed out, in its efforts to gain power by transforming society, late imperial Russia can be seen as a modernizing empire, even though it rejected the liberal modern values of equality and popular sovereignty.[5]

Spiritual Christianity and Modernity

The first Spiritual Christians appear in the historical record in the middle of the eighteenth century as both agents and products of modernization. In 1768, influenced by pietistic theological trends from Ukraine and their own interpretation of the Slavonic Bible (newly edited under Empress Elizabeth, r. 1741–62), some nominally Orthodox Christians in Voronezh and Tambov Provinces openly rejected the authority of the state church and petitioned Empress Catherine the Great (r. 1762–96) about their concerns. Convinced that God demanded spiritual worship (John 4:24), they refused to venerate icons and preached that the sacraments should be understood in a spiritual, rather than a literal, sense. The Orthodox Eucharist was mere bread and wine and provided no salvation; the true Christian fed on spiritual bread, the Word of God. They rejected physical baptism with water and embraced instead baptism by the Holy Spirit. Marriage did not require a priest, but simply the mutual consent of the bride and groom. Spiritual Christians gathered for their religious meetings in private homes, where they sang biblical psalms as well as hymns of their own composition. Encouraged by Catherine II's initiatives to introduce religious toleration at the beginning of her reign, these spiritual rebels sent a delegation to St. Petersburg to seek recognition for their convictions. Despite an apparently promising initial reception by the empress's personal secretary, the Freemason Ivan Perfil'evich Elagin, ultimately the state harshly repressed the movement, separating children from their parents and condemning the leaders to hard labor in exile.[6]

By demanding freedom of conscience (however unsuccessfully), these early Spiritual Christians sought the individual autonomy promised by liberal modernity. Explaining their own rejection of church authority with an appeal to a higher truth, the Spiritual Christians anticipated the American and French

Revolutions with their more elaborate justifications for resistance to illegitimate authority. Throughout the first half of the nineteenth century, the Russian state responded to this resistance by exiling and deporting large numbers of Spiritual Christians to the frontiers of Tauride Province and the Caucasus. On the frontier, they were free to form their own communities and to develop their own culture, including distinctive dress and music.

With no central ecclesiastical authority, Spiritual Christianity split into two main branches: the Dukhobors and the Molokans. The Dukhobors (*dukhobortsy* or *dukhobory*, "spirit-wrestlers") emphasized the direct leading of the Holy Spirit as more important than the Bible. By contrast, the Molokans, who drank milk (*moloko*) during the Orthodox fasts, insisted on the authority of the canonical scriptures, including the apocryphal or deutero-canonical books. Despite their common commitment to the Bible, Molokans differed over specific theological doctrines, such as the Trinity, and practices, such as the ritual fraternal kiss that some congregations exchanged.[7] In particular, beginning in the 1830s, Molokans were divided into the Jumpers (*pryguny*), who held that the Holy Spirit spoke through their prophets and inspired their members to dance ecstatically, and the Constants (*postoiannye*), who rejected these extraordinary divine manifestations. Several Jumper prophets predicted the end of the world, the return of the Christ, and the imminence of his millenarian kingdom. To prepare for the kingdom, these prophets called their fellow Molokan-Jumpers to repentance and to action, including migration to the land of the promised coming (often Mount Ararat in the Caucasus, the final resting place of Noah's ark).

With their millenarian prophecies and their openness to God's spontaneous and direct intervention, the Molokan-Jumpers embodied two important aspects of modernity: a forward-looking conception of time and the possibility of individual transformation or self-fashioning. As the sociologist Göran Therborn has argued, modernity is best defined as a culture with "a time conception looking forward to this worldly future, open, novel, reachable or constructable, a conception seeing the present as a possible preparation for a future, and the past either as something to leave behind or as a heap of ruins, pieces of which might be used for building a new future."[8] Unlike the large body of amillennial Old Believers—Orthodox Christians who rejected the liturgical reforms of the seventeenth century and idealized the golden age of the Muscovite past—the Molokan-Jumpers sought their golden age in Christ's future terrestrial kingdom foretold by their prophets. In this respect, they resembled the millenarian Calvinists whose theological vision gave birth to Western modernity, according to Weber. Likewise, God's spontaneous, direct, unmediated intervention in the world opened up dramatic possibilities for individual transformation.

Were the Molokans agents of modernity? Russian Orthodox heresiologists and policy makers who dealt with the Spiritual Christians on the contrary initially portrayed them as ignorant, rude, unlearned peasants, whose religious dissent was an expression of their primitive, atavistic state. Alexander I's instructions in 1816 to the governor of Kherson concerning the Dukhobors illustrate this attitude. The error of the Dukhobors, the tsar explained, arose from their "lack of enlightenment: for they have zeal for God, but not according to reason." The tsar then drew the logical conclusion from the premise that religious dissenters needed education administered by wise and patient teachers: "The teaching of the savior of the world, who came to earth to seek and save the lost, cannot be imparted by violence and executions. . . . The true faith is birthed by the grace of God through conviction, through instruction, through meekness, and above all through kind examples."[9] A standard Orthodox approach toward religious dissent also emphasized the backwardness and ignorance of those who had willfully departed from the true faith. Andrei Filippovich Leopol'dov (1800–1875), in his 1839 statistical description of the Saratov diocese, condemned Molokanism as "rude superstition and obstinate ignorance."[10] Likewise, in the first major published study of the Molokans in Russia, which appeared anonymously in the church journal *Orthodox Conversationalist (Pravoslavnyi sobesednik)* in 1858, Grigorii Pokrovskii chided the Molokans for their "blind faith."[11]

Public attitudes toward the Molokans (and religious dissent in general) began to change during the Great Reforms of the 1860s and 1870s, when the Russian state sought to modernize after its humiliating defeat in the Crimean War (1853–56). The reforms affected every area of public life and included the abolition of serfdom (1861), a new university statute (1863), implementation of public jury trials (1864), the institution of limited self-government (1864), introduction of universal military service (1874), major investments in primary education, the expansion of the press, relaxation of censorship, and the legalization of new voluntary philanthropic and service organizations. With a freer press and public trials of religious dissenters, educated Russians debated the question of religious freedom on the pages of their newspapers and gazettes. In this new atmosphere, some progressive voices portrayed the Molokans as champions of rationality and modernity. In 1865, Aleksandr Herzen's Russian Free Press, based in Geneva, published (anonymously) the Saratov Molokan Ivan Andreevich Pashatskii's *Confession of Faith of the Spiritual Christians, Commonly Known as Molokans.*[12] Arguing for a reasonable religion of the mind as well as the heart, Pashatskii proclaimed that "a faith is good not because it is old, but because it is true."[13] In 1869, the historian of Ukrainian and Russian culture Nikolai Ivanovich Kostomarov published a sympathetic sketch of the Molokans of Saratov Province in the liberal journal *Notes of the Fatherland.*

A few months later, in the same journal, Anna Petrovna Philibert (née Shipilova), the wife of a wealthy landowner of Swiss extraction in Tauride Province, lauded the local Molokans as harbingers of modernity, who were disciplined, hardworking, successful entrepreneurs, running large and profitable ranches in "beautiful and well-constructed villages."[14]

Populist intellectuals echoed this praise. Aleksandr Stepanovich Prugavin (1850–1920), in his idealized vision of Molokan life, observed:

> The Molokans are strangers to fanaticism and are distinguished by their tolerance, which is unusual in the sectarian world. In their meetings, they invite each visitor to speak, and they allow representatives of other religions to make speeches and sermons, no matter how much they differ from their teaching.
>
> They are almost all literate. Many are learned and intellectually developed. . . . In their everyday domestic life, Molokans are distinguished by their work ethic, sobriety, and devotion to home. Mutual aid is so well developed in their congregations that, thanks to it, one never finds poor, homeless, or landless peasants in their midst.[15]

The modern values of tolerance, reasoned debate, literacy, and a strong work ethic characterized the Molokans as Prugavin knew them.

Conservatives, too, increasingly recognized the close connection between the religious dissenters and the "modernity" of the Great Reforms. In a sermon delivered at the local seminary, A. Spasskii, an archpriest of Voronezh Province (an important center of the Molokan movement), complained about the naive views of Russian liberals, who denied the pernicious nature of religious dissent:

> Our quasi-liberal world not only doesn't see anything condemnable in this heresy but is even ready to regard it as the awakening of Russian popular thought, which is striving to achieve a rational, conscious understanding of faith and morality and which wants to shake off the tight shackles of false clericalism. Behind this pious pretext, the worshippers of freedom of conscience make every effort to increase the rights of the schismatics or in other words to give honor and protection to schism.[16]

In fact, Spasskii continued, religious freedom was nothing more than license. Religious sectarianism was simply part of the pernicious pathology of modernity, a consequence of the rapid pace of reform:

> The sharp transition from the strict regime of the past to the new autonomous life (which has been poorly prepared) has had a debilitating

effect on the entire structure of the moral life of society. A person who is enticed by freedom cannot understand that he doesn't yet know how to use his freedom. Instead of freedom he makes personal caprice the watchword of his actions. Morally and spiritually weak, a slave to sensuality and passions, he gives himself over completely to his lower impulses. To justify his carnal life, he begins to seek a new political structure, a new religion, and a new church.[17]

The Molokans' refusal to venerate icons, observe the fasts, or obey their priests was simply their way of satisfying human lusts. Reacting to the increasing numbers of religious sectarians who rejected Russia's official religions after the 1861 emancipation, Spasskii underscored the political implications of the Molokans' religious views. Yes, the Molokans were agents of modernity, but this modernity was a social ill.

Like their conservative rivals, Russian revolutionaries also saw the Molokans as potential allies in the struggle against autocracy. So promising were these Russian peasants who eschewed Orthodox rituals for the reasoned pursuit of truth through the study of scripture that many populist revolutionaries hoped to find a sympathetic ear for socialism among the Molokans. Such hopes were generally disappointed. During the 1873 "Going to the People" movement, for example, the young Lev Grigor'evich Deich (1855–1941) found that the Constant Molokans of Astrakhanka near Melitopol' were not at all receptive to his message. Rather than blame the tsar or the government for their troubles, the Molokans blamed alcoholism. One Molokan explained to Deich the real reason for their most recent problems: "Debauchery has arrived among us. In times past, none of us ever even mentioned anything about drinking wine, but nowadays a tavern has opened. Someone who goes in can never get out, and his household turns to ashes."[18] They also extolled the virtues and the rewards of hard work, and they rejected Deich's call for common ownership of the land. Deich himself concluded, "The conception we had formed [of the Molokans] by reading old books and journal articles did not correspond in any way to reality. The living conditions of the followers of this sect and their personal qualities did not make them any more receptive to socialist propaganda than Orthodox peasants. Freed from state persecution, the Molokans were satisfied by their conviction of the perfection of their religion and the relatively high prosperity that they had achieved."[19]

And yet, many Molokans did harbor strong resentments against state and church officials who discriminated against them. In the 1830s, when the Russian state forcibly deported thousands of Molokans from their homes to the violent frontier in the Caucasus, the aggrieved believers found comfort in the words of the prophet Isaiah, who spoke of a day when men would cast away their images and "Assur" would fall (31:7–8). The Slavonic word for Assyrian (Assur) was the prophet's code word for Russia: spelled backward, Assur became "Russa."[20] The police also uncovered evidence that Molokans forged passports, smuggled goods, and hid deserters as they waited for God's judgment on the idolatrous Russian Orthodox Church.[21] Molokan prophets identified the seven Orthodox ecumenical councils with the seven heads of the beast of Revelation 13. In 1857, the most influential of the Jumper prophets, the peasant wheelwright Maksim Gavrilovich Rudometkin (ca. 1818–1877), declared himself to be the "king of spirits"; he fervently denounced the tsars as the forerunners of the Antichrist and the state church as a fomenter of idolatry. Arrested in 1858, Rudometkin spent the next nineteen years in monastic confinement, which ended only with his death—or his mysterious occultation—in 1877. (Even today, some of Rudometkin's followers claim that he has never died and await his return to establish the millennial kingdom.) While imprisoned, Rudometkin stayed in contact with his followers by smuggling out small notebooks of prophetic writings, which condemned Orthodox monks and priests, arrayed "in purple and in heels like a woman prostitute."[22] Alluding to the Russian state symbol of the two-headed eagle, Rudometkin lamented, "Now all our land is everywhere and in every way occupied by the proud, two-headed authority of the Devil and Satan—or to speak more directly, of the monks and tsars cursed by God."[23] Copied, recopied, and circulated in Molokan communities for decades, Rudometkin's prophecies only began to be published after the 1905 revolution.[24]

Yet even Rudometkin's bitter critique of the Russian state and church would have disappointed Deich and his revolutionary colleagues. The Molokans looked to God for their salvation in both this world and the next; Rudometkin called not for a revolutionary uprising but for faithful obedience to God's commands. Divine intervention, not the force of human arms, would usher in the millennial kingdom. Of all the Molokans, the Jumpers issued the fiercest condemnations of the tsarist regime, but they also were the strongest proponents of pacifism. Identifying their community with the apocalyptic woman, clothed with the sun, whom Satan tried to destroy (Rev. 12), the Molokan-Jumpers trusted that God would miraculously provide a refuge for them, just as he had for her. This conviction and the sacred narrative of divinely mandated exodus (*pokhod*) led the Molokans to mass migration—first, to Russia's frontiers on the Volga and in the Caucasus and, later, to the United States.

In the last decades of the Russian Empire, the Molokans were not only products of modernity but also agents of modernity. Their forward-looking conception of time, their vision of a this-worldly kingdom of God on earth, their spiritual techniques of self-fashioning, and their defense of their rights as a community had powerful implications for the development of Russian society as a whole. Leading intellectuals, from the Bolshevik Vladimir Bonch-Bruevich to the novelist Count Leo Tolstoy, recognized the significance of the "sectarians," who offered alternative worldviews, politics, and sense of justice. By the 1905 revolution, even some Orthodox clerics expressed admiration for the Molokans' success in business, evangelism, community building, and sobriety.[25]

The Molokans in America: A Test of Liberal Modernity

The Molokan spiritual vision of human equality and of the possibility of direct communication with the divine often placed them in conflict with the Russian authorities. This was especially true of the Jumpers, that branch of the Molokan faith that held to the eschatological promise that Christ would soon establish his thousand-year reign on earth. This promise led some Molokans to seek a new life in the United States, where they believed that they would be free from the universal military obligation that the modernizing Russian state had imposed on them as part of the Great Reforms. Beginning in 1904, approximately five thousand Molokans made the trek to the United States. Most traveled to the cities of Los Angeles and San Francisco, where they were able to find work, but many still longed to create an agrarian community. By growing their own food, they could more easily follow the Old Testament dietary restrictions that they continued to observe. Farming also offered a defense against the wiles of the Antichrist, whose imminent reign would create a worldwide famine. In the late summer of 1911, a group of 170 Molokans arrived in Glendale, Arizona, where they planned to establish their community of faith.[26]

The promised *freedom* of liberal modernity enticed the Molokans to the United States, but the *power* of the modern state to mobilize its population in wartime led to conflict with the new immigrants. In moving from the Russian Caucasus to the United States, the Spiritual Christians fled not only the draft but also the social and legal categories that had marginalized them. In Russia, where religion was a public matter of state and recorded in each subject's internal passport, the Molokans were classified as dangerous sectarians, and neither their religion (before 1905) nor their pacifism (before 1917) was legally recognized. By contrast in the United States, religion was a private affair and certainly not recorded in state-issued identification cards; in their adopted country, which admitted no established church, the Molokans could reasonably hope to escape the legal burdens of being heretics. But the Molokans also found themselves in the middle of a changing racialized hierarchy that was becoming encoded into law and economic policy. In 1917, the Molokans' objections to registration for the draft led them to be prosecuted in their adopted country.

Although the principle of equality under law was clearly stated in its founding documents, the United States also enshrined white male supremacy into its legal and social codes. Laws forbade miscegenation and enforced racial segregation; real estate covenants and the rules, written or unwritten, of elite social clubs prevented members of "undesirable" races from threatening white dominance. By contrast, the Russian Empire, which, like the United States, had an extremely diverse population, rejected equality out of hand. The rights and privileges of a subject of the autocratic tsar-father were determined largely by religion, gender, and social estate (*soslovie*). The dominant Russian social hierarchies were not race and class, as in the United States, but religion and *soslovie*. While the US Constitution enjoined Congress from prohibiting the free exercise of religion, which was regarded as a protected individual right, the Russian state openly favored the established Orthodox Church and extended certain rights only to recognized religious confessions. On the one hand, unlike the United States, the Russian state strictly regulated religion and sought to discourage and eliminate "heretical" groups that lay outside the list of privileged faiths. On the other hand, race played almost no role in Russian social hierarchies; the great-grandfather of Russia's illustrious national poet, Aleksandr Sergeevich Pushkin (1799–1837), was Abram Petrovich Gannibal (1696–1781), a black African slave who was adopted by Peter the Great and who became a privileged member of the Russian gentry.[27] Many Russian nobles, such as the Iusupovs and the Kasimovs, proudly traced their ancestry back to the great Mongol conqueror Genghis Khan at the same time that the United States was passing legislation such as the Chinese Exclusion Act (1882) to keep Chinese, Japanese, and Mongolians from coming to its shores.

These Russian pacifists arrived in the Arizona territory, where race and gender hierarchies were being developed in legal, social, and scientific discourse. By 1911, the growing numbers of Slavic immigrants in the mining industry, and the radicalization of the mining laborers by the International Workers of the World, led local elites to express greater anxiety about these ethnic groups and their alien religions, customs, and languages. Significantly, local newspapers initially welcomed the Molokans as "progressive men" who would soon become "able and influential citizens."[28]

When they first arrived, the Molokans were celebrated as successful, far-sighted entrepreneurs, agents of liberal modernity. Real estate developers, anxious to make a profit on farmland near Glendale, Arizona, arranged an entire media campaign to ensure that their clients would be accepted by the civic leaders who read and wrote for the newspapers in the territorial capital. A month before the Spiritual Christians came to Glendale, the *Arizona Republican* reported on their expected arrival. A. A. Betts, a representative of the Santa Fe railroad, which conveyed the Molokans from Los Angeles, noted, "They are a good class of people . . . and just the kind of people that will be able to take hold of things and make a success of farming here. They dress very quietly, but they dress well, but not in such a way that the strength of their bodies is in the least concealed." In his effort to prepare the civil society of Phoenix, Arizona, for the arrival of these Russian immigrants, Betts articulated the values of modernity. The immigrants were strong, hardworking, and self-disciplined. Their dress was unusual (later reporters will speak of the "quaint garb" of the Molokans' native land), but did not hide the essential strength that would allow them to succeed on the Arizona soil. In his efforts to reassure the newspaper readers, Betts hastened to add, "No one must expect to see a crowd of peasant hoodlums." On the contrary, the Russian immigrants "are an extraordinary race in their physical development." They are "as moral a crowd of men as I have ever seen," he stated, and "will give the police courts no trouble for they are law abiding, and industrious, not addicted to drink, or any form of dissipation." Moreover, they valued education, and had requested their own school from the territorial superintendent of public instruction. They were frugal and financially responsible, for they were able to put a 20 percent down payment on the land that they bought for $200,000. Most importantly, their labor was needed for the new Glendale sugar beet factory: "The arrival of these people in the valley will effectually settle the labor problem for the Southwestern Sugar and Land company, as they are hard workers, and will be ready for the mill every day during the rush season." In short, Betts concluded, "These people are intelligent, religious, and the very material from which the best grade of American citizenship is manufactured."[29]

Like the Italians and Serbs who had come to work in Arizona's flourishing mines, these Russian farmers were prime candidates for entry into the dominant white race. But when, in 1917, their pacifist convictions led the Spiritual Christians to protest collectively against registration for the selective service, Arizonan civil society deliberately compared them to Indian "savages" or to the despised Chinese. The Molokans' religious convictions against war, their vision of a collective Christian community, and their apocalyptic understanding of world history alienated them from the Arizona mainstream. This historical example demonstrates how religion—as well as race, gender, class, and language—was used in the "invention of the white race."[30]

In fact, the very notion of "whiteness" as a racial category was in the process of being constructed both formally, as a legal category, and less formally, in habits, usages, and customs. Race was a fluid category in the early twentieth century, and in Arizona different systems of racial hierarchies competed with one another. For example, the racial system in Tucson, with its elite Mexican creole families, was radically different than the one that prevailed in the mining town of Bisbee, founded in 1881 as a "white man's camp," where Mexicans were deliberately excluded from the privileges conferred by "whiteness." Different ecologies also affected racial hierarchies; the ranching culture, which had been largely created by Mexicans, promoted a different concept of "whiteness" from the increasingly dominant industrialized mining culture.[31] Different racial hierarchies, different conceptions of race, might be dominant in different contexts. For example, Arizona's anti-miscegenation law of 1901 (and its adjudication in the courts) implicitly classified Mexican Americans as "whites," but Mexican Americans increasingly suffered institutional discrimination on the job and in schools.[32]

The Spiritual Christian Molokan-Jumpers sought to fit into this new landscape. They took out deeds, insured their homes, and informed the local newspapers about their activities. In 1912, when Mikhail Pivovarov (Mehaeel Pivavaroff), the preceptor of the Arizona congregation, traveled to Los Angeles to celebrate the Feast of Tabernacles (*kushcha*) with the Spiritual Christian Jumper Molokans there, the *Arizona Republican* dutifully reported that he had "returned from an 8 day celebration in the Los Angeles Russian colony," just as it reported on the vacations, marriages, divorces, and business trips of other members of Phoenix society.[33] The paper did not explain that the eight-day celebration had been commanded by God through the prophet Maksim Rudometkin while he was in monastic imprisonment; it did not say that the feast represented the coming thousand-year reign of Christ, which the Jumpers believed was imminent. In other words, the newspaper did not give any clue about the apocalyptic hope that would lead to conflict in June 1917, when the men of the Arizona Jumper Molokan colony refused to register for the draft.

Shaped by this vision, which included the formation of an egalitarian Christian commune, the Glendale Molokans proved to be the most uncompromising opponents of selective service registration. When the First World War broke out in 1914, the Glendale Molokans began preparing to resist military service. In the summer of 1915, as their brothers in Russia were compelled to fight on the Allied side, the Molokans of Glendale demonstrated their commitment to pacifism by publicly burning their single firearm in a park outside the Phoenix courthouse.[34] Less than two years later, on April 6, 1917, the

United States declared war on the German Empire and began mobilizing its population; the Selective Service Act of May 18, 1917, required all men between the ages of twenty-one and thirty to register for the draft.[35] The large community of Molokan-Jumpers in Los Angeles responded immediately to the threat of conscription by formally registering a protest with the county clerk. In their formal affidavit, 259 Molokans declared that "their religious convictions . . . do not admit military service or carrying of arms" and that they "cannot on the strength of these religious views, enter any existing armies."[36] A few days later, a delegation including the leaders of the Los Angeles and Glendale communities traveled to Washington, DC, to present their petition in person. After meeting with the delegation, General Enoch H. Crowder (1859–1932), the US provost marshal, assured the Molokans: "Registration is not enlistment in military service. It creates in and of itself no obligation to perform any military service." On the contrary, it offered the opportunity for adherents of pacifist religious movements to be identified so that they could be excused from combatant service.[37]

Such assurances (which were also given by the Arizona authorities) held little sway with the most radical members of the Spiritual Christian community in Glendale, however. The Selective Service Act exempted religious pacifists from combatant service, but not from all service; all Americans were expected to support the war effort. But the spiritual revival that swept Molokan congregations in the 1910s emphasized the absolute value of peace, the imminence of Christ's millennial kingdom, the need for individual purity, and the preciousness of life. Although most Molokans were not vegetarian, the most committed members in Arizona gave up meat. In preparation for their response to the registration requirement, the Glendale colony began a communal, three-day fast. God's answer was clear and unambiguous. One prophet declared the registration was the mark of the Beast. The next day, the prophet Masha Valova assured her community of God's support: "The Lamb is amongst you. He shall go with you. Do not have any doubts, for not one hair on your head will be lost."[38]

On the day appointed for registration, June 5, 1917, the community held a prayer service and then marched together to downtown Glendale to protest.[39] Like the elect souls standing before the throne of the Lamb (Rev. 7:8), the Molokans were dressed in white clothing. The men wore a traditional shirt, the long-sleeved *kosovorotka*, buttoned on the left side with a short, stand-up collar. Women wore white ankle-length skirts with a high-necked blouse and a headscarf. After singing a hymn, about three hundred members of the community marched to the registration site in downtown Glendale.[40] A local businessman, Dwight B. Heard (1869–1929), the publisher of a local newspaper and chair of the State Council of Defense, tried for three hours to convince the Molokans to obey the law. His efforts, hampered by a large language barrier, succeeded in persuading twenty men to register, but thirty-seven others maintained their principled stance.[41] The newly elected Republican governor of Arizona, Thomas Campbell (1878–1944), met with Molokan leaders on the following day. A strong supporter of the war, Campbell was unable to win over the Molokans, despite the law's provisions for religious pacifists. The Molokans explained to the governor that "their religion forbade them from taking part in a war in any manner whatever."[42]

In August, thirty-four Molokan men who had refused registration were tried, found guilty, and sentenced to serve one year in the Yavapai County jail in Prescott, Arizona. Newspaper coverage racialized the resisters, portraying them as ignorant aliens—a stark contrast to the welcome they had received a few years earlier. One witness admitted that she could not distinguish the Russian colonists as individuals because "they all looked alike to her."[43] After reporting on the Molokans' resistance, one journalist excluded them from the white race by declaring, "So far there has not been a single white man marked as a slacker in this district."[44] During the trial, a large group from the Molokan-Jumper community prayed, sang, and danced outside the federal building on Van Buren Street in downtown Phoenix.[45] Reporters described their hymns and dances as "wild" and "weird," "an orgy of wild jumping," "not unlike that done by Indians at ceremonials."[46] Someone with a movie camera filmed their "fanatical worship"; a few weeks later, two Phoenix cinemas showed footage of the Molokan prayer service as an added bonus for those who bought tickets to see the regular feature—"positively the last opportunity" to see "their queer religious observances," as one advertisement proclaimed.[47]

The modern state exercised its powers of persuasion over the Molokan prisoners, twenty-eight of whom eventually agreed to register by submitting a questionnaire while serving their sentences in the Yavapai County jail. The remaining six recalcitrants refused to provide even this much support for the war effort. Forcibly inducted into the army, they continued their principled refusal to obey the orders that they were given. In the fall of 1918, all six men were court-martialed and given sentences ranging from fifteen years to life at hard labor. Only in 1919, several months after the end of the war, did they receive clemency and were able to return to their homes.[48]

The Molokans' experience in Russia and the United States highlights varieties of modernity in the first decades of the twentieth century. In the modernizing Russian Empire, the Molokans struggled as a persecuted religious minority that only slowly acquired limited legal recognition of its rights. But the modernizing reforms that offered greater freedom for religious dissenters (abolition of serfdom, institution of an independent judiciary, and public trials) also included universal military service, an obligation that bore especially heavily on Spiritual Christian pacifists. For those Molokans most radically devoted to nonviolence (especially the Jumpers who adhered to Maksim Rudometkin's millennial hopes), emigration to a liberal modern republic, with its guarantees of religious freedom, offered one possible solution to the contradictions of Russian modernization. But even the liberal modernity of the United States imposed limits on freedom of conscience, especially in time of war. The uncompromising position of the most radical Molokan-Jumpers of Arizona tested those limits.

The educated elites of imperial Russia cast the Spiritual Christians in three different roles in their grand narratives about modernity. For Tsar Alexander I, the Molokans were obstacles to modernity who needed education, above all, in order to abandon their false doctrines and take their proper place as subjects of an enlightened empire. Russian progressives and revolutionaries, on the contrary, styled the Molokans as heroic agents of liberal modernity. Models of sobriety and self-discipline, they refused to blindly accept authority and instead insisted on thinking for themselves. By the late nineteenth century, conservatives, alarmed by the dramatic growth in the numbers of Christian dissenters, cited the Molokans as a disease of modernity. Russian peasants were simply not ready for the freedom unleashed by the Great Reforms and especially by the emancipation of 1861. In the conditions of modernity, freedom quickly degenerated into license, and lazy sinners turned to heresies that catered to their lusts. The Molokans' unwillingness to submit to true Orthodox pastors was no act of heroism, but a refusal to exercise the virtue of self-control.

Grand narratives of modernity also shaped the reception of the Molokan immigrants to their new home in Arizona. Local real-estate developers portrayed them initially as hardworking, freedom-loving newcomers—the raw material of citizenship for the forty-eighth state. Yet under the exigencies of war, Arizona newspapers turned against the Molokans and sounded very much like Tsar Alexander I. Ignorant fanatics, the Molokans required education and discipline; their stubborn adherence to pacifism in the face of an existential threat to the republic was simply not acceptable.

The biblical vision of peace and equality that some of the Spiritual Christian Jumper Molokans shared challenged the modernizing societies of both Russia and the United States. In Russia, the Spiritual Christians' rejection of the state church led to their exile. In Arizona, where the Jumpers were guaranteed freedom of religious expression, the rhetoric of race played a powerful role in the efforts of the political and social elite to control and repress the

Molokan protest against war. In both cases, the Molokans suffered under modernizing (but not completely "modern") states; the hierarchies of race in the United States and those of religion in the Russian Empire seem out of place in the ideal type of a modern political system. At the same time, it was precisely modernization—the need of the state to control and mobilize its manpower—that led to the persecution of these dissenters.

Devoted to a God who spoke through the scriptures and their prophets, the Molokan community was more complex than any of these grand narratives of modernity allowed. Neither purely "rationalistic" nor purely "mystical" (to use the taxonomies of Russian Orthodox heresiologists), the Molokans became agents of modernity primarily by acting on their vision of the future, Christ's eschatological kingdom of peace. Whether in forming an agrarian commune or publicly protesting against military service, the Molokans acted in light of their divine revelation of the future. By preserving their community of faith, they bore witness to the prophetic promise and sought to reconcile the modernity of freedom with the modernity of power.

CHAPTER 12

Vseedinstvo

A Russian Project of Religious Modernity

Clemena Antonova

The philosophy of "full unity" (*vseedinstvo*), as it was developed within Russian Orthodox religious thought, has its origins in the middle of the nineteenth century and its high point toward the end of the Russian Silver Age (the period roughly between the 1880s and 1920s), when it was explored in greater depth by some of the leading Russian thinkers of the early twentieth century. In brief, it is a philosophy that rests on several key principles. Human consciousness is unified and, therefore, knowledge is unified. The process whereby the "whole man," or, to borrow Fyodor Dostoyevsky's expression, *vsechelovek*, strives to achieve integral knowledge of the Truth is a step on the road to man's union with God, which is the purpose of Christian life. At heart, "full unity" is Sophia, or Divine Wisdom, which penetrates the creaturely world. The deification of man understood as the union of God and man is predicated on Sophia being present in humanity as the image of God in man, a truth that, in turn, confers essential dignity and worth to the human being.

As such, this is a philosophy that contains numerous pitfalls, and it is also one that is not as uniquely Russian as its representatives and its followers claim. However, within this philosophy are insights that can contribute to a new way of looking at contemporary debates on religion, secularism, and modernity. In particular, this philosophy can add a new dimension to two twenty-first century intellectual trends: the discussion surrounding the "religious turn" in present-day culture and the religious genealogy of modern, ostensibly secular, concepts (such as human rights, for example). These present-day debates have largely ignored the insights of Russian Orthodox religious philosophers, but interlocutors could benefit from engaging with this aspect of the Russian intellectual experience.

In essence, the Orthodox Russian philosophical project of the late nineteenth and early twentieth centuries was one of "religious modernity."[1] This contradicts a conventional, but unexamined, view that Orthodox Christian religious thought is, almost by definition, traditionalist and anti-modern. What makes Orthodox religious philosophy unique, in my view, is the brand of "religious modernity" it offers—a religiosity that embraces, and even presupposes, characteristics that are commonly seen as aspects of secularity. In this way, it challenges the much-debated concept of secularism.[2]

It is well-known that the period referred to as the Russian Silver Age was one of the most vibrant and exciting in twentieth-century cultural history. Avant-garde experiments in painting, the cinema, the theater, and music put Russia in the forefront of the emergence of modernism. Symbolism, the revival of occultism and of Platonic idealism, and the renewed interest in German romantic philosophy and in Friedrich Nietzsche further enriched the intellectual landscape. Uniting all these seemingly disparate developments was the idea that religion and modernity belonged together. In many ways and under different forms, there was a fusion of a revived religiosity (in many cases, Orthodox Christian) with an ostensibly secular modernism.

It is noteworthy that these developments, when reflected within the religious philosophy of the *vseedintsy* (the representatives of *vseedinstvo*), frequently ran counter to the positions of the Russian Orthodox Church. In fact, almost all the members of the movement had a tense or at least an ambiguous relationship with the official church. Sergei Bulgakov was almost excommunicated in the 1930s by the Russian Church Abroad. Pavel Florenskii, a priest, who never broke with the church was, at the same time, a vocal supporter of teachings that the Russian Church had declared heretical in no uncertain terms.[3] In other words, it cannot be emphasized enough that the most exciting ideas during what was called "the Russian Religious Renaissance" at the beginning of the twentieth century were formulated almost entirely outside the channels provided by the church and frequently were opposed by the church hierarchy.[4]

The Russian Concept of Full Unity: Problems and Potential

Russian philosophers and theologians have described the "philosophical school of full unity" as "distinguishable from other schools and philosophical trends in Russia."[5] This school, founded by Vladimir Solov'ev (1853–1900), is based on the "originality of the conception of full unity."[6] Its main representatives were the brothers Sergei and Evgenii Trubetskoi, Bulgakov, V. F. Ern, and Florenskii. In *The Russian Idea*, Nikolai Berdiaev, probably the best-known Russian philosopher in the West, proposed already in the late 1940s that the "totalitarian character" of thought (a description he derived from the term *total unity*) constitutes a "peculiar originality" of Russian religious philosophy.[7] Similarly, another Russian émigré, Vasilii Zenkovsky, also discusses what he calls the "metaphysics of total-unity."[8]

The English translation of *vseedinstvo* has varied from "total unity" and "pan-unity" to "spiritual unity."[9] My own preference for "full unity" is dictated by a concern to avoid the association with pantheism ("pan-unity"), with the political totalitarianism that came to be associated with Stalinism and Nazism ("total unity"), and with the value-laden opposition between the spiritual and the material ("spiritual unity"). Keeping these connotations at bay is important. Indeed, Russian *vseedinstvo* was used to combat pantheism, totalitarian politics (especially in the 1930s and 1940s), and the dichotomy between spiritual and material. "Full unity" is also meant to convey the idea of indivisibility, that is, a whole as prior to its parts in contrast to a whole as divisible and an aggregate.[10]

Now, while it is noticeable that some of the figures associated with "full unity" have received extensive scholarly attention both in Russia and, to a lesser extent, in the West, they are rarely studied against the background of the *vseedinstvo* movement, nor, in the cases when "full unity" is mentioned, does the critical literature make it clear what the concept means. There are several major studies on Solov'ev, the founder of the movement, by thinkers who were profoundly influenced by "full unity," but also by later scholars, both in Russia and in the West.[11] The émigré philosopher Bulgakov is the subject of a few major monographs in English and dozens of studies in Russian.[12] There is an enormous literature on Florenskii in Russia, where he is considered by some scholars as the country's most important thinker of the twentieth century.[13] At the same time, little effort has been made to study these thinkers precisely as proponents of the philosophy of "full unity."[14]

There are two main factors, I believe, that plague any serious engagement with the Russian philosophy of "full unity." The first is the understandable suspicion of holistic theories in the aftermath of the "totalitarian experiment in the twentieth century."[15] After all, as history has demonstrated, holistic conceptions have hovered in the background of progressive, positive, even if sometimes utopian, philosophical and political beliefs but also of some of the most repugnant and destructive ideologies in modern times. The ideals of communality, togetherness, and man as an all-rounded and complete being have their counterpart in totalitarianism and related ideas. In a major study of the origins of Nazism, Richard Evans finds that "the most important aspect of Nazi ideology was its emphasis on social solidarity,"[16] an aspect that predominated over the cult of Hitler or antisemitism. All this is relevant to the Russian project and not only because it explains why "full unity" sounds much more ambivalent today than it did at the end of the nineteenth and the beginning of the twentieth centuries. An awareness of the dangers inherent in totalitarian projects makes one realize the need for a constructive development of ideas, associated with "full unity." This is especially so when we take into account the overall philosophical positions of the *vseedinstsy*. Florenskii was openly antisemitic, as was Dostoyevsky. There is an undercurrent of nationalism and xenophobia in much of the movement, while the rejection of Enlightenment rationalism cuts across the writings of all of the *vseedintsy*, from Solov'ev to Florenskii.

The second factor, especially pertinent for theologians, is the discomfort with the Sophiology at the root of many conceptions of full unity, often because Sophiology has been dogged by repeated accusations of heresy. This is a problem, because it seems to me that any serious study of "full unity" in the Russian context will touch on a Sophiological, Eastern Orthodox religious perspective of the world. It is not by accident that all the *vseedintsy*, from Solov'ev to Florenskii, were Sophiologists.[17]

Why attract attention to the Russian project at all in this case? The answer is that with all the problems that it poses, it also advances valuable ideas, which can be developed in ways that are meaningful to present-days situations.

For these Russian thinkers, the concept of *vseedinstvo* was used to cover a wide range of phenomena; it was applied to human consciousness, to the world as a whole, to the relationship between the subject and object in the process of knowledge, to the relationship between the imminent and the transcendent, between man and God, also to the notion of a universal church, and so on. All these connotations, however, are interconnected and represent a belief in the underlying connectedness of Being. Though different figures within the movement focused on different aspects of *vseedinstvo*, all of them were interested in the question of how "full unity" could become a value accessible to man.

One of the most important practical values of the philosophy of "full unity" was its assistance in attaining *"tsel'noe znanie,"* that is, "integral knowledge."[18] The notion that knowledge is one and that it is revealed to the whole man, who exercises all his powers of cognition (rationality, mystical intuition, aesthetic perception, and so forth), was very important for the earlier, so-called Slavophile philosophers, Aleksei Khomiakov (1804–1860) and Ivan Kireevskii (1806–1856). The Slavophiles wrote about the "inner wholeness of self-consciousness" and condemned Western thought for separating reason from "its original unity with the other faculties of the human spirit."[19] They called for an "inner wholeness of the mind for the comprehension of integral truth" through a "coordination of all cognitive powers into a single force."[20] Solov'ev, who was the direct intellectual descendant of the Slavophiles, never tired of emphasizing the need for an "organic synthesis of theology, philosophy, and the experimental sciences." "Only such a synthesis," in his view, "can comprise the whole truth of knowledge."[21]

The discussion of full unity and, especially, of integral knowledge, from Khomiakov and Kireevskii, through Solov'ev and to Florenskii, was invariably couched in terms of the opposition between the allegedly fragmented nature of Western philosophy and the full unity of Russian religious philosophical inquiry. As Kireevskii wrote in his essay "On the Nature of European Culture and on Its Relationship to Russian Culture" (1852), in Western philosophy reason was "separated from its original unity with the other faculties of the human spirit."[22] The twin towers of Gothic churches became "the symbol of this dichotomy."[23] Later in the century, the notion of "the universal and all-unifying Russian soul," which underlay Dostoyevsky's famous speech on Aleksandr Pushkin, belonged to the same discourse and formed the background of Dostoyevsky's definition of the Russian as a "universal man" (*vsechelovek*), whose task was to "bring an ultimate reconciliation to Europe's contradictions."[24]

Ironically, most Russian thinkers failed to acknowledge the Western philosophical contributions to the concept of full unity.[25] Ultimately, the origins of full unity go back at least to Plato and the Neo-Platonists, and full unity owes a considerable debt to the church fathers and medieval Christian mysticism.[26] More centrally, the works of German romantic philosophy (the term in German is *All-Einheit*) directly influenced the Slavophiles and their intellectual progeny.[27] G. W. F. Hegel's philosophy, much of which can be read as an elaboration of his slogan "The true is the whole" was important, though not always acknowledged.[28] The German *All-Einheit* resonated among nineteenth-century theologians such as Jakob Sengler, who in his *Der Idee Gottes* (1845) interpreted the term as a pantheistic, anti-Christian concept. No one, however, had an influence comparable to that of Friedrich Schelling.[29] Schelling's powerful evocation of aesthetic unity/wholeness, and his notion of art as "theurgy" (that is, the ability of art to embody transcendental form), made him indispensable, for example, to Florenskii's critique of the medieval icon. More surprising perhaps is the contribution of Baruch Spinoza, who rejected the traditional Judeo-Christian concepts of the divine, to the Russian religious philosophical understanding of full unity.

In short, the Russian religious-philosophical concept of "full unity" was developed out of a philosophical heritage that was largely Western, pagan (or outside mainstream Christianity), or even anti-religious. In this sense, it illustrates once again the futility of attempting to draw a clear-cut opposition between Russia and the West. As we saw, the Russians themselves—the representatives of full unity, as well as Russian scholars, mostly émigrés to the West, who have been promoting the movement abroad—have passionately insisted on the uniqueness and originality of *vseedinstvo*. Their motivation largely grows from the inherited Slavophile tradition, first articulated in the 1820s, of viewing Russia and the Russian people (*narod*) as having a special role to play in world history. These nineteenth-century ideas of national purpose cast a shadow over the Silver Age as well and provided the background against which the opposition between Russia and the West was formulated.

Russian Orthodox intellectuals believed that their mission lay in Christianizing the Western intellectual tradition, precisely because the crisis of modernity was seen very much as a consequence of modern man's turning away from God. As Solov'ev wrote in a letter of 1873: "It is now clear to me as two times two is four that the whole great development of Western philosophy and science, apparently indifferent and often hostile to Christianity, has in fact merely elaborated for Christianity a new form—one that is worthy of it."[30] What the Orthodox philosophers attempted to do was to take the concept of full unity, thoroughly Christianize it, and make it more compatible with Orthodox Christianity, while keeping and further developing the modern idiom. The originality of the Russian project very likely lies in the specific ways in which Russian philosophers infused a Christian Orthodox religious spirit into a holistic modernist framework of meaning. Probably no one had a better right than Florenskii, who was deeply immersed in Western philosophy and science and was at the same time whole-heartedly committed to a Christian worldview, to say along with Saint Paul, "I capture every thought to make it obedient to Christ" (2 Cor.). Indeed, for Florenskii and for the whole Russian tradition, it is faith that is "the pillar and the ground of truth."[31] It is, therefore, important to realize that all studies on art, philosophy, mathematics, and so on by representatives of the school of full unity are grounded in a profoundly felt and thought-through Christian worldview. Florenskii's call that "we should philosophize *in* religion" and his view that philosophy is "valuable not in itself . . . but for the life in Christ" apply to all fields of intellectual investigation.[32] Thus, with the whole Russian religious-philosophical tradition that we are looking at, "full unity" has an unmistakably positive, religious, and salvific coloring.

It is largely because of figures like Florenskii—a mathematician turned priest and theologian with dozens of technological patents in his name—that there is a danger of becoming fascinated by the Russian philosophical enterprise as an interdisciplinary exercise. This, however, would be misleading. If we understand interdisciplinarity as insights from different disciplines that, when brought together, can illuminate a certain problem in frequently unexpected and intellectually exciting ways, then it is not a good description of the Russian philosophical project at the turn of the century. For the Russian philosophers, it was the duty of man to strive to know the Truth by bringing together the scattered facets of the one Truth, and this duty was religious in nature. Florenskii expressed this in a letter to his mother, in which he vowed to "conduct a synthesis of ecclesiastical and profane culture, to integrate with the church, but without compromise and with honesty, to apprehend the positive doctrine of the church, the scientific and philosophical worldviews, and so on."[33] The mission of restoring the lost unity of secular and religious reason that he refers to was common to all the *vseedintsy*. In the language of Eastern Orthodox theology that the Russians themselves were using, the whole project of integral knowledge and the implied unity of secular and religious reason were part of the process of *theosis*, or deification, the aim of which was the union between man and God.[34]

This philosophy—of the unified human consciousness, of the "whole" man, of the universal penetration of Divine Wisdom into the created world, and of the deification of man as the union of God and man—can be interpreted as a specifically Christian Orthodox response to secularization, which the *vseedintsy* saw as lying at the heart of the crisis of modernity. To secularization, understood as the death of God in modern times, the Russians opposed a profoundly thought-through philosophy of the Sophianization of the world, an awareness of God's presence through Sophia in the whole of creation. In this sense, "full unity" is very much a project of "religious modernity." In many ways, this project failed, as it could not produce a convincing philosophical explanation of the world that would decisively supplant the Western, Enlightenment, and post-Enlightenment framework. It proved too vague, too utopian, and it was riddled with various philosophical and theological problems. The main contribution of the philosophy of full unity, in my reading, was to further open Christian thought to modernity. Philosophers such as Solov'ev and Bulgakov may not have come out with the solutions to the problems of modernity, but they attracted attention, to an unprecedented extent, to questions that are still relevant and urgent, especially to those concerned with the role of religion in the modern world.

The Relevance of Russian Religious Philosophy Today: Religion and Modernity

Unlike Russian literature, which holds a significant place within the Western canon, Russian philosophy has remained highly marginal and is, generally, familiar only to a small group of specialists. It is certainly likely that a person well-read in Leo Tolstoy and Dostoyevsky would have little or no idea about Sophiology, "full unity," "integral knowledge," and so forth. Interestingly, some Russian scholars have suggested that there was a moment at the beginning of the twentieth century when it seemed that "philosophy was definitely ready to replace literature in the role of the leading branch of national culture" in Russia.[35] Communism interrupted abruptly these developments. After all, a philosophy, most of which was of a religious orientation, had no place under the rule of a militantly atheistic regime.

There was a short time during the late Soviet period and especially after 1989 when religious thinkers such as Solov'ev, Florenskii, Evgenii Trubetskoi, and others attracted intense, passionate, and widespread interest. There was even a hope for a "religious renaissance" of the sort that had taken place, in the view of some, at the beginning of the twentieth century.[36] However, this phenomenon soon ended. As Sergei Khoruzhii has noticed, there is no longer the expectation of the late Soviet period that "philosophical wisdom, as well as the solutions to most acute social problems" would come from this quarter.[37] If the Russian philosophical tradition from the late nineteenth and the first half of the twentieth centuries was expected to fill the void left by the disintegrated Soviet system, it has certainly failed to do so. Indeed, the situation in Russia in the past few years shows nationalism and fundamentalism taking center stage rather than the religious-philosophical ideal of "full unity."

At the same time, I believe that there is another contemporary context in which Russian religious philosophy and particularly the movement of "full unity" could prove to be relevant. To an extraordinary degree, Russian religious thinkers at the end of the nineteenth and the beginning of the twentieth centuries were consistently and deeply engaged with some of the very same questions at the intersection of religion, secularism, and modernity that have been at the center of the attention of philosophers and social scientists in the last several decades. It is strikingly obvious that, at present, there is an almost complete lack of a Russian perspective on these questions and very little constructive input from the Eastern Orthodox tradition in general. We need to look more seriously and systematically into the tradition of Russian religious philosophy, which may well offer valuable insights to ongoing discussions on the role of religion in modernity.

The Russian tradition, partly because of the different historical circumstances in which it developed and the different intellectual framework, gave its specific answers to questions that are urgent to us. In the late 1950s, for example, the Russian thinkers whom I have been referring to were among the sources, mainly via French authors, of the discussions leading to the Second Vatican Council.[38] After this period, interest in Russian religious figures noticeably decreased, and, as a rule, at present we do not hear of them in any of the major debates on religion and modernity. Here, I would like to draw attention to several, closely interconnected themes that have become prominent in contemporary debates that were foreshadowed in the trend of Russian religious philosophy under our attention.

In the first place, new secularization theories have challenged and practically left behind the notion that a modern, secular worldview has triumphantly supplanted the old, religious one. As Talal Asad put it, "If anything is agreed upon, it is that a straightforward narrative of progress from the religious to the secular is no longer acceptable."[39] The realization that religion is still a major factor in modernity has become glaringly obvious since 2001 and has been reflected in developments in philosophy, frequently described as the "religious turn."[40]

In the second place, one of the most interesting trends in the history of ideas is the attention being paid to the religious genealogy of what are usually thought of as secular, modern concepts. This trend, going back to Hegelian philosophy, is evident in the work of Charles Taylor, Michael Gillespie, Jürgen Habermas, Samuel Moyn, and others. It has not gone unchallenged, and the debate around it is illuminating on several levels.[41] Peter Gordon, for example, has highlighted some of the problems that he finds in the secularization theory to which Taylor and others subscribe. Most important seems to be Gordon's observation that for Taylor, what offers transcendence is "always and only" a Christian, monotheistic God.[42] For the Russian thinkers under our attention here, this was also very much the case, and this is one of the reasons why the analogies between them and the understanding of secularization exemplified by Taylor is especially relevant.

Both themes—the role of religion in modernity and the religious origins of modern, secular concepts—have their counterparts in the earlier Russian tradition under our attention, which was, as we saw, passionately combating the separation between religious and secular reason and promoting, instead, the claim that religion, secularism, and modernity belonged together. In this context, it was natural to approach modern concepts in their *longue durée* history rather than as fundamentally new responses to modern situations.

The "Religious Turn" in Present-Day Culture

Modernity has been frequently understood as defined by the "death of God" (Nietzsche) and by the "disenchantment of the world" (Max Weber). It is allegedly profoundly secular. This is certainly true in the sense that we no longer live in the unquestioningly religious world of older times. It is, however, just as clear that religion, in one form or another, remains important to millions of people around the world. Some authors have even suggested that we live in "a new age of religious searching, whose outcome no one can foresee."[43] Not only on the level of the individual, but on the level of society at large, religion has taken a new, public role. José Casanova has written about the "deprivatization" of religion since the 1980s, that is, the fact that "religious traditions throughout the world are refusing to accept the marginal and privatized role which theories of modernity as well as theories of secularization had reserved for them."[44] As a result, if religion could be described as "invisible," that is, existing on the margins of culture a couple of decades earlier, it has now become clearly noticeable that religion has entered the "public sphere."[45]

Habermas, the philosopher largely responsible for the popularization of the term, has sought the origins of the "public sphere" in the eighteenth century, particularly in Britain, Germany, and France. What facilitated the rise of the "public sphere" at the time in these countries was exactly the separation between church and state and the distinction between public norms and private beliefs, which was one of the results of this separation.[46] In other words, the initial definition of "public sphere" implies a social space that is radically secularized in a certain sense of the term. However, Habermas himself and other thinkers have drawn attention to the role that religion plays in the public sphere. In an article of 2006, Habermas noted the "unexpected political importance" of religious movements since 1989–90, not only in the Middle East and Africa but also in the United States.[47] Thus, in the words of Taylor, we have ended up with "a kind of public space of a modern kind, . . . a religious identity that fits . . . within a modern-type public space."[48] Authors continue to debate the extent and the various ways in which religion has become an element of the modern public sphere.[49]

It seems to me that it is becoming increasingly obvious that we cannot stick to a worldview that radically excludes the transcendental dimension from human existence. At the same time, there is no way back to a pre-Enlightenment and pre-Reformation Christianity. In *Religion in the Modern World*, Steve Bruce observes that "the fragmentation of religious culture was, in time, to see the widespread, taken-for-granted, and unexamined Christianity of the pre-Reformation period replaced by an equally widespread, taken-for-granted, and unexamined indifference to religion."[50] It is this "taken-for-granted" and "unexamined indifference to religion" that is, I believe, no longer viable in a globalized world in which religion, sometimes in dramatic ways, shows itself increasingly capable of determining many people's identities, allegiances, and worldviews. As Leszek Kołakowski remarked in his essay "Anxiety about God in an Ostensibly Godless Age" (1981), "The breakdown of the old faith and the collapse of the Enlightenment are taking place simultaneously."[51]

The Religious Genealogy of Modern Concepts

The complex role that religion plays in modernity has meant, among other things, that religion faces the need to open itself up to critique, while philosophy, too, has become aware of its religious heritage and of the need to engage with religion. This came across, for instance, in the 2004 dialogue between Joseph Ratzinger (later Pope Benedict XVI) and Habermas, in which the latter commented on the need for philosophy's "self-reflection with regard to its own religious-metaphysical origins."[52] Taylor's award-winning *A Secular Age* (2007) tells the story of the rise of secularism from the spirit of reform within Latin Christianity in the late Middle Ages. Gillespie's *The Theological Origins of Modernity* (2008) is a masterful elaboration of the idea that there is a "metaphysical, theological core of the modern project" and that religion and theology have played a "central role" in "the formation of the idea of modernity."[53] Without reflecting on this, modern man would find himself in the position of "Sophocles' Oedipus, who did not remember his origin."[54] The notion that modernity is the result of the secularization of Christian ideas was voiced earlier, most famously and provocatively by Nietzsche in the late nineteenth century. Nietzsche's observation that "the democratic movement is the inheritance of the Christian movement" was certainly not meant as a compliment to either democracy or Christianity and should be understood in the context of his larger understanding of Christianity as "embodiment of slave-morality, giving advantage to the inferior classes over the better classes of men."[55] In the first half of the twentieth century, several historians concerned themselves with the Christian roots of modern concepts that we tend to think of as secular—Étienne Gilson and Alexandre Koyré in the 1920s and 1930s and Karl Löwith in his *The Meaning of History* (1949).[56] More recently, in 2010, Moyn put forward the controversial argument that the very concept of "human rights" is developed from Catholic personalism, and others have gone so far as to suggest that human rights have become a "secular religion."[57]

The religious genealogy of modern concepts is probably nowhere as striking as in the field of aesthetics. After all, the very possibility for the rise of aesthetics in the eighteenth century has been commonly understood to come as a result of the radical separation of art from religion. In this way, aesthetics needed to develop its own terminology and conceptual apparatus that would be modern and, by definition, secular. Immanuel Kant's aesthetics and its elaboration of the idea of art as "disinterested aesthetic experience," a notion that goes back to eighteenth-century British writers, were largely unchallenged in the Western tradition until the 1960s. At the same time, it is noticeable that while making clear that the aesthetic develops in an entirely different framework than the religious, art critics from the very beginning would consistently describe aesthetic experience in religious terms. The influential eighteenth-century German art critic Karl Philipp Moritz described the "forgetting" of the self in the process of contemplation of the work of art and, thus, as a form of transcendence and revelation. Later on, within the same tradition of formalist thought, the famous art historian Bernard Berenson talks of the experience afforded by the artwork in a language that carries clearly Christian overtones: "In visual art the aesthetic moment is that fleeting instant, so brief as to be almost timeless, when the spectator is at one with the work of art he is looking at. . . . The two become one entity; time and space are abolished. . . . In short, the aesthetic moment is a moment of mystic vision."[58]

However brief and sketchy this overview may be, what comes across almost immediately is that all of the authors cited, who write on the relationship between secularism and Christianity, do so from within an exclusively Western intellectual tradition. Taylor's impressive narrative of the rise of secularism is the story of developments within Latin Christianity. So is Gillespie's study that looks at figures such as William of Ockham, Petrarch, Erasmus, and Luther. The Western perspective is shared by practically all of the major authors in the field of secularization theories nowadays (Habermas, Taylor, Peter L. Berger, and others), apart from those working specifically on the case of Islam (Talal Asad and Tariq Modood, for instance). Of course, already Nietzsche's "death of God" and Weber's "disenchantment of the world" were envisioning developments in Western European civilization.

Russian, or more generally Eastern Orthodox, material is almost entirely missing from these discussions. Of course, some may feel that if modern secularity comes at a certain stage of the development of an exclusively Western Christian tradition, one of the defining features of which was the Reformation, then we do not need a Russian perspective at all. I am suggesting something else. The very absence in Russia of some of the defining moments of the Western secularizing process—the Renaissance, the Reformation, the Counter-Reformation, the Enlightenment—means that for the Russian tradition at the turn of the twentieth century the relationship between religion, secularism, and modernity was much more closely interwoven than in the reigning paradigm in the West at the time. In this way, when contemporary authors suggest that religion, secularism, and modernity exist in a much closer relationship than the mainstream of Western philosophy has implied, they find natural allies in the Russian *vseedintsy*. In fact, many of the questions that are confronting us today were at the heart of Russian religious philosophy, indeed, were part of the repertoire of a national philosophy that understood itself, mainly and above all, as religious thought. At the same time, these problems—in many ways they coincide with the "accursed questions" of Dostoyevsky—were discussed within an intellectual tradition that, while not disconnected from the West, followed its own, very distinct, development. Indeed, to stick with the example of human rights—there is good evidence to suggest that the Catholic personalist origins of human rights are themselves indebted to an older, Russian religious defense of human rights, as found, for example, in Solov'ev and in the work of the Russian philosophical contributions to the *Problems of Idealism* volume. Precisely the absence of rights in the Russian context led Russian religious thinkers to insist on the universality of rights based on the religious defense of the dignity of human beings.[59] A better understanding of this legacy would perhaps change the contemporary debate on the place of rights within a modern, secular context.

Partly because of their frequent use of theological terminology—*theosis*, *energies* versus *essence*, and so forth—Russian religious philosophers can leave the initial impression that they are backward-looking, traditionalist, and even conservative and illiberal. There may be such tendencies with some of the representatives of the Russian philosophical tradition. However, what makes the Russian project interesting are those aspects of it that are intensely concerned with working out a Christianity for modernity. When Berdiaev, Florenskii, and others speak of the "New Middle Ages," the emphasis falls on "new," not on "Middle Ages." This is why I feel convinced that Russian religious philosophy can be genuinely relevant, especially in a postmodern context.

More concretely, I will mention several themes while there are, of course, many others. Russian Sophiology can be conceptualized to serve as a specific model of divine presence in the world. The quintessentially Eastern Orthodox doctrine of *theosis*, or deification, and its elaboration in Solov'ev's "*bogochelovechestvo*," usually translated as "Godmanhood," offers an understanding of individualism, human dignity, and worth that presupposes the relationship between God and man. In this way, it brings an alternative to some forms of modern individualism that radically exclude a transcendental perspective. In fact, I do not see why a notion of individualism that posits the possibility that man can, in some way, become like God in a world penetrated by divine presence should be weaker than the exclusive individualism of a Nietzschean type.[60]

What are sometimes called "communitarian philosophers," such as Alasdair MacIntyre, Charles Taylor, Michael Walzer, Michael Sandel, and others with their stress on the importance of the community versus the exclusive value of some varieties of modern individualism, touch on the cluster of problems around the Russian idea of *sobornost'*. Further, there are notions of solidarity, which we are witnessing at the present—think of the refugee crisis in Europe—that can be understood, it seems to me, only if we take into account a perspective on the world, which is, in one way or another, religiously inspired.[61] As Taylor has noted, these "world-wide movements of sympathy and practical solidarity" are "without precedent in history," and this is so in the sense that they involve extending help and assistance to people thousands of miles away, whom one has never met, and who belong to a different culture.[62] The Russian religious idea of "full unity" understood as the unity of humankind, held together by Sophia, can be very relevant here. It underlines Dostoyevsky's otherwise incomprehensible "everyone is responsible for everyone and for everything."

There is also the age-old tradition of Eastern Orthodox theology of the image and its development by Russian religious philosophy, which can offer constructive insights in the aftermath of a discredited formalist aesthetics that had allied itself with Kantian philosophy. The foremost figure in such an enterprise would undoubtedly be Florenskii. His fragmented but extremely rich writings on the theory of the icon have the potential to be developed toward an Eastern Orthodox aesthetics that could address the concerns and dissatisfaction of many with traditional accounts of art.[63]

In short, while the Russian project does not offer a complete philosophical system, it does contain ideas that could advance contemporary debates on the role of religion in modernity in interesting and important ways. However, at this stage, Russian religious philosophy is still too little known among Western scholars and, as a result, has been almost completely ignored as a possible model of "religious modernity."

Afterword

Russian Religious Modernity

Randall A. Poole

Among the many different ways of defining secularism, two are most important for understanding the Russian experience. The first is political and favorable to religion; the second is intellectual and unfavorable to religion. The first conception of secularism is separation of church and state, based on the principle of freedom of conscience. It recognizes that faith, by its very nature as freely held inner beliefs and convictions, rests on freedom of conscience. It sees the main purpose of the state as providing the ordered external liberty necessary for the enjoyment of religious and other personal freedoms. As a historical movement, secularism in this sense—which is closely aligned with classic liberalism—traces its origins to the struggle for religious freedom in early modern Europe and colonial North America. Its main theorists include Roger Williams, William Penn, Baruch Spinoza, Pierre Bayle, and John Locke.[1] The first, political conception of secularism has a certain normative status, reflected in the recognition of freedom of conscience as a basic human right. It holds that church-state relations *ought to be* ordered in a way that protects this right.

The second, intellectual conception of secularism takes the view that religion is contrary to reason and should be discouraged. Its first modern advocates were Enlightenment *philosophes* such as Denis Diderot and Baron d'Holbach, both atheists. In the nineteenth century its champions included George Jacob Holyoake, who seems to have coined the term *secularism*, and his stridently atheistic contemporary Charles Bradlaugh. Today the "new atheists" (Richard Dawkins, Daniel Dennett, and others) take an extreme position, but the terms *secularist* and *secular humanism* are generally associated with an irreligious view, if not always with hard-core materialism or naturalism.

Secularism as atheism (to put it succinctly) has a long history in Russia, beginning with the nineteenth-century radical intelligentsia and continuing through the Soviet period, when it was the official ideology of the Communist Party.[2] The relevance of secularism as separation of church and state, as the defense of freedom of conscience, is less immediately obvious to Russian history. Rather the opposite situation—autocratic subordination of church to state—characterized the imperial period after Peter the Great's creation of the Holy Synod; this subordination took a new and very violent form in the Soviet period. Under Vladimir Putin, the Moscow Patriarchate has aligned itself with the Russian state (and, deplorably, with its war on Ukraine). In response to the dominant statist tradition, there emerged, however, a Russian religious "counter-tradition," which generally extolled the principle of freedom of conscience. It appreciated that violation of this principle, perhaps more than anything else, was what made the Russian state (whether tsarist or Soviet) autocratic and that, by contrast, respect for freedom of conscience was essential for a state under the rule of law—for a secular state that, as such, respects religious freedom.

Kristina Stoeckl, in her chapter in this book, distinguishes between Russian Orthodoxy as a state church and Russian Orthodoxy as a people's church. The latter took many forms, both genuinely popular ("lived Orthodoxy" such as monasticism and icon veneration) and more elite (religious philosophy, theology, art).[3] Sometimes popular and elite forms were combined, as in Kazimir Malevich's aesthetic-religious metaphysics, which, as Tatiana Levina shows in her daring chapter, was inspired by iconography. Russian Orthodoxy as a people's church was a broad-based and multifaceted movement of religious dissidence, in opposition to the Synodal Church in the imperial period and to Communist atheism in the Soviet period. Russia's rich history of religious dissent also included persecuted religious minorities such as the Spiritual Christian Molokans, whose fascinating history is told here by J. Eugene Clay. As a whole, the Russian religious counter-tradition stood for "the individual autonomy promised by liberal modernity," as Clay puts it. Soviet "spiritual dissident" Father Aleksandr Men' (the subject of April L. French's fine chapter) recognized that freedom of conscience was "the holy of holies within humanity" and must be protected by "the honest and consistent application of the principle of a secular state . . . that serves the interests of its citizens regardless of their religious affiliations." The autocratic context of the Russian religious counter-tradition gave it a keen appreciation of the normative principle of secularism as separation of church and state and as freedom of conscience.

Beginning with the Slavophiles, Russian Orthodoxy as a people's church developed a robust, independent tradition of religious thought that flourished especially in the few decades before the Russian Revolution and that formed the philosophical core of the Russian religious counter-tradition. As Ana Siljak and Clemena Antonova suggest in their contributions to the present book, Russian religious-philosophical thought offers key insights into the relationship among modernity, religion, and the secular.[4] Antonova refers to a Russian philosophical model of "religious modernity"—"a religiosity that embraces, and even presupposes, characteristics that are commonly seen as aspects of secularity." What are some of the main insights or principles of this model? Following Antonova's lead, let me suggest four.

First is the rationality of theism: the belief that there is more to reality than the natural world (*contra* naturalism), or the belief in the ontological reality of the spiritual. Russian religious philosophers thought that theism (or more broadly spiritualism) was the worldview or conception of reality that best accorded with our experience of the world and of ourselves as persons. They followed the traditional proofs for the existence of God, but as a whole their approach was not rationalistic, but experiential.[5] The experience underlying the cosmological proof, for example, is that of the giftedness or createdness of the world, which follows immediately from experience of the world's contingency rather than necessity—the world exists, but not by its own nature, thus Gottfried Wilhelm Leibniz's famous question, "Why is there something rather than nothing?"—an experience behind all the great creation myths. Similarly with the ontological proof; the idea of the absolute entails its ontological reality (God), but not so much because of the logic of the argument but because the absolute is basic (intrinsic) to human consciousness and experience and because its presence is otherwise inexplicable (the positive, finite data of sensory experience suggest nothing of the absolute). Semyon Frank, whom Vasilii Zenkovsky famously ranked as the "most outstanding" Russian philosopher, devoted much attention to the ontological proof.[6] He thought that proofs of God were superfluous because the absolute, "in its immediacy in living experience," is a self-evident reality, but he respected the ontological proof for recognizing that and for bringing "the full, living self-evident truth of Divinity onto the plane of thought."[7]

Russian philosophers cast the moral proof within a broader idealist conception of human nature, which was central to their whole theological approach: they believed that personhood itself had metaphysical or theistic implications. According to this (Kantian) conception, human beings are persons by virtue of their reason, which has a remarkable dual power: first, to recognize or posit absolute ideals (for example, truth, the good, and beauty), and, second, to determine the will according to them.[8] This type of philosophical anthropology was advanced by Boris Chicherin and Vladimir Solov'ev, the two greatest philosophers of nineteenth-century Russia. It formed one of the basic frameworks for the further development of Russian religious-philosophical thought in the twentieth century. Russian philosophers identified the capacity for "ideal self-determination" (as Sergei Trubetskoi called it) as the core of personhood.[9] They believed it defeated naturalism—the absolute ideals of consciousness invalidated positivism, while free will refuted physical determinism—and entailed a theistic metaphysics. Precisely this belief is what made them *religious idealists*.[10]

Solov'ev is generally regarded as Russia's greatest religious philosopher. In his version of the Russian idealist conception of human nature, human beings combine in themselves three principles: the absolute or divine principle, the material principle, and (between them) the distinctively human principle, which is rational autonomy or the capacity for self-determination.[11] Together the divine and human principles form "divine humanity" (*Bogochelovechestvo*), the central concept of Solov'ev's religious philosophy.[12] It is the free human realization of the divine principle in ourselves and in the world—in patristic terminology, *theosis* (deification).

Bogochelovechestvo describes both the process of human perfectibility, or infinite progress toward the *telos* of perfection (the absolute), and its transcendent culmination. The concept contains a distinctively Kantian "argument from human perfectibility."[13] In *Lectures on Divine Humanity*, Solov'ev wrote that the human capacity for "infinite development" (or perfectibility) presupposes an ultimate end toward which it is directed, which he called the positive absolute of all-unity or perfect "fullness of being." Infinite human striving toward the absolute ideal convinced Solov'ev of the ontological reality of the absolute. He formulated this in striking terms: "Thus, belief in oneself, belief in the human person, is at the same time belief in God."[14]

Following Solov'ev, this "argument from personhood" or "personological proof" was advanced by other Russian religious thinkers and forms part of the Russian school of personalism. Nikolai Berdiaev, himself a prominent Russian personalist, wrote, "The existence of personality presupposes the existence of God; its value presupposes the supreme value—God."[15] Another example is Semyon Frank. The title of his last major work captures the personalist approach: *Reality and Man: An Essay in the Metaphysics of Human Nature*. In it he wrote: "The only completely adequate 'proof of the existence of God' is the existence of the human person taken in all its depth and significance as an entity that transcends itself." This argument was utterly convincing to Frank: "If the human being is aware of himself as a person, i.e., as a being generically distinct from all external objective existence and transcending it in depth, primacy and significance, if he feels like an exile having no true home in this world—that means that he *has* a home in another sphere of being," the sphere, that is, of ultimate reality. "The apprehension of the reality of God is, thus, immanently given in the apprehension of my own being as a person."[16]

The second principle of the Russian philosophical conception of religious modernity is clear from the above exposition: religious humanism.[17] It holds that human beings are capable of recognizing the divine *image* (or ideal) in themselves and of working progressively to realize the divine *likeness* in themselves and in the world. In short, religious humanism affirms the possibility of human progress toward union with the divine, that is, toward salvation conceived as *theosis*. It puts the emphasis on human capabilities (reason, conscience, free will)—on human dignity rather than human depravity. It is clear that Solov'ev's concept of *Bogochelovechestvo* was the vehicle, as Paul Valliere has written, "for a principled and profound Orthodox Christian humanism."[18] In 1934, Sergei Bulgakov used the term *Christian humanism* to characterize the main direction of his theology and of modern Russian religious thought as a whole. Its distinctiveness, he wrote, is that "it includes the creativity of man in the means of his salvation."[19]

The third principle of Russian religious modernity is liberalism, understood as a philosophy of human rights upheld through the rule of law.[20] As a normative political philosophy, liberalism recognizes that the highest value of social and political life is the human person. The good of society consists in the good of every person in it, in every person's fullest possible self-realization and flourishing. The intrinsic worth of the human person is the principle of human dignity, the idea that every person is an end-in-itself who ought never to be treated merely as a means to other ends. Human dignity is the source of human equality and of human rights. Solov'ev, in his entry on *lichnost'*, or "personhood," for the Brogauz-Efron encyclopedia, wrote, "Human personhood has in principle an *unconditional dignity*, upon which are based *its inviolable rights*."[21] If human dignity is the source of human rights, what is the source of human dignity? Russian religious idealists generally followed Immanuel Kant in locating the source within human nature, specifically in the capacity or potential for ideal self-determination (which Kant also calls autonomy or practical reason).[22] However, as we have seen, they thought this human source entailed a theistic metaphysics—not unlike Kant, who derived from it the "metaphysical postulates" of the soul's immortality and the existence of God.

Beginning with Chicherin, Russian religious idealists regarded freedom of conscience as the "first and most sacred" human right, because of its central bearing on human dignity. The concept has a dual meaning: inner freedom as self-determination according to freely recognized ideals, and external freedom as the right to seek, express, and live according to one's ideals or beliefs. In his masterpiece *Philosophy of Right* (1900), Chicherin wrote: "The great moral significance of the secular enlightenment was never expressed so clearly as in the modern recognition of freedom of conscience as the most sacred and inviolable of human rights. It is the cornerstone of the inner freedom of man, and therefore of human dignity as well."[23]

The modern recognition of freedom of conscience is earlier than Chicherin suggests here. In 1895, the German legal philosopher Georg Jellinek, perhaps the first historian of human rights, published his classic book *Die Erklärung der Menschen- und Bürgerrechte: Ein Beitrag zur modernen Verfassungsgeschichte* (*The Declaration of the Rights of Man and of Citizens: A Contribution to Modern Constitutional History*). Despite the title's reference to the French Revolution, Jellinek's thesis is that human rights, developing out of a long tradition of natural law, first acquired their modern constitutional and institutional forms in colonial North America, and there as a result of the struggle of Protestant dissenters for religious freedom. He came to a bold conclusion: "The idea of legally establishing inalienable, inherent and sacred rights of the individual is not of political but religious origin."[24] The hero of Jellinek's story is the Puritan preacher Roger Williams, who founded the colony of Rhode Island on the principle of unlimited religious freedom. Williams recognized that freedom of conscience goes to the heart of what it means to be a person. Conscience is "indeed the man," he said.[25]

Russian liberal theorists knew Jellinek's work, of course. In 1901, Peter Struve, the leader of the Russian Liberation Movement that would culminate in the Russian revolution of 1905, published an important essay, "What Is True Nationalism?," which lays out his liberal theory and which draws on Jellinek.[26] Struve calls Williams the first apostle of the idea of the inalienable rights of man, beginning with freedom of conscience—"the first word of liberalism," in Struve's phrase. He refers in this connection to the work of his Russian colleague Pavel Novgorodtsev, who devoted a few pages of his *History of the Philosophy of Law* to Williams.[27] Struve and Novgorodtsev were then organizing the collective volume *Problems of Idealism*, conceived as a defense of freedom of conscience and its importance in liberalism.[28] Among its contributors were several of Russia's most important philosophical thinkers (then or soon-to-be). They recognized that freedom of conscience was religious both in its metaphysical implications (as the human capacity for ideal self-determination) and in its historical origins (as the foundational human right, arising from the struggle for religious freedom). Their insights have much to offer for today's debates over the theory and history of human rights, over their contested secular and religious genealogies and interpretations.

For Russian religious philosophers, freedom of conscience had another meaning, which is the fourth principle of Russian religious modernity: an integral worldview based on respect for the relative autonomy of the various distinct spheres of human need, experience, inquiry, and aspiration, not only church and state, or religion and politics, but also morality, philosophy, science, economy, and art.[29] Each of these spheres is legitimate in its own domain; one cannot be substituted for the others; they are parts of a whole in which each has its own place. An integral worldview strives to achieve a higher unity among them while respecting their autonomy. As Bulgakov formulated it in *Problems of Idealism*: "Man cannot be satisfied by exact science alone, to which positivism hoped to limit him; metaphysical and religious needs are ineradicable and have never been removed from the life of man. Precise knowledge, metaphysics, and religion must exist in a certain harmonious relation, the establishment of which always comprises the task of philosophy."[30] Bulgakov's case study here is positivism (in both its Comtean and Marxist versions). He shows how it, denying the absolute, becomes a secular "religion of progress"; it gives science a salvific mission in imagining that science can predict the laws of history that (allegedly) will automatically bring about a future state of perfected humanity. Instead of such conflation, it is necessary, Bulgakov says, "to return to Caesar what is Caesar's, and to God what is God's. The correct formulation of the theory of progress must . . . delimit and, within the proper sphere, restore in their own rights science, metaphysics, and religion."[31]

Bulgakov and other Russian religious idealists believed that the idea of the absolute was a constituent element of human consciousness. They thought that attempts to deny it—and freedom of conscience in the process—led only to "unconscious metaphysics," to false absolutes, and to various forms of reductionism and utopianism, including the phenomenon of secular or political religions (which they were the first to analyze). But recognition of the absolute is not disdain for the relative; rather the absolute is the source of the value of the relative and the ideal for its development and improvement (that is, for progress). For this very reason the relative must not be made into its own absolute. As the legal philosopher Sergei Kotliarevskii put it, "The world of the relative must be decisively secularized, freed from the conflation of *spiritualia* and *temporalia*, which (true, not quite in medieval form) so often comes back to life in science and art, politics and the social sphere, in all branches of human activity."[32] Thus Kotliarevskii's view was that an integral worldview, recognizing the absolute and respecting the relative, reflects the normative type of secularism. By contrast, secularism as atheism typically results in the phenomenon of "secular religions." (Two examples of this phenomenon are the Moscow Methodological Circle and Maxim Gorky's God-building, expertly presented in this book by Peter A. Safronov and Erich Lippman, respectively. Certain conceptions of nationalism also fall into this category, while national messianism imputes to a chosen nation a more transparently religious, and exclusive, vocation. These ideas are discussed in the excellent chapters by Kåre Johan Mjør and Vassili Schedrin.)

These four principles—the rationality of theism, religious humanism, liberalism, and an integral worldview—converge on a complex understanding of freedom of conscience as the capacity for ideal self-determination (the inner core of personhood) and as the "first and most sacred" human right. The principles demonstrate that the Russian philosophical understanding of religious modernity forms a very rich intellectual and spiritual tradition. In Russia today, it sadly remains a counter-tradition.

Notes

Introduction. Religion and Secularism in Russia

1. Orlando Figes, *The Story of Russia* (London: Bloomsbury, 2022) 9; Gaziza Shakhanova and Petr Kratochvíl, "The Patriotic Turn in Russia: Political Convergence of the Russian Orthodox Church and the State?," *Politics and Religion* 15, no. 1 (2022): 114–41. For a discussion of the persistent binaries involved in the history of the concept of a "Holy Russia," see Laura Engelstein, "Holy Russia in Modern Times: An Essay on Orthodoxy and Cultural Change," *Past & Present*, no. 173 (2001): 129–56.

2. Ian Hunter, "Secularization: The Birth of a Modern Combat Concept," *Modern Intellectual History* 12, no. 1 (2015): 1.

3. See Phil Zuckerman and John R. Shook, "Introduction: The Study of Secularism," 1–14, esp. 2–4, quote on p. 2, and Joseph Blankholm, "Secularism, Humanism, and Secular Humanism: Terms and Institutions," 689–702, esp. 690–91, both in *The Oxford Handbook of Secularism*, ed. Phil Zuckerman and John R. Shook (New York: Oxford University Press, 2017).

4. William H. Swatos and Kevin J. Christiano, "Secularization Theory: The Course of a Concept," *Sociology of Religion* 60, no. 3 (1999): 209–28, esp. 211–14, quote 209. Zuckerman and Shook, "Introduction: The Study of Secularism," 5–6.

5. Swatos and Christiano, "Secularization Theory," 219–20; José Casanova, "The Secular, Secularizations, Secularisms," in *Rethinking Secularism*, ed. Craig Calhoun, Mark Juergensmeyer, and Jonathan VanAntwerpen (New York: Oxford University Press, 2011), 54–74, esp. 60–61. Ian Hunter has gone so far as to call conceptions of secularization "combat concepts" because they were "the instruments of competing cultural-political programs advanced by factions engaged in multisided struggles to determine the shape of the religious and political order." Hunter, "Secularization," 3–4.

6. Charles Taylor, *A Secular Age* (Cambridge, MA: Belknap Press of Harvard University Press, 2007), 22. Swatos and Christiano, "Secularization Theory," 214–15; Ahmet T. Kuru, "Passive and Assertive Secularism: Historical Conditions, Ideological Struggles, and State Policies toward Religion," *World Politics* 59, no. 4 (2007): 568–94, esp. 572.

7. Walter Capp cited in Jonathan Z. Smith, "Religion, Religions, Religious," in *Critical Terms for Religious Studies*, ed. Mark C. Taylor (Chicago: University of Chicago Press, 1998), 274, 281.

8. William T. Cavanaugh, *The Myth of Religious Violence: Secular Ideology and the Roots of Modern Conflict* (New York: Oxford University Press, 2009), 80–85.

9. See David Martin, *On Secularization: Towards a Revised General Theory* (Aldershot: Ashgate, 2005), 26–27; Craig Calhoun, Mark Juergensmeyer, and Jonathan

VanAntwerpen, introduction to *Rethinking Secularism*, ed. Craig Calhoun, Mark Juergensmeyer, and Jonathan VanAntwerpen (New York: Oxford University Press, 2011), 3–4; Peter L. Berger, "The Desecularization of the World: A Global Overview," in *The Desecularization of the World: Resurgent Religion and World Politics*, ed. Peter L. Berger (Washington, DC: Ethics and Public Policy Center; Grand Rapids, MI: William B. Eerdmans, 1999), 2–3.

10. Taylor, *Secular Age*, 3, 20.

11. Taylor, *Secular Age*, 727.

12. Craig Calhoun, Mark Juergensmeyer, and Jonathan VanAntwerpen, eds., *Rethinking Secularism* (New York: Oxford University Press, 2011); Michael Warner, Jonathan VanAntwerpen, and Craig Calhoun, eds., *Varieties of Secularism in a Secular Age* (Cambridge, MA: Harvard University Press, 2013).

13. Talal Asad, *Formations of the Secular: Christianity, Islam, Modernity* (Stanford, CA: Stanford University Press, 2003); David Scott and Charles Hirschkind, eds., *Powers of the Secular Modern: Talal Asad and His Interlocutors* (Stanford, CA: Stanford University Press, 2006).

14. Saba Mahmood, "Secularism, Hermeneutics, and Empire: The Politics of Islamic Reformation," *Public Culture* 18, no. 2 (2006): 326–27.

15. Michael Burleigh, *Earthly Powers: The Clash of Religion and Politics in Europe, from the French Revolution to the Great War* (New York: HarperCollins, 2005) 2, 10.

16. Peter van der Veer, *The Modern Spirit of Asia: The Spiritual and the Secular in China and India* (Princeton, NJ: Princeton University Press, 2014); Azzam Tamimi and John L. Esposito, eds., *Islam and Secularism in the Middle East* (New York: New York University Press, 2000).

17. There is a good collection of essays on the secular and society in Zuckerman and Shook, *The Oxford Handbook of Secularism*, 499–625. See also K. Moti Gokulsing, "Without Prejudice: An Exploration of Religious Diversity, Secularism and Citizenship in England (with Particular Reference to the State Funding of Muslim Faith Schools and Multiculturalism)," *Journal of Education Policy* 21, no. 4 (2006): 459–70; Hilal Elver, *The Headscarf Controversy: Secularism and Freedom of Religion* (New York: Oxford University Press, 2012); Alev Çınar, "Subversion and Subjugation in the Public Sphere: Secularism and the Islamic Headscarf," *Signs: Journal of Women in Culture and Society* 33, no. 4 (2008): 891–913.

18. For exceptions, see Gordon Graham, *The Re-enchantment of the World: Art versus Religion* (Oxford: Oxford University Press, 2007); and the chapters by Victor V. Bychkov, Rebecca Mitchell, Martha M. F. Kelly, and Clemena Antonova in *The Oxford Handbook of Russian Religious Thought*, ed. Caryl Emerson, George Pattison, and Randall A. Poole (Oxford: Oxford University Press, 2020).

19. In the Russian context, see Victoria Frede, *Doubt, Atheism, and the Nineteenth-Century Russian Intelligentsia* (Madison: University of Wisconsin Press, 2011).

20. Hunter, "Secularization," 1–9. A major exception to this omission is Massimo Rosati and Kristina Stoeckl, eds., *Multiple Modernities and Postsecular Societies* (New York: Routledge, 2016).

21. V. Dal', *Tolkovyi slovar' zhivogo velikorusskogo iazyka* [Elektronnyi resurs], s.v. "svetskii," accessed February 20, 2024, http://slovardalja.net/word.php?wordid=37226.

22. Valerie A. Kivelson and Robert H. Greene, "Introduction: Orthodox Russia," in *Orthodox Russia: Belief and Practice under the Tsars*, ed. Valerie A. Kivelson and Robert H. Greene (University Park: Pennsylvania State University Press, 2003), 6–7; Ernest A. Zitser, *The Transfigured Kingdom: Sacred Parody and Charismatic Authority at the Court of Peter the Great* (Ithaca, NY: Cornell University Press, 2004), 6–7.

23. Robert D. Crews, *For Prophet and Tsar: Islam and Empire in Russia and Central Asia* (Cambridge, MA: Harvard University Press, 2009), 31–91. It is telling that there are few stand-alone books on religions in Russia during the era of Peter and Catherine. For exceptions, see Elise Kimerling Wirtschafter, *Religion and Enlightenment in Catherinian Russia: The Teachings of Metropolitan Platon* (DeKalb: Northern Illinois University Press, 2013); Gary M. Hamburg, *Russia's Path toward Enlightenment: Faith, Politics, and Reason, 1500–1801* (New Haven, CT: Yale University Press, 2016).

24. *Istoricheskii slovar' gallitsizmov russkogo iazyka* (Moscow: Slovarnoe izdatel'stvo ETS, 2010), s.v., "religiia," accessed February 20, 2024, https://rus-gallicismes-dict.slovaronline.com/. Translations are mine unless otherwise noted.

25. *Istoricheskii slovar'*, s.vv., "sekuliarizovat'," "sekuliarizatsiia"; Dal', *Tolkovyi slovar'*, s.v. "sekuliarizatsiia," accessed February 20, 2024, http://slovardalja.net/word.php?wordid=37452.

26. Sergey Horujy, "Slavophiles, Westernizers, and the Birth of Russian Philosophical Humanism," in *A History of Russian Philosophy, 1830–1930: Faith, Reason, and the Defense of Human Dignity*, ed. Gary M. Hamburg and Randall A. Poole (Cambridge: Cambridge University Press, 2010), 27–51, esp. 29–30. Ivan Kireevskii complained that reason was no longer serving as the foundation of "religion" and that philosophical concepts were "increasingly replacing religious concepts." I. V. Kireevskii, "O neokhodimosti i vozmozhnosti novykh nachal dlia filosofii," in *Izbrannye stat'i*, ed. V. A. Kotel'nikov (Moscow: Sovremennik, 1984), 256. And Aleksei Khomiakov contended that "Religion is one sun, one light for all; but its blessed rays do not equally shine over all the earth." A. S. Khomiakov, "Neskol'ko slov o 'Filosofskom pis'me' napechatannom v 15 knizhke 'Teleskopa,'" in *Sochineniia v dvukh tomakh*, ed. V. A. Koshelev (Moscow: Moskovskii filosofskii fond, 1994), vol. 1, 454.

27. Patrick Lally Michelson, "Slavophile Religious Thought and the Dilemma of Russian Modernity, 1830–1860," *Modern Intellectual History* 7, no. 2 (2010): 252; *Istoricheskii slovar'*, s.v. "sekuliarizatsiia."

28. Erich Haberer, *Jews and Revolution in Nineteenth-Century Russia* (New York: Cambridge University Press, 1995).

29. Frede, *Doubt, Atheism*, 180, 135, 167.

30. Gregory L. Freeze, "Subversive Piety: Religion and the Political Crisis in Late Imperial Russia," *Journal of Modern History* 68, no. 2 (1996): 308–50; Jennifer Hedda, *His Kingdom Come: Orthodox Pastorship and Social Activism in Revolutionary Russia* (DeKalb: Northern Illinois University Press, 2008); Irina Paperno and Joan Delaney Grossman, eds., *Creating Life: The Aesthetic Utopia of Russian Modernism* (Stanford, CA: Stanford University Press, 1994); Randall A. Poole, trans. and ed., *Problems of Idealism: Essays in Russian Social Philosophy* (New Haven, CT: Yale University Press, 2003); Judith Deutsch Kornblatt and Richard F. Gustafson, eds., *Russian Religious Thought* (Madison: University of Wisconsin Press, 1996).

31. P. L. Lavrov, "Mir bogov nemetskikh i severnykh narodov," in *O religii*, by P. L. Lavrov, ed. A. I. Volodin (Moscow: Mysl', 1989), 73, 83. The "secular commune" quote is found in Peter Lavrov, *Historical Letters*, trans. James P. Scanlan (Berkeley: University of California Press, 1967), 53.

32. V. S. Solov'ev, *Chteniia o Bogochelovechestve; Stat'i; Stikhotvoreniia i poema*, ed. A. B. Muratov (St. Petersburg: Khudozh. lit-ra, 1994), 34, 55.

33. F. A. Brokgauz, *Entsiklopedicheskii slovar'*, ed. I. E. Andreevskii (St. Petersburg: F. A. Brokgauz, I. A. Efron, 1890–1907), vol. 29, s.v. "sekuliarizatsiia"; vol. 26A, s.v. "religiia."

34. See Randall A. Poole and Paul W. Werth, eds., *Religious Freedom in Modern Russia* (Pittsburgh: University of Pittsburgh Press, 2018), especially Randall A. Poole, "Introduction: Faith, Freedom, and the Varieties of Russian Religious Experience, 1–43; Richard Stites, *Revolutionary Dreams: Utopian Vision and Experimental Life in the Russian Revolution* (New York: Oxford University Press, 1989), esp. 101–3.

35. Stites, *Revolutionary Dreams*, 101–3.

36. The 1918 "Decree on Separation of Church from State and School from Church" is quoted in Paul Gabel, *And God Created Lenin: Marxism vs. Religion in Russia, 1917–1929* (Buffalo, NY: Prometheus Press, 2010), 141.

37. Catherine Wanner, introduction to *State Secularism and Lived Religion in Soviet Russia and Ukraine*, ed. Catherine Wanner (Washington, DC: Woodrow Wilson Center Press; New York: Oxford University Press, 2012), 6.

38. See Wanner, introduction to *State Secularism*, esp. 10–23.

39. Andrzej Walicki, *Marxism and the Leap to the Kingdom of Freedom: The Rise and Fall of the Communist Utopia* (Stanford, CA: Stanford University Press, 1995); Igal Halfin, *From Darkness to Light: Class, Consciousness, and Salvation in Revolutionary Russia* (Pittsburgh: University of Pittsburgh Press, 2000), esp. 2–4; Jochen Hellbeck, "The New Man in Stalinist Russia and Nazi Germany," in *Beyond Totalitarianism, Stalinism and Nazism Compared*, ed. Michael Geyer and Sheila Fitzpatrick (Cambridge: Cambridge University Press, 2008), 302–342. Victoria Smolkin, *A Sacred Space Is Never Empty: A History of Soviet Atheism* (Princeton, NJ: Princeton University Press, 2018); Yuri Slezkine, *The House of Government: A Saga of the Russian Revolution* (Princeton, NJ: Princeton University Press, 2017), esp. xii.

40. Sergei Filatov and Roman Lunkin, "Statistics on Religion in Russia: The Reality behind the Figures," *Religion, State & Society* 34, no. 1 (2006): 33–49. See also Zoe Knox, *Russian Society and the Orthodox Church: Religion in Russia after Communism* (London: RoutledgeCurzon, 2005); J. Eugene Clay, "Multiculturalism and Religious Education in the Russian Federation: The Fundamentals of Religious Cultures and Secular Ethics," *State, Religion and Church* 2, no. 1 (2015): 44–74.

41. Kivelson and Greene, "Introduction: Orthodox Russia," 4–5.

42. Even subtle and comprehensive treatments of the Jewish minority in Russia and the Soviet Union mostly emphasize the ethnic/national identities of the Jewish population. See John Doyle Klier, *Imperial Russia's Jewish Question, 1855–1881* (Cambridge: Cambridge University Press, 2005); Benjamin Nathans, *Beyond the Pale: The Jewish Encounter with Late Imperial Russia* (Berkeley: University of California Press, 2004); Benjamin Pinkus, *The Jews of the Soviet Union: The History of a National Minority* (Cambridge: Cambridge University Press, 1990).

43. Gregory L. Freeze, *The Russian Levites: Parish Clergy in the Eighteenth Century* (Cambridge, MA.: Harvard University Press, 1977); Gregory L. Freeze, *The Parish Clergy in Nineteenth-Century Russia: Crisis, Reform, Counter-Reform* (Princeton, NJ: Princeton University Press, 1983); Gregory L. Freeze, "Handmaiden of the State? The Church in Imperial Russia Reconsidered," *Journal of Ecclesiastical History* 36, no. 1 (1985): 82–102; Freeze, "Subversive Piety." In 2001, Freeze put out a useful review of the state of the field: Gregory L. Freeze, "Recent Scholarship on Russian Orthodoxy: A Critique," *Kritika: Explorations in Russian and Eurasian History* 2, no. 2 (2001): 269–78. Vera Shevzov, "Miracle-Working Icons, Laity, and Authority in the Russian Orthodox Church, 1861–1917," *Russian Review* 58, no. 1 (1999): 26–48; Vera Shevzov, "Chapels and the Ecclesial World of Prerevolutionary Russian Peasants," *Slavic Review* 55, no. 3 (1996): 585–613; Kornblatt and Gustafson, *Russian Religious Thought*; Paul Valliere, "Theological Liberalism and Church Reform in Imperial Russia," in *Church, Nation and State in Russia and Ukraine*, ed. Geoffrey A. Hosking (London: Palgrave Macmillan, 1991), 108–30; Paul Valliere, *Modern Russian Theology: Bukharev, Soloviev, Bulgakov: Orthodox Theology in a New Key* (Grand Rapids, MI: William B. Eerdmans, 2000). See also Joan Delaney Grossman, "Khrushchev's Anti-religious Policy and the Campaign of 1954," *Soviet Studies* 24, no. 3 (1973): 374–86; Brenda Meehan, *Holy Women of Russia: The Lives of Five Orthodox Women Offer Spiritual Guidance for Today* (Crestwood, NY: St. Vladimir's Seminary Press, 1997).

44. Valerie A. Kivelson and Robert H. Greene, eds., *Orthodox Russia: Belief and Practice under the Tsars* (University Park: Pennsylvania State University Press, 2003); Mark D. Steinberg and Heather J. Coleman, eds., *Sacred Stories: Religion and Spirituality in Modern Russia* (Bloomington: Indiana University Press, 2007).

45. Patrick Lally Michelson and Judith Deutsch Kornblatt, eds., *Thinking Orthodox in Modern Russia: Culture, History, Context* (Madison: University of Wisconsin Press, 2014); Patrick Lally Michelson, *Beyond the Monastery Walls: The Ascetic Revolution in Russian Orthodox Thought, 1814–1914* (Madison: University of Wisconsin Press, 2017); Leonid Heretz, *Russia on the Eve of Modernity: Popular Religion and Traditional Culture under the Last Tsars* (Cambridge: Cambridge University Press, 2008); Scott M. Kenworthy, *The Heart of Russia: Trinity-Sergius, Monasticism, and Society after 1825* (Washington, DC: Woodrow Wilson Center Press; New York: Oxford University Press, 2010). See also Vera Shevzov, *Russian Orthodoxy on the Eve of Revolution* (New York: Oxford University Press, 2004); Judith Deutsch Kornblatt, *Doubly Chosen: Jewish Identity, the Soviet Intelligentsia, and the Russian Orthodox Church* (Madison: University of Wisconsin Press, 2004); Robert P. Geraci and Michael Khodarkovsky, eds., *Of Religion and Empire: Missions, Conversion, and Tolerance in Tsarist Russia* (Ithaca, NY: Cornell University Press, 2001); Irina Paert, *Spiritual Elders: Charisma and Tradition in Russian Orthodoxy* (DeKalb: Northern Illinois University Press, 2010); Robert H. Greene, *Bodies like Bright Stars: Saints and Relics in Orthodox Russia* (DeKalb: Northern Illinois University Press, 2010); Nadieszda Kizenko, *A Prodigal Saint: Father John of Kronstadt and the Russian People* (University Park: Pennsylvania State University Press, 2000); Chris J. Chulos, *Converging Worlds: Religion and Community in Peasant Russia, 1861–1917* (DeKalb: Northern Illinois University Press, 2003).

46. Frede, *Doubt, Atheism*; See also Wirtschafter, *Religion and Enlightenment*; Hamburg, *Russia's Path toward Enlightenment*.

47. Teresa Obolevitch, *Faith and Science in Russian Religious Thought* (Oxford: Oxford University Press, 2019); Teresa Obolevitch and Randall A. Poole, eds., *Evgenii Trubetskoi: Icon and Philosophy* (Eugene, OR: Pickwick Publications, 2021); Smolkin, *Sacred Space*; Caryl Emerson, George Pattison, and Randall A. Poole, eds., *The Oxford Handbook of Russian Religious Thought* (Oxford: Oxford University Press, 2020).

48. See Paul Froese, *The Plot to Kill God: Findings from the Soviet Experiment in Secularization* (Berkeley: University of California Press, 2008); Sonja Luehrmann, *Religion in Secular Archives: Soviet Atheism and Historical Knowledge* (New York: Oxford University Press, 2015); Wanner, *State Secularism*; Smolkin, *Sacred Space*; Victoria Smolkin-Rothrock, "The Ticket to the Soviet Soul: Science, Religion, and the Spiritual Crisis of Late Soviet Atheism," *Russian Review* 73, no. 2 (April 2014): 171–97; and the multiple works of Alexander Agadjanian, including Victor Roudometof, Alexander Agadjanian, and Jerry G. Pankhurst, eds., *Eastern Orthodoxy in a Global Age: Tradition Faces the Twenty-First Century* (Walnut Creek, CA: AltaMira Press, 2005).

49. See Wanner, *State Secularism*; Froese, *Plot to Kill God*; Luehrmann, *Religion in Secular Archives*; and Smolkin-Rothrock, "Ticket to the Soviet Soul."

50. Michelson, "Slavophile Religious Thought"; Paul W. Werth, "The Emergence of 'Freedom of Conscience' in Imperial Russia," *Kritika: Explorations in Russian and Eurasian History* 13, no. 3 (2012): 585–610; Paul W. Werth, "Toward 'Freedom of Conscience': Catholicism, Law, and the Contours of Religious Liberty in Late Imperial Russia," *Kritika: Explorations in Russian and Eurasian History* 7, no. 4 (2006): 843–63; Paul W. Werth, *The Tsar's Foreign Faiths: Toleration and the Fate of Religious Freedom in Imperial Russia* (Oxford: Oxford University Press, 2014); Crews, *For Prophet and Tsar*; Poole and Werth, *Religious Freedom*; Laurie Manchester, *Holy Fathers, Secular Sons: Clergy, Intelligentsia, and the Modern Self in Revolutionary Russia* (DeKalb: Northern Illinois University Press, 2008); Halfin, *From Darkness to Light*; Smolkin, *Sacred Space*; Alexander Agadjanian, "Russia's 'Cursed Issues,' Post-Soviet Religion, and the Endurance of Secular Modernity," in *Multiple Modernities and Postsecular Societies*, ed. Massimo Rosati and Kristina Stoeckl (New York: Routledge, 2016), 79–96; William G. Wagner, "Religion in Modern Russia: Revival and Survival," *Kritika: Explorations in Russian and Eurasian History* 15, no. 1 (2014): 151–68; Shevzov, "Miracle-Working Icons"; Michelson, *Beyond the Monastery Walls*; Kenworthy, *Heart of Russia*; Roudometof, Agadjanian, and Pankhurst, *Eastern Orthodoxy*; Alexander Agadjanian, "Breakthrough to Modernity, Apologia for Traditionalism: The Russian Orthodox View of Society and Culture in Comparative Perspective," *Religion, State & Society* 31, no. 4 (2003): 327–46.

51. Paul W. Werth, "Lived Orthodoxy and Confessional Diversity: The Last Decade on Religion in Modern Russia," *Kritika: Explorations in Russian and Eurasian History* 12, no. 4 (2011): 849–65; Christine D. Worobec, "Lived Orthodoxy in Imperial Russia," *Kritika: Explorations in Russian and Eurasian History* 7, no. 2 (2006): 329–50.

1. Confession and Modernity in Imperial Russia

1. Peter Brooks, *Troubling Confessions: Speaking Guilt in Law and Literature* (Chicago: University of Chicago Press, 2000), 92. W. David Meyers argues that, at Trent, confession went from being a seasonal ritual meant to purify the community and "set it straight" with God to an act of personal self-examination. W. David Meyers, *"Poor,*

Sinning Folk": Confession and Conscience in Counter-Reformation Germany (Ithaca, NY: Cornell University Press, 1996), 116, 134.

2. The argument for "novoe vremia" as something close to "early modern" in Western Europe is advanced by, among others, S. A. Vaigachev, "Dukhovnaia kul'tura perekhodnoi epokhi ot srednevekov'ia k novomu vremeni v Rossii i v zapadnoi Evrope: Nekotorye tipologicheskie paralleli," in *Russkaia kul'tura v perekhodnyi period ot srednevekov'ia k novomu vremeni; Sbornik statei* (Moscow: Institut rossiiskoi istorii RAN, 1992), 46–78.

3. In 1768, a combined religious-secular commission began to explore how to punish "actions contrary to both sacred and civil laws, but which carry different penalties." These included adultery, incest, sodomy, bestiality, rape, magic, infanticide by unwed mothers from shame, and suicide. Although the commission was closed in 1771, its discussions helped create the system of parallel criminal sentences and church penances. See B. V. Titlinov, *Gavriil Petrov, mitropolit Novgorodskii i Sankt-Peterburgskii (1730–1801): Ego zhizn' i deiatel'nost', v sviazi s tserkovnymi delami togo vremeni* (Petrograd, 1916), 244–50. All translations are the author's own.

4. "Pouchenie Fotiia, mitropolita Kievskogo," *Pravoslavnyi sobesednik*, ch. III (September–December 1860), 235–37.

5. Jan Joseph Santich, *Misso Moscovitica: The Role of the Jesuits in the Westernization of Russia, 1582–1689* (New York: Peter Lang, 1995). See also V. S. Del'vig, "Vliianie inozemtsev iz stran zapadnoi Evropy na razvitie rossiiskogo obshchestva v 1652–1740 gg." (PhD diss., Ivanovo State University, 2011).

6. Russian State Archive of Early Acts (RGADA), f. 396 (Oruzheinaia palata), op. 1, d. 40283, ll. 1–25 (1627).

7. *Polnoe sobranie zakonov* (St. Petersburg: tip. II otdeleniia, 1830), vol. 1, no. 47, 246. RGADA, f. 210, Novgorodskii stol, d. 96 (Mery k izkoreniiu bezchiniia vo vremia posta i suevernykh obychaev), fols. 1–13, 251–54, 316 (1645).

8. For the proceedings of the council, see *Dopolneniia k aktam istoricheskim, otnosiashchimsia k Rossii: Sobrany v inostrannykh arkhivakh i bibliotekakh* (St. Petersburg: E. Prats, 1848), vol. 5, 463, 469.

9. N. I. Subbotin, ed., *Materialy dlia istorii raskola za pervoe vremia ego sushchestvovaniia* (Moscow: Bratstvo sviatogo Petra Metropolita, 1894), vol. 2, 132–33.

10. See, for example, RGADA, f. 210, Prikaznyi stol, d. 799, fols. 23–57, Razsprosnye rechi trekh raskolnits (1680–81). This argument would persist through the early nineteenth century. See "O sovrativshikhsia v raznykh mestakh v raskol'nicheskoe zabluzhdenie zhiteliakh, i o nevzyskivaemom s nikh za nebytie u ispovedi shtraf," May 1, 1800, no. 461, in *Polnoe sobranie postanovlenii i rasporiazhenii po vedomostvu pravoslavnago veroispovedaniia Rossiiskoi imperii* (henceforth cited as *PSPRPV*) (St. Petersburg: v sinodal'noi tipografii, 1910), vol. 14, 561–62.

11. "Rezoliutsiia Sviateishego Sinoda na dokladnye punkty," June 15, 1722, no. 1323, in *PSPRPV*, vol. 2, 161–63.

12. See in particular James Cracraft, *The Petrine Revolution in Russian Culture* (Cambridge, MA: Belknap Press of Harvard College, 2004), 175–80; Alexander V. Muller, trans. and ed., *The Spiritual Regulation of Peter the Great* (Seattle: University of Washington Press, 1972), 10; Viktor Zhivov, "Pokaiannaia distsiplina i individual'noe blagochestie," in *Druzhba: Ee formy, ispytaniia i dary: Uspenskie chteniia* (Kyiv: Dukh i litera,

2008), 303–43; Oleg Kharkhordin, *The Collective and the Individual in Russia: A Study of Practices* (Berkeley: University of California Press, 1999), 5.

13. Alexander Murray, "Confession as a Historical Source in the Thirteenth Century," in *The Writing of History in the Middle Ages: Essays Presented to Richard William Southern*, ed. R. H. C. Davis and J. M. Wallace-Hadrill (Oxford: Clarendon Press, 1981), 322; Meyers, *"Poor, Sinning Folk,"* 119–22.

14. Gerald Strauss, ed., *Manifestations of Discontent in Germany on the Eve of the Reformation* (Bloomington: Indiana University Press, 1971), 146.

15. "O dopolnenii ob"iavleniia Sviateishego Sinoda ot 30 Aprelia 1722 goda raz"iasneniiami, kak postupat' po delam, otkryvaemym sviashchennikam kaiushchimisia na ispovedi," September 4, 1723, no. 1350, in *PSPRPV*, vol. 3, 190–92. For denunciation in the Muscovite period, see Valerie A. Kivelson, "Muscovite 'Citizenship': Rights without Freedom," *Journal of Modern History* 74, no. 3 (2002): 465–89.

16. "Ob izmenenii 2go punkta opredeleniia Sv. Sinoda," revised on September 30, 1723, no. 1379, in *PSPRPV*, vol. 3, 224–26.

17. Russian State Historical Archive (RGIA), f. 796 (Holy Synod), op. 15, d. 144 (1734), and RGIA, f. 796, op. 23, d. 366, l. 83 (1742).

18. See the facsimile of the 1669 Innokentii (Gizel'), Archimandrite, *Mir s bogom chelovieku ili pokaianie sviatoe, primiriaiushchee bogovi chelovieka ucheniem ot pisaniia sviatogo i ot uchitelei tserkovnykh* (Kyiv-L'viv: Vyd. "Svichado," 2009), t. 1, kn. 2, 27–30. The rejection of satisfaction in the 1776 *O dolzhnostiakh presviterov prikhodskikh*, attributed to Archbishop Georgii (Konisskii) of Mogilev and Bishop Parfenii (Sopkovskii) of Smolensk, is available in a reprint edition is *O dolzhnostiakh presviterov prikhodskikh* (Moscow: Izd. Sretenskogo monastyria, 2004).

19. "Ob uchinenii v Sinodal'noi kantseliarii zhenie, pozhelavshei, s razresheniia muzha, postrichsia v monashestvo . . . i o doprosie po semu eia muzha i dukhovnika," April 1, 1730, no. 2432, in *PSPRPV*, vol. 6, 252.

20. "Ob otvete na ispovedi, dannom sviashchenniku kuptsom Moskvinym po voprosu: Ne povinen li on, Moskvin, v sozhzhenii korablia," May 28, 1731, no. 2711, in *PSPRPV*, vol. 7, 75–76

21. On previous practices, see "Ob otpravlenii takogo chisla sviashchennikov, dlia uveshchanii i ispovedi osuzhdennykh k natural'nym ekzekutsiiam kolodnikov, kakoe budet naznachenno," August 30, 1730, no. 2476, in *PSPRPV*, vol. 7, 324.

22. "O naznachenii osobago sviashchennika dlia uveshchanii, ispovedi, i Sv. prichastiia kolodnikov," September 29, 1735, no. 2918, in *PSPRPV*, vol. 9, 146–47.

23. See the discussion of Russian legal precedent by Senator Tagantsev, in State Archive of the Russian Federation (Gosudarstvennyi Arkhiv Rossiiskoi Federatsii), f. 564, op. 1, d. 641, ll. 1–3 (1909).

24. S. Smirnov, "Kak goveli v drevnei Rusi?," *Tserkovnye vedomosti*, no. 8 (February 24, 1901): 266–79; no. 9 (March 3, 1901): 305–11; no. 10 (March 10, 1901): 343–51.

25. For Nikonov, see RGADA, f. 7, op. 1, d. 2285; for Frolov, see RGADA, f. 7, op. 1, d. 316a. Anikiev's case has since vanished, but a record of its contents still appears in RGADA, as f. 7, op. 1, d. 1509.

26. Mark Cruse and Hilde Hoogenboom, trans., *The Memoirs of Catherine the Great* (New York: Modern Library, 2005), 47.

27. Cruse and Hoogenboom, *The Memoirs of Catherine the Great*, 201–7.

28. A. G. Lebedintsev, *Russkie gosudari v Kieve* (Kiev, 1896), 115–16.

29. "O sobranii svedienii, gde v inostrannykh gosudarstvakh imeiutsia i na kakom soderzhanii pravoslavnyia tserkvi pri russkikh posol'stvakh," December 12, 1744, no. 797, in *PSPRV*, vol. 10, 297; RGIA, f. 796, op. 25, d. 726, ll. 1–2.

30. All quotations in this case come from RGADA, f. 18, op. 1, d. 134, ll. 4–32ob.

31. This and all other references to this case are from RGADA, f. 7 (Dela Preobrazhenskogo prikaza i tainoi kantseliarii), op. 1, d. 134. An account is also in *PSPRPV*, Reign of Elizaveta Petrovna, no. 975, vol. 11, 33–43.

32. See Akilina Kobeleva's 1733 claim along these lines: no. 3074, in *PSPRPV*, vol. 8, 467–74.

33. See, for example, National Archive of the Republic of Tatarstan (NART), f. 4, op. 1, d. 1531 (on the assignment of a penance to Stefan Danilov for his absence at confession and communion) (1823).

34. NART, f. 4, op. 1, d. 945 (on the assignment of a penance to Merkul Ksenofontov Kondrat'ev for not having gone to confession), ll. 1–9 (1819).

35. For examples from the Kyiv Consistory, see Central State Historical Archive of Kyiv, f. 127, op. 28 (1825), d. 88 (on collecting a fine from the peasant F. Kuplenko for not going to confession); from St. Petersburg, see Central State Historical Archive of St. Petersburg, f. 19, op. 32, d. 142 (on assigning the townsman *meshchanin* Timofei Vorobiev a penance for not going to confession and Holy Communion in 1837) (1840–1847); from Moscow, see Central Historical Archive of Moscow, f. 203, op. 341 (1869–79), d. 9 (on assigning penances to peasants A. Kharlamov and A. Sukov for not having gone to confession).

36. NART, f. 4, op. 1, d. 121323 (on the assignment of penances to criminals) (1906–9), l. 12.

37. NART, f. 4, op. 1, d. 121323 (on the assignment of penances to criminals) (1906–9), l. 20.

38. NART, f. 4, op. 1, d. 121323, ll. 37, 43, 71.

39. NART, f. 4, op. 149 (1917), d. 41 (on the assignment of a church penance to the personal honorable citizen Aleksei Surkov), l. 3ob.

40. While Maria Korogodina argues that confessional manuals had become a mass phenomenon by the sixteenth century, and that changes in questions asked reflected changes in actual behavior, there is still no way of determining how often these manuals were used or how often people went to confession. See M. V. Korogodina, *Ispoved' v Rossii v XIV–XIX vekakh: Issledovanie i teksty* (St. Petersburg: Dmitrii Bulanin, 2006), 310–32.

2. Church and State versus Church and People

1. This chapter was first published in German as "Staatskirche und Diaspora. Die zwei Erscheinungsformen von Zivilgesellschaft in der russischen Orthodoxie," in *Zwischen Fürsorge und Seelsorge. Christliche Kirchen in den europäischen Zivilgesellschaften seit dem 18. Jahrhundert*, ed. Arnd Bauerkämper and Jürgen Nautz (Frankfurt: Campus Verlag, 2009), 237–58. The present version has been revised and updated for the English translation. Translation by Deborah Fölsche-Forrow.

2. Quoted in Petros Vassiliades, "Orthodox Christianity," in *God's Rule: The Politics of World Religions*, ed. Jacob Neusner (Washington, DC: Georgetown University Press, 2003), 99.

3. Kristina Stoeckl, "Russian Orthodoxy and Secularism," *Religion and Politics* 1, no. 2 (2020): 11.

4. Alexandros K. Papaderos, "Aspekte orthodoxer Sozialethik," in *Perspektiven ökumenischer Sozialethik. Der Auftrag der Kirchen im größeren Europa*, ed. Ingeborg Gabriel, Alexandros K. Papaderos, and Ulrich H. J. Körtner (Ostfildern: Matthias Grünewald-Verlag, 2006), 113–15.

5. On this dual role of public religions, see José Casanova, *Public Religions in the Modern World* (Chicago: University of Chicago Press, 1994); José Casanova, "Public Religions Revisited," in *Religion: Beyond a Concept*, ed. Hent de Vries (New York: Fordham University Press, 2008), 101–19.

6. See John T. S. Madeley and Zsolt Enyedi, *Church and State in Contemporary Europe: The Chimera of Neutrality* (New York: Routledge, 2003).

7. Konstantin Kostjuk, *Der Begriff des Politischen in der russisch-orthodoxen Tradition* (Paderborn: Schöningh, 2005), 58–61. In this chapter, I frequently draw on Kostjuk's excellent study, which has so far been published only in German.

8. On these different distinctions, for church versus believers, see Vera Shevzov, *Russian Orthodoxy on the Eve of Revolution* (New York: Oxford University Press, 2004), esp. chap. 1. For elite versus peasant church, see Laura Engelstein, "Old and New, High and Low: Straw Horsemen of Russian Orthodoxy," in *Orthodox Russia: Belief and Practice under the Tsars*, ed. Valerie A. Kivelson and Robert H. Greene (University Park: Pennsylvania State University Press, 2003), 23–32; Nadieszda Kizenko, review of *Letters from Heaven: Popular Religion in Russia and Ukraine*, ed. by John-Paul Himka and Andriy Zayarnyuk, and *Ispoved' v Rossii v XIV–XIX vekakh: Issledovanie i teksty*, by M. V. Korogodina, *Kritika: Explorations in Russian and Eurasian History* 9, no. 3 (2008): 641–54. For authority versus lived religion, see Catherine Wanner, ed., *State Secularism and Lived Religion in Soviet Russia and Ukraine* (Washington, DC: Woodrow Wilson Center Press; New York: Oxford University Press, 2012); Thomas N. Tentler, "Epilogue: A View from the West," in *Orthodox Russia: Belief and Practice under the Tsars*, ed. Valerie A. Kivelson and Robert H. Greene (University Park: Pennsylvania State University Press, 2003), 253–75.

9. Randall A. Poole, "Introduction: Faith, Freedom, and the Varieties of Russian Religious Experience," in *Religious Freedom in Modern Russia*, ed. Randall A. Poole and Paul W. Werth (Pittsburgh: University of Pittsburgh Press, 2018), 11.

10. Alexander V. Muller, trans. and ed., *The Spiritual Regulation of Peter the Great* (Seattle: University of Washington Press, 1972), cited in Poole, "Introduction: Faith, Freedom," 12.

11. José Casanova, "Private and Public Religions," *Social Research* 59, no. 1 (1992): 55.

12. Gregory L. Freeze, "Handmaiden of the State? The Church in Imperial Russia Reconsidered," *Journal of Ecclesiastical History* 36, no. 1 (1985): 82–102.

13. Poole, "Introduction: Faith, Freedom," 12.

14. See Scott M. Kenworthy, "Archbishop Nikon (Rozhdestvenskii) and Pavel Florenskii on Spiritual Experience, Theology, and the Name-Glorifiers Dispute," in *Thinking Orthodox in Modern Russia: Culture, History, Context*, ed. Patrick Lally Michelson and Judith Deutsch Kornblatt (Madison: University of Wisconsin Press, 2014), 85–107. A detailed description and interpretation of events is also given by Metropolitan Hilarion Alfeev in his Italian publication *La gloria del nome* (Magnano: Edizioni Qiqajon, 2002).

15. Shevzov, *Russian Orthodoxy*.

16. On this stipulation, see Kostjuk, *Begriff des Politischen*, 108.

17. Kostjuk, *Begriff des Politischen*, 62.

18. Freeze, "Handmaiden."

19. Fyodor Dostoyevsky, *The Brothers Karamazov*, trans. Constance Garnett (New York: Penguin Books, 1958), 400.

20. See Patrick Lally Michelson, *Beyond the Monastery Walls: The Ascetic Revolution in Russian Orthodox Thought, 1814–1914* (Madison: University of Wisconsin Press, 2017); Scott M. Kenworthy, *The Heart of Russia: Trinity-Sergius, Monasticism, and Society after 1825* (Washington, DC: Woodrow Wilson Center Press; New York: Oxford University Press, 2010).

21. Jutta Scherrer, *Die Petersburger religiös-philosophischen Vereinigungen* (Wiesbaden: Otto Harrassowitz, 1973).

22. On religious philosophy in the prerevolutionary period, see Randall A. Poole, trans. and ed., *Problems of Idealism: Essays in Russian Social Philosophy* (New Haven, CT: Yale University Press, 2003).

23. For a detailed analysis, see Daniela Kalkandjieva, *The Russian Orthodox Church, 1917–1948: From Decline to Resurrection* (London: Routledge, 2017).

24. Sergei Bulgakov, "Social Teaching in Modern Russian Orthodox Theology," in *Orthodoxy and Modern Society*, ed. Robert Bird (New Haven, CT: Yale University Press, 1995), 5–26; Rowan Williams, ed., *Sergii Bulgakov: Towards a Russian Political Theology* (Edinburgh: T&T Clark, 1999); Georges Florovsky, *The Ways of Russian Theology*, vols. 5–6 of *The Collected Works of Georges Florovsky* (Belmont, MA: Nordland, 1987). See also Brandon Gallaher, "'Waiting for the Barbarians': Identity and Polemicism in the Neo-Patristic Synthesis of Georges Florovsky," *Modern Theology* 27, no. 4 (2011): 659–91.

25. Cf. John Meyendorff, *Byzantine Theology: Historical Trends and Doctrines* (New York: Fordham University Press, 1983); John Meyendorff, *St. Gregory Palamas and Orthodox Spirituality* (Crestwood, NY: St. Vladimir's Seminary Press, 1998).

26. Williams, *Sergii Bulgakov*, 230.

27. For studies concerned with the theological debate among Russian émigrés, see, for example, Robert Bird, "The Tragedy of Russian Religious Philosophy: Sergei Bulgakov and the Future of Orthodox Theology," in *Orthodox Christianity and Contemporary Europe*, ed. Jonathan Sutton and Wil van den Bercken (Leuven: Peeters, 2003), 211–28; Alexander Schmemann, "Russian Theology: 1920–1972; An Introductory Survey," *St. Vladimir's Theological Quarterly* 16, no. 4 (1972): 172–94; Kristina Stoeckl, "Modernity and Its Critique in 20th Century Russian Orthodox Thought," *Studies in East European Thought* 58, no. 4 (2006): 243–69; Paul Valliere, *Modern Russian Theology: Bukharev, Soloviev, Bulgakov: Orthodox Theology in a New Key* (Grand Rapids, MI: William B. Eerdmans, 2000); Nathaniel Wood, "'I Have Overcome the World': The Church, the Liberal State, and Christ's Two Natures in the Russian Politics of Theosis," in *Christianity, Democracy, and the Shadow of Constantine*, ed. George E. Demacopoulos and Aristotle Papanikolaou (New York: Fordham University Press, 2017), 155–73.

28. See Michael Bourdeaux, "Zoya Krakhmalnikova: Christian Writer Jailed for Her Beliefs by the Soviet Authorities," obituary, *Guardian*, May 12, 2008. On the persecution of Orthodox Christians in the USSR, see Jane Ellis, *The Russian Orthodox Church: A Contemporary History* (London: Routledge, 1988).

29. Oleg Kharkhordin, *The Collective and the Individual in Russia: A Study of Practices* (Berkeley: University of California Press, 1999); Oleg Kharkhordin, "Civil Society and Orthodox Christianity," *Europe-Asia Studies* 50, no. 6 (1998): 949–68.

30. Shevzov, *Russian Orthodoxy*, 8.

31. On the 1997 bill and the events leading to its becoming law, see Zoe Knox, *Russian Society and the Orthodox Church: Religion in Russia after Communism* (London: RoutledgeCurzon, 2005). On the post-Soviet Russian Orthodox Church, see Irina Papkova, *The Orthodox Church and Russian Politics* (Washington, DC: Woodrow Wilson Center Press; New York: Oxford University Press, 2011); Katja Richters, *The Post-Soviet Russian Orthodox Church: Politics, Culture and Greater Russia* (London: Routledge, 2013); Zoe Knox and Anastasia Mitrofanova, "The Russian Orthodox Church," in *Eastern Christianity and Politics in the Twenty-First Century*, ed. Lucian N. Leustean (London: Routledge, 2014), 38–66.

32. Irina Papkova, "The Freezing of Historical Memory? The Post-Soviet Russian Orthodox Church and the Council of 1917," in *Religion, Morality, and Community in Post-Soviet Societies*, ed. Mark D. Steinberg and Catherine Wanner (Washington, DC: Woodrow Wilson Center Press; Bloomington: Indiana University Press, 2008), 55–84.

33. The Bases of the Social Concept (Official Translation)," official website of the Department for External Church Relations of the Moscow Patriarchate, accessed February 8, 2024, http://www.mospat.ru/en/documents/social-concepts

34. Social Concept.

35. Zoe Knox, "The Symphonic Ideal: The Moscow Patriarchate's Post-Soviet Leadership," *Europe-Asia Studies* 55, no. 4 (2003): 575–96.

36. Social Concept.

37. Kristina Stoeckl, "*Political Hesychasm?* Vladimir Petrunin's Neo-Byzantine Interpretation of the Social Doctrine of the Russian Orthodox Church," *Studies in East European Thought* 62, no. 1 (2010): 125–33.

38. For an early description of this organization, see John B. Dunlop, "The Russian Orthodox Church as an 'Empire-Saving' Institution," in *The Politics of Religion in Russia and the New States of Eurasia*, ed. Michael Bourdeaux (Armonk, NY: M. E. Sharpe, 1995), 15–41.

39. See Aleksandr Filonenko, "The Russian Orthodox Church in Twentieth-Century Britain: Laity and 'Openness to the World,'" *Religion, State & Society* 27, no. 1 (1999): 59–71.

40. Maria Hämmerli and Edmund Mucha, "Innovation in the Russian Orthodox Church: The Crisis in the Diocese of Sourozh," in *Orthodox Identities in Western Europe: Migration, Settlement and Innovation*, ed. Maria Hämmerli and Jean-François Mayer (Farnham, UK: Ashgate, 2014), 291–302.

41. Dmitry Uzlaner, "The Pussy Riot Case and the Peculiarities of Russian Post-Secularism," *State, Religion and Church* 1, no. 1 (2014): 46–47.

3. Russian Religious Thought and the Christian Justification of the Nation

1. Carlton J. H. Hayes, "Nationalism as a Religion," in *Essays on Nationalism* (New York: Macmillan, 1926), 93–125; Reinhard Wittram, *Nationalismus und Säkularisation:*

Beiträge zur Geschichte und Problematik des Nationalgeistes (Lüneburg: Heliand-Verlag, 1949), 10–12, 30–32.

2. Elie Kedourie, *Nationalism* (London: Hutchinson, 1960).

3. Eric Hobsbawn, *Nations and Nationalism since 1780: Programme, Myth Reality* (Cambridge: Cambridge University Press, 1990), 14.

4. Adrian Hastings, *The Construction of Nationhood: Ethnicity, Religion and Nationalism* (Cambridge: Cambridge University Press, 1997), 3–4.

5. Anthony D. Smith, *Chosen Peoples: Sacred Sources of National Identity* (Oxford: Oxford University Press, 2003). Note that "sacred foundation" for Smith, as I read him, does not necessarily mean a covenant in the manner of the Old Testament, but means the belief in an origin that has a sacred function. In modern nationalism, "religious sanctity, the category of the sacred in traditional religions, has become *transmuted* in the nationalist belief-system into a secular authenticity" (40; emphasis added).

6. In addition to the religious current, late imperial Russia saw also a predominantly secular current of liberal, civic nationalism, represented by figures such as Boris Chicherin, Peter Struve, and Pavel Miliukov. For an analysis of these thinkers—in company with Solov'ev—as "liberal nationalists," see Ol'ga Malinova, *Liberal'nyi natsionalizm* (Moscow: RIK Rusanova, 2000), chap. 3. Interestingly, the secular Struve, too, described his own grounding of what he called "true nationalism" (which comes close to the "nationality" of the religious thinkers) in the human personality (*lichnost'*) as Christian. See P. B. Struve, *Na raznye temy* (St. Petersburg: Tip. A. E. Koltinskogo, 1902), 549. On the emergence of the terms *narodnost'* and *natsional'nost'* and their increasing popularity in late imperial Russia, see Nathaniel Knight, "Ethnicity, Nationality and the Masses: *Narodnost'* and Modernity in Imperial Russia," 41–64, and Charles Steinwedel, "To Make a Difference: The Category of Ethnicity in Late Imperial Russian Politics, 1861–1917," 67–86, both in *Russian Modernity: Politics, Knowledge, Practices*, ed. David L. Hoffmann and Yanni Kotsonis (New York: St. Martin's Press, 2000).

7. Yael Tamir, *Liberal Nationalism* (Princeton, NJ: Princeton University Press, 1993), 79.

8. Malinova, *Liberal'nyi natsionalizm*, 10 (pagination refers to the online edition at http://rss.archives.ceu.hu/archive/00001095/01/101.pdf).

9. The liberal interpretation of Russian religious philosophy of late imperial Russia can be found in Paul Valliere, *Modern Russian Theology: Bukharev, Soloviev, Bulgakov: Orthodox Theology in a New Key* (Grand Rapids, MI: William B. Eerdmans, 2000); Greg Gaut, "A Practical Unity: Vladimir Solov'ev and Russian Liberalism," *Canadian Slavonic Papers* 43, no. 3 (2000): 295–314; Randall A. Poole, "Religion, War, and Revolution: E. N. Trubetskoi's Liberal Construction of Russian National Identity, 1912–20," *Kritika: Explorations in Russian and Eurasian History* 7, no. 2 (2006): 195–240. For a critique of this approach, see Patrick Lally Michelson, "Freedom of Conscience and the Limits of the Liberal Solovyov," *Solov'evskie issledovaniia* 41, no. 1 (2014): 25–46. Andrzej Walicki, *The Slavophile Controversy: History of a Conservative Utopia in Nineteenth-Century Russian Thought* (Notre Dame, IN: University of Notre Dame Press, 1989), 575. Walicki notes that Solov'ev's utopia was "certainly not a liberal utopia"; he devotes a chapter to Solov'ev in Andrzej Walicki, *Legal Philosophies of Russian Liberalism* (Oxford: Clarendon Press, 1987), 195–212. See, moreover, the remarks in Oliver Smith, review of *A History of Russian Philosophy, 1830–1930: Faith, Reason, and the Defense of Human Dignity*, ed. Gary M. Hamburg and

Randall A. Poole, *Forum for Modern Language Studies* 49, no. 1 (2013): 111–17; and Christopher Stroop, "Nationalist War Commentary as Russian Religious Thought: The Religious Intelligentsia's Politics of Providentialism," *Russian Review* 72, no. 1 (2013), 94–115. Stroop's analyses question the "liberal" emphasis on human agency exclusively in historical interpretations of Russian religious thought.

10. Ernest Gellner, *Nations and Nationalism*, 2nd ed. (Ithaca, NY: Cornell University Press, 2006), 1–2. From here on, I omit the quotation marks around "universalistic" when using Gellner's concept, while being fully aware of the challenges inherent in this position.

11. See, for instance, John Stuart Mill, "Of Nationality, as Connected with Representative Government," chap. 16 in *Considerations on Representative Government* (London, 1861). As argued in Malinova, *Liberal'nyi natsionalizm* (80), Solov'ev showed little interest in nations' self-determination. As for Mill, he too was not only a "liberal nationalist" but also a "liberal imperialist" in that he actively promoted the British Empire, while his nationality theory was meant for the Western world. See Uday Singh Metha, *Liberalism and Empire: A Study in Nineteenth-Century British Liberal Thought* (Chicago: University of Chicago Press, 1999), 7.

12. On the Russian liberals' views on this issue in general, see Theodore R. Weeks, *Nation and State in Late Imperial Russia: Nationalism and Russification on the Western Frontier, 1863–1914* (DeKalb: Northern Illinois University Press, 1996), 24. On Solov'ev more specifically, see Greg Gaut, "Can a Christian Be a Nationalist? Vladimir Solov'ev's Critique of Nationalism," *Slavic Review* 57, no. 1 (1998): 87. On Trubetskoi, see Poole, "Religion, War, and Revolution," 215.

13. Their "expressivism" was, thus, indebted to the Herderian and Hegelian legacy. See Charles Taylor, *Sources of the Self: The Making of the Modern Identity* (Cambridge, MA: Harvard University Press 1989), 368–93.

14. Craig Calhoun, Mark Juergensmeyer, and Jonathan VanAntwerpen, introduction to *Rethinking Secularism*, ed. Craig Calhoun, Mark Juergensmeyer, and Jonathan VanAntwerpen (New York: Oxford University Press, 2011), 15.

15. Smith, *Chosen Peoples*, 10, 15–16.

16. On these and other central concepts in Solov'ev's philosophy, see Randall A. Poole's chapter in this book. For a systematic overview of Solov'ev's writings on nationalism, see Gaut, "Can a Christian Be a Nationalist?"

17. V. S. Solov'ev, *Sochineniia v dvukh tomakh* (Moscow, 1989), vol. 1, 281. Except where noted, all translations from Russian are my own.

18. Ernest Renan, *Qu'est-ce qu'une nation?* (Paris, 1882).

19. Solov'ev, *Sochineniia*, vol. 1, 262.

20. Manon de Courten, *History, Sophia and the Russian Nation: A Reassessment of Vladimir Solov'ëv's Views of History and His Social Commitment* (Bern: Peter Lang, 2004), 157.

21. Solov'ev, *Sochineniia*, vol. 1, 345.

22. Solov'ev, *Sochineniia*, vol. 1, 281–82.

23. Solov'ev, *Sochineniia*, vol. 1, 326–27.

24. Solov'ev, *Sochineniia*, vol. 1, 285.

25. Joep Leerssen, *National Thought in Europe: A Cultural History* (Amsterdam: Amsterdam University Press, 2006), 230–31.

26. Solov'ev, *Sochineniia*, vol. 1, 299–301.

27. Solov'ev, *Sochineniia*, vol. 1, 309.

28. Solov'ev, *Sochineniia*, vol. 2, 219–20.

29. Walicki, *Slavophile Controversy*, 573. Cf. Solov'ev, *Sochineniia*, vol. 1, 289.

30. Solov'ev, *Sochineniia*, vol. 1, 336. This formulation is italicized in the original. Solov'ev regarded Immanuel Kant's moral law as "one of the greatest achievements of the human mind." Quoted in Randall A. Poole, "Kant and the Kingdom of Ends in Russian Religious Thought (Vladimir Solov'ev)," in *Thinking Orthodox in Modern Russia: Culture, History, Context*, ed. Patrick Lally Michelson and Judith Deutsch Kornblatt (Madison: University of Wisconsin Press, 2014), 216.

31. Cf. Immanuel Kant, *Perpetual Peace and Other Essays*, trans. Ted Humphrey (Indianapolis: Hackett, 1983), 108. Solov'ev does not refer to this work by Kant.

32. Solov'ev, *Sochineniia*, vol. 1, 264.

33. Solov'ev, *Sochineniia*, vol. 1, 261; vol. 2, 220.

34. Judith Deutsch Kornblatt, "Vladimir Solov'ev on Spiritual Nationhood, Russia and the Jews," *Russian Review* 56, no. 2 (1997): 174, 176.

35. Solov'ev, *Sochineniia*, vol. 1, 269; vol. 2, 228–29.

36. Solov'ev, *Sochineniia*, vol. 1, 301.

37. Vladimir Solovyov, *The Justification of the Good: An Essay in Moral Philosophy*, trans. Natalie Duddington, ed. Boris Jakim (Grand Rapids, MI: William B. Eerdmans, 2005), 241. Original Russian text available in Solov'ev, *Sochineniia*, vol. 1, 360. References to this edition appear in brackets in subsequent citations.

38. Solov'ev. *Sochineniia*, vol. 2, 220. On perennialism and primordialism, see Anthony D. Smith, *Nationalism: Theory, Ideology, History* (Cambridge, UK: Polity Press, 2001), 49–57.

39. Kornblatt, "Solov'ev on Spiritual Nationhood," 172.

40. Solovyov, *Justification of the Good*, 246 (365).

41. Solovyov, *Justification of the Good*, 247 (366).

42. Solovyov, *Justification of the Good*, 248 (367).

43. Poole, "Kant and the Kingdom of Ends," 218.

44. Solovyov, *Justification of the Good*, 256 (376).

45. Solovyov, *Justification of the Good*, 257 (377).

46. Malinova, *Liberal'nyi natsionalizm*, 78. See also Courten, *History, Sophia and the Russian Nation*, 155. Mazzini's view can be found in Stefano Recchia and Nadia Urbinati, eds., *Cosmopolitanism of Nations: Giuseppe Mazzini's Writings on Democracy, Nation Building and International Relations* (Princeton, NJ: Princeton University Press, 2009), 53–65.

47. Sonia Sikka, *Herder on Humanity and Cultural Difference: Enlightened Relativism* (Cambridge: Cambridge University Press, 2011), 219–47. That Herder saw all nations as belonging to the Kingdom of God was something he stated in his *Letters for the Advancement of Humanity* (written in the 1790s, quoted in Sikka, *Herder on Humanity and Cultural Difference*, 238), but without citing biblical texts in the extensive way that Solov'ev did.

48. On Providentialism in Russian thought of the late imperial period, see Stroop, "Nationalist War Commentary."

49. The phrase is borrowed from José Casanova, "The Secular, Secularizations, Secularisms," in *Rethinking Secularism*, ed. Craig Calhoun, Mark Juergensmeyer, and Jonathan VanAntwerpen (New York: Oxford University Press, 2011), 65.

50. As argued in Michelson, "Freedom of Conscience," 41.

51. Charles Taylor, *A Secular Age* (Cambridge, MA: Belknap Press of Harvard University Press, 2007).

52. Solov′ev's attitude to scripture is therefore a traditional, if radical, Orthodox one. See Theodore G. Stylianopoulos, "Scripture and Tradition in the Church," in *The Cambridge Companion to Orthodox Christian Theology*, ed. Mary B. Cunningham and Elizabeth Theokritoff (Cambridge: Cambridge University Press, 2008), 24, 30. On the "dual allegiance" of reason and scripture in Solov′ev, see Jonathan Sutton, *The Religious Philosophy of Vladimir Solovyov: Towards a Reassessment* (Basingstoke: Macmillan Press, 1988), 130–40.

53. Poole, "Kant and the Kingdom of Ends," 219.

54. Sean Gillen, "V. D. Kudriavtsev and the Making of Russian Orthodox Theism," in *Thinking Orthodox in Modern Russia: Culture, History, Context*, ed. Patrick Lally Michelson and Judith Deutsch Kornblatt (Madison: University of Wisconsin Press, 2014), 119. For a theist interpretation of Solov′ev, see Poole, "Kant and the Kingdom of Ends." Whether Kant was a theist or deist is disputed.

55. On Bulgakov's (and others') reception of Solov′ev, see Kåre Johan Mjør, "Philosophy, Modernity and National Identity: The Quest for a Russian Philosophy at the Turn of the Twentieth Century," *Slavonic and East European Review* 92, no. 4 (2014): 622–52.

56. This essay, which first was published in *Questions of Philosophy and Psychology*, no. 66–67 (1903), is quoted in S. N. Bulgakov, *Ot marksizma k idealizmu: Sbornik statei* (St. Petersburg: Tovarishchestvo "Obshchestvennaia pol′za," 1903), 240, 250.

57. Bulgakov, *Ot marksizma k idealizmu*, 252.

58. Bulgakov, *Ot marksizma k idealizmu*, 258–59. It is difficult to see the difference between Bulgakov and Solov′ev here, since the former's formulation clearly echoes the latter's as quoted earlier.

59. Marshall S. Shatz and Judith E. Zimmerman, trans. and eds., *Vekhi/Landmarks: A Collection of Articles about the Russian Intelligentsia* (Armonk, NY: M. E. Sharpe, 1994), 44.

60. For an extensive treatment, see Robin Aizlewood and Ruth Coates, eds., *Landmarks Revisited: The Vekhi Symposium 100 Years On* (Boston: Academic Studies Press, 2013).

61. The essay first appeared in *Questions of Philosophy and Psychology*, no. 103 (2010). References here are made to S. N. Bulgakov, *Dva grada: Issledovaniia o prirode obshchestvennykh idealov* (Moscow: Put′, 1911), vol. 2, 280–81.

62. Bulgakov, *Dva grada*, vol. 2, 281.

63. See Catherine Evtuhov, *The Cross and the Sickle: Sergei Bulgakov and the Fate of Russian Religious Philosophy, 1890–1920* (Ithaca, NY: Cornell University Press, 1997), 159–62.

64. Bulgakov, *Dva grada*, vol. 2, 296.

65. Bulgakov, *Dva grada*, vol. 2, 287.

66. See N. A. Berdiaev, *Dusha Rossii* (Moscow: Tip. Sytina, 1915), 31. On the Hegelian concept of "historical nations" in Russian thought, see Ana Siljak, "Between East and West: Hegel and the Origins of the Russian Dilemma," *Journal of the History of Ideas* 62, no. 2 (2001): 335–58.

67. Bulgakov, *Dva grada*, vol. 2, 278–79, 298, 300.

68. See Stroop, "Nationalist War Commentary," 111; Evtuhov, *The Cross and the Sickle*, 141. On nationalism, together with Orthodoxy and statehood, as a central component of the program of these writers and their publishing house Put', see E. A. Gollerbakh, *K nezrimomu gradu: Religiozno-filosofskaia gruppa "Put'" (1910–1919) v poiskakh novoi russkoi identichnosti* (St. Petersburg: Aleteiia, 2000), 37–56.

69. Bulgakov, *Dva grada*, vol. 2, 281, 289, 298.

70. E. N. Trubetskoi, "Staryi i novyi natsional'nyi messianizm," *Russkaia mysl'*, no. 3 (1912): 86.

71. Trubetskoi, "Staryi i novyi natsional'nyi messianizm," 98.

72. Trubetskoi, "Staryi i novyi natsional'nyi messianizm," 96.

73. This typology was not invented by Trubetskoi or Solov'ev, however; it appeared at least as early as in Aleksandr Lopukhin's 1885 lectures on the "contemporary West." See Vera Shevzov, "The Burdens of Tradition: Orthodox Constructions of the West in Russia (Late 19th–Early 20th cc.)," in *Orthodox Constructions of the West*, ed. George E. Demacopoulos and Aristotle Papanikolaou (New York: Fordham University Press, 2013), 95.

74. Trubetskoi, "Staryi i novyi natsional'nyi messianizm," 93.

75. Trubetskoi, "Staryi i novyi natsional'nyi messianizm," 96.

76. Trubetskoi, "Staryi i novyi natsional'nyi messianizm," 97.

77. Trubetskoi, "Staryi i novyi natsional'nyi messianizm," 101.

78. E. N. Trubetskoi, *Mirosozertsanie Vladimira Solov'eva* (Moscow: Put', 1913), vol. 2, 115.

79. Trubetskoi, *Mirosozertsanie Vladimira Solov'eva*, vol. 2, 156.

80. Stroop, "Nationalist War Commentary," 108. On Trubetskoi's response to the war, see also Poole, "Religion, War, and Revolution," 203–15; and Gollerbakh, *K nezrimomu gradu*, 38. Bulgakov resonates along similar lines in "Reflections on Nationality," regarding the Russian nationality as the first among equals in the common house of the Russian state. Such views became even more prominent in his wartime writings.

81. See, for instance, Hugh McLeod, "Christianity and Nationalism in Nineteenth-Century Europe," *International Journal for the Study of the Christian Church* 15, no. 1 (2015): 7–22; Halvor Moxnes, "The Nation and Nationalism," in *The Oxford Handbook of Nineteenth-Century Christian Thought*, ed. Joel D. S. Rasmussen, Judith Wolfe, and Johannes Zachhuber (Oxford: Oxford University Press, 2017), 246–63.

82. McLeod, "Christianity and Nationalism," 9. McLeod does not make explicit who these "Christian nationslists" were.

83. Arndt and Scheleiermacher quoted in A. J. Hoover, "German Nationalism and Religion," *History of European Ideas* 20, nos. 4–6 (1995): 765–66.

84. Hoover, "German Nationalism and Religion," 770.

85. Gerard Delanty, "An Interview with S. N. Eisenstadt: Pluralism and the Multiple Forms of Modernity," *European Journal of Social Theory* 7, no. 3 (2004): 394.

86. George E. Demacopoulos and Aristotle Papanikolaou, "Orthodox Naming of the Other: A Postcolonial Approach," in *Orthodox Constructions of the West*, ed. George E. Demacopoulos and Aristotle Papanikolaou (New York: Fordham University Press, 2013), 1–22. On the (post)colonial epistemology and situation, see Ilya Gerasimov, Sergey Glebov, and Marina Mogilner, "The Postimperial Meets the Postcolonial: Russian Historical Experience and the Postcolonial Moment," *Ab Imperio*, no. 2 (2013): 97–135.

87. Demacopoulos and Papanikolaou, "Orthodox Naming of the Other," 11. See also Shevzov, "Burdens of Tradition." On nationalism as a "weakness of Orthodoxy," see Ernst Benz, *Geist und Leben der Ostkirche* (Hamburg: Rowohlt, 1957), 174–75.

88. On how the Orthodox churches in this region took an active part in nation-building processes and enaged with nationalist ideology, see Lucian N. Leustean, ed., *Orthodox Christianity and Nationalism in Nineteenth-Century Southeastern Europe* (New York: Fordham University Press, 2014).

89. As argued in Victor Roudometof, *Globalization and Orthodox Christianity: The Transformation of a Religious Tradition* (New York: Routledge, 2014), chap. 5 ("Nationalism and the Orthodox Church: The Modern Synthesis").

90. On Russian post-reform nationalism, see Andreas Renner, *Russischer Nationalismus und Öffentlichkeit im Zarenreich 1855–1875* (Cologne: Böhlau Verlag, 2000).

91. Hastings, *Construction of Nationhood*, 196. See also Roudometof, *Globalization and Orthodox Christianity*, 81.

92. Bulgakov, *Dva grada*, vol. 2, 297.

4. "Dark" Intellectuals

I would like to express my gratitude to the participants of the "Varieties of Russian Modernity" conference held in the Russian Presidential Academy of National Economy and Public Administration (RANEPA) in 2013, Christopher Stroop, Vyatcheslav Danilov, Irina Dudenkova, Dmitri Kralechkin, and the book's anonymous reviewers.

1. Peter Galison and Emily Thompson, eds., *The Architecture of Science* (Cambridge, MA: MIT Press, 1999).

2. Post-Soviet Russian intellectual communities as well as some universities often represent themselves as "islands" of true freedom or academic quality imported from the West. See T. Shanin, "O pol'ze inogo: Britanskaia akademicheskaia traditsia i rossiiskoe universitetskoe obrazovanie," Polit.ru, January 23, 2006, http://www.polit.ru/article/2006/01/23/shan/. The distance between (modern) West and (archaic) East thus acquires the status of constitutive parameter for ideological mapping of educational institutions and particular academic communities during the Soviet period and well after it. (Quasi)naturalization and spatialization of cultural and social divides facilitated the making of education as another world fully detached from the outer everyday reality.

3. Emilio Gentile and Robert Mallett, "The Sacralisation of Politics: Definitions, Interpretations and Reflections on the Question of Secular Religion and Totalitarianism, *Totalitarian Movements and Political Religions* 1, no. 1 (2000): 20. http://doi.org/10.1080/14690760008406923. See also Michael Burleigh, *Earthly Powers: The Clash of Religion and Politics in Europe, from the French Revolution to the Great War* (New York: HarperCollins, 2009).

4. Yuri Slezkine, *The House of Government: A Saga of the Russian Revolution* (Princeton, NJ: Princeton University Press, 2017), esp. xii. There is a significant literature on Soviet Communism appropriating aspects of religion. See Igal Halfin, *From Darkness to Light: Class, Consciousness, and Salvation in Revolutionary Russia* (Pittsburgh: University of Pittsburgh Press, 2000), esp. 2–4; Andrzej Walicki, *Marxism and the Leap to the Kingdom of Freedom: The Rise and Fall of the Communist Utopia* (Stanford, CA: Stanford

University Press, 1995); Victoria Smolkin, *A Sacred Space Is Never Empty: A History of Soviet Atheism* (Princeton, NJ: Princeton University Press, 2018).

5. Barbara Walker, "*Kruzhok* Culture: The Meaning of Patronage in the Early Soviet Literary World," *Contemporary European History* 2, no. 1 (2002): 107–22.

6. Walker, "*Kruzhok* Culture," 113.

7. Cf. Walker, "*Kruzhok* Culture," 115–16.

8. Sheila Fitzpatrick, *Education and Social Mobility in the Soviet Union, 1921–1934* (Cambridge: Cambridge University Press, 1979).

9. The labels "Russian" and "Soviet" have to be used rather cautiously in order to avoid imaginary construction of Soviet or Russian per se. It is all too easy to identify ideas with some features of particular spatial areas. A geographical way of argumentation is often inscribed in the judgments made on mental differences. We need to distinguish between Russian or Soviet as cultural qualifications and Russian or Soviet as a geographical marker attached to a territory having no clear-enough borders. In this chapter, I use the notion "Soviet" in referring to the Soviet Union as a legal entity.

The history of universities of tsarist Russia had not abruptly come to end with the October Revolution. Corporate academic culture in the universities remained secure from the interventions of official ideology till the midst of the 1920s. Yet it is worth mentioning that, if before 1917 universities were often under suspicion for nihilism and a radical atheist spirit, after the revolution they were sometimes vice versa treated as potential allies of "reactionary religious elements." See M. M. Novikov, *Ot Moskvy do N'iu-Iorka. Moya zhizn' v nauke i politike* (Moscow: Izdatel'stvo Moskovskogo universiteta, 2009), chap. 9.

10. N. S. Khrushchev, "Ob ukreplenii sviazi shkoly s zhizn'iu i o merakh po dal'neishemu razvitiiu sistemy narodnogo obrazovaniia v strane," *Izvestia*, September 21, 1958.

11. Cf. Alexei Yurchak, *Everything Was Forever, Until It Was No More: The Last Soviet Generation* (Princeton, NJ: Princeton University Press, 2006), 139–40.

12. Yurchak, *Everything Was Forever*, 97–100. The case of the prominent Russian Soviet philosopher and historian of philosophy Alexei Fedorovitch Losev, a "monk in the world," is especially interesting as an example of an escapist stance. See V. I. Postovalova, "Isikhazm v tvorcheskom osmyslenii A. F. Loseva (monakha Andronika)," in *Sofiia: Al'manakh. Vyp. 2: P.A. Florenskii u A.F. Losev: rod, mif, istoriia*, ed. R. R. Vakhitov et al., 207–22 (Ufa: Ufimskoe religiozno-filosofskoe obshchestvo im. A.F. Loseva 2007). http://synergia-isa.ru/wp-content/uploads/2011/05/postovalova_losev.pdf. Apparent neglect for everyday life was also manifested by the renowned dissident philologist Sergei Sergeevitch Averintsev and many other representatives of the Soviet intelligentsia. O. A. Sedakova, "Rassuzhdenie o metode. Sergei Sergeevich Averintsev i ego kniga 'Poety,'" in *Moralia*, ed. Ol'ga Sedakova, 769–94 (Moscow: Universitet Dmitriia Pozharskogo, 2010). http://www.olgasedakova.com/Moralia/296. Apart from the collection of particular life histories, there is a general need for a comprehensive analysis of the "secularity" of Soviet culture.

13. On nuclear cities, see Kate Brown, *Plutopia: Nuclear Families, Atomic Cities, and the Great Soviet and American Plutonium Disasters* (New York: Oxford University Press, 2013).

14. Cf. Benjamin Tromly, *Making the Soviet Intelligentsia: Universities and Intellectual Life under Stalin and Khrushchev* (New York: Cambridge University Press, 2013).

15. A. D. Kosichev, *Filosofiia, vremia, liudi. Vospominaniia i razmyshleniia dekana filosofskogo fakul'teta MGU im. M. V. Lomonosova* (Moscow: OLMA-Press, 2003).

16. Y. V. Gromyko, "Moskovskaia metodologicheskaia shkola," *Voprosy metodologii*, no. 4 (1991): 3.

17. See Gromyko, "Moskovskaia metodologicheskaia shkola," 3.

18. See Moskovskii metodologicheskii kruzhok (MMK), accessed February 13, 2024, http://www.fondgp.ru/mmk. This page contains also some articles dedicated to the history of the methodological movement as well as a number of comments on its current state.

19. See International Biography Initiative, Center for Democratic Culture, University of Nevada, Las Vegas, http://cdclv.unlv.edu//programs/bios.html. This website also hosts autobiographies of some well-known Soviet philosophers and sociologists. Sociology in the Soviet Union was closely connected with philosophy, as almost all of the elder generation of sociologists in the USSR graduated from the faculties of philosophy of Moscow and Leningrad State Universities. Vladimir Shlapentokh, *The Politics of Sociology in the Soviet Union* (Boulder, CO: Westview Press, 1997).

20. James A. Holstein and Jaber F. Gubrium, *The Active Interview* (Thousand Oaks, CA: Sage, 1995).

21. D. Jean Clandinin, and F. Michael Connelly, *Narrative Inquiry: Experience and Story in Qualitative Research* (San Francisco: Jossey-Bass, 2000).

22. Gromyko, "Moskovskaia metodologicheskaia shkola," 4.

23. I. M. Fil'shtinskiy, "Glazami druga," *Otechestvennye zapiski*, no. 6 (2005): 130–45. All translations from Russian hereafter are my own.

24. V. A. Kostelovskii, MMK, see https://www.fondgp.ru/mmk/persons; N. I. Nepomniashchaa, MMK, https://www.fondgp.ru/mmk/persons.

25. Barbara H. Rosenwein, *Emotional Communities in the Early Middle Ages* (Ithaca, NY: Cornell University Press, 2006).

26. That point raises an interesting question of the "secularity" of Soviet intelligentsia. We still lack a comprehensive account of the secularization process with respect to the Soviet history. Anyway, a secularist stance should not be taken for granted while examining Soviet culture. For an overview of literature regarding secularization, see Philip S. Gorski and Ateş Altınordu, "After Secularization?," *Annual Review of Sociology* 34 (2008): 55–85. Most of this literature is preoccupied with the European Union, North America, or Islamic and/or postcolonial areas. The same is true for various conceptions of secular, including the influential book by Charles Taylor, *A Secular Age* (Cambridge, MA: Belknap Press of Harvard University Press, 2007).

27. G. E. Belyaeva, MMK, https://www.fondgp.ru/mmk/persons; P. V. Malinovskii, MMK, accessed February 13, 2024, https://www.fondgp.ru/mmk/persons.

28. Due to the collectivist style of thinking that dominated all *kruzhok* activities, there was no place for the authorship of ideas. Concepts were produced together and therefore by no one in particular. The traditional way of doing intellectual history through reading texts turns out to be rather inappropriate, since it is apparently much harder to detect any traces of an individual intellectual production in the *kruzhok* culture.

29. On alienation, cf. A. A. Piskoppel', MMK, accessed February 13, 2024, https://www.fondgp.ru/mmk/persons.

30. Piskoppel', MMK

31. IU. M. Novikov, MMK, accessed February 13, 2024, https://www.fondgp.ru/mmk/persons.

32. Quotation from V. E. Lepskii, MMK, accessed February 13, 2024, https://www.fondgp.ru/mmk/persons. On Shchedrovitskiy's style of leadership, see V. M. Rozin, MMK, accessed February 13, 2024, https://www.fondgp.ru/mmk/persons.

33. V. Shlapentokh, "Sotsiolog: Zdes' i tam," Center for Democratic Culture Archives, University of Nevada, Las Vegas, accessed February 13, 2024, http://cdclv.unlv.edu//archives/Interviews/shlapentokh.html.

34. Cf. I. Kukulin, "Al'ternativnoe sotsial'noe proektirovanie v sovetskom obshchestve 1960–1970-kh godov, ili pochemu v sovremennoi Rossii ne prizhilis' levye politicheskie praktiki," *Novoe literaturnoe obozrenie*, no. 6 (2007): 172.

35. Arpad Szakolczai, "Moving beyond the Sophists: Intellectuals in East Central Europe and the Return of Trancendence," *European Journal of Social Theory* 8, no. 4 (2005): 417–33.

36. N. Mitrokhin, "Zametki o sovetskoi sotsiologii (po prochtenii knigi Borisa Firsova)," *Novoe literaturnoe obozrenie*, no. 4 (2009): 111–22.

37. Yurchak, *Everything Was Forever*, 137.

38. Michel Foucault, "Of Other Spaces (1967), Heterotopias," Michel Foucault, Info., accessed February 13, 2024, http://foucault.info/documents/heteroTopia/foucault.heteroTopia.en.html.

39. Cf. Kukulin, "Al'ternativnoe sotsial'noe proektirovanie."

40. One of the oldest members of the methodological movement, Boris Sazonov, stresses in his memoir that Shchedrovirskiy "always perceived himself as a part of the elite." B. V. Sazonov, MMK, accessed February 13, 2024, https://www.fondgp.ru/mmk/persons. The "creation" reference is from N. I. Kuznetsova, MMK, accessed February 13, 2024, https://www.fondgp.ru/mmk/persons.

41. O. B. Alexeyev, MMK, accessed February 13, 2024, https://www.fondgp.ru/mmk/persons.

42. Cf. Kuznetsova.

43. Kukulin, "Al'ternativnoe sotsial'noe proektirovanie," 189–90.

44. Jan Plamper, *The Stalin Cult: A Study in the Alchemy of Power* (Stanford, CA: Hoover Institution, Stanford University; New Haven, CT: Yale University Press, 2012). Soviet intellectual history provides an abundance of examples of affective cults of circle organizers. On the cult of the sociologist Yuri Levada, supported by a number of his disciples and friends and maintained by Boris Doktorov and Dmitry Shalin, see the Yuri Levada Archives, Center for Democratic Culture, University of Nevada, Las Vegas, http://cdclv.unlv.edu//yla/index.html. On the cult of the philosopher Mikhail Rozov, see the amateur memorial website "Teoriia sotsial'nykh estafet" http://cumatoid.narod.ru/index.htm.

45. Cf. Kuznetsova.

46. Cf. Walker, "*Kruzhok* Culture," 112–13.

47. Cf. F. F. Dudyrev, MMK, accessed February 13, 2024, https://www.fondgp.ru/mmk/persons.

5. Father Aleksandr Men' and Jewish-Christian Identities under Soviet Secularism

The research on which this chapter is based was funded by the Tauber Institute for the Study of European Jewry and the Keston Institute. Thanks to the following people for feedback on drafts: Shimshon Ayzenberg, ChaeRan Freeze, Geraldine Gudefin, Nadieszda Kizenko, Katie Loveland, Bronwyn and Nathan McLellan, Randall A. Poole, Nomi Pritz-Bennett, and Jan Therkildsen; participants in the "Varieties of Russian Modernity" conference at the Russian Presidential Academy of National Economy and Public Administration in Moscow (June 2013; and participants in the Helsinki Consultation in Moscow (June 2015).

1. Aleksandr Men', "The Jews and Christianity," trans. Emma Watkins, *Religion, State & Society* 23, no. 1 (1995): 25.

2. Aleksandr Men', "Ob"iasnitel'naia zapiska," in *O sebe: Vospominaniia, interv'iu, besedy, pis'ma* (Moscow: Fond imeni Aleksandra Menia [FiAM], 2007), 245–46; Sergei Bychkov, *Khronika neraskrytogo ubiistva* (Moscow: Russkoe reklamnoe izdatel'stvo, 1996), 69. Aleksandr Men', "Evrei i khristianstvo," interview by A. Shoikhet, *Evrei v SSSR*, no. 11 (1975), reprinted as appendix 10 in *Khronika neraskrytogo ubiistva*, by Sergei Bychkov (Moscow: Russkoe reklamnoe izdatel'stvo, 1996), 184–89; Aleksandr Men', "Evrei i khristianstvo," interview by A. Shoikhet, *VRKhD*, no. 117 (1976): 112–17. The Jewish visitor was likely Aleksandr Shoikhet (b. 1946), who was just beginning journalistic samizdat work in the mid-1970s.

3. Men', "Jews and Christianity," 26. On one early antisemitic encounter, see David Remnick, "Black September," in *Lenin's Tomb: The Last Days of the Soviet Empire* (New York: Random House, 1993), 362.

4. Bychkov, *Khronika*; Judith Deutsch Kornblatt, *Doubly Chosen: Jewish Identity, the Soviet Intelligentsia, and the Russian Orthodox Church* (Madison: University of Wisconsin Press, 2004); Dominic Rubin, *Holy Russia, Sacred Israel: Jewish-Christian Encounters in Russian Religious Thought* (Brighton, MA: Academic Studies Press, 2010), 511–26; Wallace L. Daniel, *Russia's Uncommon Prophet: Father Aleksandr Men and His Times* (DeKalb: Northern Illinois University Press, 2016).

5. Charles Taylor, *A Secular Age* (Cambridge, MA: Belknap Press of Harvard University Press, 2007), 3.

6. For a critical examination of the use of civil religion within post-Soviet Eastern Orthodox spaces, see Cyril Hovorun, "Civil Religion in the Orthodox Milieu," in *Political Theologies in Orthodox Christianity: Common Challenges–Divergent Positions*, ed. Kristina Stoeckl, Ingeborg Gabriel, and Aristotle Papanikolaou (London: T&T Clark, 2017), 253–62.

7. Alexander Agadjanian, "Reform and Revival in Moscow Orthodox Communities: Two Types of Religious Modernity," *Archives de sciences sociales des religions*, no. 162 (2013): 88n24.

8. Men' also mentions a matrilineal forebear who was a Cantonist in Nicholas I's army (a Jewish conscript required to serve 25 years in the Russian army) and a paternal great-grandfather who was "an Odessan contrabandist of the Babel type." Aleksandr Men', "O moikh predkakh," appendix 6 in *Khronika neraskrytogo ubiistva*, by Sergei Bychkov (Moscow: Russkoe reklamnoe izdatel'stvo, 1996), 134–36. On the history of

Jewish Cantonists, see Yohanan Petrovsky-Shtern, "Military Service in Russia," in *The YIVO Encyclopedia of Jews in Eastern Europe*, https://yivoencyclopedia.org/article.aspx /Military_Service_in_Russia (accessed February 21, 2024).

9. Elena Semenovna Men', "Moi put'," in *I bylo utro: Vospominaniia ob ottse Aleksandre Mene*, ed. M. V. Sergeeva (Moscow: AO "Vita Tsentr," 1992), 126–27; Aleksandr Men', "O moikh predkakh," 137. All translations are by April L. French, unless otherwise noted.

10. Nadieszda Kizenko, *A Prodigal Saint: Father John of Kronstadt and the Russian People* (University Park: Pennsylvania State University Press, 2000).

11. Elena Men', "Moi put'," 125; Vera Iakovlevna Vasilevskaia, "Vospominaniia: Fragmenty iz knigi *Katakomby XX veka*," in *I bylo utro: Vospominaniia ob ottse Aleksandre Mene*, ed. M. V. Sergeeva (Moscow: AO "Vita Tsentr," 1992), 43–44, 42, 65–66.

12. On this required subject for all pupils in Russian imperial public schools, including Jewish children, see Zvi Gitelman, *A Century of Ambivalence: The Jews of Russia and the Soviet Union, 1881 to the Present*, 2d ed. (Bloomington, IN: Indiana UP, 2001), 6.

13. Elena Men', "Moi put'," 137–40; Vasilevskaia, "Vospominaniia," 73. Father Serafim led a branch of the "Catacomb" church, which had gone underground in the late 1920s during a theo-political conflict involving the new Bolshevik government, a group of "red priests" who sought renewal in the ROC by "blending Orthodoxy with Soviet Communism," and laypeople and priests like Father Serafim, who aimed "to preserve Orthodoxy's purity." Edward E. Roslof, *Red Priests: Renovationism, Russian Orthodoxy, and Revolution, 1905–1946* (Bloomington: Indiana University Press, 2002), 169; Vasilevskaia, "Vospominaniia," 76.

14. Elena Men', "Moi put'," 134–36. On Vladimir's name change, see "Vladimirovich ili Vol'fovich?," FiAM website, accessed October 31, 2014, http://www.alexandrmen .ru/biogr/vladvolf.html.

15. Pavel Men', informal interview by author, Aleksandr Men' Foundation at the Church of Saints Kosmos and Damian, Moscow, May 23, 2013; Pavel Men', e-mail correspondence with author, October 2014; Pavel Men', "Prepodobnyi Sergii ne dopustit: Vspominaet Pavel Men'," by Aleksandr Zorin, *Vyshgorod*, no. 2–3 (2015): 19.

16. Aleksandr Men', "O moikh predkakh," 138.

17. Aleksandr Men' ("Ob"iasnitel'naia zapiska," 245) later claimed he had neither visited a synagogue nor blessed anyone else to do so. If he did attend the synagogue with his father as a child, he may have stopped attending once he became an altar server.

18. Pavel Men', e-mail, October 2014.

19. Yaacov Ro'i, "The Role of the Synagogue and Religion in the Jewish National Awakening," in *Jewish Culture and Identity in the Soviet Union*, ed. Yaacov Ro'i and Avi Beker (New York: New York University Press, 1991), 112–35.

20. Anna Vinogradov, "Religion and Nationality: The Transformation of Jewish Identity in the Soviet Union," *Penn History Review* 18, no. 1 (2010): 51. See also Zvi Gitelman, "Jewish Nationality and Religion in the USSR and Eastern Europe," in *Religion and Nationalism in Soviet and East European Politics*, ed. Pedro Ramet (Durham, NC: Duke University Press, 1989), 59–80; Kornblatt, *Doubly Chosen*, 33–51.

21. For more on Soviet nationalities policy, see Terry Martin, *The Affirmative Action Empire: Nations and Nationalism in the Soviet Union, 1923–1939* (Ithaca, NY: Cornell University Press, 2001); Francine Hirsch, *Empire of Nations: Ethnographic Knowledge and the Making of the Soviet Union* (Ithaca, NY: Cornell University Press, 2005).

22. The class was held at the home of Boris Vasil'ev and Tat'iana Kupriianova, a cousin of Pavel Florenskii (1882–1937, a polymath philosopher and Russian Orthodox priest who was a friend of Russian Symbolists including Andrei Bely and Silver Age philosophers including Sergei Bulgakov). Aleksandr Zorin, *Angel chernorabochii*, ed. Roza Adamiants (Moscow: Put', Istina i Zhizn', 2004), 67–68; Aleksandr Men', "Delo Tserkvi—delo Bozhie," interview by Sergei Bychkov, autumn 1982–January 1984, appendix 9 in *Khronika neraskrytogo ubiistva*, by Sergei Bychkov (Moscow: Russkoe reklamnoe izdatel'stvo, 1996), 156.

23. Zoia Maslenikova, *Aleksandr Men': Zhizn'*, 2nd ed. (Moscow: Zakharov, 2001), 195; Men', "Delo Tserkvi," 156.

24. Michael Meerson, "The Life and Work of Father Aleksandr Men," in *Seeking God: The Recovery of Religious Identity in Orthodox Russia, Ukraine, and Georgia*, ed. Stephen K. Batalden (DeKalb: Northern Illinois University Press, 1993), 15–16. See also Kornblatt, *Doubly Chosen*, 72. Father Aleksandr was instrumental in the conversion of Meerson, a Jew, to Christianity. Meerson is now an Orthodox priest at Christ the Savior Church in New York City.

25. Shimshon (Ignat) Ayzenberg, in research for his forthcoming dissertation at Stanford, has discovered that Vol'f/Vladimir Men' was actively involved in the Poale Zion Party from 1924 to 1926 (just before he met Elena Tsuperfein). This party, whose leaders were all executed in 1932, espoused a form of Marxist Zionism called "Palestinism." According to Pavel Men', his father never told them of his involvement in this group. Pavel Men', informal interview by author, Aleksandr Men' Foundation at the Church of Saints Kosmos and Damian, Moscow, August 14, 2015.

26. Pavel Men' (e-mail, October 2014) claims that Vladimir discovered Aleksandr was a priest in the early 1960s from a "saboteur" neighbor. For a biography of Aleksandr Men', see Daniel, *Uncommon Prophet*.

27. An extensive exploration of Men''s theology is a desideratum. Alena Kharko has completed a doctoral dissertation in 2023 at Westfälische Wilhelms-Universität (Münster, Germany) concerning Men''s soteriology.

28. A. Bogoliubov [Aleksandr Men'], *Syn Chelovecheskii* (Brussels: La Vie avec Dieu, 1968); Emmanuil Svetlov [Aleksandr Men'], *V poiskakh Puti, Istiny i Zhizni: Istoriia religii*, 6 vols. (Brussels: La Vie avec Dieu, 1970–83). On the writing and reception of these works, see April L. French, "Spiritual Dissident: The Writings of Father Aleksandr Men' as Dissent from Soviet Ideology" (master's thesis, Regent College, Vancouver, BC, 2011), 27–30, 31–35, 59–61; 77–89, 92–95.

29. Aleksandr Men', *Istoki religii*, vol. 1 of *V poiskakh Puti, Istiny i Zhizni* (Moscow: EKSMO, 2004), 12.

30. Aleksandr Men', *Syn Chelovecheskii*, 4th ed. (Moscow: FiAM, 2000), 39, 72, 132–33, 177–78, 116.

31. Aleksandr Men', letter to Mikhail Galperin, April 1982. Unpublished letters provided to author by Pavel Men'.

32. Men', letter to Galperin, autumn 1980.

33. Men', letter to Galperin, August 1981.

34. Men', letter to Galperin, January 1980. See also Aleksandr Men', *Pervye apostoly* (Moscow: FiAM, 1998), 108.

35. Quoted by Bychkov (*Khronika*, 76). See also Men', "Ob''iasnitel'naia zapiska," 246.

36. Serge Ruzer, "Jewish Christianity in Russia after the Six-Day War: Israeli Factor, Eschatology and *Nostra Aetate*," *Revue des études juives* 168, nos. 3–4 (2009): 556. See Aleksandr Men', "Khristianstvo" (lecture, September 8, 1990), accessed October 28, 2014, http://alexandrmen.ru/sounds/index.html#lectures.

37. Men''s thought falls in line with Eastern Orthodox ecclesiology, particularly his understanding of ancient Israel as "the Old Testament Church" and his view of the *eschaton* beginning with Christ's Incarnation and having both an ongoing reality (of the in-breaking of the Kingdom of God in the midst of competing evil) and a future-but-unknowable consummation. On the Eastern Christian view of the *eschaton*, see John Panteleimon Manoussakis, "The Anarchic Principle of Christian Eschatology in the Eucharistic Tradition of the Eastern Orthodox Church," *Harvard Theological Review* 100, no. 1 (2007): 29–46. A scholarly exploration of Men''s eschatology is a desideratum. He claims an affinity for certain eschatological conceptions of Sergei Bulgakov, Nikolai Federov, and Pierre Teilhard de Chardin. Men', "Delo Tserkvi," 159; Aleksandr Men', *Chitaia Apokalipsis* (Moscow: FiAM, 2000). Men''s eschatology differs greatly from the dispensationalist views of evangelical Christians in the West; he holds something akin to an amillennialist position. See Richard Harvey, *Mapping Messianic Jewish Theology: A Constructive Approach* (Milton Keynes, UK: Paternoster, 2009), 223–61.

38. Edith Stein's beatification (1987) and canonization (1998) created a controversy among Jewish commentators. See Zev Garber, "Jewish Perspectives on Edith Stein's Martyrdom," in *The Unnecessary Problem of Edith Stein*, ed. Harry J. Cargas (Lanham, MD: University Press of America, 1994), 61–76; Emily Leah Silverman, "On the Frontiers of Faith: Edith Stein Encounters Herself as a Burnt Offering," *Hebrew Studies* 51 (2010): 375–78.

39. Garber, "Edith Stein's Martyrdom," 69.

40. Men', "Jews and Christianity," 27.

41. Ruzer, "Jewish Christianity," 553.

42. Kornblatt, *Doubly Chosen*, 69–82, 84, 103.

43. Kornblatt, *Doubly Chosen*, 73, 156–57; Meerson, "Life and Work," 14.

44. Among those who have acknowledged Men''s significance are Ruzer, "Jewish Christianity"; Simeon Charny, "Judaism and the Jewish Movement," in *The Jewish Movement in the Soviet Union*, ed. Yaacov Ro'i (Baltimore: Johns Hopkins University Press, 2012), 325–8; Yohanan Petrovsky-Shtern, "Contextualizing the Mystery: Three Approaches to *The Protocols of the Elders of Zion*," *Kritika: Explorations in Russian and Eurasian History* 4, no. 2 (2003): 395–409. An example of a scholar who has dismissed him is Benjamin Pinkus, *The Jews of the Soviet Union: The History of a National Minority* (Cambridge: Cambridge University Press, 1988), 304. And among those who have ignored him is Zvi Gitelman, "Glasnost, Perestroika and Antisemitism," *Foreign Affairs* 70, no. 2 (Spring 1991): 141–59.

45. *Vykrest* (literally "baptized out") is an archaic term used for a baptized Jew, with a connotation of apostasy.

46. According to Mikhail Meerson (e-mail to author, November 7, 2014), who compiled and distributed "Dva Zaveta" soon before his emigration to the United States, it was "a substantial collection of original Russian and translated articles . . . [including] some forgotten articles by Russian religious thinkers, one by Sergei Bulgakov." He states outright that Men' did not contribute to this collection. Copies of "Dva Zaveta"

prove difficult to locate, but quotations from the text are in Natan Faingol'd, *Dialog ili missionerstvo? O "dialogicheskoi" forme russkogo pravoslavnogo missionerstva sredi evreev i o doktrine neoiudekhristianstva* (Jerusalem: Shamir, 1977), 25–26, 28–30.

47. Aleksandr Men', "Interv'iu na sluchai aresta," by "Correspondent N.," *Vestnik Russkogo Khristianskogo Dvizheniia [VRKhD]*, no. 159 (1990): 305.

48. Information on family members' deaths at Babi Yar provided by Pavel Men', informal interview by author, Aleksandr Men' Foundation at the Church of Saints Kosmos and Damian, Moscow, January 23, 2015; Pavel Men', "Prepodobnyi Sergii," 19. Aleksandr Men''s views on the Shoah can be found in: Aleksandr Men', "Rasizm pered sudom khristianstva," *Zhurnal Moskovskoi Patriarkhii*, no. 3 (March 1962): 24; Aleksandr Men', "Kratkaia istoriia antisemitizma" [1982], in *Blagoslovenie na genotsid: Mif o vsemirnom zagovore evreev i "Protokolakh sionskikh mudretsov,"* by Norman Kon [Cohn], trans. S. S. Bychkov, with a foreword and appendix by Aleksandr Men' (Moscow: Rudomino, 2000), 163. In Dominic Rubin's (*Holy Russia, Sacred Israel*, 513) analysis of Men''s recording and the 1975 "interview," he regrettably misquotes Men' as referring "in one [unattributed] place" to "Jewish, German, and Russian holocausts" and consequently claims that Men' likely did not understand the Holocaust, due to Soviet "internationalist ideology." Nowhere does Men' make such a statement.

49. Men', "Jews and Christianity," 25, 27. On Jewish converts' discussions during this period, see Mikhail Agursky, "O perspektivakh khristianstva sredi evreev," *Moskovskii sbornik* 1 (1974): 80–87; Mikhail Agursky, "Epizody vospominanii," *Ierusalimskii zhurnal* 4 (2000): 260; Mikhail Meerson-Aksenov, "V gostiakh u o. Il'i Shaina v Ierusalime," *Novyi zhurnal* no. 254 (2009), accessed October 24, 2014, http://magazines.russ.ru/nj/2009/254/pr16.html.

50. Anonymous, "Pis'mo sviashchenniku Aleksandru Meniu" (Moscow: [samizdat], 1976), appendix 13 in *Khronika neraskrytogo ubiistva*, by Sergei Bychkov (Moscow: Russkoe reklamnoe izdatel'stvo, 1996), 194–207; Gennadii Shimanov, Feliks Karelin, and L. Ibragimov [Vladimir Ibragimovich Prilutskii], "K chitateliu," in *Priglashenie k dialogu* (Moscow: [samizdat], 1978), 1–2, Keston Center for Religion, Politics, and Society (KCRPS), Baylor University, Waco, TX, SU/Ort 11–10 S. Three of the six essays and the appendix of the 1978 collection focused on Men''s interview. Shimanov, Karelin, and Prilutskii were future contributors to the nationalistic almanac *Mnogaia leta*. John B. Dunlop, "*Mnogaya leta*: Advocate of a Russian Church–Soviet State Concordat," *Religion in Communist Lands* 11, no. 2 (1983): 146–60; Mikhail D. Suslov, "The Fundamentalist Utopia of Gennady Shimanov from the 1960s–1980s," *Demokratizatsiya* 17, no. 4 (2009): 324–48.

51. Men', "Evrei i khristianstvo" (*VRKhD*), 114, 117.

52. Feliks Karelin, "O domostroitel'nykh predelakh bogoizbrannosti evreiskogo naroda (diptikh)," in *Priglashenie k dialogu* (Moscow: [samizdat], 1978), 23–37, KCRPS, SU/Ort 11–10 S. These quotations are taken from a post-Soviet reprints of Karelin's article: "O domostroitel'nykh predelakh bogoizbrannosti evreiskogo naroda (diptikh)," in *O bogoslovii protoiereia Aleksandra Menia* by Feliks Karelin, Sergei Antiminsov, and Andrei Kuraev (Zhitomir: NI-KA, 1999), 10–11.

53. Karelin, "O domostroitel'nykh predelakh" (1999), 17. Karelin was an avowed apocalyptic enthusiast. In the late 1960s, he convinced several of Men''s friends and parishioners that Jesus would return on a certain day to Novyi Afon (New Athos) in

Abkhazia. Men', who considered Karelin "a pathological fanatic" led by "either the KGB or Satan," tried to save his friends from Karelin's influence. Karelin's article, therefore, likely carried a tone of personal animosity. Aleksandr Men', "Vspominaiu 60-e gody," in *O sebe*, 146–50, 152, 155–57, 161, 169–74. See the post-Soviet reprint of Nilus's 1905 work: Sergei Nilus, *Velikoe v malom: Zapiski pravoslavnogo* (Moscow: Sviato-Troitskaia Sergievaia Lavra, 1992). Karelin wrote a "theological manifesto" in *Mnogaia leta* further espousing such ideas. Dunlop, "*Mnogaya leta*," 148.

54. Men', "Jews and Christianity," 26; Aleksandr Men', "Po povodu otklika na interv'iu (otvet I. Shafarevichu)," *VRKhD*, no. 122 (1977): 89. Men' ("Ob"iasnitel'naia zapiska," 248) later wrote that Metropolitan Filaret had said these two saints had never formally been canonized.

55. Igor Shafarevich, "Po povodu interv'iu prot. Aleksandra Menia 'Evrei i khristianstvo,'" *VRKhD*, no. 120 (1977): 100; Men', "Po povodu otklika," 89–90. For an alternative analysis of this exchange, see Krista Berglund, *The Vexing Case of Igor Shafarevich, a Russian Political Thinker* (Basel: Birkhäuser, 2012), 167–74.

56. G. M. Shimanov, "Pokhvala o. Aleksandru Meniu," in *Priglashenie k dialogu* (Moscow: [samizdat], 1978), 20, KCRPS, SU/Ort 11–10 S.

57. L. Ibragimov [Vladimir Ibragimovich Prilutskii], "Otkrytoe pis'mo protoireiu Aleksandru Meniu," [May 1978], in *Priglashenie k dialogu* (Moscow: [samizdat], 1978), 15–19, KCRPS, SU/Ort 11–10 S. I have chosen to translate *iudaist* here as Judaizer, due to its negative connotation. Even after Men''s death, Russian nationalist hard-liners "vilified [him] as the one primarily responsible for the revival of the Judaizing heresy, and a spiritual father to Judaizers." Several priests were accused of this heresy, but Men' was at the top of the list. Vadim Rossman, *Russian Intellectual Antisemitism in the Post-Communist Era* (Lincoln: University of Nebraska Press, 2002), 229–30; Dimitry Pospielovsky, "The Russian Orthodox Church in the Postcommunist CIS," in *The Politics of Religion in Russia and the New States of Eurasia*, ed. Michael Bourdeaux (Armonk, NY: M. E. Sharpe, 1995), 52, 69–70n30.

58. Men', "Jews and Christianity," 26. Men' makes similar comments in letters to Galperin, autumn 1978 and January 1980. See Ruzer's ("Jewish Christianity," 554–56) discussion of Men''s emphasis on Hanukkah over Passover.

59. Men', "Evrei i khristianstvo" (*VRKhD*), 115–16. Some think Men' mentioned a hypothetical church of St. James, misunderstanding his reference to a specific Jewish Christian community in Israel. See Yurii Tabak's statement in a conversation led by Mikhail Edel'shtein and Afanasii Mamedov, "Meneva oikumena," *Lekhaim*, no. 290 (May 31, 2016), accessed June 10, 2016, http://www.lechaim.ru/8872.

60. Bychkov, *Khronika*, 69. The letter was reprinted as P. I. Ivanov, "Pis'mo sviashchenniku Aleksandru Meniu," in *Mnogaia leta*, ed. Gennadii Shimanov (Moscow: [samizdat], 1980), 217–28, KCRPS, SU/Ort 11–10 S. The Aleksandr Men' Foundation considers the claim that the author of the letter was Metropolitan Antonii (Mel'nikov) of Leningrad a libelous accusation, since his writing style is so different from the anonymous author's. See Men', "Ob"iasnitel'naia zapiska," 240n2.

61. Anonymous, "Pis'mo sviashchenniku," 195, 196, 198. On this forgery, see Richard Landes and Steven T. Katz, ed., *The Paranoid Apocalypse: A Hundred-Year Retrospective on "The Protocols of the Elders of Zion"* (New York: New York University Press, 2012); Christopher Partridge and Ron Geaves, "Antisemitism, Conspiracy Culture, Christianity, and

Islam: The History and Contemporary Religious Significance of *The Protocols of the Learned Elders of Zion*," in *The Invention of Sacred Tradition*, ed. James R. Lewis and Olav Hammer (Cambridge: Cambridge University Press, 2007), 75–95; Vadim L. Skuratovskii, *Problema avtorstva "Protokolov sionskikh mudretsov"* (Kiev: Dukh i Litera, 2001).

62. Anonymous, "Pis'mo sviashchenniku," 194, 197, 198–207.

63. Bychkov, *Khronika*, 69, 71, 74; Sergei Bychkov, "K izdaniiu 2000 goda," in *Blagoslovenie na genotsid: Mif o vsemirnom zagovore evreev i "Protokolakh sionskikh mudretsov*," by Norman Kon [Cohn], trans. S. S. Bychkov (Moscow: Rudomino, 2000), 168, 170.

64. Men', "Ob"iasnitel'naia zapiska," 240, 248, 249.

65. See Noah Lewin-Epstein, Yaacov Ro'i, and Paul Ritterband, eds., *Russian Jews on Three Continents: Migration and Resettlement* (London: Frank Cass, 1997).

66. Aleksandr Men', "60-e gody," 177–78; Pavel Men', interview, May 23, 2013; Kornblatt, *Doubly Chosen*, 75–76.

67. Such activity "symbolized the hope of young activists and refuseniks" (Soviet Jews whose applications for emigration were refused) and, therefore, drew the ire of Soviet authorities. Efraim Sicher, "Soviet-Jewish culture," in *Encyclopedia of Modern Jewish Culture*, 2nd ed., ed. Glenda Abramson (New York: Routledge, 2005), vol. 1, 865. According to Pavel Men', his brother was unenthusiastic about him teaching Hebrew briefly in the 1960s. Father Aleksandr studied biblical Hebrew privately and in theological school and then modern Hebrew briefly with a tutor, Ernst Trakhtman (who changed his name to Moshe Palkhan when he made aliyah). Pavel met Trakhtman while both served in the Soviet army in Cuba. Pavel Men', interview, May 23, 2013; Pavel Men', e-mail, October 2014; Pavel Men', interview, January 23, 2015; Aleksandr Men', "60-e gody," 166.

68. Pavel Men', e-mail, October 2014. The latter question posed by Pavel's friends may speak to the reception of "Dva Zaveta" among Soviet Jewish readers (see note 46).

69. The dating of this meeting has not been precise before now, but given (1) Pavel Men''s insistence that he shared this recording the night Jewish activist Iosif Begun was arrested at the apartment after participating in the discussion, (2) Aleksandr Men''s citation of a 1975 David Flusser work, (3) the mention of Jewish pride in "recent military events" likely referring to the Yom Kippur War (1973), and (4) the claim of Serge Ruzer (who was involved in this meeting) that it took place in 1977, one can place the meeting in March 1977, Begun's earlier arrests having taken place in May 1972 or at other locations. Pavel Men', interview, May 23, 2013; Pavel Men', e-mail, October 2014; Ruzer, "Jewish Christianity," 556n27.

70. The audio lecture is available on the Aleksandr Men' Foundation's website (http://alexandrmen.ru/sounds/index.html#besedy) as "Iudaizm i khristianstvo." This analysis is based on a transcript of the lecture: "Vozmozhno li iudeokhristianstvo?," Aleksandr Men' Foundation, accessed April 14, 2012, http://www.alexandrmen.ru/besedy/judcrist.html. The audio title is better suited to the lecture's content than the transcript title.

71. See thesis 56 in David Flusser, "Theses on the Emergence of Christianity from Judaism," *Immanuel*, no. 5 (Summer 1975): 83. In late 1975 or 1976, Men' received a copy of Flusser's "Theses" from Father Vsevolod Roshko, a Catholic priest in Israel. Men' to Roshko, "Dorogoi moi Otche," in *Iz sovremennykh problem Tserkvi: Fragmenty chastnoi perepiski* (Moscow, FiAM: 2004), 141. Flusser and Men' later corresponded. After Men''s death, Flusser told a reporter in Israel that he "was greatly impressed by

Men"s profound understanding of the Jewish sources of Christianity." Ruzer, "Jewish Christianity," 551n13.

72. See Flusser, "Theses," 74 (thesis 1).

73. Here, Men' is using the Targum's meaning of *Memra* to refer to "the Word" ("Logos" in Greek), which is used in John 1 to refer to Jesus Christ, the Son. He is using the Kaballah meaning of *Chochmah* to refer to the Father, and a long-held Jewish understanding of *Ruach ha-kodesh* referring to a "holy spirit." On these meanings, see Kaufmann Kohler, "Memra," *Jewish Encyclopedia,* https://www.jewishencyclopedia .com/articles/10618-memra#anchor4 (accessed February 21, 2024); Imry GalEini, "Basics of Kaballah: Chochmah," *Gal Einei: The Gateway to the Inner Dimention* [sic] *of the Torah,* January 27, 2014, https://inner.org/sefirot/sefchoch.htm; Joseph Jacobs and Ludwig Blau, "Holy Spirit," *Jewish Encyclopedia,* https://jewishencyclopedia.com /articles/7833-holy-spirit (accessed February 21, 2024).

74. See, for example, Men', *Syn Chelovecheskii* (2000), 262, 286–89, 298–99, 301.

75. Pavel Men', e-mail, October 2014. After the March 1977 meeting, Pavel shared the recording with a few other interested persons, but he did not distribute it further; the transcript was published well after Aleksandr Men"s death.

76. Men', "Evrei i khristianstvo" (*VRKhD*), 117.

77. Men', "Vozmozhno li?"; emphasis added.

78. Men', "Vozmozhno li?"

79. Men', "Vozmozhno li?"; emphasis added.

80. Men', "Vozmozhno li?" See also Men', "Jews and Christianity," 25.

81. Men', "Vozmozhno li?" Pavel Men' (interview, May 23, 2013) states that Father Daniel and Father Aleksandr corresponded; to his knowledge, no letters remain extant.

82. Men', "Vozmozhno li?" Men' also wrote to Galperin (autumn 1978), "Judeo-Christianity does not yet exist. There is no need yet to capture a bird in the bush. The Lord accepts us within the law by which we live, but in and of themselves, these laws are futile. . . . The main thing is faith and trust." Men' appears not to have been aware of the then fledgling movement "Jews for Jesus," and his statement indicates that he did not believe the community of St. James in Haifa constituted true "Judeo-Christianity."

83. Men', "Na sluchai aresta," 305.

84. Men', "Evrei i khristianstvo" (*VRKhD*), 114, 112.

85. See Kornblatt, *Doubly Chosen,* esp. 15. The term *spiritual children* is used by and about those to whom Father Aleksandr ministered and who came under his authority as a spiritual director.

86. Maxim D. Shrayer, *Waiting for America: A Story of Emigration* (Syracuse, NY: Syracuse University Press, 2007), 7–8.

87. See, for example, Mikhail Meerson's description of how he found Father Aleksandr. Kornblatt, *Doubly Chosen,* 76.

88. Men', "Vozmozhno li?"

89. Jean-Paul Sartre, *Anti-Semite and Jew: An Exploration of the Etiology of Hate,* trans. George J. Becker (New York: Schocken Books, 1948), 00.

90. I am grateful to ChaeRan Freeze for the concept of "genealogy of authority." Aleksandr Alekseev was born Vul'f Iudkovich Nakhlas. See Aleksandr Alekseev, *Upotrebliaiut-li evrei khristianskuiu krov' s religioznoi tsel'iu?* (Novgorod, 1886). Lustiger met

Men' in 1989 and considered him "a brother and a friend." Kardinal Zhan-Mari Liustizhe [Lustiger], "Predislovie," in *Otets Aleksandr Men': Khristov svidetel' v nashe vremia*, by Iv Aman [Yves Hamant] (Moscow: Rudomino, 1994), accessed November 9, 2014, http://www.alexandrmen.com/books/aman/aman00.html.

91. Men', "Na sluchai aresta," 305.

92. In the throes of Nikita Khrushchev's anti-religious campaign, such a breadth of publication was only possible because Men' knew the journal's editorial secretary, Anatolii Vasil'evich Vedernikov (1901–1992). Men', "60-e gody," 110–11, 118–20; French, "Spiritual Dissident," 28, 31–32n16.

93. Men', "Rasizm." Men' stopped writing regularly for the journal after a change in editorial leadership in 1963. Maslenikova, *Zhizn'*, 140; French, "Spiritual Dissident," 78n5.

94. Men', "Rasizm," 23, 27, 22.

95. S. V. Lur'e, "'Druzhba narodov' v SSSR: Natsional'nyi proekt ili primer spontannoi mezhetnicheskoi samoorganizatsii," *Obshchestvennye nauki i sovremennost'*, no. 4 (2011): 145–56. Men' ("Rasizm," 23) avoids the term *druzhba narodov* (friendship of the peoples); in addition to the term *bratstvo* (brotherhood), he varies his language with the words *edinstvo* (unity), *ravenstvo* (equality), and *ravnopravie* (equal rights).

96. On the censorship of *Zhurnal Moskovskoi Patriarkhii* in this period, see Jane Ellis, *The Russian Orthodox Church: A Contemporary History* (Bloomington: Indiana University Press, 1986), 158–63.

97. Men', "Rasizm," 23.

98. See Jonathan Frankel, "The Soviet Regime and Anti-Zionism: An Analysis," in *Jewish Culture and Identity in the Soviet Union*, ed. Yaacov Ro'i and Avi Beker (New York: New York University Press, 1991), 310–54; William Korey, "The Soviet Public Anti-Zionist Committee," in *Soviet Jewry in the 1980s: The Politics of Anti-Semitism and Emigration and the Dynamics of Resettlement*, ed. Robert O. Freedman (Durham, NC: Duke University Press, 1989), 26–50.

99. Men' ("Kratkaia istoriia," 167) said *The Protocols* had arisen once again "like a Phoenix from the ashes of time to play its evil role in fomenting international animosity."

100. Bychkov, "K izdaniiu 2000 goda," 168–69; Zoia Maslenikova, "Moi Dukhovnik," in *Zhizn'*, 322 (September 6, 1979). Men''s insistence on combating *The Protocols* by the end of the 1970s reveals the inaccuracy of Vadim Rossman's claim (*Russian Intellectual Antisemitism*, 288n4, 172–74) that this document was only "rediscovered after perestroika."

101. Men', "Kratkaia istoriia," 167. Norman Cohn, *Warrant for Genocide: The Myth of the Jewish World-Conspiracy and the Protocols of the Elders of Zion* (London: Eyre & Spottiswoode, 1967). Of Cohn's original eleven chapters and four appendixes, Bychkov's translation retained six chapters and one original appendix. Bychkov and Men' added an appendix on Freemasonry based on encyclopedic sources: "Chto takoe masonstvo," in *Blagoslovenie na genotsid: Mif o vsemirnom zagovore evreev i "Protokolakh sionskikh mudretsov,"* by Norman Kon [Cohn], trans. S. S. Bychkov (Moscow: Rudomino, 2000), 157–62.

102. Norman Kon [Cohn], *Blagoslovenie na genotsid: Mif o vsemirnom zagovore evreev i "Protokolakh sionskikh mudretsov,"* ed. E. N. Samoilo, trans. S. S. Bychkov, with an af-

terword by T. A. Karasova and D. A. Cherniakhovskii (Moscow: Progress, 1990); Kon [Cohn], *Blagoslovenie na genotsid* (2000). For a review of Men'′s contributions to the 2000 edition, see Petrovsky-Shtern, "Contextualizing the Mystery," 395–98, 409. On the publication, see Bychkov, "K izdaniiu 2000 goda," 168–71. In the period between the two publications, the publishing arms of Trinity–St. Sergius Monastery and Optina Pustyn published *The Protocols* and the apocalyptic works of Sergei Nilus. Michael Hagemeister, "*The Protocols of the Elders of Zion* and the Myth of a Jewish Conspiracy in Post-Soviet Russia," in *Nationalist Myths and Modern Media: Contested Identities in the Age of Globalization*, ed. Jan Herman Brinks, Stella Rock, and Edward Timms (London: Tauris Academic Studies, 2006), 246.

103. Men', "Po povodu otklika," 90–91.

104. Men', "Evrei i khristianstvo" (*VRKhD*), 117.

105. Petrovsky-Stern ("Contextualizing the Mystery," 398) offers a nuanced example of this view. See historical analyses in Men', "Rasizm"; Men', "Kratkaia istoriia."

106. Men', "Kratkaia istoriia," 164–65.

107. Men', "Evrei i khristianstvo" (*VRKhD*), 117. This statement provoked one aspect of the exchange between Shafarevich ("Po povodu interv'iu," 100–101) and Men' ("Po povodu otklika," 90–91).

108. Men', "Kratkaia istoriia," 163. See similar statements in Men', "Kratkaia istoriia," 166; Aleksandr Men', "Predislovie" [1990], in *Blagoslovenie na genotsid: Mif o vsemirnom zagovore evreev i "Protokolakh sionskikh mudretsov,"* by Norman Kon [Cohn], trans. S. S. Bychkov (Moscow: Rudomino, 2000), 4, 5; Alexander Men, "The Russian Orthodox Church Today," interview by Pilar Bonet, in *Christianity for the Twenty-First Century: The Prophetic Writings of Alexander Men*, ed. Elizabeth Roberts and Ann Shukman (New York: Continuum, 1996), 170.

109. Men', "Po povodu otklika," 91.

110. Men', "Rasizm," 27.

111. Men', "Rasizm," 22.

112. Aleksandr Men', "Religiia, kul't lichnosti i sekuliarnoe gosudarstvo: Zametki istorika religii," in *Na puti k svobode sovesti*, ed. D. E. Furman and Father Mark (Smirnov) (Moscow: Progress, 1989), 110, 136.

113. Maslenikova, "Dukhovnik," 352 (August 27, 1981), 330–31 (February 15, 1980).

114. Bychkov, *Khronika*, 83–85. See also Maslenikova, "Dukhovnik," 366 (April and July 1982). A priest from a nearby parish also preached a sermon against Men', calling him a "Yid-Mason" and heretic. Andrei Eremin, "Ty ne uznal vremeni poseshcheniia tvoego," in *Pamiati protoiereia Aleksandra Menia*, ed. T. V. Gromova (Moscow: Rudomino, 1991), 61.

115. Official copy of Tsentral'nyi Gosudarstvennyi Arkhiv Moskovskoi Oblasti, f. 7383, op. 3, d. 108, ll. 25–26: A. A. Trushin, "Informatsionnyi otchet o deiatel'nosti religioznykh ob''edinenii i sostoianii kontrolia za sobliudeniem zakonodatel'stva kul'takh v Moskovskoi oblasti za 1982 god," KCRPS, drawer file no. 95.

116. French, "Spiritual Dissident," 124–31.

117. Men', *O sebe*, 295.

118. Men, "Russian Orthodox Church Today," 168–69.

119. William Korey, *Russian Antisemitism, Pamyat, and the Demonology of Zionism*, Studies in Antisemitism 2, ed. Yehuda Bauer (Chur, Switzerland: Harwood Academic

Publishers, 1995); Walter Laqueur, *Black Hundred: The Rise of the Extreme Right in Russia* (New York: HarperCollins, 1993), 204–21.

120. Remnick, "Black September," 365; Vladimir Fainberg, "Otets Aleksandr, Aleksandr Vladimirovich, Sasha," in *Reki vody zhivoi: Vospominaniia ob ottse Aleksandre Mene*, ed. Roza Adamiants, Marina Kopylova, Pavel Men', and Marina Nasonova (Moscow: Put', Istina i Zhizn', 2003), 89–90; Alexander Men, "Russian Orthodox Church Today," 169–70; Maslenikova, "Dukhovnik," 404 (April 4, 1990).

121. Bychkov, *Khronika*, 43–44, 46; Sergei Bychkov, "KGB protiv sviashchennika Aleksandra Menia," *VRKhD*, no. 196 (2010): 127.

122. Elena Svetlova, "On Whose Conscience a Cross?," *Sovershenno sekretno*, no. 6 (1991): 16–17, reprinted by *U.S.S.R. Today*, no. 929 (October 16, 1991): 20.

123. Maslenikova, "Dukhovnik," 406–7. See also G. Paprotski, "Taina smerti ottsa Aleksandra," in *Pamiati protoiereia Aleksandra Menia*, ed. T. V. Gromova (Moscow: Rudomino, 1991), 105; Fainberg, "Otets Aleksandr," 89.

124. Western commentators link Men''s death to the "conservative political backlash" from summer 1990 through 1991. Jane Ellis, *The Russian Orthodox Church: Triumphalism and Defensiveness* (New York: St. Martin's Press, 1996), 8–9, 113; Remnick, "Black September," 359–61, 365–67.

125. Men, "Russian Orthodox Church Today," 164–70. For the term *sionistofobia*, see Aleksandr Men', "Iz besedy s P. Bonet," in *Kul'tura i dukhovnoe voskhozhdenie*, ed. L. I. Vasilenko (Moscow: Iskustvo, 1992), 449. On antisemitism in the late Soviet and early post-Soviet ROC, see Bychkov, *Khronika*, 95–96; Z. A. Krakhmal'nikova, ed., *Russkaia ideia i evrei: Rokovoi spor: Khristianstvo, antisemitizm, natsionalizm* (Moscow: Nauka, 1994).

126. The murder weapon was either an axe, as widely reported, or a *sapernaia lopatka* (a military shovel), as suggested by an independent medical examiner. Bychkov, "KGB protiv sviashchennika," 128.

127. Mikhail Aksenov-Meerson, "Zhizn' svoiu za drugi svoia," *Russkaia mysl'*, no. 3846 (September 21, 1990): 7; Vladimir Iliushenko, "Syn Chelovechestva," in *Pamiati protoiereia Aleksandra Menia*, ed. T. V. Gromova (Moscow: Rudomino, 1991), 127–28.

128. Bychkov, *Khronika*; Ellis, *Triumphalism*, 115.

129. Bychkov, *Khronika*, 90–94.

130. These theories are discussed at length in Bychkov, *Khronika*, esp. 16–26.

131. Men', "Delo Tserkvi," 157, 177–78. See Vladimir Solov'ev, *Russia and the Universal Church* (London: Centenary Press, 1948), 12, 41, 85, 90, 177, 180–81, 183–85. Men' (*Istoki religii*, 10) dedicated the first volume of his history of religions to Solov'ev. See also E. B. Rashkovskii, "Vladimir Solov'ev i Aleksandr Men' v dinamike rossiiskoi istorii," *Obshchestvennye nauki i sovremennost'*, no. 5 (2011): 118–28; Daniel, *Uncommon Prophet*, 80–82, 172–73, 276–77; Paul Valliere, *Modern Russian Theology: Bukharev, Soloviev, Bulgakov—Orthodox Theology in a New Key* (Grand Rapids, MI: Eerdman's Publishing, 2000), 402.

132. Rubin, *Holy Russia, Sacred Israel*, 512n2, 515.

133. On Men''s stance on freedom, see E. B. Rashkovskii, "Istoriia i svoboda: Aleksandr Men' i kul'turnye gorizonty Rossii kontsa XX stoletiia," in *Osoznannaia svoboda: Materialy k istorii mysli i kul'tury XVIII–XX stoletii* (Moscow: Novyi khronograf, 2005), 231–49; Wallace L. Daniel, "Aleksandr Men, Intellectual Freedom and the Russian Orthodox Church," *Kirchliche Zeitgerchichte / Contemporary Church History* 24, no. 1 (2011): 92–119.

134. Luehrmann offers insightful analysis of the Mari El region of Russia by utilizing the concept of "elective affinity," which was first coined by Johann Goethe and extended by Max Weber, regarding "a lively back-and-forth between religious and secular approaches to solving social problems by means of personal transformation." Sonja Luehrmann, *Secularism Soviet Style: Teaching Atheism and Religion in a Volga Republic* (Bloomington: Indiana University Press, 2011), 15. Although Luehrmann was analyzing entire subcultures within Mari El, the concept of "elective affinity" can also be used to describe specific individuals who dynamically interface with both religious and secular in their identity formation.

6. Zinaida Gippius and "Christian Infatuation"

1. Jenifer Presto has written on the subject; see Jenifer Presto, *Beyond the Flesh: Alexander Blok, Zinaida Gippius, and the Symbolist Sublimation of Sex* (Madison: University of Wisconsin Press, 2008); Jenifer Presto, "The Androgynous Gaze of Zinaida Gippius," *Russian Literature* 48, no. 1 (July 2000): 87–115; Jenifer Presto, "Reading Zinaida Gippius: Over Her Dead Body," *Slavic and East European Journal* 43, no. 4 (Winter 1999): 621–35; Jenifer Presto, "The Fashioning of Zinaida Gippius," *Slavic and East European Journal* 42, no. 1 (Spring 1998): 58–75. Presto particularly (and unfortunately) relies on the testimony of male memoir writers regarding the image of Gippius; see Presto, *Beyond the Flesh*, 145–47. Olga Matich is a recognized scholar on the subject of Gippius and sexuality; see Olga Matich, *Erotic Utopia: The Decadent Imagination in Russia's Fin de Siècle* (Madison: University of Wisconsin Press, 2005); Olga Matich, "Androgyny and the Russian Silver Age," *Pacific Coast Philology* 14 (October 1979): 42–50; Olga Matich, "Zinaida Gippius: Theory and Practice of Love," in *Readings in Russian Modernism: To Honor Vladimir Fedorovich Markov*, ed. Ronald Vroon and John E. Malmstad (Moscow: Nauka / Oriental Research Publishers, 1993); Philippa Hetherington, "Zinaida Gippius and Vyliublennost: An Early Modernist's Sexual Revolution" (presentation, "Revolutions and Sexualities: Cultural and Social Aspects of Political Transformations," eighth conference in the "Socialism and Sexuality" series, Krakow, Poland, September 26, 2007). Temira Pachmuss is the scholar who tries hardest to understand Gippius from a religious and philosophical standpoint. She is also good at discussing Gippius's views on sexuality; see especially the introduction to Temira Pachmuss, ed., *Intellect and Ideas in Action: Selected Correspondence of Zinaida Gippius* (Munich: Wilhelm Fink Verlag, 1972), 17–58.

2. Matich, *Erotic Utopia*, 4–7. Philippa Hetherington argues for her as a "revolutionary" in matters of sexuality; see Hetherington, "Gippius," 1. The concept of "sublimation" is used by Matich and Presto; see Matich, *Erotic Utopia*, 211; Presto, *Beyond the Flesh*, 9–10.

3. Presto, *Beyond the Flesh*, 7–8.

4. Eve Levin, *Sex and Society in the World of the Orthodox Slavs, 900–1700* (Ithaca, NY: Cornell University Press, 1989), x; see also Laura Engelstein, *The Keys to Happiness: Sex and the Search for Modernity in Fin-de-Siècle Russia* (Ithaca: Cornell University Press, 1992), 17, 27–28; Jane T. Costlow, Stephanie Sandler, and Judith Vowles, introduction to *Sexuality and the Body in Russian Culture*, ed. Jane T. Costlow, Stephanie Sandler, and Judith Vowles. (Stanford, CA: Stanford University Press, 1998), 1–40, 10.

5. An excellent discussion of this complicated attitude toward sexuality, in the case of the Silver Age poet Mikhail Kuzmin, is found in Martha M. F. Kelly, *Unorthodox Beauty: Russian Modernism and Its New Religious Aesthetic* (Evanston, IL: Northwestern University Press, 2016), esp. 69–70.

6. Irina Paperno, introduction, 1–11, and "The Meaning of Art: Symbolist Theories," 13–23, in *Creating Life: The Aesthetic Utopia of Russian Modernism*, ed. Irina Paperno and Joan Delaney Grossman (Stanford, CA: Stanford University Press, 1994); Steven Cassedy, *Flight from Eden: The Origins of Modern Literary Criticism and Theory* (Berkeley: University of California Press, 1990), esp. 99–120.

7. D. Merezhkovskii, "O prichinakh upadka i o novykh techeniiakh sovremennoi russkoi literatury," in *L. Tolstoi i Dostoevskii. Vechnye sputniki* (Moscow: Izdatel'stvo "Respublika," 1995), 522–604, 537. Translations are the author's unless otherwise noted.

8. Z. Gippius, "Dva slova ran'she," in *Literaturnyi dnevnik (1899–1907)*, by Anton Krainii (Z. Gippius) (Munich: Wilhlem Fink Verlag, 1970), v.

9. On the rise of a new "ascetic" approach to Orthodoxy in the second half of the nineteenth century, see Patrick Lally Michelson, *Beyond the Monastery Walls: The Ascetic Revolution in Russian Orthodox Thought, 1814–1914* (Madison: University of Wisconsin Press, 2017), esp. 145–49.

10. Z. Gippius, "Khleb zhizni," in Krainii, *Literaturnyi dnevnik*, 15, 18–19.

11. Z. Gippius, "Kritika liubvi," in Krainii, *Literaturnyi dnevnik*, 60.

12. Paperno, "Meaning of Art," 1.

13. Cassedy, *Flight from Eden*, 107–8.

14. Paperno, "Meaning of Art," 13.

15. Cassedy, *Flight from Eden*, 103.

16. Clemena Antonova, "'The World Will Be Saved by Beauty': The Revival of Romantic Theories of the Symbol in Pavel Florenskii's Works," *Slavonica* 14, no. 1 (2008): 44–56.

17. Paperno, introduction to *Creating Life*, 1.

18. V. Bryusov, "A Holy Sacrifice," in *The Russian Symbolists: An Anthology of Critical and Theoretical Writings*, ed. and trans. Ronald E. Peterson (Ann Arbor, MI: Ardis, 1986), 68–69.

19. Zinaida N. Gippius, "O liubvi," in *Mechti i koshmar (1920–1925)* (St. Petersburg: Izdatel'stvo "Rostok," 2002), 2.

20. Interpretation and contextualization of "The Kreutzer Sonata" can be found in Cynthia Hooper, "Forms of Love: Vladimir Solov'ev and Lev Tolstoy on Eros and Ego," *Russian Review* 60, no. 3 (July 2001): 360–80; Engelstein, *Keys to Happiness*, 218–20.

21. See Anna Lisa Crone, *Eros and Creativity in the Russian Religious Renewal* (Leiden: Brill, 2010), 70–71; Evgenii Bershtein, "The Notion of Universal Bisexuality in Russian Religious Philosophy," in *Understanding Russianness*, ed. Risto Alapuro, Arto Mustajoki, and Pekka Pesonen (London: Routledge, 2012), 210–31.

22. S. M. Polovinkin, *Zapiski peterburgskikh Religiozno-filosofskikh sobranii, 1901–1903* (Moscow: Respublika, 2005), 214–353, esp. 215, 228, 251–55.

23. Kelly, *Unorthodox Beauty*, 70.

24. Hooper, "Forms of Love," 361.

25. Vladimir Solov'ev, *The Meaning of Love*, ed. and trans. Thomas R. Beyer Jr. (Hudson, NY: Lindisfarne Press, 1985), 76, 79.

26. Solov'ev, *Meaning of Love*, 82–83; Hooper, "Forms of Love," 362–63. On the Platonic origins of Solov'ev's philosophy, see Judith Deutsch Kornblatt, "The Transfiguration of Plato in the Erotic Philosophy of Vladimir Solov'ev," *Religion & Literature* 24, no. 2 (Summer 1992): 35–50. Olga Matich, "The Symbolist Meaning of Love: Theory and Practice," in *Creating Life: The Aesthetic Utopia of Russian Modernism*, ed. Irina Paperno and Joan Delaney Grossman (Stanford, CA: Stanford University Press, 1994), esp. 26–32. Matich argues that Solov'ev champions an "erotic utopia," but her conception of his work relies on a theory of sublimation, which I address in Ana Siljak, "Sigmund Freud, Sublimation, and the Russian Silver Age," *Modern Intellectual History* 15, no. 2 (August 2018): 443–70.

27. Solov'ev, *Meaning of Love*, 51, 92–93.

28. Solov'ev, *Meaning of Love*, 93, 83.

29. V. Bryusov, "A Review of K. D. Balmont's *Let's Be like the Sun*," in *The Russian Symbolists: An Anthology of Critical and Theoretical Writings*, ed. and trans. Ronald E. Peterson (Ann Arbor, MI: Ardis, 1986), 46; Viacheslav Ivanov, "Thoughts about Symbolism," in *Russian Silver Age Poetry: Texts and Contexts*, ed. Sibelan E. S. Forrester and Martha M. F. Kelly (Boston: Academic Studies Press, 2015), 323.

30. See Nicolas Berdyaev, *The Meaning of the Creative Act* (San Rafael, CA: Semantron Press, 2009), 214–24. Berdiaev borrowed heavily from Solov'ev, but retained, in places, much of the spirit/flesh dualism that Solov'ev sought to overcome.

31. See Siljak, "Freud."

32. Z. Gippius, "Vliublennost'," in Krainii, *Literaturnyi dnevnik*, 194.

33. Gippius, "Vliublennost'," 195.

34. Gippius, "Vliublennost'," 197–98.

35. Gippius, "Vliublennost'," 198.

36. Berdiaev, *Creative Act*, 201. The anti-procreative and chaste ideal of the Silver Age is discussed extensively in Matich, *Erotic Utopia*, and in Presto, *Beyond the Flesh*.

37. For Matich (*Erotic Utopia*, 211), Gippius's argument is one for straightforward sexual repression, which leads to "sublimation." Presto (*Beyond the Flesh*, 159) argues that Gippius had a "problematic relationship with the body and self" and that she wrote "against the female body and sex." Hetherington ("Gippius," 8), by contrast, sees Gippius as a straightforward champion of "sexual freedom," in the contemporary sense of the word. For Merezhkovskii's influence on Freud, see Siljak, "Freud."

38. Gippius, "Vliublennost'," 198–99.

39. Gippius, "Vliublennost'," 199.

40. Gippius, "Vliublennost'," 201–2.

41. Gippius, "Vliublennost'," 206–7.

42. Gippius, "Vliublennost'," 203–5.

43. Gippius, "Vliublennost'," 208–9.

44. Z. Gippius, "Contes d'Amour," in *Dnevniki* (Moscow: Intelvak, 1999), vol. 1, 35–88.

45. Gippius, "Contes d'Amour," 38, 52–53, 62.

46. Gippius, "Contes d'Amour," 53, 60, 68.

47. Z. Gippius, correspondence with Filosofov, in Pachmuss, *Intellect and Ideas*, 64–65, 70–71.

48. Gippius, correspondence with Filosofov, 91, 96–98.

49. The quotations are from Presto's prose translation of the poem in *Beyond the Flesh*, 178.

50. Z. Gippius, "Iabloni tsvetut," in *Novye liudi / Pobediteli* (Munich: Wilhelm Fink Verlag, 1973), 14–15, 25, 22, 26.

51. Z. Gippius, "Miss Mai," in *Novye liudi*, 399, 426–27, 430.

52. I examine this topic in my article on Merezhkovskii and Freud; see Siljak, "Freud," esp. 27–28.

7. Disbelief and Piety

1. Viktor Shklovskii, *Sentimental'noe puteshestvie* (Moscow: Novosti, 1990), 198. All translations are those of the author unless otherwise noted.

2. See Erich Lippman, "Co-opting Orthodoxy: Orthodox Symbolism in Gorky's God-building Works, 1905–1909," *Modern Greek Studies Yearbook* 24/25 (2008/9): 181–200.

3. José Casanova, "The Secular, Secularizations, Secularisms," in *Rethinking Secularism*, ed. Craig Calhoun, Mark Juergensmeyer, and Jonathan VanAntwerpen (New York: Oxford University Press, 2011), 64. Nicholas Zernov, *The Russian Religious Renaissance of the Twentieth Century* (New York: Harper & Row, 1963).

4. Casanova, "Secular, Secularizations, Secularisms," 56.

5. Casanova, "Secular, Secularizations, Secularisms," 64.

6. Alexander Schmemann, "Worship in a Secular Age," in *For the Life of the World: Sacraments and Orthodoxy* (Crestwood, NY: St. Vladimir's Seminary Press, 1998), 128.

7. Charles Taylor, "Western Secularity," in *Rethinking Secularism*, ed. Craig Calhoun, Mark Juergensmeyer, and Jonathan VanAntwerpen (New York: Oxford University Press, 2011), 32.

8. Taylor, "Western Secularity," 39.

9. Donald Fanger, "Introduction: The Singularity of M. Gorky," in *Gorky's Tolstoy and Other Reminiscences: Key Writings by and about Maxim Gorky*, trans. and ed. Donald Fanger (New Haven, CT: Yale University Press, 2008), 1.

10. See K. Chukovskii, *Dve dushi Gor'kogo* (Leningrad: A. F. Marks, 1924), 50.

11. Bertram D. Wolfe, *The Bridge and the Abyss: The Troubled Friendship of Maxim Gorky and V. I. Lenin* (London: Pall Mall Press, 1967), vii, 18.

12. Nina Berberova, *Moura: The Dangerous Life of the Baroness Budberg*, trans. Marian Schwartz and Richard D. Sylvester (New York: New York Review of Books, 2005), 111.

13. For the first specific articulation, see George L. Kline, "'Nietzschean Marxism' in Russia," in *Demythologizing Marxism: A Series of Studies on Marxism*, ed. Frederick J. Adelmann, Boston College Studies in Philosophy 2 (The Hague: Martinus Nijhoff, 1969), 166–83.

14. George L. Kline, "Changing Attitudes toward the Individual," in *The Transformation of Russian Society*, ed. Cyril Black (Cambridge, MA: Harvard University Press, 1960), 606.

15. Kline, "'Nietzschean Marxism' in Russia," 166.

16. Kline, "'Nietzschean Marxism' in Russia," 169.

17. George L. Kline, *Religious and Anti-religious Thought in Russia* (Chicago: University of Chicago Press, 1968), 106.

18. Bernice Glatzer Rosenthal, ed., *Nietzsche in Russia* (Princeton, NJ: Princeton University Press, 1986), 249–311.

19. Bernice Glatzer Rosenthal, *New Myth, New World: From Nietzsche to Stalinism* (University Park: Pennsylvania State University Press, 2002), 68–93.

20. See Mary Louise Loe, "Godbuilding in Gorky's Early Work," *Modern Greek Studies Yearbook* 24/25 (2008/9): 210.

21. Kline, *Religious and Anti-religious Thought*, 109.

22. See, for example, Tovah Yedlin, *Maxim Gorky: A Political Biography* (Westport, CT: Praeger, 1999), 90.

23. Andrew Barratt and Barry P. Scherr, trans. and eds., *Maksim Gorky: Selected Letters* (Oxford: Clarendon Press, 1997), 9.

24. V. A. Posse, *Moi zhiznennyi put'* (Moscow-Leningrad, 1929), 126; quoted in Barratt and Scherr, *Maksim Gorky*, 9n5.

25. Yedlin, *Maxim Gorky*, 10.

26. Yedlin, *Maxim Gorky*, 228.

27. Ana Siljak, *Angel of Vengeance: The "Girl Assassin," the Governor of St. Petersburg, and Russia's Revolutionary World* (New York: St. Martin's Press, 2008), 29–30.

28. Shklovskii, *Sentimental'noe puteshestvie*, 199. Nikolai Mikhailovsky was a well-known populist writer.

29. Maksim Gor'kii, "O polemike," *Novaia zhizn'*, April 25 (May 8), 1917, 6.

30. Gor'kii, "O polemike."

31. K. I. Chukovskii, *Dnevnik v trekh tomakh*, vol. 1, *1901–1921* (Moscow: PROZAiK, 2012), 247.

32. Chukovskii, *Dnevnik*, vol. 1, 302.

33. State Archive of the Russian Federation, 1764–1—56, p. 2.

34. E. N. Nikitin, *"Ispoved'" M. Gor'kogo* (Moscow: Nasledie, 2000); L. Spiridonova, *M. Gor'kii: Novyi vzgliad* (Moscow: IMLI RAN, 2004); *Kontseptsiia mira i cheloveka v tvorchestve M. Gor'kogo*, M. Gor'kii, materialy i issledovaniia, vyp. 8 (Moscow: IMLI RAN, 2009).

35. M. M. Dunaev, "Aleksei Maksimovich Gor'kii," in *Pravoslavie i russkaia literatura* (Moscow: Khristianskaia literatura, 2003), vol. 5, 363–507.

36. See Zernov, *Russian Religious Renaissance*.

37. Andrei Siniavskii, *"Opavshie list'ia" Vasiliia Vasil'evicha Rozanova* (Moscow: Zakharov, 1999), 14.

38. Irina Gutkin, *The Cultural Origins of the Socialist Realist Aesthetic, 1890–1934* (Evanston, IL: Northwestern University Press, 1999), 18–19.

39. For a more substantive look at this article, see Erich Lippman, "'Undivided yet Merged': Maxim Gorky's Concept of Personhood in 'The Disintegration of Personality,'" in *"A Convenient Territory": Russian Literature at the Edge of Modernity; Essays in Honor of Barry Scherr*, ed. John M. Kopper and Michael Wachtel (Bloomington, IN: Slavica, 2015), 259–74.

40. M. Gor'kii, "Razrushenie lichnosti," in *Ocherki filosofii kollektivizma*, ed. A. A. Bogdanov (St. Petersburg: Izd. tovarishchestva "Znanie," 1909), 353–403.

41. See Lippman, "Co-opting Orthodoxy" (192–93), for my argument about Gorky's tendency to co-opt Orthodox terminology and symbols in his work. The pages listed deal specifically with his use of the word *lichnost'* in his articles "O tsinizme" and "Razrushenie lichnosti."

42. Aleksandr Bogdanov, "Sobiranie cheloveka," in *Novyi mir: Stat'i 1904–1905* (Moscow, 1905), 7–54; Kline, "Changing Attitudes toward the Individual," 623.

43. For a further explication of Gorky's Christology in *Confession*, see Lippman, "Co-opting Orthodoxy," 189–91.

44. Maksim Gor'kii, *Ispoved'* (Berlin: J. Ladyschnikow Verlag, 1909), 170.

45. Maksim Gor'kii to E. P. Peshkova, Capri, around March 6 (19), 1908, in *Polnoe sobranie sochinenii. Pis'ma v dvadtsati chetyrekh tomakh* (Moscow: Nauka, 2000), vol. 6, 196.

46. Gor'kii, *Ispoved'*, 194.

47. For an example of Marxist attacks on Gorky's *Confession*, see G. Plekhanov, "O tak nazyvaemykh religioznykh iskaniiakh v Rossii," in *Izbrannye filosofskie proizvedeniia* (Moscow, 1957), vol. 22, 326–437.

48. The reference is to the title of the article by P. Pertsov, "Religiia Gor'kogo," *Novoe vremia*, no. 11757 (December 3, 1908).

49. Barry P. Scherr, "God-Building or God-Seeking? Gorky's *Confession* as Confession" *The Slavic and East European Journal* 44, no. 3 (Autumn, 2000), 448–469, quote 453; see also Barry P. Scherr, "Gorky and God-Building," in *William James in Russian Culture*, ed. Joan Delaney Grossman and Ruth Rischin (Lanham, MD: Lexington Books, 2003), 196.

50. See A. A. Blok, "Rossiia i intelligentsiia," in *Religiozno-filosofskoe obshchestvo v Sankt-Peterburge (Petrograde): Istoriia v materialakh i dokumentakh*, vol. 1, *1907–1909* (Moscow: Russkii put', 2009), 359–67; Dmitrii Filosofov, "Druz'ia ili vragi," *Russkaia mysl'*, no. 8 (1909): 120–47.

51. Russian State Archive for Literature and Art, 419–1—125, p. 8. For reference, see V. V. Rozanov, "O 'narodo'-bozhii kak novoi idee Maksima Gor'kogo," *Russkoe slovo*, no. 289 (December 13, 1908).

52. For the full text of both presentations, see *Religiozno-filosofskoe obshchestvo v Sankt-Peterburge (Petrograde)*, vol. 1, *1907–1909* (Moscow: Russkii put', 2009), 419–73.

53. Dmitrii Filosofov, "Bogostroitel'stvo i bogoiskatel'stvo," in *Religiozno-filosofskoe obshchestvo v Sankt-Peterburge (Petrograde)*, vol. 1, *1907–1909* (Moscow: Russkii put', 2009), 441.

54. V. Bazarov [Vladimir Aleksandrovich Rudnev], "Bogoiskatel'stvo i bogostroitel'stvo," in *Vershiny* (St. Petersburg, 1909), 354–57.

55. Originally published as V. V. Rozanov, "V religiozno-filosofskom obshchestve," *Novoe vremia*, no. 11806 (January 23, 1909). Reprinted in V. V. Rozanov, *Staraia i molodaia Rossii: Stat'i i ocherki 1909 g.*, ed. Aleksandr Nikoliukin (Moscow: Respublika, 2004), 39.

56. Rozanov, *Staraia i molodaia Rossii*, 40.

57. Rozanov, *Staraia i molodaia Rossii*, 39.

58. Rozanov, *Staraia i molodaia Rossii*, 41; italics in the original.

59. Maksim Gor'kii, "O Karamazovshchine," in *O literature* (Moscow: Gosudarstvennoe izd-vo khudozhestvennoi literatury, 1961), 66–69.

60. Lenin to Gorky, Krakow to Capri, November 13 or 14, 1913, in *V. I. Lenin i A. M. Gor'kii: Pis'ma, vospominaniia, dokumenty* (Moscow: Izd. Akademii nauk SSSR, 1961), 109.

61. *V. I. Lenin i A. M. Gor'kii*, 109.

62. *V. I. Lenin i A. M. Gor'kii*, 110.

63. *V. I. Lenin i A. M. Gor'kii*, 115n1. Apparently, the last paragraph was published in *Russkoe slovo* but not in *Rech'*.

64. Pavel Basinskii, "Logika gumanizma: Ob istokakh tragedii Maksima Gor'kogo," *Voprosy literatury* 2 (1991): 136.

65. Despite the fact that Gorky's primary Old Believer contact in Moscow was his devotee Savva Morozov, supporters of the "religious roots of Russian Communism" argument have found Gorky's connection to this prominent Old Believer family meaningful. Robert Williams strongly implies a connection between the Old Believers' long history of opposition to the Russian state and Gorky's religious approach to socialism. See Robert Williams, *The Other Bolsheviks: Lenin and His Critics, 1904–1914* (Bloomington: Indiana University Press, 1986), 49–62. For a more direct argument that Gorky's religious worldview was heavily influenced by positive perceptions of Russian sectarians, see Mikhail Agurskii, "Velikii eretik (Gor'kii kak religioznyi myslitel')," *Voprosy filosofii* 8 (1991): 54–74.

66. Gorky to Rozanov, April 8 or 9 (21 or 22), 1912, in *Polnoe sobranie sochinenii. Pis'ma v dvadtsati chetyrekh tomakh* (Moscow: Nauka, 2003), vol. 9, 9.

67. Barratt and Scherr, *Maxim Gorky*, 167n5.

68. Gorky to Rozanov, Capri, August 3 or 4 (16 or 17), 1911, in *Polnoe sobranie sochinenii*, vol. 9, 81.

69. The soldiers, despite their imperfections, became unwitting disciples of Christ, furthering the cause of Christ and the apocalypse with their advance, despite not understanding it themselves.

70. Judith Deutsch Kornblatt, ed., *Divine Sophia: The Wisdom Writings of Vladimir Solovyov* (Ithaca, NY: Cornell University Press, 2009), 144.

71. Rozanov to Gorky, near the end of 1911, in V. V. Rozanov, *Mysli o literature* (Moscow: Sovremennik, 1989), 520.

72. See, for example, Aleksei Khomiakov, "The Church Is One," in *On Spiritual Unity: A Slavophile Reader*, trans. and ed. Boris Jakim and Robert Bird (Hudson, NY: Lindisfarne Books, 1998), 31–53.

73. This phrase is one of Solov'ev's favorites and can be found throughout many of his works. For a discussion of his philosophy with frequent reference to this phrase, see Kornblatt, *Divine Sophia*, 3–97.

74. Vasilii Rozanov, *Uedinennoe*, ed. V. G. Sukach (Moscow: Russkii put', 2002), 128–29.

75. Siniavskii, *"Opavshie list'ia,"* 14.

76. Casanova, "Secular, Secularizations, Secularisms," 73.

77. K. I. Chukovskii, *Dnevnik v trekh tomakh*, vol. 3, *1936–1969* (Moscow: PROZAiK, 2012), 21.

78. Gutkin, *Cultural Origins*, 19.

79. Nikolai Berdiaev, *O rabstve i svobode cheloveka: Opyt personalisticheskoi filosofii* (Paris: YMCA Press, 1972), 10–11.

80. See Zernov, *Russian Religious Renaissance*, 131–64.

81. Casanova, "Secular, Secularizations, Secularisms," 64; Taylor, "Western Secularity," 32.

82. Shklovskii, *Sentimental'noe puteshestvie*, 198.

8. The Dazzling Darkness of *Black Square*

This research was carried out in 2015 and supported by the National Research University Higher School of Economics Academic Fund Program, grant no. 15-09-0276. I thank David Conolly for his editorial suggestions.

1. An abstract painter and art theoretician (1878–1935).

2. Alexandra Shatskikh, "Aspects of Kazimir Malevich's Literary Legacy: A Summary," in *Rethinking Malevich: Proceedings of a Conference in Celebration of the 125th Anniversary of Kazimir Malevich's Birth*, ed. Charlotte Douglas and Christina Lodder (London: Pindar Press, 2007), 323.

3. Shatskikh, "Malevich's Literary Legacy," 325–26.

4. Alexei Kurbanovsky, "Malevich's Mystic Signs: From Iconoclasm to New Theology," in *Sacred Stories: Religion and Spirituality in Modern Russia*, ed. Mark D. Steinberg and Heather J. Coleman (Bloomington: Indiana University Press, 2007), 372.

5. Dmitrii Sarabyanov and Alexandra Shatskikh, *Kazimir Malevich. Zhivopis' teoriia* (Moscow: Iskusstvo, 1993), 363. Translations are the author's unless otherwise noted.

6. Suprematism, an art movement founded by Malevich, focused on basic geometrical forms. The agenda of suprematism was manifested in his theoretical works, in "Suprematism: World as Objectlessness, or Eternal Peace," "From Cubism and Futurism to Suprematism: The New Realism in Painting," and many others.

7. Shatskikh, "Malevich's Literary Legacy," 321.

8. See Siljak's introduction to this book.

9. Valery Podoroga, "Byt' vozvishennim segodnia—eto byt' nemodnym," *Kriticheskaia massa*, no. 3 (2003), http://magazines.russ.ru/km/2003/3/fil.html.

10. Yekaterina Dyogot', "Dnevnik VIP na iarmarke Frieze," vypusk 3, October 20, 2008, http://os.colta.ru/art/projects/89/details/3760; italics added.

11. See James Elkins, *On the Strange Place of Religion in Contemporary Art* (New York: Routledge, 2004), 22 and Mark Rothko, *Writings on Art: Mark Rothko*, edited by Miguel López-Remiro (New Haven: Yale University Press, 2006), 119. On color-field paintings, see Karen Wilkin and Carl Belz, *Color as Field: American Painting, 1950–1975* (New Haven, CT: Yale University Press, 2007).

12. Donald Judd, "Questions to Stella and Judd," interview by Bruce Glaser, in *Minimal Art: A Critical Anthology*, ed. Gregory Battcock (Berkeley: University of California Press, 1995), 151.

13. Helen E. Scott, "Crime or Creation?: Iconoclasm in the Name of Art," *St Andrews Journal of Art History and Museum Studies*, no. 13 (2009): 25–34.

14. Helen E. Scott, "'Wholly Uninteresting'? The Motives behind Acts of Iconoclasm," in *Perspectives on Power: An Inter-disciplinary Approach*, ed. Heather M. Morgan, Jernej Letnar Černič, and Lindsay Milligan (Newcastle, UK: Cambridge Scholars Publishing, 2010), 21–40.

15. Or without a very direct understanding of Malevich's revolutionary manifesto: "All forms of heavenly bliss are rejected, as are those on this earth of kingdoms, and as are also all their representations by art workers: they are a lie concealing reality." Kazimir Malevich, "On New Systems in Art," in *Essays on Art, 1915–1933*, trans. Xenia Glowacki-Prus and Arnold McMillin, ed. Troels Andersen (London: Rapp & Whiting, 1968), vol. 1, 118.

16. Pavel Florensky, *Iconostasis*, trans. Donald Sheeh and Olga Andrejev (Crestwood, NY: St. Vladimir's Seminary Press, 1996). Steven Cassedy specifies: "Every iconic image was meant to be an imitation of a previous image, which was itself an imitation of a previous image, and so on, back to an image based on an actual physical view of the person represented." Steven Cassedy, *Flight from Eden: The Origins of Modern Literary Criticism and Theory* (Berkeley: University of California Press, 1990), 104.

17. Clemena Antonova, "Re-contextualizing Holy Images in Early Soviet Russia: Florensky's Response to Lenin's Plan for Monumental Propaganda," in *Der Sturm der Bilder*, ed. U. Fleckner (Berlin: Schriften des Internationalen Warburg-Kollegs, 2011), 107.

18. Lunacharsky, quoted in Antonova, "Re-contextualizing Holy Images," 106.

19. See Viktor Bychkov, *2000 let khristianskoi kul'tury sub specie aesthetica*, vol. 2, *Slavianskii mir. Drevniaia Rus'. Rossiia* (Moscow, 2007); Alexander Inshakov, *Mikhail Larionov: Russkie gody* (Moscow: Gnosis, 2010); Myroslava M. Mudrak, "Kazimir Malevich and the Liturgical Tradition of Eastern Christianity," in *Byzantium/Modernism: The Byzantine as Method in Modernity*, ed. Roland Betancourt and Maria Taroutina (Leiden: Brill, 2015), 37–72; Anthony Parton, *Mikhail Larionov and the Russian Avant-Garde* (Princeton, NJ: Princeton University Press, 1993); Dmitrii Sarabyanov, *Russkaia zhivopis'. Probuzhdenie pamiati* (Moscow: Isskustvovedenie, 1998); Andrew Spira, *The Avant-Garde Icon* (London: Lund Humphries, 2008); Oleg Tarasov, *Icon and Devotion: Sacred Spaces in Imperial Russia* (London: Reaktion Books, 2002).

20. The term *primitivism* is often applied to professional painters working in the style of naive or folk art such as Paul Gauguin, Henri Rousseau, Larionov, Paul Klee, and others. Russian avant-garde primitivism is often called "neo-primitivism." See also Jane Ashton Sharp, "Primitivism, 'Neoprimitivism,' and the Art of Natalia Goncharova, 1907–1914" (PhD diss., Yale University, 1992).

21. Alexandra Shatskikh translates Malevich's term *bespredmetnost'* as "objectlessness," while Troels Andersen, translator of Malevich's collected volume, translates it as "non-objectivity." I will use the term *objectlessness* except in citations translated by Andersen.

22. E. H. Gombrich, *Art and Illusion* (Princeton, NJ: Princeton University Press, 2001). Kazimir Malevich, "From Cubism and Futurism to Suprematism: The New Realism in Painting,", in *Essays on Art 1915–1933*, Vol. I, ed. Troels Andersen (London: Rapp & Whiting, 1968), vol. 1, 24.

23. Kazimir Malevich, "From Cubism and Futurism to Suprematism: The New Realism in Painting," in *Essays on Art*, vol. 1, 24, 27, 36. See also.

24. Kazimir Malevich, "Zapiska o granitsakh real'nosti," in *Sobranie sochinenii v 5 tt.*, vol. 5, *Proizvedeniia raznyh let*, comp. Alexandra Shatskikh (Moscow: Gileia, 2004), 193.

25. Kazimir Malevich, "God Is Not Cast Down," in *Essays on Art*, vol. 1, 194.

26. Malevich, "God Is Not Cast Down," 195.

27. Kazimir Malevich, "Vystavka Professional'nogo soiuza khudozhnikov-zhivopistsev. Levaia fraktsiia (molodaia fraktsiia)," in *Sobranie sochinenii v 5 tomakh*, vol. 1, *Stat'i, manifesty, teoreticheskie sochineniia i drugie raboty, 1913–1929*, comp. A. S. Shatskikh (Moscow: Gileia, 1995), 121; Alexei Kurbanovsky, "Malevich's Mystic Signs: From Iconoclasm to New Theology," in Mark. D. Steinberg and Heather J. Coleman, eds., *Sacred Stories: Religion and Spirituality in Modern Russia*, (United States: Indiana University Press, 2007), 366.

28. Kazimir Malevich, "Non-objectivity," in *The World as Non-objectivity: Unpublished Writings 1922–25*, trans. Xenia Glowacki-Prus and Edmund T. Little, ed. Troels Andersen (Copenhagen: Borgen, 1976), 59.

29. Malevich, "Non-objectivity," 35–36.

30. Malevich, "Non-objectivity," 38.

31. Kazimir Malevich, "Zapisi i zametki," in *Sobranie sochinenii v 5 tt.*, vol. 5, 403.

32. I have analyzed Meister Eckhart's mysticism, in Tatiana Levina, "'Liberated Nothingness.' Eckhart of Avant-Garde," *RSUH/RGGU Bulletin. Series Philosophy. Social Studies. Art Studies* 4 (2019): 34–47.

33. Malevich, *World as Non-objectivity*, 67.

34. Alexandra Shatskikh, "Kazimir Malevich: volia k slovesnosti," in Malevich, *Sobranie sochinenii v 5 tt*, vol. 3, 00.

35. Kazimir Malevich, "The Philosophy of the Kaleidoscope" in *World as Non-objectivity*, 13.

36. Kazimir Malevich, "Appendix from the Book on Non-objectivity," in *World as Non-objectivity*, 315. See Eph. 1:5: "This then is the message which we have heard of him, and declare unto you, that God is light, and in him is no darkness at all."

37. See Eph. 5:13; Kazimir Malevich, "Vypiski iz Evangeliyi i kommentarii k nim," in *Sobranie sochinenii v 5 tt.*, vol. 5, 400.

38. Andrew Spira mentions this connection; see Spira, *Avant-Garde Icon*, 147. An explicit connection would require more concrete evidence that Malevich read Palamas.

39. The "Palamite disputes" related to the teaching of hesychasm (the mystical tradition of prayer in the Eastern Orthodox Church) continued for many years; Gregory Palamas responded to the criticism from Barlaam and his followers, which found expression in the "Triads in Defense of the Holy Hesychasts." Florenskii cites several works of Palamas in his bibliography in "The Pillar and the Ground of the Truth" (1914), but without any analysis. Florenskii acknowledges his ideas later. See Vasily Lourie, introduction to *Zhizn' i trudy Sv. Grigoriia Palamy: Vvedenie v izuchenie*, by Ioann Meiendorf, trans. N. G. Nachinkina, ed. I. P. Medvedeva and V. M. Lurie (St. Peterburg: Vizantinorossika, 1997), 338–39.

40. Pseudo-Dionysius, "The Letters," in *The Complete Works*, trans. Colm Luibheid (Mahwah, NJ: Paulist Press, 1987), 265, Letter 5, 1073A.

41. Gregory Palamas, *The Triads*, ed. John Meyendorff, trans. Nicholas Gendle (Mahwah, NJ: Paulist Press, 1983), I.iii.18, 36.

42. Kliun, quoted in Alexandra Shatskikh, *Black Square: Malevich and the Origin of Suprematism* (New Haven, CT: Yale University Press, 2012), 45.

43. Kurbanovsky, "Malevich's Mystic Signs," 367.

44. Kurbanovsky, "Malevich's Mystic Signs," 369.

45. Malevich, *Essays on Art*, 214, quoted in Kurbanovsky, "Malevich's Mystic Signs," 371.

46. Kurbanovsky, "Malevich's Mystic Signs," 371.

47. Malevich, *Essays on Art*, 204, quoted in Alain Besançon, *The Forbidden Image: An Intellectual History of Iconoclasm* (Chicago: University of Chicago Press, 2000), 370.

48. Besançon, *Forbidden Image*, 372.

49. A schism appeared after new liturgical revisions, initiated by Patriarch Nikon of Moscow, were made. Those who refused to support the revised rite—and iconog-

raphy that accompanied it—were anathematized. See Jefferson J. A. Gatrall, introduction to *Alter Icons: The Russian Icon and Modernity*, ed. Jefferson J. A. Gatrall and Douglas Greenfield (University Park: Pennsylvania State University Press, 2011), 11.

50. Vladimir Lazarev, *Russkaia ikonopis' ot istokov do nachala XVI veka* (Moscow: Iskusstvo, 2000), 13.

51. Rodchenko, quoted in Gatrall, introduction to *Alter Icons*, 6.

52. Larionov, quoted in Spira, *Avant-Garde Icon*, 59.

53. Benois, quoted in Besançon, *Forbidden Image*, 362. Benois (1870–1960) was a promoter of art nouveau in Russia. He lived in the Soviet Union until 1927.

54. Nikolai Berdiaev, *Krizis iskusstva* (Moscow: SP Interprint, 1990), 3.

55. Berdiaev, *Krizis iskusstva*, 16.

56. Berdiaev, *Krizis iskusstva*, 15;

57. Gershenzon (1869–1925) was the author of *Troistvennyi obraz sovershenstva* (Triple image of perfection) and the editor of *Vekhi* and other publications.

58. Alexandra Shatskikh, "Kazimir Malevich: volia k slovesnosti," in Malevich, *Sobranie sochinenii v 5 tt.*, vol. 3, 44.

59. Shatskikh, "Malevch," in Malevich, *Sobranie sochinenii v 5 tt.*, vol. 3, 48–49.

60. Malevich expressed his mistrust of bookish culture: "I am myself a wise book, and . . . all the books emerged from me. . . . I bear within me all the wisdom of everything." Quoted in Shatskikh, "Malevich's Literary Legacy," 323.

61. Besançon, *Forbidden Image*, 369.

62. Besançon, *Forbidden Image*, 369.

63. Malevich, *World as Non-objectivity*, 25.

64. Malevich, "God Is Not Cast Down," 196.

65. Immanuel Kant, *The Critique of Pure Reason*, edited and translated by Paul Guyer, Allen W. Wood (Cambridge University Press, 1998), 116.

66. Kant, *Critique of Pure Reason*, 117.

67. Malevich, "God Is Not Cast Down," 211; italics added.

68. Malevich, "God Is Not Cast Down," 212.

69. As compared to other philosophical works, which were known to Malevich only in their general ideas, Malevich had read Gershenzon's writings and had written about them in his notebooks by way of short aphorisms.

70. Malevich, "God Is Not Cast Down," 193.

71. Nicholas of Cusa, "On Learned Ignorance," in *Complete Philosophical and Theological Treatises*, trans. J. Hopkins (Minneapolis: Banning Press, 2001), 196; italics added.

72. Kazimir Malevich, "Suprematizm Mir kak bespredmetnost' ili vechnyi pokoi," in *Sobranie sochinenii v 5 tt.*, vol. 3, 290.

73. Malevich, "God Is Not Cast Down," 197.

74. Plato, "Symposium," in *Complete Works*, edited by John M. Cooper and D. S. Hutchinson (Indianapolis/Cambridge: Hackett Publishing Company, 1997), 211c–d.

75. Metaphysical realism (or Platonism) is the view that properties, relationships, or concepts exist independently of our world and human consciousness.

76. Kazimir Malevich, "Letter to Mikhail Gershenzon," March 18, 1920, Cultural Foundation "Khardzhiev-Chaga Center," Stedelijk Museum, Amsterdam; reprinted in Kazimir Malevich, *Chernyi kvadrat*, ed. A. Shatskikh (St. Petersburg: Azbuka-klassika, 2003), 439.

9. Magnitogorsk as Jerusalem

1. Solomon Mikhoels, "V studii," in *Evreiskii kamernyi teatr. K ego otkrytiiu v iiule 1919 goda* (Petrograd: Evreiskoe teatral'noe obshchestvo, 1919), 15. Translations here are the author's unless otherwise noted.

2. Solomon Mikhoels, "Sluzhu sovetskomu narodu!," in *Mikhoels: Stat'i, besedy, rechi*, ed. Konstantin Rudnitskii (Moscow: Iskusstvo, 1981), 311.

3. Jeffrey Veidlinger, *The Moscow State Yiddish Theater: Jewish Culture on the Soviet Stage* (Bloomington: Indiana University Press, 2000), 12–13. See also Kenneth Moss, *Jewish Renaissance in the Russian Revolution* (Cambridge, MA: Harvard University Press, 2009); David Shneer, *Yiddish and the Creation of Soviet Jewish Culture, 1918–1930* (New York: Cambridge University Press, 2004).

4. Veidlinger, *Moscow State Yiddish Theater*, 196–97.

5. The play has been performed once, in 1919, and has been considered lost since then. In 1993, I discovered the original manuscript at the manuscript department of the Bakhrushin Central State Theatrical Museum in Moscow (Rukopisnyi otdel GTsTM, f. 584, d. 51). *The Builder*, originally written in Russian, was first published in Yiddish translation by Dov-Ber Kerler with an introduction by Vassili Schedrin. See Vassili Schedrin, "Der boyer tsvishn khurbos. Di ershte teg fun Sovetishen Yiddishen teater un di kurtse piese fun Shloyme Mikhoels," *Yerushalaimer almanakh* 28 (2008): 306–22. The Russian original was published in Vassili Schedrin, "Vozvrashchenie 'Stroitelia.' Solomon Mikhoels kak dramaturg. Publikatsiia rukopisi p'esy 'Stroitel'' (1919)," in *Dokumenty po istorii teatra v knizhnykh i arkhivnykh sobraniiakh* (Moscow: Rossiiskaia gosudarstvennaia biblioteka iskusstv, 2017), 289–302. Two comprehensive histories of Soviet Yiddish theater in Russian and English mention the play only briefly. See Vladislav Ivanov, *GOSET: Politika i iskusstvo. 1919–1928* (Moscow: GITIS, 2007), 46–47; Veidlinger, *Moscow State Yiddish Theater*, 33. This chapter introduces the play to English-language scholarship for the first time.

6. "The Basel Declaration (1897)," in *The Israel-Arab Reader: A Documentary History of the Middle East Conflict*, ed. Walter Laqueur and Barry Rubin (New York: Penguin Books, 1985), 11–12.

7. 1 Sam. 8:20.

8. Abraham Isaac Kook, "The Lamentation in Jerusalem," *Hama'ayan*, accessed April 9, 2018, https://www.machonso.org/uploads/images/13-D-10-lamentation.pdf.

9. Kook, "Lamentation in Jerusalem."

10. Ahad Ha-Am, "The Jewish State and the Jewish Problem (1897)," in *The Zionist Idea. A Historical Analysis and Reader*, ed. Arthur Hertzberg (New York: Atheneum, 1971), 262–69.

11. Moss, *Jewish Renaissance*, 14.

12. Beynush Steiman, "Meshiekh ben Yoysef. Dramatishe poeme," *Eygns* 2 (1920): 55–61; also see Moss, *Jewish Renaissance*, 242–43.

13. Mikhoels, "Sluzhu sovetskomu narodu!," 311.

14. The source—Efros's article "Evreiskii teatr" (1922)—is quoted and discussed in Veidlinger, *Moscow State Yiddish Theater*, 22. It is noteworthy, that, according to Dan Miron, Sholem Aleichem, the classic writer of Yiddish literature, almost single-handedly created the "history" of modern Yiddish literature in the 1880s by inventing "the grand-

father myth" about Mendele Mocher Sforim (S.Y. Abramovitsh), another great Yiddish writer, who "started it all." Such "historicization of Yiddish literature" helped to integrate it as valuable "tradition" into modern Jewish life. See Dan Miron, *A Traveler Disguised: The Rise of Modern Yiddish Fiction in the Nineteenth Century* (Syracuse, NY: Syracuse University Press, 1996), 32.

15. Mark Rivesman, "Proshloe i budushchee evreiskogo teatra," in *Evreiskii kamernyi teatr. K ego otkrytiiu v iiule 1919 goda* (Petrograd: Evreiskoe teatral'noe obshchestvo, 1919), 9, 10, 12–13.

16. Lev Levidov, "Evreiskoe teatral'noe obshchestvo i Evreiskii kamernyi teatr," in *Evreiskii kamernyi teatr. K ego otkrytiiu v iiule 1919 goda* (Petrograd: Evreiskoe teatral'noe obshchestvo, 1919), 4.

17. Aleksei Granovskii, "Nashi tseli i zadachi," in *Evreiskii kamernyi teatr. K ego otkrytiiu v iiule 1919 goda* (Petrograd: Evreiskoe teatral'noe obshchestvo, 1919), 6.

18. Mikhoels, "V studii," 16.

19. Rivesman, "Proshloe i budushchee," 13. According to Jewish tradition, redemption after the exile comes as a daybreak after a long night. Jerusalem Talmud's (Berachot 4b) Rabbi Hiyya says: "[Like the break of day] so is the redemption of Israel. It begins little by little and, as it proceeds, it grows greater and greater." [Scripture says,] 'When I sit in darkness the Lord will be a light to me' (Micah 7:8). So at the outset it proceeded slowly. . . . And thereafter it grew greater. . . . And thereafter, 'The Jews had [the] light [of redemption] and gladness and joy and honor' (Esther 8:16)." Moreover, these "first flashes of light" could also be seen as an allusion to kabbalistic sparks of Divine Light—pieces of God's wisdom scattered throughout the world.

20. Levidov, "Evreiskoe teatral'noe obshchestvo," 3.

21. Mikhoels, "V studii," 15.

22. Mikhoels, "V studii," 16.

23. Mikhoels, "V studii," 19–20. Mikhoels refers to the biblical story of Jacob and Esau. Jacob was in full control of his own voice, but in order to obtain the blessing of his father, Isaac, Jacob impersonated Esau by virtually using Esau's hands. Jacob put goat skins on his hands so, when touched, they felt like Esau's hairy hands. The Torah says, "And Jacob went near unto Isaac his father; and he felt him, and said, the voice is Jacob's voice, but the hands are the hands of Esau. And he discerned him not, because his hands were hairy, as his brother Esau's hands: so he blessed him" (Gen. 27:22–23). So, there is an obvious mistake—"the hands of Jacob" in Mikhoels's quotation should be "the hands of Esau." Since the early Middle Ages, Jacob and Esau were the symbols of Jews and Christians in Jewish tradition and popular imagination. Hence the additional symbolism of Mikhoels's observation; it was easy for newly minted Yiddish actors to master the spiritual Jewish skill of speech ("Jacob's voice"), while it was hard to master the physical non-Jewish skill of movement and action ("hands of Esau").

24. Mikhoels, "V studii," 19, 24.

25. Granovskii, "Nashi tseli i zadachi," 7.

26. Rivesman, "Proshloe i budushchee," 15.

27. Granovskii, "Nashi tseli i zadachi," 7.

28. Nikolai Minskii, *Genrikh Ibsen. Ego zhizn' i literaturnaia deiatel'nost'* (Moscow: Direkt-Media, 2014), 10.

29. For analysis of relationships between symbolism and avant-garde in Russian and European art, see John Bowlt, *Moscow and St. Petersburg in Russia's Silver Age, 1900–1920* (London: Thames & Hudson, 2008), 10, 27.

30. Knut Ove Arntzen, "The Revolutionary Avant-Garde: What Drama?," in *Ibsen and Russian Culture: Ibsen Conference in St. Petersburg, 2003 1 October–4 October*, ed. Knut Brynhildsvoll, Acta Ibseniana 3 (Oslo: Centre for Ibsen Studies, University of Oslo, 2005), 16.

31. Gerhart Hauptmann's *The Sunken Bell* (*Die versunkene Glocke*, 1896) might have been an alternative under consideration. However, Hauptmann did not match Ibsen's status of a symbolic and influential figure in Russian culture. Additionally, the universalistic setting of *The Master Builder* may have been more suitable for the task than *The Sunken Bell*'s folkloristic style.

32. Minskii, *Genrikh Ibsen*, 92.

33. Rukopisnyi otdel GTsTM, f. 584, d. 51, l. 7.

34. Rukopisnyi otdel GTsTM, f. 584, d. 51, ll. 7–8.

35. The history of modern Russian theater already had a considerable record of such a utilitarian approach to Ibsen's ideas and dramas prior to the debut of Granovskii's studio. For example, according to Osip Mandelshtam, Komissarzhevskaia, by establishing her own symbolist theater, "used Ibsen as a mere foreign hostel. It helped her to escape from the mental asylum of Russian theater routines; it helped her to become free at last." Osip Mandelshtam, *Sochineniia* (Moscow: Khudozhestvennaia literatura, 1990), vol. 2, 44. In 1906, Meyerhold directed *Hedda Gabler*, deliberately rejecting, reversing, or disregarding each of many meticulous stage directions provided by Ibsen in the text of his play. See Margarita Odesskaya, "*Hedda Gabler*: Life in Time," in *Ibsen and Russian Culture: Ibsen Conference in St. Petersburg, 2003 1 October–4 October*, ed. Knut Brynhildsvoll, Acta Ibseniana 3 (Oslo: Centre for Ibsen Studies, University of Oslo, 2005), 85–96.

36. Abram Efros, "Nachalo," in *Mikhoels: Stat'i, besedy, rechi*, ed. Konstantin Rudnitskii (Moscow: Iskusstvo, 1981), 328.

37. Ivanov, *GOSET*, 39.

38. Ivanov, *GOSET*, 42.

39. Ivanov, *GOSET*, 46–47.

40. Gen. 11:1–9.

41. Pirkei DeRabbi Eliezer 24.

42. 2 Sam. 13:1–29.

43. Pirkei Avot 5:19.

44. Derech Chaim 107.

45. Traditionally, the Jewish people are seen as a bride of God.

46. Isaac Goldberg, English translator and editor of Yiddish plays including *In Winter*, wrote that "to the Western mind [these plays] would seem to lack climax, whereas the truth is that the Jewish reader or spectator regards the work as a picture, rather than a progress. Indeed the regular name for the popular Yiddish melodramas . . . is still Lebensbild, a picture from life." See David Pinski, Sholom Ash, Perez Hirschbein, and Solomon J. Rabinowitsch, *Six Plays of the Yiddish Theater*, ed. and trans. Isaac Goldberg (Boston: John W. Luce, 1916), 121.

47. See Nikolai Berdiaev, "Tsarstvo Bozhie i tsarstvo kesaria," *Put'* 1 (September 1925): 31–52.

48. Moshe Litvakov, *Finf yor Melukhisher Idisher kamer teatr. 1919–1924* (Moscow: Shul un Bukh, 1924), 10–11.

49. Mikhoels replaced Granovskii, who defected to France in 1929, as a head of GOSET in the early 1930s.

50. Soviet authorities issued the movie's release certificate on December 6, 1932. See *Vse belorusskie fil'my* (Minsk: Belaruskaia navuka, 1996), vol. 1, 52. For analysis of the movie's script, see Gennady Estraikh, *In Harness: Yiddish Writers' Romance with Communism* (Syracuse, NY: Syracuse University Press, 2005), 145–49; Harriet Murav, "Peretz Markish in the 1930s: Socialist Construction and the Return of the Luftmentsh," in *A Captive of the Dawn: The Life and Work of Peretz Markish (1895–1952)*, ed. Joseph Sherman, Gennady Estraikh, Jordan Finkin, and David Shneer (London: Legenda, 2011), 114–26.

51. "Pervyi v mire evreiskii zvukovoi fil'm," *Vecherniaia Moskva*, October 30, 1932. The full movie, both Yiddish and Russian versions, included nine parts (35 mm film reels). Only one Yiddish part (the first) and eight Russian parts (the first to eighth) survived. See *The Return of Nathan Becker* (*Nosn Becker fort aheym*), USSR, 1932. Restored and distributed by the National Center for Jewish Film, Brandeis University, Waltham, MA.

52. "Pervyi v mire evreiskii zvukovoi fil'm."

53. *Vse belorusskie fil'my*, 52–53.

54. H.T.S., "A Soviet Yiddish Picture," *New York Times*, April 15, 1933. Concerned with the propaganda message of the movie, the US Department of State reluctantly approved the release of *The Return of Nathan Becker* in the United States. See Veidlinger, *Moscow State Yiddish Theater*, 133.

55. Miron Chernenko, *Krasnaia zvezda, zheltaia zvezda. Kinematograficheskaia istoriia evreistva v Rossii, 1919–1999* (Vinnitsa, Ukraine: Globus-Press, 2001), 89; B. Kolomarov, "Vozvrashchenie Neitana Bekkera," *Rabochii i teatr* 17 (1939).

56. Chernenko, *Krasnaia zvezda, zheltaia zvezda*, 87.

57. Yuri Slezkine, *The House of Government: A Saga of the Russian Revolution* (Princeton, NJ: Princeton University Press, 2017), xii.

58. See the analysis of similar imaginary topography in modern Yiddish literature in Dan Miron, *The Image of the Shtetl and Other Studies of Modern Jewish Literary Imagination* (Syracuse, NY: Syracuse University Press, 2000), 1–48.

59. Iurii Lotman and Boris Uspenskii, "'Pis'ma russkogo puteshestvennika' Karamzina i ikh mesto v razvitii russkoi kul'tury," in *Pis'ma russkogo puteshestvennika*, ed. Nikolai Karamzin (Leningrad: Nauka, 1984), 561–62.

60. Lotman and Uspenskii, "'Pis'ma russkogo puteshestvennika' Karamzina," 533.

61. See Yuri Slezkine, *The Jewish Century* (Princeton, NJ: Princeton University Press, 2004), 204–371.

62. The song in the movie is an abridged version of an actual Yiddish folk song, "Ten Brothers" ("Tsen brider"). Its full Yiddish text, Russian translation, and musical score were published in *Evreiskaia narodnaia pesnia. Antologiia*, comp. M. Goldin, ed. I. Zemtsovskii, A. Kaplan, and E. Khazdan (St. Petersburg: Kompozitor, 1994), 136–37.

63. Mikhoels often used such details and gestures onstage. As the Deaf, he stretched his arm toward the heavens in a silent prayer (*The Deaf*, 1930); as Lear, he repeatedly touches his head trying to find the crown he lost (*King Lear*, 1935). See Konstantin Rudnitskii, ed. *Mikhoels: Stat'i, besedy, rechi* (Moscow: Iskusstvo, 1981), 62, 64, 138–39.

64. Ilya Ehrenburg, *Neobychainye pokhozhdeniia* (St. Petersburg: Kristall, 2001), 522.

65. Rukopisnyi otdel GTsTM, f. 584, d. 51, l. 7.

66. Kh. Dunets, *Far magnitboen fun der literatur* (Minsk: Belorusskaia Akademiia Nauk, 1932). See also Estraikh, *In Harness*, 166.

67. Chernenko, *Krasnaia zvezda, zheltaia zvezda*, 88.

68. "Answers to Napoleon (1806). The Assembly of Jewish Notables," in *The Jew in the Modern World: A Documentary History*, ed. Paul Mendes-Flohr and Jehuda Reinharz, 3rd ed. (New York: Oxford University Press, 2011), 154.

69. "The Reform of Judaism," in *Heritage: Civilization and the Jews; Source Reader*, ed. William W. Hallo, David Ruderman, and Michael Stanislawski (New York: Praeger, 1984), 223.

70. Methods used in anti-religious campaigns against Judaism included reframing of traditional religious ritual to become a ceremony infused with the folk (*narodnyi*) spirit, such as the "Soviet" Passover seder, and rewriting traditional religious texts and infusing them with socialist substance, such as "red" haggadah (a collection of prayers, commentaries, and stories traditionally read at the Passover table). See Anna Shternshis, *Soviet and Kosher: Jewish Popular Culture in the Soviet Union, 1923–1939* (Bloomington: Indiana University Press, 2006).

10. "Holy Russia" and British Conservatism at the Turn of the Twentieth Century

The chapter is based on research supported by the Russian Foundation for Humanities (RGNF), grant no. 12-01-00183.

1. I thank the anonymous reviewer for this particular expression.

2. For an overview of the secularization theories, see Philip S. Gorski and Ateş Altınordu, "After Secularization?," *Annual Review of Sociology* 34 (2008): 55–85.

3. On the globalization tendencies in the period before World War I, see Martin H. Geyer and Johannes Paulmann, "Introduction: The Mechanics of Internationlism," in *The Mechanics of Internationalism: Culture, Society, and Politics from the 1840s to the First World War*, ed. Martin H. Geyer and Johannes Paulmann (New York: Oxford University Press, 2001), 1–25. On the religious aspects of globalization, see Abigail Green and Vincent Viaene, eds., *Religious Internationals in the Modern World: Globalization and Faith Communities since 1750* (Basingstoke: Palgrave Macmillan, 2012).

4. José Casanova, "The Secular, Secularizations, Secularisms," in *Rethinking Secularism*, ed. Craig Calhoun, Mark Juergensmeyer, and Jonathan VanAntwerpen (New York: Oxford University Press, 2011), 64, 71.

5. Hugh McLeod, introduction to *The Decline of Christendom in Western Europe, 1750–2000*, ed. Hugh McLeod and Werner Ustorf (Cambridge: Cambridge University Press, 2003), 18.

6. For an overview of the scholarship on religion and the church in Russia, see Paul W. Werth, "Lived Orthodoxy and Confessional Diversity: The Last Decade on Religion in Modern Russia," *Kritika: Explorations in Russian and Eurasian History* 12, no. 4 (2011): 849–65. The new approach to religion and the church in modern Russia is conceptualized in the following collections: Valerie A. Kivelson and Robert H. Greene, eds., *Orthodox Russia: Belief and Practice under the Tsars* (University Park: Pennsylvania State University Press, 2003); Mark D. Steinberg and Heather J. Coleman, eds., *Sacred Stories:*

Religion and Spirituality in Modern Russia (Bloomington: Indiana University Press, 2007); Amy Singleton Adams and Vera Shevzov, eds., *Framing Mary: The Mother of God in Modern, Revolutionary, and Post-Soviet Russian Culture* (Ithaca, NY: Cornell University Press, 2018).

7. Nadieszda Kizenko, *A Prodigal Saint: Father John of Kronstadt and the Russian People* (University Park: Pennsylvania State University Press, 2000); Vera Shevzov, *Russian Orthodoxy on the Eve of Revolution* (New York: Oxford University Press, 2004); Scott M. Kenworthy, *The Heart of Russia: Trinity-Sergius, Monasticism, and Society after 1825* (Washington, DC: Woodrow Wilson Center Press; New York: Oxford University Press, 2010); Jennifer Hedda, *His Kingdom Come: Orthodox Pastorship and Social Activism in Revolutionary Russia* (DeKalb: Northern Illinois University Press, 2008); Laurie Manchester, *Holy Fathers, Secular Sons: Clergy, Intelligentsia, and the Modern Self in Revolutionary Russia* (DeKalb: Northern Illinois University Press, 2008); Page Herrlinger, *Working Souls: Russian Orthodoxy and Factory Labor in St. Petersburg, 1881–1917* (Bloomington, IN: Slavica, 2007); Irina Paert, *Spiritual Elders: Charisma and Tradition in Russian Orthodoxy* (DeKalb: Northern Illinois University Press, 2010); Patrick Lally Michelson, *Beyond the Monastery Walls: The Ascetic Revolution in Russian Orthodox Thought, 1814–1914* (Madison: University of Wisconsin Press, 2017); Patrick Lally Michelson and Judith Deutsch Kornblatt, eds., *Thinking Orthodox in Modern Russia: Culture, History, Context* (Madison: University of Wisconsin Press, 2014).

8. William John Birkbeck, *Birkbeck and the Russian Church: Containing Essays and Articles by the Late W. J. Birkbeck*, comp. and ed. Athelstan Riley (New York: Macmillan, 1917), 5, 8. Important information on Birkbeck's activities in Russia can be found in the obituaries written by his Russian friends: V. A. Sokolov, "Iskrennii drug Pravoslavnoi Tserkvi i Rossii (pamiati V. D. Birkbeka)," *Bogoslovskii vestnik* 2, no. 9 (1916): 59–87 (2nd pagination); K. N. Faminskii, "Dorogoi pamiati druga Rossii i Vostochnoi Tserkvi I. V. Birkbeka," *Khristianskoe chtenie* 1–2 (1917): 112–20; N. N. Glubokovskii, "Svetloi pamiati druga Rossii i russkogo pravoslaviia Ivana Vasil'evicha Birkbeka," *Trudy Kievskoi dukhovnoi akademii* 11–12 (1916): 226–57.

9. For these opinions of the British public, see Herbert Barry, *Russia in 1870* (London: Wyman & Sons, 1871); Geoffrey Drage, *Russian Affairs* (London: J. Murray, 1904); Charles Sarolea, *The French Revolution and the Russian Revolution* (Edinburgh: Oliver & Boyd, 1906); Maurice Baring, *The Russian People* (London: Methuen, 1911). On the British stereotypes concerning the Russian Church, see A. N. Zashihin, *"Gliadia iz Londona." Rossiia v obshchestvennoi mysli Britanii; Vtoraia polovina XIX–nachalo XX v.* (Arhangel'sk: Izdatel'stvo Pomorskogo mezhdunarodnogo pedagogicheskogo universiteta, 1995), 44–57.

10. William John Birkbeck, *Life and Letters of W. J. Birkbeck*, collected and ed. by Rose Katherine Birkbeck (London: Longmans, Green, 1922), 20, 22. The diplomatic activities of Hardinge are described in his memoirs: Arthur H. Hardinge, *A Diplomatist in Europe* (London: J. Cape, 1927); Arthur H. Hardinge, *A Diplomatist in the East* (London: J. Cape, 1928).

11. Birkbeck, *Russian Church*, 230.

12. Viscount Halifax, preface to *Life and Letters of W. J. Birkbeck*, ed. Rose Katherine Birkbeck (London: Longmans, Green, 1922), v–vi. On Birkbeck's travels to Russia, see Sokolov, "Iskrennii drug," 67–68.

13. Rossiiskii gosudarstvennyi istoricheskii arhiv (RGIA), f. 797, op. 67, otd. 2, st. 3, d. 167 (o poezdke arkhiepiskopa Antoniia v London), l. 45. Faminskii, "Dorogoi pamiati," 114. Translations are the author's unless otherwise noted.

14. On the visits of Anglican and Episcopal bishops to Russia, see V. A. Sokolov, "Poseshchenie Moskovskoi dukhovnoi akademii primasom Anglii arkhiepiskopom Iorkskim (15 aprelia 1897 g.)," *Bogoslovskii vestnik* 2 (1897): 216–24 (3rd pagination); V. A. Sokolov, "Otklik na prizyv (po povodu priezda v Rossiiu Ch. Graftona, episkopa Amerikanskoi episkopal'noj tserkvi)," *Bogoslovskii vestnik* 3 (1904): 484–521 (3rd pagination); Ernest C. Miller, "Bishop Grafton of Fond du Lac and the Orthodox Church," *Sobornost* 4, no. 1 (1982): 38–48; RGIA, f. 797, op. 63, otd. 2, st. 3, d. 364 (o poezdke v Rossiiu Charl'za Graftona).

15. Michael Hughes, "The English Slavophile: W. J. Birkbeck and Russia," *Slavonic and East European Review* 82, no. 3 (2004): 699.

16. Birkbeck, *Russian Church*, 103, 109–10; Birkbeck, *Life and Letters*, 176; Hughes, "English Slavophile," 692.

17. On Archbishop Antonii's trip to Britain: RGIA, f. 797, op. 67, otd. 2, st. 3, d. 167 (o poezdke arkhiepiskopa Antoniia v London); Birkbeck, *Russian Church*, 155–63.

18. RGIA, f. 797, op. 67, otd. 2, st. 3, d. 167, l. 45.

19. Glubokovskii, "Svetloi pamiati druga Rossii," 239.

20. On Novikoff, see William T. Stead, *The M.P. for Russia: Reminiscences and Correspondence of Madame Olga Novikoff*, 2 vols. (London: Andrew Melrose, 1909); Joseph Baylen, "Madame Olga Novikov, Propagandist," *American Slavic and East European Review* 10, no. 4 (December 1951): 255–71.

21. Michael Hughes, "Stephen Graham and Russian Spirituality: The Pilgrim in Search of Salvation," in *A People Passing Rude: British Responses to Russian Culture*, ed. Anthony Cross (Cambridge, UK: Open Book Publishers, 2012), 164, 166–67.

22. Theofanis G. Stavrou, *Russian Interests in Palestine, 1882–1914* (Thessaloniki: Institute for Balkan Studies, 1963), 100; Derek Hopwood, *The Russian Presence in Syria and Palestine, 1843–1914* (Oxford: Clarendon Press, 1969), 116. The sympathy shown to Russian pilgrims was most visible in works such as Theodor Dowling, *The Orthodox Greek Patriarchate of Jerusalem* (London: Society for Promoting Christian Knowledge, 1913); and Arthur C. Headlam, *Teaching of the Russian Church* (London: Rivingtons, 1897).

23. For an overall account of the views and activities of Stephen Graham, see Hughes, "Graham and Russian Spirituality"; and the website Stephen Graham: World Traveller, http://www.stephengrahamworldtraveller.com/, maintained by Michael Hughes.

24. Hughes, "Graham and Russian Spirituality," 170–71.

25. Hughes, "Graham and Russian Spirituality," 163, 171.

26. Andrzej Walicki, *A History of Russian Thought from the Enlightenment to Marxism* (Stanford, CA: Stanford University Press, 1993), 101, 107.

27. Birkbeck, *Russian Church*, 139.

28. K. P. Pobedonostsev to Olga Novikova, September 6, 1889, Otdel rukopisei Rossiiskoi gosudarstvennoi biblioteki, f. 126, k. 8479, edinitsa khraneniia 10, l. 13ob.

29. Birkbeck, *Russian Church*, 79.

30. Birkbeck, *Russian Church*, 82.

31. Birkbeck, *Russian Church*, 224. The traditional notion of the "enslavement" of the Orthodox Church in imperial Russia has to some extent been revised by the modern scholarship. See Gregory L. Freeze, "Handmaiden of the State? The Church in Imperial Russia Reconsidered," *Journal of Ecclesiastical History* 36, no. 1 (1985): 82–102.

32. Birkbeck, *Russian Church*, 85. On the participation of Birkbeck in the discussions on religious freedom in Russia, see A. Yu. Polunov, "Poniatiia 'svoboda sovesti' i 'veroterpimost'" v obshchestvenno-politicheskom diskurse Rossii kontsa XIX–nachala XX v.," in *"Poniatiia o Rossii": K istoricheskoi semantike imperskogo perioda* (Moscow: NLO, 2012), vol. 1, 559–573.

33. On the history of the relationship between the Russian Church and the Church of England, see I. K. Smolich, *Istoriia russkoi tserkvi, 1700–1917* (Moscow: Izdatel'stvo Spaso-Preobrazhenskogo Valaamskogo monastyria, 1996), pt. 1, 368–75; J. A. Douglas, *The Relations of the Anglican Churches with the Eastern-Orthodox, Especially in Regard to Anglican Orders* (London: Faith Press, 1921); *Po puti sblizheniia anglikanskoi tserkvi s pravoslavno-vostochnoi* (Riga: Pravoslavnoe religiozno-prosvetitel'skoe obshchestvo pri kafedre Rizhskogo episkopa, 1911).

34. On the discussion in Russian theological journals concerning the papal bull, see V. A. Sokolov, "Po povodu bully papy L'va XIII ob anglikanskikh rukopolozheniiakh" *Bogoslovskii vestnik*, 1 (1897); "Otvet Anglii Rimu po voprosu ob anglikanskom sviashchenstve," *Khristiankoe chtenie* 6 (1897).

35. For an account of Birkbeck's travel to Arkhangel'sk Province in 1889, see Birkbeck, *Russian Church*, 17–50. On the development of public speaking in post-reform Russia that included the revitalizing of church preaching, see Stephen Lovell, "*Glasnost'* in Practice: Public Speaking in the Era of Alexander II," *Past & Present*, no. 218 (2013): 127–58.

36. Birkbeck, *Russian Church*, 238–39.

37. On the Il'minskii system, see Robert P. Geraci, *Window on the East: National and Imperial Identities in Late Tsarist Russia* (Ithaca, NY: Cornell University Press, 2001).

38. Birkbeck, *Life and Letters*, 131; Birkbeck, *Russian Church*, 210.

39. Hughes, "English Slavophile," 687.

40. It was Birkbeck who proposed that Antonii should represent Russia at the celebrations for Queen Victoria's Diamond Jubilee. See Birkbeck, *Life and Letters*, 178.

41. Birkbeck, *Russian Church*, 120–25, 153, 210–17; Birkbeck, *Life and Letters*, 248–49.

42. Birkbeck, *Russian Church*, 120–25; Birkbeck, *Life and Letters*, 28.

43. On the religious policy of Pobedonostsev, see Alexander Polunov, "Church, Regime, and Society in Russia (1880–1895)," *Russian Studies in History* 39, no. 4 (2001): 33–53; A. Yu. Polunov, *Pod vlast'iu ober-prokurora. Gosudarstvo i tserkov' v epokhu Aleksandra III* (Moscow: AIRO-XX, 1995).

44. Polunov, *Pod vlast'iu ober-prokurora*, 75.

45. On the popular religiosity in late imperial Russia, see Shevzov, *Russian Orthodoxy*; Chris J. Chulos, *Converging Worlds: Religion and Community in Peasant Russia, 1861–1917* (DeKalb: Northern Illinois University Press, 2003).

46. Polunov, *Pod vlast'iu ober-prokurora*, 72–82.

47. Robert F. Byrnes, *Pobedonostsev: His Life and Thought* (Bloomington: Indiana University Press, 1968), 291, 335–57; A. Yu. Polunov, "K. P. Pobedonostsev i

obshchestvenno-politicheskaia zhizn' Velikobritanii," in *Konstantin Petrovich Pobedonostsev: Myslitel', uchenyi, chelovek* (St. Petersburg: Sankt-Peterburgskaia metropoliia, 2007), 87–93.

48. Hughes, "English Slavophile," 687.

49. On contradictions in Pobedonostsev's views and activities, see John D. Basil, "Konstantin Petrovich Pobedonostsev: An Argument for a Russian State Church," *Church History* 64, no. 1 (March 1995): 44–61; John D. Basil, "K. P. Pobedonostsev and the Harmonius Society," *Canadian-American Slavic Studies* 37, no. 4 (2003): 415–26.

50. Hughes, "English Slavophile," 695.

51. Hugh McLeod, *Secularisation in Western Europe, 1848–1914* (New York: St. Martin's Press, 2000), 28.

52. Polunov, *Pod vlast'iu ober-prokurora*, 72–82.

53. On the ideological meaning of the construction of "neo-Russian" churches, see Richard S. Wortman, *Scenarios of Power: Myth and Ceremony in Russian Monarchy from Peter the Great to the Abdication of Nicholas II* (Princeton, NJ: Princeton University Press, 2000), vol. 2, 244–56.

54. Stavrou, *Russian Interests*, 71. On the foundation of the IOPS, see N. N. Lisovoi, *Russkoe dukhovnoe i politicheskoe prisutstvie v Sviatoi zemle i na Blizhnem Vostoke v XIX–nachale XX v.* (Moscow: Indrik, 2006), 348–57.

55. On the publications devoted to Palestine for ordinary people, see E. A. Chach, "Khristianskii Vostok v izdaniiakh dlia naroda kontsa XIX–nachala XX veka: K postanovke problemy," *Vestnik Omskogo gosudarstvennogo universiteta* 1 (2012): 129–35. On the social activities of the IOPS, see Simon Dixon, "Nationalism versus Internationalism: Russian Orthodoxy in Nineteenth-Century Palestine," in *Religious Internationals in the Modern World: Globalization and Faith Communities since 1750*, ed. Abigail Green and Vincent Viaene (Basingstoke: Palgrave Macmillan, 2012), 148–57.

56. Nikolaos Chrissidis, "The Athonization of Pious Travel: Shielded Shrines, Shady Deals, and Pilgrimage Logistics in Late Nineteenth-Century Odessa," *Modern Greek Studies Yearbook* 28/29 (2012/13): 169–76.

57. On the history of Russian monasteries on Mount Athos, see L. A. Gerd, *Russkii Afon. 1878–1914: Ocherki tserkovno-politicheskoi zhizni* (Moscow: Indrik, 2010).

58. Chrissidis, "Athonization of Pious Travel," 174, 182.

59. Casanova, "Secular, Secularizations, Secularisms," 58.

11. Power, Freedom, and Modernity

1. See the illuminating discussion in Maikl David-Foks [Michael David-Fox], "Modernost' v Rossii i SSSR: Otsutstvuiushchaia, obshchaia, al'ternitivnaia ili perepletennaia," *Novoe literaturnoe obozrenie* 140, no. 4 (2016), and the ten responses by Timur Atnashev, Andy Byford, Aleksandr Etkind, Bruce Grant, Catriona Kelly, Kirill Kobrin, Stephen Lovell, Aleksandr Markov, Douglas Rogers, and Mark D. Steinberg, https://www.nlobooks.ru/magazines/novoe_literaturnoe_obozrenie/140_nlo_4_2016/.

2. W. W. Rostow, *The Stages of Economic Growth: A Non-Communist Manifesto* (Cambridge: Cambridge University Press, 1960); Stephen Kotkin, *Stalin*, vol. 1, *Paradoxes of Power, 1878–1928* (New York: Penguin, 2014), 63; Mark Elvin, "A Working Definition

of 'Modernity'?," *Past & Present*, no. 113 (1986): 209; Bernard Lewis, *What Went Wrong? Western Impact and Middle Eastern Response* (New York: Oxford University Press, 2002).

3. John Stuart Mill, *On Liberty* (London: John W. Parker and Son, West Strand, 1859); Jürgen Habermas, "Modernity—an Incomplete Project," in *Postmodernism: A Reader*, ed. Thomas Docherty (New York: Columbia University Press, 1992), 51–61; Laura Engelstein, *The Keys to Happiness: Sex and the Search for Modernity in Fin-de-Siècle Russia* (Ithaca, NY: Cornell University Press, 1992); Stephen Eric Bronner, *The Bigot: Why Prejudice Persists* (New Haven, CT: Yale University Press, 2014).

4. Max Weber, *The Protestant Ethic and the Spirit of Capitalism*, trans. Talcott Parsons (London: George Allen and Unwin, 1930); Julia Berest, "J. S. Mill's *On Liberty* in Imperial Russia: Modernity and Democracy in Focus," *Slavonic and East European Review* 97, no. 2 (April 2019): 266–98; Kristina Stoeckl, "European Integration and Russian Orthodoxy: Two Multiple Modernities Perspectives," in *Multiple Modernities and Postsecular Societies*, ed. Massimo Rosati and Kristina Stoeckl (Burlington, VT: Ashgate, 2012), 97–114.

5. Shmuel N. Eisenstadt, *Comparative Civilizations and Multiple Modernities* (Leiden: Brill, 2003); Valerie A. Kivelson and Ronald Grigor Suny, *Russia's Empires* (New York: Oxford University Press, 2017), 234–40.

6. Svetlana Aleksandrovna Inikova, "Tambovskie dukhobortsy v 60-e gody XVIII veka," *Vestnik Tambovskogo universiteta, Seriia: Gumanitarnye nauki* 2, no. 1 (1997): 39–53; Svetlana Aleksandrovna Inikova, "The Tambov Dukhobors in the 1760s," *Russian Studies in History* 46, no. 3 (Winter 2007–8): 10–19; J. Eugene Clay, "Russian Spiritual Christianity and the Closing of the Black-Earth Frontier: The First Heresy Trials of the Dukhobors in the 1760s," *Russian History* 40, no. 2 (January 2013): 221–43.

7. [Ivan Andreevich Pashatskii], *Veroispovedanie dukhovnykh khristian obyknovenno nazyvaemykh molokanami* (Geneva: Vol'naia russkaia tipografiia, 1865), 5; Iv. Fedos. Kolesnikov, "Iubileinyi s"ezd v Vorontsovke, *Dukhovnyi khristianin*, no. 3 (February 1906): 31–33; "Iz Tiflisa: Samobytnoe molokanstvo," *Dukhovnyi khristianin*, no. 11 (October 1906): 63–64.

8. Göran Therborn, "Entangled Modernities," *European Journal of Social Theory* 6, no. 3 (August 1, 2003): 293.

9. *Sobranie postanovlenii po chasti raskola* (St. Petersburg: Tip. Ministerstva vnutrennikh del, 1875), 47–48. Translations are the author's unless otherwise noted.

10. Andrei Leopol'dov, *Statisticheskoe opisanie Saratovskoi gubernii*, 2 vols. in one (Moscow: Tip. Departamenta vneshnei torgovli, 1839), 1:170.

11. [Grigorii Iakovlevich Pokrovskii], "Istoricheskie svedeniia o molokanskoi sekte," *Pravoslavnyi sobesednik*, September 1858, 43; November 1858, 291–327. On the authorship of this article, see P. V. Znamenskii, *Istoriia Kazanskoi dukhovnoi akademii za pervyi (doreformennyi) period eia sushchestvovaniia (1842–1870 gody)*, 3 vols. (Kazan': Tipografiia Imperatorskogo universiteta, 1891–92), 3: 333, 394–95.

12. Soviet scholars mistakenly attributed this anonymously published work to Herzen's acquaintance, the adventurist Nikolai Aleksandrovich Shevelev (ca. 1826–after 1881). L. R. Lanskoi, "Strannoe proshchanie," *Literaturnoe nasledstvo* 99, no. 1 (1997): 251–349.

13. [Pashatskii], *Veroispovedanie*, III.

14. Anna Filibert, "Neskol'ko slov o molokanakh v tavricheskikh stepiakh," *Otechestvennye zapiski* 190, no. 6, (June 1870): 292, second pagination.

15. Aleksandr Stepanovich Prugavin, "Molokane," in *Entsiklopedicheskii slovar' Granat*, 7th ed., vol. 29 (Moscow: T-va Br. A. i I. Granat i Ko; Petrograd: Obshchestvennaia pol'za, [1916]), col. 228.

16. A. Spasskii, "Ob usloviiakh proiskhozhdeniia i razvitiia sovremennogo russkogo raskola," *Voronezhskie eparkhial'nye vedomosti*, god 23, no. 1 (January 1, 1888): 1–2.

17. Spasskii, "Ob usloviiakh," 11.

18. Lev G. Deich, *Khozhdenie v narod: Iz vospominanii* (Petrograd: Izdanie Petrogradskogo soveta rabochikh i krasnoarm. deputatov; Gosudarstvennoe izdatel'stvo, 1919), 23. On Deich, see Ana Siljak, *Angel of Vengeance: The Girl Who Shot the Governor of St. Petersburg and Sparked the Age of Assassination* (New York: St. Martin's Griffin, 2009), chap. 7.

19. Deich, *Khozhdenie v narod*, 33. .

20. [Pokrovskii], "Istoricheskie svedeniia," 304.

21. Gosudarstvennyi arkhiv Rossiiskoi Federatsii, f. 109, op. 63 (2-aia ekspeditsiia, 1833 g.), edinitsa khraneniia 695, ll. 2–3ob.

22. Maksim Gavrilovich Rudometkin, *Utrenniaia zvezda* (Los Angeles: Tip. t-va Raduga v Amerikie, 1915), 36. This attack on the clergy includes an untranslatable pun that turns the word for a monk's headdress, *klobuk*, into an item of woman's fashion, the heel, *kabluk*.

23. M. G. Rudometkin et al., *Bozhestvennyia izrecheniia nastavnikov i stradal'tsev za slovo Bozhie* (Los Angeles: I. G. Samarin & Son, 1928), 181.

24. According to the Orthodox missionary Mikhail Aleksandrovich Kal'nev, in 1906 Molokan-Jumpers secretly published the ritual manual that Rudometkin compiled for his followers; Maksim Gavrilovich Rudometkin, *Molitvennik s pesniami*, ed. I. I. Portnov, A. I. Portnov, and Petr Cheremisin (Aleksandropol', 1906), cited in M. A. Kal'nev, *Sluzhebnik i trebnik prygunov* Riazan': tip. Bratstva sv. Vasiliia, 1913), 3–4. The Molokan colony in Los Angeles published a brief twenty-page pamphlet of Rudometkin's apocalyptic prophecies in 1910. Maksim Gavrilovich Rudometkin, *Izrechenie Maksima Gavrilovicha Rudometkina* (Los Angeles: Izdanie Molokanskoi kolonii, 1910). Five years later, two different publishing houses produced rival editions of Rudometkin's writings: Rudometkin, *Utrenniaia zvezda*, and Maksim Gavrilovich Rudometkin, *Kamen' gorlion: Bogoslovskiia izrecheniia Maksima Gavrilovicha Rudometkina, vozhdia sionskago naroda Zakavkazskikh khristian-prygunov, sochinennye im v monastyrskikh zatocheniiakh v period 1858–1877 gg.* (Los Angeles: Dukh i zhizn', 1915). The latter work became the basis of a second revised and supplemented authoritative edition published in 1928, which is often simply called the *Dukh i zhizn'* (*Spirit and Life*): Community of Spiritual Christian Jumpers in America, *Bozhestvennyia izrecheniia nastavnikov i stradal'tsev za slovo Bozhie, veru Iisusa i dukh sviatoi religii dukhovnykh khristian molokan-prygunov*, 2nd ed. (Los Angeles: Dukh i zhizn', 1928).

25. "Mneniia i otzyvy," *Tserkovnyi vestnik* 25, no. 6, February 11, 1899, cols. 202–6; "Mneniia i otzyvy," *Tserkovnyi vestnik* 33, no. 20, May 17, 1907, col. 642.

26. "Advent of Russians in 'Promised Land': Over Two Hundred Chaperoned by Greene & Griffin Settle at Glendale," *Arizona Republican* (Phoenix), August 31, 1911; "Russians Will Make Good Citizens: Description of One Time Subjects of White Czar Who Will Settle at Glendale," *Arizona Republican*, August 2, 1911; J. Eugene Clay, "The

Woman Clothed in the Sun: Pacifism and Apocalyptic Discourse among Russian Spiritual Christian Molokan-Jumpers," *Church History* 80, no. 1 (March 31, 2011): 109–38.

27. Mikhail Longinov, "Abram Petrovich Gannibal," *Russkii arkhiv*, no. 2, 1864, cols. 180–91; Catharine Theimer Nepomnyashchy, Nicole Svobodny, and Ludmila A. Trigos, eds., *Under the Sky of My Africa: Alexander Pushkin and Blackness* (Evanston, IL: Northwestern University Press, 2006).

28. "Russian Colonists Find in Salt River Valley an Ideal Place to Make Their Homes and Till the Soil," *Arizona Gazette* (Phoenix), September 8, 1911.

29. "Russians Will Make Good Citizens," *Arizona Republican*, 4.

30. Theodore W. Allen, *The Invention of the White Race*, 2 vols. (New York: Verso, 2012).

31. Katherine Benton-Cohen, *Borderline Americans: Racial Division and Labor War in the Arizona Borderlands* (Cambridge, MA: Harvard University Press, 2009).

32. Peggy Pascoe, "Miscegenation Law, Court Cases, and Ideologies of 'Race' in Twentieth-Century America," *Journal of American History* 83, no. 1 (June 1996): 44–69.

33. "Glendale," *Arizona Republican*, October 12, 1912, A2.

34. Alex F. Wren, *True Believers: Prisoners for Conscience; A History of Molokan Conscientious Objectors in World War One; The Absolutists of Arizona; "You Shall Not Lose One Hair on Your Head"* (Australia: n.p., 1991), 28–30; Alex Joseph Valoff and Tanya Andrew Valoff, "[Memoirs]" (1973), 10–13, personal archive of Andrew J. Conovaloff. I am grateful to Conovaloff for generously sharing this manuscript with me. Alex Valoff, who participated in the arms-burning, dates it to 1914.

35. United States, *Selective Service Regulations Prescribed by the President under the Authority Vested in Him by the Terms of the Selective Service Law (Act of Congress Approved May 18, 1917)* (Washington, DC: Govt. Print. Off., 1917), 26, pt. 3, sec. 53.

36. John K. Berokoff, *Molokans in America* (Los Angeles: John K. Berekoff, 1969), 158; "Men Mobilized for Draft Day: Mounted Rangers Carry Word to Up-Country Homes; Aliens Must Register, Though Don't Have to Serve; Russian Religionists File a Protest against It," *Los Angeles Times*, May 29, 1917, II-7.

37. Berokoff, *Molokans in America*, 161.

38. Wren, *True Believers*, 41. The Molokans had received other prophecies against registration as early as 1915. "Jail for Anti-war Russians," *Arizona Republican*, June 10, 1917, 1–2; Berokoff, *Molokans in America*, 69.

39. Wren, *True Believers*, 42–43.

40. "Glendale Molokans Decline," *Arizona Republican*, June 6, 1917.

41. "Will Swear Out Warrants for Molokanas in County: Russian Members of Religious Sect, Who Refused Yesterday to Register, Must Answer to the Law," *Arizona Gazette*, June 6, 1917.

42. "Molokanas Maintain Registering Is an Act of War on Their Part," *Arizona Gazette*, June 7, 1917; "Gives Molokanas One More Chance," *Arizona Gazette*, June 8, 1917. On Campbell, see James W. Byrkit, *Forging the Copper Collar: Arizona's Labor-Management War of 1901–1921* (Tucson: University of Arizona Press, 1982), 89–92; John S. Goff, *George W. P. Hunt and His Arizona* (Pasadena, CA: Socio Technical Publications, 1973), 95–97.

43. "Trial of Molokanas for Slackering Goes on Today," *Arizona Gazette*, August 7, 1917.

44. "Fifty Slackers Will Face Court Here Tomorrow," *Arizona Gazette*, July 30, 1917.

45. "Molokans Entertain Crowd by Dancing and Howling in Front of Federal Building," *Arizona Republican*, August 7, 1917, 10.

46. "Molokanas in Jail Worship Fervently to the Annoyance of Other Prisoners," *Arizona Gazette*, June 11, 1917; "Jail for Anti-war Russians," *Arizona Republican*, June 10, 1917, 8.

47. "Molokan Pictures," *Arizona Republican*, September 15, 1918, 2.

48. William Haas Moore, "Prisoners in the Promised Land: The Molokans in World War I," *Journal of Arizona History* 14, no. 4 (1973): 281–302; Walter Guest Kellogg, *The Conscientious Objector* (New York: Boni and Liveright, 1919), 43–48; Norman Thomas, *The Conscientious Objector in America* (New York: B. W. Huebsch, 1923), 50–53, 150–55.

12. *Vseedinstvo*

Some of the research for this chapter was done during my Lise Meitner Fellowship at the Institute for the Human Sciences in Vienna, where I was attached to Charles Taylor's project "Religion and Secularism." I thank Christopher Stroop for inviting me to take part in the conference at the Russian Presidential Academy of National Economy and Public Administration (RANEPA) in Moscow, where I had the opportunity to present this material and discuss it with colleagues in the field.

1. I am borrowing the phrase from the book on Dostoyevsky by Rowan Williams, *Dostoevsky: Language, Faith, and Fiction* (Waco, TX: Baylor University Press, 2011).

2. There is enormous literature on the subject. On the different connotations of *secularism* and related terms, see Karel Dobbelaere, *Secularization: A Multi-dimensional Concept* (Beverly Hills, CA: Sage, 1981); David Martin, *The Religious and the Secular* (New York: Routledge, 1969), especially the chapters "Secularization: The Range of Meaning" and "Towards Eliminating the Concept of Secularization." I have found useful Charles Taylor's work—*A Secular Age* (Cambridge, MA: Belknap Press of Harvard University Press, 2007); and "What Is Secularism?," in *Secularism, Religion and Multicultural Citizenship*, ed. Geoffrey Brahm Levey and Tariq Modood (Cambridge: Cambridge University Press, 2009), xi–xxii.

3. For example, Florenskii became a defender of *imiaslavie* (name-worshipping), a movement that started among the Russian monks on Mount Athos and which the Russian Church declared heretical.

4. The period takes its name from the book by Nicholas Zernov, *The Russian Religious Renaissance of the Twentieth Century* (New York: Harper & Row, 1963).

5. V. N. Akulinin, *Filosofiia vseedinstva: Ot V. S. Solov'eva k P. A. Florenskomu* (Novosibirsk: Sibirskoe otd-nie, 1990), 3, 7; my translation. Translations are the author's unless otherwise noted.

6. Akulinin, *Filosofiia vseedinstva*, 13.

7. Nicolas Berdyaev, *The Russian Idea* (New York: Macmillan, 1948), 159.

8. V. V. Zenkovsky, *A History of Russian Philosophy*, trans. George L. Kline, 2 vols. (London: Routledge and Kegan Paul, 1953).

9. For instance, "total unity" is the rendition of George L. Kline in his translation of Zenkovsky's book, as well as the translation of Alexander Schmemann's edited vol-

ume, *Ultimate Questions: An Anthology of Modern Russian Religious Thought* (New York: Holt, Rinehart, and Winston, 1965), 4. Robert Slesinski prefers to use "pan-unity"; see Robert Slesinski, "The Metaphysics of Pan-Unity in P. A. Florensky: A Worldview," in *P. A. Florenskii i kul'tura ego vremeni*, ed. Michael Hagemeister and Nina Kauchtschis-chwili (Marburg: Blaue Horner Verlag, 1995), 467–75. "Spritual unity" is used by Boris Jakim and Robert Bird, trans. and eds., *On Spiritual Unity: A Slavophile Reader* (Hudson, NY: Lindisfarne Books, 1998).

10. See Aristotle's definition of "to holon" in the *Metaphysics*, where "to holon" refers to "the whole" not as the sum of its parts, but as possessing an inner cause of unity (that is, Form). See Aristotle, Metaphysics, 1-984a, accessed February 17, 2024, https://www.perseus.tufts.edu/hopper/text?doc=Aristot.+Met.+1.984a&fromdoc=Perseus%3Atext%3A1999.01.0052.

11. P. Gaidenko, *Vladimir Solov'ev i filosofiia Serebrianogo veka.* (Moscow: Progress-Traditsiia, 2001); Jonathan Sutton, *The Religious Philosophy of Vladimir Solovyov: Towards a Reassessment* (Basingstoke: Macmillan Press, 1988); Oliver Smith, *Vladimir Soloviev and the Spiritualization of Matter* (Boston: Academic Studies Press, 2011); Thomas Nameth, *The Early Solov'ev and His Quest for Metaphysics* (Cham: Springer, 2014).

12. Catherine Evtuhov, *The Cross and the Sickle: Sergei Bulgakov and the Fate of Russian Religious Philosophy, 1890–1920* (Ithaca, NY: Cornell University Press, 1997); Aiden Nichols, *Wisdom from Above: A Primer in the Theology of Father Sergei Bulgakov* (Leominster, UK: Gracewing, 2005).

13. Some of the major scholars working on Florenskii in Russia are Viktor Bychkov, Boris Uspensky, Sergei Khoruzhii, and Konstantin Usupov. Khoruzhii has taken a highly critical view of Florenskii. I offer an overview of Russian criticism in the twentieth century and until now in Clemena Antonova, "Changing Perceptions of Pavel Florensky in Russian and Soviet Scholarship," in *In Marx's Shadow: Knowledge, Power, and Intellectuals in Eastern Europe and Russia*, ed. Costica Bradatan and Serguei Alex. Oushakine (Lanham, MD: Lexington Books, 2010), 73–95. In the West, the first biography of Florenskii is by Avril Pyman, *Pavel Florensky: A Quiet Genius* (New York: Continuum, 2010). Other scholars working on Florenskii are Robert Slesinski, Michael Hagemeister, and Christoph Schneider.

14. I approach Florenskii's writings on the icon through the prism of two intersecting themes, visuality and unity, in Clemena Antonova, *Visual Thought in Russian Religious Philosophy: Pavel Florensky's Theory of the Icon* (New York: Routledge, 2019).

15. See David D. Roberts, *The Totalitarian Experiment in Twentieth-Century Europe: Understanding the Poverty of Great Politics* (New York: Routledge, 2006).

16. Richard Evans, *The Coming of the Third Reich* (New York: Penguin Books, 2003), 218.

17. On the Gnostic roots of the concept of Sophia (Holy Wisdom), see the classic study by Elaine Pagels, *The Gnostic Gospels* (New York: Random House, 1979). On the idea of Sophia as bringing together the immanent and the transcendent in the German mystic Jakob Boehme and his influence of the *vseedintsy*, see David Zdenek, "The Influence of Jacob Boehme on Russian Religious Thought," *Slavic Review* 21, no. 1 (1962): 43–64.

18. The term *"tsel'noe znanie"* derives from Solov'ev and especially his *Philosophical Principles of Integral Knowledge* (Grand Rapids, MI: William B. Eerdmans, 2008).

19. Ivan Kireevsky, "On the Nature of European Culture and on Its Relationship to Russian Culture," in *On Spiritual Unity: A Slavophile Reader*, trans. and ed. Boris Jakim and Robert Bird (Hudson, NY: Lindisfarne Books, 1998), 223, 193.

20. Ivan Kireevsky, "On the Necessity and Possibility of New Principles in Philosophy," in *On Spiritual Unity: A Slavophile Reader*, trans. and ed. Boris Jakim and Robert Bird (Hudson, NY: Lindisfarne Books, 1998), 240.

21. V. Solov'ev, *Sobranie sochineniia*, 10 vols. (St. Petersburg, 1911–14), vol. 1, (1911) 290–91; my translation. Solov'ev developed his understanding of integral knowledge most fully in his *Principles of Integral Knowledge* (1877).

22. Kireevsky, "Nature," 193.

23. Kireevsky, "Nature," 229.

24. Dostoyevsky, quoted in Marina Kostalevsky, *Dostoevsky and Soloviev* (New Haven, CT: Yale University Press, 1997), 74.

25. For the origins of "full unity" in the Western tradition, see Martin Jay, "The Discourse of Totality before Western Marxism," in *Marxism and Totality* (Berkeley: University of California Press, 1984), 21–81.

26. See A. Avramov, "Otsenka filosofii Platona v russkoi idealisticheskoi filosofii," in *Platon i ego epokha* (Moscow: Nauka, 1979), 212–38. For the notion of "holon," see F. E. Peters, *Greek Philosophical Terms* (New York: New York University Press, 1967), 84ff. See also G. N. Giordano Orsini, "The Ancient Roots of a Modern Idea" in *Organic Form: The Life of an Idea*, ed. G. S. Rousseau (London: Routledge and Kegan Paul, 1972).

27. For the role of the German romantics in Russian intellectual history, see Isaiah Berlin, "German Romanticism in Petersburg and Moscow," in *Russian Thinkers* (Harmondsworth: Penguin, 1978), 136–56. According to Berlin, in the second half of the nineteenth century Eastern Europe and Russia were "in effect, intellectual dependencies of Germany" (136). On the influence of romantic philosophy on Florenskii in particular, see Clemena Antonova, "'The World Will Be Saved by Beauty': The Revival of Romantic Theories of the Symbol in Pavel Florenskii's Works," *Slavonica* 14, no. 1 (2008): 44–56.

28. G. W. F. Hegel, *The Phenomenology of Spirit*, trans. A. V. Miller (Oxford: Oxford University Press, 1979), 11.

29. V. F. Pustarnikov, ed., *Filosofiia Schellinga v Rossii* (St. Petersburg: Izdatel'stvo Russkogo Khristianskogo gumanitarnogo instituta, 1998); D. K. Burlaka, ed., *Schelling: Pro et Contra* (St. Petersburg: Izdatel'stvo Russkogo Khristianskogo gumanitarnogo instituta, 2001).

30. Solov'ev, quoted in Zenkovsky, *History of Russian Philosophy*, 481–82.

31. Florenskii largely made his reputation, almost overnight, with the publication of the revised version of his master's thesis: Pavel Florenskii, "Stolp i utverzhdenie istiny" [The pillar and the ground of truth] (Moscow Theological Academy, 1914).

32. Pavel Florenskii, "Razum i dialektika" (1912), in *Filosofiia vseedinstva: Ot V. S. Solov'eva k P. A. Florenskomu*, by V. N. Akulinin (Novosibirsk: "Nauka," Sibirskoe otdnie, 1990), 153, 155; my translation.

33. Florenskii, quoted in Igumen Andronik, "Zhizn' i sud'ba," in *Sochineniia v chetyrekh tomakh*, by P. Florenskii (Moscow, 1994), vol. 1, 8; English translation in Nicoletta Misler, "Pavel Florensky as Art Historian," in *Beyond Vision: Essays on the Perception of Art*, by Pavel Florensky, comp. and ed. Nicoletta Misler, trans. Wendy Salmond (London: Reaktion Books, 2002), 75.

34. There is a vast literature of *theosis*. See especially Norman Russell, *The Doctrine of Deification in Greek Patristic Thought* (Oxford: Oxford University Press, 2004); but see also Michael J. Christensen and Jeffrey A. Wittung, *Partakers of the Divine Nature: The History and Development of Deification in the Christian Traditions* (Grand Rapids, MI: Baker Academic, 2008); Stephen Finlan and Vladimir Kharlamov, eds., *Theosis: Deification in Christian Theology* (Eugene, OR: Wipf & Stock, 2006); Stephen Thomas, *Deification in the Eastern Orthodox Tradition: A Biblical Perspective* (Piscataway, NJ: Gorgias Press, 2007).

35. Sergei Khoruzhii, "Breaks and Links: Prospects for Russian Religious Philosophy Today," *Studies in Eastern European Thought* 53, no. 4 (2001): 272.

36. See Zernov's celebrated book *Russian Religious Renaissance*. The appropriateness of the term is debatable, though, as the religious revival remained confined to a rather small group of intellectuals and, by no means, represented a widespread phenomenon.

37. Khoruzhii, "Breaks and Links," 273.

38. There is mention of the direct influence of Russian émigré philosophy on the Vatican II in Alexander Agadjanian, "Breakthrough to Modernity, Apologia for Traditionalism: The Russian Orthodox View of Society and Culture in Comparative Perspective," *Religion, State & Society* 31, no. 4 (2003): 338. In general, this is an intriguing and massively understudied topic.

39. Talal Asad, *Formations of the Secular: Christianity, Islam, Modernity* (Stanford, CA: Stanford University Press, 2003), 1.

40. See Hent de Vries's book dealing exclusively with continental philosophers: Hent de Vries, *Philosophy and the Turn to Religion* (Baltimore: John Hopkins University Press, 1999). Nicholas Wolterstorff has attracted attention to the "turn to religion" in analytical philosophy; see Nicholas Wolterstorff, "The Religious Turn in Philosophy and Art," in *Religion nach der Religionskritik*, ed. Ludwig Nagl (Vienna: R. Oldenbourg; Berlin: Akademie Verlag, 2003), 273–83.

41. On the debate in the mid-twentieth century between Karl Löwith and Hans Blumenberg on exactly this issue of the religious genealogy of secular concepts, see Peter Gordon, "The Idea of Secularization in Intellectual History," in *A Companion to Intellectual History*, ed. Richard Whatmore and Brian Young (Malden, MA: Wiley Blackwell, 2016), 230–46.

42. Peter Gordon, "The Place of the Sacred in the Absence of God: Charles Taylor's *A Secular Age*," *Journal of the History of Ideas* 69, no. 4 (2008): 670.

43. Taylor, *Secular Age*, 535.

44. José Casanova, *Public Religions in the Modern World* (Chicago: University of Chicago Press, 1994), 5.

45. See Thomas Luckmann, *The Invisible Religion* (New York: Macmillan, 1967).

46. See Nick Crossley and John Michael Roberts, introduction to *After Habermas: New Perspectives on the Public Sphere*, ed. Nick Crossley and John Michael Roberts (Oxford, UK: Blackwell, 2004), 1–5. There is a good summary of some of these ideas in L. Antonov, *Kritika na monologichniia razum* (Blagoevgrad: Universitetsko izdatel'stvo "Neofit Rilski," 2011), chap. 4.

47. Jürgen Habermas, "Religion in the Public Sphere," *European Journal of Philosophy* 14, no. 1 (2006): 1–25.

48. Charles Taylor, "The Future of the Religious Past," in *Religion: Beyond a Concept*, ed. Hent de Vries (New York: Fordham University Press, 2008), 230.

49. See, for instance, Jens Köhrsen, "How Religious Is the Public Sphere? A Critical Stance on the Debate about Public Religion and Post-Secularity," *Acta Sociologica* 55, no. 3 (2012): 273–88.

50. Steve Bruce, *Religion in the Modern World* (Oxford: Oxford University Press, 1996), 4.

51. Leszek Kołakowski, "Anxiety about God in an Ostensibly Godless Age," in *Is God Happy? Selected Essays* (Harmondsworth: Penguin Books, 2012), 193.

52. Jürgen Habermas and Joseph Ratzinger, *The Dialectics of Secularization: On Reason and Religion* (San Francisco: Ignatius Press, 2005), 38.

53. Michael Gillespie, *The Theological Origins of Modernity* (Chicago: University of Chicago Press, 2008), xii, xi.

54. Gillespie, *Theological Origins*, 293.

55. Friedrich Nietzsche, *Beyond Good and Evil: Prelude to a Philosophy of the Future*, trans. Helen Zimmern (1885; Edinburgh: T. N. Foulis, 1909), 127, xi.

56. Alexander Koyré, *Descartes und die Scholastik* (Bonn: Friedrich Cohen Verlag, 1923).

57. Samuel Moyn, *The Last Utopia: Human Rights in History* (Cambridge, MA: Harvard University Press, 2012); Samuel Moyn, *Christian Human Rights* (Philadelphia: University of Pennsylvania Press, 2015); Henri Féron, "Human Rights and Faith: A 'World-Wide Secular Religion'?," *Ethics & Global Politics* 7, no. 4 (2014): 181–200.

58. Bernard Berenson, *Aesthetics and History* (New York: Doubleday, 1954), 93; I have discussed this question of religious aesthetics in greater detail in Clemena Antonova, "Towards a Christian Aesthetics: An Eastern Orthodox Perspective," *Cithara* 54, no. 1 (2014): 21–38.

59. Randall A. Poole, trans. and ed., *Problems of Idealism: Essays in Russian Social Philosophy* (New Haven, CT: Yale University Press, 2003); Randall A. Poole, "Integral Humanisms: Jacques Maritain, Vladimir Soloviev, and the History of Human Rights," *Filosofiia i konfliktologiia*, no. 1 (2019): 92–106. For the case of Berdiaev, see Ana Siljak, "The Personalism of Nikolai Berdiaev," in *The Oxford Handbook of Russian Religious Thought*, ed. Caryl Emerson, George Pattison, and Randall A. Poole (Oxford: Oxford University Press, 2020), 309–26.

60. The frequently repeated formula, first used by Saint Irenaus, whence it entered the Orthodox tradition, was "God made Himself man that man might become God." See Russell, *Doctrine of Deification*.

61. On this subject, see Clemena Antonova, "'Everyone Is Responsible for Everyone and Everything': Insights on the Refugee Crisis Drawn from Russian Religious Philosophy," *Sobornost* 38, no. 1 (2016): 20–34.

62. Taylor, *Secular Age*, 370–71.

63. See Antonova, "Towards a Christian Aesthetics," 21–38.

Afterword. Russian Religious Modernity

1. Of course, there is a very large literature, but a very good study is Perez Zagorin, *How the Idea of Religious Toleration Came to the West* (Princeton, NJ: Princeton University Press, 2003).

2. See Victoria Frede, *Doubt, Atheism, and the Nineteenth-Century Russian Intelligentsia* (Madison: University of Wisconsin Press, 2011); Victoria Smolkin, *A Sacred Space Is Never Empty: A History of Soviet Atheism* (Princeton, NJ: Princeton University Press, 2018).

3. I discuss many of these forms in Randall A. Poole, "Introduction: Faith, Freedom, and the Varieties of Russian Religious Experience," in *Religious Freedom in Modern Russia*, ed. Randall A. Poole and Paul W. Werth (Pittsburgh: University of Pittsburgh Press, 2018), 1–43.

4. See also Kåre Johan Mjør, "Russkaia religioznaia filosofiia v sekuliarnyi vek," *Istoriko-filosofskii ezhegodnik 35* (2020): 263–82.

5. Boris Chicherin provided an influential account of the proofs in his book *Nauka i religiia*, 2nd ed. (Moscow: Kushnerev, 1901), 84–102, 114–16. Paul Gavrilyuk has shown how the classic arguments from natural theology were developed into a tradition of Russian philosophical theism. See Paul Gavrilyuk, "Natural Theology in Modern Russian Religious Thought," in *Natural Theology in the Eastern Orthodox Tradition*, ed. David Bradshaw and Richard Swinburne (St. Paul, MN: IOTA Publications, 2021), 89–123. Sergius Bulgakov emphasized the experiential basis of religious belief in his classic work of religious philosophy, *Unfading Light: Contemplations and Speculations*, trans. and ed. Thomas Allan Smith (Grand Rapids, MI: William B. Eerdmans, 2012), 7–20.

6. V. V. Zenkovsky, *A History of Russian Philosophy*, trans. George L. Kline, 2 vols. (New York: Columbia University Press, 1953), vol. 2, 853. Gavrilyuk, "Natural Theology," 115–19, provides a fine overview of Frank's version of the ontological argument.

7. S. L. Frank, *The Unknowable: An Ontological Introduction to the Philosophy of Religion*, trans. Boris Jakim (Athens: Ohio University Press, 1983), 215, 217.

8. Kant's most influential exposition of his idealist conception of human nature is *Groundwork of the Metaphysics of Morals* (1785). See Immanuel Kant, *Practical Philosophy*, trans. and ed. Mary J. Gregor, with an introduction by Allen Wood (Cambridge: Cambridge University Press, 1996).

9. S. N. Trubetskoi, "O prirode chelovecheskogo soznaniia" (1889–1991), in *Sobranie sochinenii Kn. Sergeia Nikolaevicha Trubetskogo*, ed. L. M. Lopatin (Moscow: Tipografiia G. Lissnera i D. Sobko, 1908), vol. 2, 108; S. N. Trubetskoi, "Psikhologicheskii determinizm i nravstvennaia svoboda" (1894), in *Sobranie sochinenii*, vol. 2, 121.

10. This group included Sergei Trubetskoi, Evgenii Trubetskoi, Pavel Novgorodtsev, Sergei Kotliarevskii, Peter Struve, Sergei Bulgakov, Nikolai Berdiaev, and Semyon Frank.

11. See Randall A. Poole, "Vladimir Solov'ëv's Philosophical Anthropology: Autonomy, Dignity, Perfectibility," in *A History of Russian Philosophy, 1830–1930: Faith, Reason, and the Defense of Human Dignity*, ed. Gary M. Hamburg and Randall A. Poole (Cambridge: Cambridge University Press, 2010), 131–49.

12. For a study of the concept in Russian religious thought, see Paul Valliere, *Modern Russian Theology: Bukharev, Soloviev, Bulgakov: Orthodox Theology in a New Key* (Edinburgh: T&T Clark, 2000).

13. Kant's version of the moral proof derives the metaphysical postulates of immortality and the existence of God from moral perfectibility. See Randall A. Poole, "Kant and the Kingdom of Ends in Russian Religious Thought (Vladimir Solov'ev)," in *Thinking Orthodox in Modern Russia: Culture, History, Context*, ed. Patrick Lally Michelson and

Judith Deutsch Kornblatt (Madison: University of Wisconsin Press, 2014), 215–34, esp. 223–28.

14. See Vladimir Solovyov, *Lectures on Divine Humanity*, trans. Peter Zouboff, revised and ed. Boris Jakim (Hudson, NY: Lindisfarne Press, 1995), 17, 23.

15. N. Berdyaev, *The Destiny of Man*, trans. Natalie Duddington (San Rafael, CA: Semantron Press, 2009), 55, as quoted in Ana Siljak, "The Personalism of Nikolai Berdiaev," in *The Oxford Handbook of Russian Religious Thought*, ed. Caryl Emerson, George Pattison, and Randall A. Poole (Oxford: Oxford University Press, 2020), 315.

16. S. L. Frank, *Reality and Man: An Essay in the Metaphysics of Human Nature*, trans. Natalie Duddington (New York: Taplinger, 1966), 104, 106 (translation modified). See also Frank, *Unknowable*, 200.

17. For further development, see Randall A. Poole, "Christian Humanism in Russian Religious Thought: Apropos *The Oxford Handbook of Russian Religious Thought*," *Solov'ëvskie issledovaniia (Solov'ëv Studies)*, no. 2 (74) (2022): 141–55.

18. Valliere, *Modern Russian Theology*, 12.

19. S. N. Bulgakov, "Social Teaching in Modern Russian Orthodox Theology," in *Sergii Bulgakov: Towards a Russian Political Theology*, ed. Rowan Williams (Edinburgh: T&T Clark, 1999), 283.

20. See Randall A. Poole, "The Liberalism of Russian Religious Idealism," in *The Oxford Handbook of Russian Religious Thought*, ed. Caryl Emerson, George Pattison, and Randall A. Poole (Oxford: Oxford University Press, 2020), 255–76. Respect for law could also be identified as a distinct principle. See Paul Valliere and Randall A. Poole, eds., *Law and the Christian Tradition in Modern Russia* (London: Routledge, 2022).

21. Solov'ev, quoted in Richard S. Wortman, *The Power of Language and Rhetoric in Russian Political History: Charismatic Words from the 18th to the 21st Centuries* (London: Bloomsbury, 2018), 109 (translation modified).

22. In *Groundwork of the Metaphysics of Morals*, Kant wrote that autonomy is "the ground of the dignity of human nature and of every rational nature." See Kant, *Practical Philosophy*, 85.

23. B. N. Chicherin, *Filosofiia prava* (Moscow: Kushnerov, 1900), 191–92. See also Gary M. Hamburg, "Boris Chicherin and Human Dignity in History," in *A History of Russian Philosophy, 1830–1930: Faith, Reason, and the Defense of Human Dignity*, ed. Gary M. Hamburg and Randall A. Poole (Cambridge: Cambridge University Press, 2010), 111–30 (he quotes the last sentence at 125).

24. Jellinek, quoted in Hans Joas, *The Sacredness of the Person: A New Genealogy of Human Rights*, trans. Alex Skinner (Washington, DC: Georgetown University Press, 2013), 24. Jellinek's thesis is the point of departure for Joas's book.

25. Williams, quoted in Martha C. Nussbaum, *Liberty of Conscience: In Defense of America's Tradition of Religious Equality* (New York: Basic Books, 2008), 52. The first chapter of this book is devoted to Williams.

26. P. Borisov [Struve], "V chem zhe istinnyi natsionalizm?," *Voprosy filosofii i psikhologii* 12 (4), kn. 59 (1901): 493–528; reprinted in Struve's collection of articles, *Na raznye temy* (St. Petersburg, 1902), 526–55. For analysis, see Richard Pipes, *Struve: Liberal on the Left, 1870–1905* (Cambridge, MA: Harvard University Press, 1970), 300–307.

27. [Struve], "V chem zhe istinnyi natsionalizm?," 505–8. Struve does not provide a specific citation for Novgorodtsev. In the fourth edition of his *Lektsii po istorii filosofii*

prava: Ucheniia novogo vremeni, XVI–XIX vv. (Moscow, 1918), Novgorodtsev's consideration of Williams is at 66–68.

28. Randall A. Poole, trans. and ed., *Problems of Idealism: Essays in Russian Social Philosophy* (New Haven, CT: Yale University Press, 2003).

29. Valliere makes this important point in his analysis of Chicherin's book *Science and Religion*. See Paul Valliere, "Theological Liberalism and Church Reform in Imperial Russia," in *Church, Nation and State in Russia and Ukraine*, ed. Geoffrey A. Hosking (London: Palgrave Macmillan, 1991), 108–30 (on Chicherin, 119–24).

30. S. N. Bulgakov, "Basic Problems of the Theory of Progress," in *Problems of Idealism: Essays in Russian Social Philosophy*, trans. and ed. Randall A. Poole (New Haven, CT: Yale University Press, 2003), 89.

31. Bulgakov, "Theory of Progress," 107.

32. S. A. Kotliarevskii, "Ob otnositel'nom i absoliutnom," in *Filosofskii sbornik. L'vu Mikhailovichu Lopatinu k tridtsatiletiiu nauchno-pedagogicheskoi deiatel'nosti. Ot Moskovskogo Psikhologicheskogo Obshchestva. 1881–1911* (Moscow, 1912), 106; my translation.

CONTRIBUTORS

Clemena Antonova works on aspects of Eastern Orthodox theology and Russian religious philosophy, with a special interest in the role of religion in modernity and in questions of visuality. Her publications include *Visual Thought in Russian Religious Philosophy: Pavel Florensky's Theory of the Icon* (2019); "Christian Philosophy as a Philosophy of Crisis: Re-reading Florensky in the Twenty-First Century," in *Eastern Christian Approaches to Philosophy*, edited by James Siemens and Joshua Mattan Brown (2022); and "The Icon and Visual Arts during the Russian Religious Renaissance," in *The Oxford Handbook of Russian Religious Thought*, edited by Caryl Emerson, George Pattison, and Randall A. Poole (2020). She is a regular contributor to the journals *Sobornost, Leonardo,* and *Cithara.* Antonova guest-curated the exhibition *Icons for Our Time: Orthodox Art from around the World* at the Museum of Russian Icons, USA (2021–22), and is organizing the lecture series "Reading Russian Philosophy in the Age of Putin" at the Institute for Human Sciences in Vienna, where she is the research director of the World in Pieces program.

J. Eugene Clay is associate professor of religious studies at the School of Historical, Philosophical, and Religious Studies at Arizona State University, where he writes and lectures about religious movements in Russia and Eurasia, the relationship between religion and nationalism, and the encounters of the world religions. He served as president of the Association for the Study of Eastern Christian History and Culture and is a research scholar of the Northwestern University Research Initiative for the Study of Russian Philosophy and Religious Thought. He is the editor of *Beasts, Humans, and Transhumans in the Middle Ages and the Renaissance* (2020) and author of "Buddhism in the Post-Soviet Religious Marketplace," *Journal of Church and State* (2023). His articles have also appeared in *Church History*; *Modern Greek Studies Yearbook*; *Religion, State & Society*; and *State, Religion and Church.* He gratefully acknowledges the support of the Social Science Research Council, National Endowment for the Humanities, National Humanities Center, International Research and Exchanges Board, Summer Research Laboratory at the University of Illinois,

Center for Jewish Studies, Center for the Study of Religion and Conflict, Melikian Center, and Institute for Humanities Research of Arizona State University.

April L. French is a historian who focuses on Russian religious history and the everyday practice of religious believers in the Soviet period. She is the editor of *An Inner Step toward God: Writings and Teachings on Prayer by Father Alexander Men* (2014), and she has also published on evangelicals in Soviet Siberia. French now works at her alma mater, the University of Wyoming.

Nadieszda Kizenko is professor of Russian history and director of the Program in Religious Studies at the State University of New York at Albany. She explores aspects of Orthodox Christianity in Russia and Ukraine, with a special focus on liturgy, gender, and identity. Her research has been supported by the National Endowment for the Humanities, International Research Exchanges Board, American Councils Research Scholar Program, National Council for Eurasian and East European Research, Social Science Research Council, and German Research Foundation. Her books include the Heldt Prize winner *A Prodigal Saint: Father John of Kronstadt and the Russian People* (2000), *Good for the Souls: A History of Confession in the Russian Empire* (2021), and the coedited *Orthodoxy in Two Manifestations? The Conflict in Ukraine as Expression of a Fault Line in World Orthodoxy* (2022).

Tatiana Levina is currently an Academy in Exile fellow at the Kulturwissenschaftliches Institut Essen (KWI). She works on Platonism in the history of philosophy and philosophy of art. She is preparing a book manuscript titled "The Abstract Revolution: Platonism in the Avant-Garde Era" for publication. She taught philosophy at the National Research University Higher School of Economics in Moscow and was involved in academic activism until her dismissal in 2020. At KWI, Levina is continuing her research project on women philosophers in the Soviet Union, with a particular focus on feminist metaphysics and epistemology. Her chapter "Sofya Yanovskaya in Defence of Abstractions: Between Soviet Ideology and Bourgeois Idealism" appears in *Stalin Era Intellectuals: Culture and Stalinism*, edited by Vesa Oittinen and Elina Viljanen (2023).

Erich Lippman is associate professor of history at Saint Mary's University of Minnesota, where he has taught since 2012. Before arriving at Saint Mary's, he taught for five years at Bethany College in West Virginia. His area of expertise is Russian intellectual history, with a focus on the interactions between religion and modernity in revolutionary Russia. He has published articles largely focused on reevaluating the legacy of Maxim Gorky's God-building period in light of his interactions with the religious thought of his day.

Kåre Johan Mjør is associate professor of Russian at the University of Bergen and senior research librarian at the Western Norway University of Applied Sciences. He is the author of *Reformulating Russia: The Cultural and Intellectual Historiography of Russian First-Wave Émigré Writers* (2011) and editor of *Russia as Civilization: Ideological Discourses in Politics, Media and Academia* (together with Sanna Turoma) (2020). He has published widely on Russian history, intellectual history, philosophy, and literature.

Alexander Polunov is professor in and head of the Department of the Management of Interethnic and Interfaith Relations at the School of Public Administration, Moscow State Lomonosov University. He is the author of *Russia in the Nineteenth Century: Autocracy, Reform, and Social Change, 1814–1914* (2005), *Pobedonostsev in the Sociopolitical and Ideological Life of Russia* (2010; in Russian), and "Spatial Utopianism and Russian Images of Distant Lands, 1880–1900," *Kritika: Explorations in Russian and Eurasian History* (2021), and coauthor of *Russian International Relations in War and Revolution, 1914–22*, book 1, *Origins and War, 1914–16* (2021). Polunov's current research is focused on the ideological and cultural aspects of Russian imperial policy toward the remote peoples of Asia and Africa.

Randall A. Poole is professor of intellectual history at the College of St. Scholastica, codirector of the Northwestern University Research Initiative for the Study of Russian Philosophy and Religious Thought, and a fellow of the Center for the Study of Law and Religion at Emory University School of Law. He is the translator and editor of *Problems of Idealism: Essays in Russian Social Philosophy* (2003) and coeditor of several volumes: *A History of Russian Philosophy, 1830–1930: Faith, Reason, and the Defense of Human Dignity* (2010), *Religious Freedom in Modern Russia* (2018), *The Oxford Handbook of Russian Religious Thought* (2020), *Evgenii Trubetskoi: Icon and Philosophy* (2021), and *Law and the Christian Tradition in Modern Russia* (2022). He is also the author of many articles and book chapters on Russian intellectual history, philosophy, and religion.

Peter A. Safronov is a guest scholar at the University of Amsterdam. He is a specialist in political philosophy and education research and has written several books and articles on these topics. He is now researching affective citizenship and caring relationships in online settings. He is a member of the European Network of Psychological Anthropology and a member of the Svobodny Universitet's faculty senate, a grassroots initiative of independent

Russian academics. He graduated from Moscow Lomonosov University with a PhD in philosophy.

Vassili Schedrin is an adjunct professor of Jewish history and director of the Russian and East European Studies Network at Queen's University in Canada. He teaches and studies topics related to the cultural history of Russian Jews from the eighteenth to the twentieth century, including Soviet Yiddish culture and theater. He is the author of *Jewish Souls, Bureaucratic Minds: Jewish Bureaucracy and Policymaking in Late Imperial Russia, 1850–1917* (2016) and coauthor of *"In America non ci sono Zar": Le relazioni russo-statunitensi: "Questione ebraica" e nascita della diplomazia umanitaria (1880–1914)* ("There are no tsars in America": Russian-US relations: The "Jewish Question" and the birth of humanitarian diplomacy [1880–1914]) (2021). His current project is a biography of Solomon Mikhoels, the brightest star of Soviet Yiddish theater and a virtual symbol of Russian Jewish culture. This project is situated at the intersection of academic scholarship and theatrical performance, of archival research and playwriting.

Ana Siljak is an associate professor of humanities at the Hamilton Center, University of Florida. She currently holds a grant from the Social Sciences and Humanities Research Council of Canada to study the philosophy and literature of the Russian Silver Age. Her essays include "The Personalism of Nikolai Berdiaev," in *The Oxford Handbook of Russian Religious Thought* (2020); "Nikolai Berdiaev and the Origin of Russian Messianism," *Journal of Modern History* (2016); "Sigmund Freud, Sublimation, and the Russian Silver Age," *Modern Intellectual History* (2018); and "Friedrich Nietzsche, Dmitrii Merezhkovskii, and the Russian Renaissance," *Canadian Slavonic Papers* (2018). She is the editor of *Nikolai Berdyaev and Jacques Maritain: An Exceptional Dialogue, 1925–1948* (2024) and is currently completing her manuscript on Nikolai Berdiaev's personalism.

Kristina Stoeckl is professor of sociology at Libera Università Internazionale degli Studi Sociali (LUISS), Rome. She conducts research in the field of political sociology and sociology of religion, with a focus on religion and human rights, value conflicts and transnational norm mobilization, religion-state relations in Russia and Orthodox Christianity. Her publications include *The Moralist International: Russia in the Global Culture Wars* (together with Dmitry Uzlaner) (2022) and *Russian Orthodoxy and Secularism* (2020).

Index

Printed in the USA
CPSIA information can be obtained
at www.ICGtesting.com
CBHW020309171024
15976CB00002B/14

9 781501 778162